INVESTMENT TRAPS EXPOSED

Navigating Investor Mistakes and Behavioral Biases

INVESTMENT TRAPS EXPOSED

Navigating Investor Mistakes and Behavioral Biases

By

H. Kent Baker
*American University, Kogod School of Business,
Washington, DC*

Vesa Puttonen
*Aalto University, School of Business,
Helsinki, Finland*

United Kingdom – North America – Japan – India – Malaysia – China

Emerald Publishing Limited
Howard House, Wagon Lane, Bingley BD16 1WA, UK

First edition 2017

British Library Cataloguing in Publication Data
A catalogue record for this book is available from the British Library

ISBN: 978-1-78714-253-4 (Print)
ISBN: 978-1-78714-252-7 (Online)
ISBN: 978-1-78714-721-8 (Epub)

ISOQAR certified
Management System,
awarded to Emerald
for adherence to
Environmental
standard
ISO 14001:2004.

Certificate Number 1985
ISO 14001

INVESTOR IN PEOPLE

CONTENTS

ACKNOWLEDGMENTS

The greatest part of a writer's time is spent in reading, in order to write; a man will turn over half a library to make one book.

Samuel Johnson

The observation aptly applies to *Investment Traps Exposed*: *Navigating Investor Mistakes and Behavioral Biases*. We owe a debt of gratitude to literally hundreds of authors whose work we read to provide a foundation for writing this book. We want to acknowledge the outstanding work by Elizabeth Caravella and Linda Baker, who diligently read each chapter providing thoughtful suggestions and edits to improve the book. Special thanks also go to Mikko Niemenmaa, Sanni Nissilä, Ilja Tauber, and Markus Weckman for research assistance in developing the various cases. We also thank our partners at Emerald Publishing Groups for their professionalism, especially Charlotte Maiorana (Senior Editor), Fiona Mattison (Editorial Assistant), and Jaya Chowdhury (Project Manager). We appreciate the research support provided by our respective institutions — the Kogod School of Business at American University and School of Business at Aalto University. Finally, we thank our families for their encouragement and support and dedicate the book to them: Linda and Rory Baker as well as Marika and Sandy Puttonen.

1

NAVIGATING THE INVESTMENT MINEFIELD

We don't have to be smarter than the rest. We have to be more disciplined than the rest.

Warren Buffett, Chairman and
CEO of Berkshire Hathaway

The investment world can be a scary place. During the past decade, investors have faced many challenges including the sub-prime mortgage crisis, a deep recession, a slow economic recovery, wars, terrorism, and much more. Investors also face a vast array of investment options with many vying for their business. However, some of those providing these "opportunities" seek to take advantage of investors. Although most investors realize they are fallible, they often have no clear idea why or what they can do about it. No wonder people often view investing as overwhelming and intimidating, especially if they attempt to tackle this task on their own. Although most individual investors are not experts, they still must take responsibility for their actions and financial lives. To be successful, investors must avoid many pitfalls along the way or risk making errors that affect their wealth.

Given the complex and challenging world of investing, what chance do less savvy investors have navigating the investment minefield and emerging unscathed? The answer is not much unless they recognize the investment traps that are strewn along their path and deliberately avoid these financial landmines. They also need to separate investment fads from tenets that stand the test of time. This, of course, is easier said than done. Awareness may lead to a small improvement in actions and decisions but any effect is likely to be short-lived unless someone can change or remove the cause of the biased actions.

In the world of investments, a *trap* is something that can lead to losses of capital or opportunities to make productive investments.[1] Although succumbing to such traps is unlikely to be fatal, it can seriously harm personal wealth, affect achieving financial goals, and damage self-esteem. However, investors can be their own worst enemies. They suffer from many behavioral or psychological biases that affect their judgment and decision-making. A *bias* is nothing more than the predisposition toward error.[2] Thus, a bias is a prejudice or a propensity to make decisions while already being influenced by an underlying belief.

Unfortunately, many individuals make rash financial decisions and commit investing sins. They make mistakes, display behavioral biases, and fall victim to investment traps because they lack the knowledge, experience, or self-discipline to make better choices. Investors may be unaware of why they make the investment decisions that they do. Poor decisions can result from bad advice, the wrong advisor or decision methodology. Many novice investors also devote little attention to understanding investing and the choices available to them. They may even spend less time managing their portfolios than planning a vacation or buying a car!

Making sound investment decisions is part of being financially literate. *Financial literacy* is the ability to understand how money works in the world: how people earn or make it, how they manage it, and how they invest it to create more wealth. Financial literacy also refers to the set of skills and knowledge that allows people to make informed and effective decisions and utilize all of their financial resources.[3] Financial literacy should command attention because many people are inadequately organizing their finances to ensure their own well-being. Johnnie Dent, Jr., author, lecturer, and motivational speaker, notes, "Financial illiteracy is like being in a rain storm and trying to jump in between the rain-drops... eventually it all catches you at the same time." A lack of financial literacy costs Americans billions of dollars every year.[4]

Becoming financially literate typically requires many hours of study and effort generally achieved over a long period. Although becoming financially fit may seem daunting, it is not a pipe dream, so long as someone is willing to seek some assistance. Although even knowledgeable investors make mistakes, let psychological biases affect their decisions, and tumble into investment traps, they do so far less often than less savvy investors. Those investors with less know-how need to sharpen their financial saw.

To help make better financial decisions, investors need to be aware of two enemies: one is external and the other is internal. External enemies involve those who try to deceive unsuspecting investors by setting investment traps. The other, and possibly more dangerous enemy, lies within investors themselves. Realizing that novice investors can be their own worst enemy can be frustrating. As Benjamin Graham, the legendary investor, scholar, and teacher, once wrote, "The investor's chief problem — and even his worst enemy — is likely to be himself." Successful investors avoid self-victimization. All investors suffer, often unknowingly, from behavioral biases that affect their sound judgment. Ultimately, yielding to either foe, be it internal or external, affects your wealth and welfare.

The purpose of this book is to help you recognize and avoid common investing mistakes, behavioral biases, and investment traps that can ensnare investors, affect sound judgment, and reduce wealth. The advice provided can help you rein in the emotional saboteur within you and enable you to become a more money savvy and successful investor. Following good financial advice is critical before making any investment decision, and this book aims to provide that type of advice. As Lao Tzu, an ancient Chinese philosopher, once wrote, "The journey of a thousand miles begins with one step." Much ground needs to be covered, so let's get started.

WHERE TO BEGIN

Investors sometimes find themselves in a similar position as Alice from Lewis Carroll's *Alice's Adventures in Wonderland*. Coming to a fork in the road, she asks the Cheshire cat:

Alice: Would you tell me, please, which way I ought to go from here?

Cheshire cat: That depends a good deal on where you want to get to.

Alice: I don't much care where.

Cheshire cat: Then it doesn't matter which way you go.

Alice: So long as I get somewhere.

Cheshire cat: Oh, you're sure to do that, if only you walk long enough.

The moral of this story is to start at the beginning — knowing which way to go. As Yogi Berra, the famous New York Yankee and member of the Baseball Hall of Fame, once said: "You've got to be careful if you don't know where you're going, 'cause you might not get there." Unlike Alice, investors should base their investment decisions on clear goals and then determine the appropriate path for achieving them. Unfortunately, many investors get caught up in the latest investment fad or on maximizing short-term investment returns instead of developing a plan with a high probability of achieving their long-term goals.

Investors can follow several paths to achieve their financial goals. One path is to "go it alone." If you are intent on managing your investments, you want to be sure that you are qualified to do so. Another path is to use the services of a qualified professional such as a financial advisor. Working with an advisor and knowing how to do your own financial planning are not mutually exclusive. Even if you decide to use the services of a financial advisor, you should have at least a basic knowledge about personal finance, especially investing, so that you understand the advice you are receiving and know what questions to ask. Just because you work with an advisor does not mean that you can abdicate your own responsibility. A third option is to use a robo-advisor. These new digital platforms can manage a portfolio for only a fraction of the cost of a human financial advisor but involve several drawbacks. Each of these paths is discussed shortly.

Regardless of which path you take, the process begins by establishing your financial goals. In general, the basic goal of investing is to build wealth. Once you are wealthy, you need to retain your wealth. What being "wealthy" means differs from person to person. What constitutes "wealthy" depends largely on your state of mind and lifestyle. Perhaps being wealthy means having no financial constraints on activities, surpassing a certain asset threshold, or not having to work again. Whatever your definition, building wealth is a key goal.

BEING A DO-IT-YOURSELFER

Taking a do-it-yourself (DIY) or self-directed approach entails managing your own money, including your investments. For most, planning their financial well-being (including retirement) has become a DIY proposition. Why? People typically do not work for organizations that offer much in the way of financial or investment advice. Hence, they need to develop competency in personal finance including investing. Even if they work for an organization that provides a retirement plan, the financial landscape has shifted away from defined benefit pension plans to defined contributions plans, which are now the dominant plan form in the private sector. With a *defined benefit pension plan* an employer promises a specified monthly benefit on retirement that is predetermined by a formula based on the employee's earnings history, tenure of service, and age. The employer bears the risk of providing these fixed payments. By contrast, in a *defined contribution plan*, employers and employees make fixed contributions into an individual account, which are then invested. The employee determines where to invest these funds and hence assumes the investment risks and rewards, not the employer. Thus, knowing how to do your own financial planning and investing is more essential than ever.

Well-informed individual investors can often do quite well on their own, especially if they have a well-thought-out investment plan and diligently execute it. Unfortunately, many individual investors unwittingly sabotage their chances of meeting their financial goals by violating the terms of prudent investment plans. On their own, the average individual investor tends to underperform the markets in which they invest. This is because the DIY approach can be fraught with danger if you lack the specialized knowledge and discipline necessary to succeed in today's highly competitive financial markets. Emotions play a big role because DIY investors often do exactly the opposite of what they should. For instance, novice investors might attempt to "time" market movements, engage in inadequate diversification, pay high and unnecessary fees to managers and advisors, and use borrowed money in an attempt to gain higher returns.

Yet, despite numerous pitfalls, you can sidestep or at least reduce making common investing mistakes and succumbing to behavioral biases as discussed in Chapters 2, 3, and 4. You can also avoid being duped into investment traps by becoming more informed about financial matters in general, and investing in particular. One of the biggest risks you face is not educating yourself about which investments can help you achieve your financial goals and how to approach the investing process. As Benjamin Franklin, one of the Founding Fathers who drafted the Declaration of Independence and the Constitution of the United States, said, "An investment in knowledge pays the best interest."

Nothing is more likely to pay off than gaining a financial education and engaging in the necessary research, study, and analysis before making investment decisions. Peter Lynch, the former manager of Fidelity Magellan Fund, one of the world's best known actively managed mutual funds, notes, "Average investors can become experts in their own field and can pick winning stocks as effectively as Wall Street professionals by doing just a little research." A lack of knowledge and awareness could result in regrettable financial decisions that diminish your wealth. If you are not an informed investor, others can and will take advantage of you. If you don't believe this statement, just ask the person with a "this can't happen to me attitude" who has fallen victim to investment fraud.

Don't underestimate your abilities or potential or cut corners when learning how to become a successful investor. You need to learn basic principles before investing. With sufficient time devoted to learning and research, you can become equipped to handle your own portfolio and investing decisions. In fact, some believe that you are better off being a do-it-yourselfer, even if you currently lack competency, than working with an incompetent or conflicted advisor.[5] Much of investing involves applying common sense and not being swayed by emotions. As H. W. Lewis writes in his book *Technological Risk*, "Those who are unwilling to invest in the future haven't earned one."

WORKING WITH AN ADVISOR

Another path to helping you achieve your financial goals is to use the services of a qualified professional such as a financial planner, investment advisor, or a wealth or money manager who has the requisite knowledge, skills, and abilities. Although differences exist among these individuals, we'll simply call them financial advisors. Unfortunately, much confusion exists over the term "financial advisor." In fact, no professional designation called financial advisor exists. Whether you should hire an investment advisor to manage your investments is a complex question that requires careful consideration before deciding. You don't have to be a financial lightweight to need a financial advisor, as almost anyone can benefit by hiring the right financial advisor. As Warren Buffett notes, "It is better to hang out with people better than you. Pick out associates whose behavior is better than yours and you will drift in that direction." For example, these professionals can help clients: (1) set reasonable financial and personal goals; (2) assess their current financial health; (3) develop a realistic, comprehensive plan to meet their financial goals; (4) put their plan into action and monitor its progress; and (5) help them stay on track to meet changing goals, personal circumstances, markets, and tax laws. Those who have a financial plan generally feel more confident and report more success managing money, savings, and investments than those who do not have a plan.[6]

Financial advisors often take a holistic view of their clients' financial needs and goals, meaning they look at the big picture. They can add value both by potentially improving investment performance and by mitigating psychological costs, such as reducing anxiety. For example, one study estimates that working with a certain type of financial advisor using "Vanguard Advisor's Alpha Framework," can add an average of about three percentage points a year in net return.[7] Clients can also benefit from their relationship with the advisor, specifically through financial planning and advice on savings and asset allocation. In fact, the true value of a financial planner or financial advisor often lies in managing the investor rather than the investments.[8]

Some financial advisors focus on offering investment advice to individuals. They counsel clients on investment opportunities that are consistent with the client's needs, goals, and risk tolerance. This requires keeping in touch with the financial markets, constantly monitoring the specific investments in a client's portfolio and being aware of new investment strategies and investment vehicles. However, finding and hiring an expert advisor is a complicated financial decision, especially if you have limited expertise. Unfortunately, many people wait until a crisis or moment of desperation before seeking an advisor. Also, some financial advisors are not investment experts and can't render good advice due to conflicts of interests.

WHO NEEDS A FINANCIAL ADVISOR?

Before explaining how to find the right financial advisor, let's discuss why you might need one. Everyone has to make decisions about managing their money. *Financial planning* deals with anything that has to do with you and your money. You might lack the expertise, time, or desire to actively plan and manage certain financial aspects of your life. However, if you have wobbly emotions, you probably shouldn't be steering your own financial future. Don't be afraid of asking for help. You should not wait for a crisis or moment of desperation to hire an advisor.

Financial advisors can provide advice on your entire financial situation, from your insurance coverage and spending habits to saving for a child's education or choosing the right mortgage. Providing investment advice is only a small part of financial planning. *Investment advice* is any recommendation or guidance that attempts to educate, inform, or guide an investor about a particular investment product or security. Just because someone offers financial planning services does not necessarily mean that they offer investment advice.

How else can financial advisors help? Working with a financial advisor can help you save time and remain disciplined when following financial strategies to achieve your goals. A good financial advisor will try to "talk you out of" doing things that might be hazardous to your wealth. People sometimes act on emotion, which often leads to negative financial consequences. For example, when the stock market plummets, so does the financial rationality of many inexperienced investors. Thus, a financial advisor can help you understand when acting on certain impulses may not be your best interest. Such advisors should have affirmative practices in place to curb harmful behaviors. Although dispassionate and prudent financial planning might not sound exciting, it can help you maximize your investing dollars.

Additionally, the right financial advisor can provide an independent and objective view of your money and how you are using it. Even if you know the basics of financial planning and investing, having someone keeping watch over your money and being interested in helping you achieve overall financial well-being can be comforting. Most financial advisors are honest and hard-working professionals who are obligated to do what is best for their clients. Finally, the right financial advisor can help you avoid making mistakes because of their knowledge and experience in working with many clients.[9]

Financial advisors often cater to different clients or to a specific niche. Some only deal with the rich and refuse clients who do not meet minimum investment requirements. For example, some financial advisors will not work with clients who do not have at least $250,000 in investable assets. Others are willing to work with those who have few assets or less to invest. Still other advisors focus on retirement planning. The skill set required for retirement planning goes beyond just financial planning or providing investment advice. A retirement planner must have a clear picture of how all pieces of the puzzle fit, including your financial assets combined with pensions, social security, home equity, and part-time work. Otherwise, a retirement planner cannot help you project how much money you will need when you retire.[10] The key is to find a financial advisor who fits your needs, whether this is to develop a comprehensive financial plan or simply to do a financial check-up. Before discussing how to find the right financial advisor, let's explore various types of advisors.

TYPES OF FINANCIAL ADVISORS

How can you find someone to best meet your needs and put your interests first or someone with whom you can build an enduring relationship based on mutual respect and trust? This is no easy task, but to start, you must first determine what type of advisor you want. There are four basic types of advisors.

- *Financial planners*: This is a vague category because almost anyone can call themselves a financial planner. Why? No minimum education, experience, training, or licensing requirement is needed to become a financial planner. More than 150 designations exist for planners, ranging from dubious to legitimate. Thus, when choosing a financial planner, you should typically focus on selecting someone who has earned highly respected designations such as the CFP, CPA/PFS, or ChFC certification. We discuss these certifications later in this chapter.

- *Financial advisors*: These individuals are registered investment advisors (RIAs) or investment advisor representatives (IARs). They are compensated with fees and are financial fiduciaries, so they are held to the highest ethical standards in the financial service industry. A *fiduciary* is an individual in whom another has placed the utmost trust and confidence to manage and protect property or money. RIAs have greater freedom to recommend investments than their counterparts in the industry because they do not work on commission. RIAs are also required to adhere to a much higher standard of conduct.

- *Money managers*: These financial professionals have the same registrations and characteristics as financial advisors but make decisions for investors without their approval in advance. Thus, money managers have discretion to make transactions for their clients.

- *Registered representatives*: These individuals, also called stock-brokers and investment representatives, are paid commissions to sell investment and insurance products.

When deciding on an advisor, don't confuse the various types. Although many brokers and insurance agents often call themselves financial advisors, they might be more interested in making a sale than offering a security or product that is best for you. Although some might offer sound financial advice, others are simply good salespeople who might not have your best interests at heart. In terms of loyalty, a broker's duty is to the broker-dealer for whom he or she works and not necessarily to the client served. Also, you should be aware that the "free" advice some offer often has commissions embedded into them. Having a securities license enables someone to receive commissions on the sale of investment or insurance products, but does not ensure the person has the knowledge to provide quality advice.

At this point, you may be asking yourself which of these types of advisors is most suitable for your investment needs. Be patient. We'll discuss this later under the topic "Finding the Right Financial Advisor." The following discussion provides the necessary background for making the right decision.

COMPENSATION STRUCTURE

Good financial advisors are not free. Before you can determine whether a financial advisor is worth the costs, you need to understand how financial advisors get paid. Financial advisors receive compensation in various ways.[11] Some charge a fee for services — a flat fee, an hourly rate, or a percentage of assets under management (AUM) and are called *fee-only advisors*. Advisors who are compensated based on a percentage of the account value have an incentive to grow your account and to minimize losses. However, this method might also entice some less scrupulous advisors to steer you toward taking additional risk to grow your assets. That is, investing in higher risk assets generally leads to higher expected returns, which can increase the payment to fee-based advisors who are compensated based on a percentage of your account value. Similarly, advisors who earn 1% on your annual AUM might be disinclined to encourage you to liquidate your investments, despite it being the right move at a particular time, because their fee would then decrease.

Fee-based advisors can also charge an hourly rate for their financial advice, such as providing an investment review for do-it-yourselfers, offering a second opinion of financial issues, and reviewing investments in 401(k). Advisors could also charge a fixed fee based on the scope of the engagement, such as developing an initial financial or retirement plan.

Such compensation methods are often highly suitable when you have limited assets and your needs are fairly simple. For example, you can view a meeting with an advisor for an agreed-upon hourly fee as a type of annual physical for your investments. Finally, you can also place the advisor on a retainer to provide continuing financial advice. This is likely to occur for more complex or on-going situations in which you are looking for a sustained relationship with a particular financial advisor who is aware of your situation. Some advisors offer a hybrid financial advisor fee structure.

At the other end of the spectrum are commission-based brokers, who make money on the products you buy or sell. Commissions can take many different forms, such as a front end sales load charged on a mutual fund, or a surrender fee on an *annuity*, which is a contract sold by an insurance company designed to provide payments to the holder at specified intervals, usually after retirement. Because this method of compensation could influence the advice given, you might want to avoid commission-based advisors. In other words, you should lean toward advisors who are fee-only, so everyone is clear about the incentives and you can better avoid conflicts of interest. As a general rule, you should avoid granting discretion to advisors who charge on a transactional basis because this enables them to generate income for themselves through excessive trading.

Don't confuse a fee-only with fee-based compensation. *Fee-only advisors*, also called no commission advisors, receive compensation directly from you and do not receive commissions from the sale of insurance or investment products. *Fee-based advisors* can switch between planning fees and commissions when they are dual-registered advisors. In other words, such advisors can receive fees paid by you and commissions paid by a brokerage firm, mutual fund, insurance company, and others.

Does either compensation model — fee-only or fee-based — truly deliver "unbiased advice"? The answer is no. Although each method has inherent flaws that could lead to potential conflicts of interest, many honest, trustworthy financial advisors operate under each compensation structure. Thus, you should focus on finding a competent, experienced, knowledgeable advisor who has your best interests in mind and has a transparent fee structure.[12] Red Adair, a world famous professional oil firefighter, probably said it best, "If you think it's expensive to hire a professional to do the job, wait until you hire an amateur."

A SHIFT IN THE ADVICE LANDSCAPE

Despite having many of the same functions, the financial advice offered by advisors such as RIAs and brokers, who act as agents for someone else, can differ due to two competing standards to which each has to adhere. Investment advisors are bound to a fiduciary standard that requires them to put their client's interest above their own. For example, they are prohibited from making trades that might result in higher commissions for them or their investment firm. In contrast, brokers can make suitable recommendations to their clients under certain circumstances, meaning that anything they sell has to be adequate and not necessarily ideal or in their client's best interests. The suitability standard can result in conflicts between a broker and the client, especially when fees are involved. Brokers are incentivized to sell their own products before competing or lower cost products. For example, under the suitability standard, a broker can recommend a mutual fund that returns a fee to the advisor, even if the advisor knows that a comparable, less expensive fund is available Thus, the fiduciary standard offers better protection to investors than the lesser suitability standard.[13]

According to Liz Skinner, the Department of Labor's (DOL) fiduciary rule is "… aimed at stopping the $17 billion a year the government claims investors waste in exorbitant fees. The idea is that the regulation will stop advisers from putting their own interests in earning high commissions and fees over clients' interests in obtaining the best investments at the lowest prices."[14] Thus, the new fiduciary rule helps to bridge the gap between the two groups by expecting all advisors to act as fiduciaries when making recommendations and/or giving advice on 401(k) plans or individual retirement accounts (IRAs). Although both are tax-advantaged retirement savings plans, a 401(k) is offered by an employer with varying levels of matching contributions, whereas an IRA enables individuals to direct pretax income, up to specific annual limits, toward investments that can grow tax-deferred.[15]

The DOL's expanded definition of advice substantially reduces brokers' ability to operate under a "suitability" standard as they once did for retirement accounts and eliminates the conflicted compensation model that led to potential abuse. However, keep in mind that this new regulation applies only to tax-advantaged retirement accounts. Thus, advisors can bypass the rule by limiting their practice to taxable accounts. The suitability standard still applies to individual retail accounts. Moreover, an exemption, called the best interest contract exception (BICE) exists for conflicting payment structures or "prohibited transactions" that allows the advisor to continue working with the client even if compensation increases. The rule became law in April 2017 and then fully phases in through January 2018.[16]

FINANCIAL SERVICES FIRMS VERSUS INDEPENDENT FINANCIAL ADVISORS

Besides the listed financial advisors, another choice involves deciding whether to work with a large financial services firm or an independent planner or advisor. Examples of financial services firms include full-service brokerage firms, online and discount brokerage firms, mutual fund companies, insurance companies, and banks. Many of these companies are household names, which may provide a pseudo sense of security and comfort knowing that your money is entrusted to a familiar firm. Large financial services companies have multiple branches as well, offering convenience and flexibility. However, some advisors in large commission-driven firms may be more skilled in making sales than in being financial experts.

Although such companies have many ethical and conscientious professionals, their chief role is to sell a specific product, whether or not it is best for you. They often receive a commission for those sales and their firms might not permit them to give their clients independent advice. This could create conflict regarding whose interests are best being served — your interests, their interests, or the interests of their employer. In financial planning, your interests should come first. Common sense suggests that how someone is compensated motivates behavior. Commission-compensated advisors make money by selling a product typically at a high cost. They make a large percentage of their income in the early stages of a relationship. In contrast, fee-based advisors make their money by developing and maintaining a relationship with clients over time. They try to increase your wealth by growing your assets in a consistent and predictable fashion over time.[17] As Mike Garry, author of *Independent Financial Planning: Your Ultimate Guide to Finding and Choosing the Right Financial Planner*, notes: "But when you go to an investment professional, you are really looking for advice, not a product."[18] Thus, you should typically avoid financial advisors who rely on commissions for their income or fees filtered through a broker-dealer because they may be a biased source of advice.

Instead of using an advisor who is part of a large financial services firm, another option is to use an independent financial advisor. However, independence is not necessarily a sign of objectivity because independent advisors can also receive commissions or referral fees from third parties. To minimize conflicts of interest, you generally should seek out fee-only advisors, meaning their only revenue comes from their clients. Such advisors do not have a financial incentive to steer you toward a product that is not in your best interests. Hence, they are motivated to provide advice and services that are consistent with your goals. Why? They don't sell products or receive a commission from a brokerage firm, a mutual fund company, or an insurance company. Instead, you pay them a fee for their counsel. Fee-only financial advisors also have a fiduciary responsibility to select investments that are right for you including those having low expenses. Although many experts recommend fee-only advisors, in some cases they could be inappropriate. For example, if you need help with annuities, life insurance or disability insurance, you should consider a firm that has a broker-dealer so that you don't have to go to multiple sources to meet all of your needs.

COSTS OF CONFLICTED OR BAD ADVICE

Although hiring a financial advisor involves costs, relying on someone who does not have your interests in mind or provides conflicted or bad advice can be even more costly.[19] In fact, it can lead to large and economically meaningful costs. As Jeffrey Zients of the National Economic Council notes, "You could end up with tens of thousands of dollars less simply because your advisor isn't required to put your best interests first."[20] However, many investors are unaware of the conflicting interests that could encourage their advisors to steer them into costly products or to take actions that could result in losses.

A report by the White House Council of Economic Advisers (CEA) examines the evidence on the cost of conflicted investment advice and its effects on Americans' retirement savings, especially IRAs. CEA's survey of the evidence suggests that conflicted advice reduces investment returns by roughly one percentage point for savers receiving that advice. In the aggregate, such savers hold about $1.7 trillion of IRA assets. Thus, the cumulative annual cost of conflicted advice is estimated to be about $17 billion each year.[21]

You also need to be mindful that not all investment advice is given with the client's best interests in mind. For example, some investors are encouraged to roll over assets from a 401(k) plan into an IRA, without receiving warning that the fees of the new plan exceed those of the old plan. Some brokers receive lucrative commissions when selling a product that is risky or inappropriate for an investor's portfolio but do not have to disclose that financial incentive. Thus, such brokers might recommend that their clients buy and sell products more often than needed, which causes investors to repeatedly pay unnecessary fees. To avoid this trap, you should demand that anyone giving advice or recommendations disclose how they are compensated.

Financial advisors who give bad advice do so for two major reasons. First, they place their interests before those of their clients. Remember, clients should always come first! Second, advisors might provide bad advice because of insufficient knowledge and failure to perform sufficient due diligence. In general, *due diligence* refers to the care a reasonable person should take before entering an agreement or a transaction with another party. An advisor can't be an expert is all aspects of finance and investments because the discipline is simply too broad and complex. This is why you need to educate yourself to recognize when an advisor may have limited expertise in certain areas.

Not surprisingly, the level of knowledge and understanding that advisors have about investing and financial markets varies markedly. Some advisors might believe that they are doing the right thing for their clients when they actually aren't. This could manifest itself in several ways, such as not fully understanding the investments they recommend, being overconfident in being able to pick winners that outperform the market, buying what's "hot," and constructing poorly diversified portfolios. Having a competent financial advisor is critical because the consequences of bad advice are likely to be poor performance or a loss of money.

FINDING THE RIGHT FINANCIAL ADVISOR

After you decide that you need a financial advisor, you have to find the right one for you. Although many people could benefit from a talented and conscientious financial advisor, they often don't know where to begin, especially since each type of advisor has some inherent risks. As Bruce Horovitz notes, "Selecting the right financial adviser is an imperfect storm of art and science."[22] Also, finding a truly low-cost, competent, and honest financial advisor requires an investment of time and effort. You want to investigate the person to confirm all material facts. However, don't fall into what Nobel laureate Daniel Kahneman calls the "planning fallacy."[23] The *planning fallacy* is the tendency to underestimate the time, costs, and risks of future actions while overestimating the potential benefits.

You might not know what you want, how much you should pay, or what you should ask before making a decision about a financial advisor. You should expect to devote at least as much time finding the right financial advisor as you would shopping for a car. You wouldn't risk buying an unreliable car because you didn't put enough time into research, so why would you risk it with the person handling your finances? You probably wouldn't look at a single vehicle or make a rushed decision without shopping around. By this analogy, you should identify and screen potential financial advisors before interviewing several candidates and making a final decision. You need to take your time and conduct sufficient due diligence to find the right person for the job. Like buying the wrong car, choosing the wrong financial advisor can come back to haunt you for years.

Identifying Potential Candidates

By taking a systematic approach, you should be able to find the right financial advisor.[24] You need to know where to look and the right questions to ask. As a first step, you should know what you want to accomplish in working with a financial advisor and your basic financial goals. Next, you need to identify several potential advisors. One way is to ask for referrals from friends, family, and work colleagues whose goals and finances are similar to yours. You should then look up these advisors online to get some sense of the nature of their firm and whether they are targeting your demographic. Treat these referrals as a starting point. Remember that just because one person likes an advisor doesn't mean that you will. Some horror stories of fraud and scams, such as the Madoff fraud discussed in Chapter 6, resulted from accepting recommendations on pure faith. Also, just because an advisor worked for your friend, does not mean they will work for you, especially if your financial goals do not align with your friend's.

Another way of finding a financial advisor is to use Internet websites and search engines such as the following:[25]

- The National Association of Personal Financial Advisors (NAPFA) (findanadvisor.napfa.org) contains fee-only advisors. Compared to other financial advisors, NAPFA members tend to be more experienced, are more credentialed, and have well-established practices, but could also have minimum fees or asset requirements. NAPFA advisors pledge to act in their clients' best interests at all times. You can locate an advisor by entering a zip code, last name, or address. NAPFA also provides a field guide on finding a financial advisor.[26]

- CFP Board (http://www.letsmakeaplan.org/choose-a-cfp-professional/find-a-cfp-professional/) provides a directory of financial advisors who hold the certified financial planner (CFP) designation along with their method of compensation.

- The Financial Planning Association (fpanet.org) enables you to search a database of CFPs by city, state, zip code, or last name. By using an "advanced search," you can select CFP professionals by specialties (i.e., major life changes, personal finances, and investments), method of compensation, and any income or asset minimums required.

- Boomerater (boomerater.com) is a free online advice network for *baby boomers*, that is, those born between 1946 and 1964. It provides a comprehensive database containing financial planners, investment advisors, and wealth managers from both independent practices and large firms. You can search for an advisor by entering your zip code and the distance you want to search or by last name. Those advisors with an enhanced listing provide additional information such as a detailed description of their firm, minimum client assets and income required, certifications and affiliations, compensation and fee structures, areas of expertise, education background, and firm size.

- Garrett Planning Network (garrettplanningnetwork.com) is a nationwide network of independent, fee-only financial planners. These planners are available for smaller projects for an hourly fee and are either CFPs or actively working toward this designation. Finding an advisor involves entering a name or zip code and clicking the "Find Advisor" bottom. A profile of each advisor is available.

- Paladin Registry (paladinregistry.com) has been providing free research and registry services to investors since 2003. Paladin screens, rates, and documents the quality of advisors' credentials, ethics, business practices, and services. The process of finding a financial advisor here is simple. After completing a form containing information on the type of services you need and your available asset range, Paladin's computers match your situation to a few select financial advisors. You receive an email containing the match results and the advisors receive your contact information.

- American Institute of CPAs (AICPA.com) provides a directory for locating certified public accountants (CPAs) who hold the personal financial specialist (PFS) designation by city and state, postal code or country.

Keep in mind that just because an advisor is listed with one of these networks does not guarantee honesty or expertise. While these searches give you a good place to start, your next step is to do some homework and narrow down your search to several potential candidates. Selecting a financial advisor is more difficult than finding one. A search of the financial advisor's website is likely to reveal important background information about the advisor and whether the person is still taking on clients. You might also try to identify those with successful experience advising clients in a similar life stage or circumstance as you. You should also look for fiduciaries and advisors with a transparent fee structure in which all fee and costs are clearly disclosed. Here are some other actions to take before meeting with several prospects.

Verifying the Advisor's Credentials

When you choose a physician, you want that person to have the proper credentials, training, and experience to offer quality medical advice. The same is true for someone providing financial advice. Before you engage an investment professional, make sure you research and understand the professional designations they use, and that these designations are current. You can conduct a web search to identify who administers the designation and then contact the administrator to verify that the credential is valid. For example, you can verify a planner's CFP status and background by contacting the CFP Board of Standards (http://www.cfp.net).

Be careful when obtaining investment advice about securities. Check out the person's background, experience, fee structure, or financial incentives. Unscrupulous individuals could make bogus or exaggerated claims about having degrees, credentials, or designations intended to imply special expertise or training in advising others on financial matters. Some securities regulators have encountered people pitching financial services or products with nonexistent law degrees, certifications, designations, and expired or nonexistent regulator registrations. Others might be unlicensed as securities brokers or investment advisors to effect securities transactions or give investment advice. Unqualified advisors or unlicensed agents might make unsuitable recommendations and place investors in underperforming products or securities. Such investments could also have hidden fees or long lock-up periods. To avoid this investment trap, you need to investigate anyone who is offering securities and investment advice before investing. You should insist that the person has the proper credentials and licenses. Most people who have valid credentials usually offer to help you verify them, if requested. If they try to convince you not to double check their credentials, this should be a red flag. If any suspicions arise, you should check with their state regulator.

Although many different certifications and designations exist in the financial services industry, the requirements for earning them differ markedly.[27] In recent years, a proliferation of designations, particularly in the financial planning field, has occurred. Some require rigorous standards while others do not. The financial industry regulatory authority (FINRA) provides a page called Investment Professional Designations that enables decoding the letters that sometimes follow a financial professional's name and lists various qualifications.[28]

Four of the most respected and recognized designations are typically the most important: the CFP, ChFC, CPA/PFS, and CFA designations. The first three designations focus on comprehensive financial planning, and the fourth mainly involves investments.

- *CFP*: The initial requirements to attain the CFP designation involve meeting the four "Es": education, examination, experience, and ethics. A person must have a bachelor's degree, pass a rigorous examination, have three years of professional experience in the financial planning process, or do a two-year apprenticeship with a CFP professional before earning the designation, and must adhere to the high standards of ethics and practice outlined by the CFP Board. The certification focuses on general principles of financial planning in addition to insurance, investment, income tax, retirement, and estate planning. Other topics include interpersonal communication and professional conduct and fiduciary responsibility. Thus, you can view a CFP as a generalist. The CFP® certification is a recognized standard of excellence for competent and ethical personal financial planning.

- *Chartered Financial Consultant (ChFC)*: This financial services credential issued by the American College of Financial Services has the same core curriculum as the CFP designation but adds several elective courses focusing on various areas of personal financial planning. A major difference between the CFP and

ChFC is that the latter does not require candidates to pass a comprehensive board exam. Thus, achieving the CHFC designation is generally viewed as less difficult than the CFP designation.

- *Certified Public Accountant/Personal Planning Specialists (CPA/PFS)*: A CPA is a well-trained accountant who is well-suited to provide advice especially in the realm of taxes. The Personal Financial Specialist (PFS) certification allows CPAs to gain and demonstrate competence and confidence in providing estate, tax, retirement, risk management, and/or investment planning advice to individuals, families, and business owners through experience, education, examination, and a resulting credential. Thus, a PFS can generally provide comprehensive financial planning.

- *Chartered Financial Analyst (CFA)*: A CFA charterholder must do the following: pass three six-hour examinations, have four years of qualified investment work experience, agree to follow the CFA Institute Code of Ethics and Standards of Professional Conduct, become a regular member of the CFA Institute, and apply for membership in a local CFA member society. The CFA credential has become the most respected and recognized investment designation in the world. Those holding this designation focus on investment analysis and decision-making in today's global financial industry.

Checking the Advisor's Record

When picking an advisor, you should check to determine whether they have complaints or disciplinary actions filed against them. Knowing whether any regulatory body or investment-industry group has ever put the person under investigation, whether being found guilty or not, is important. The procedure differs depending on the security licenses or credentials the individual holds.

For example, you can verify an individual's CFP certification and any disciplinary actions on the CFP website.[29]

Financial advisors involved in either managing assets or providing advice to clients have two choices: (1) be sponsored by a broker-dealer and become licensed under FINRA regulations to become a stockbroker or (2) register directly with the Securities and Exchange Commission (SEC) as an investment advisor.[30] Some financial advisors and their firms can have dual registration with both regulatory agencies. Those meeting a certain level of AUM must file Form ADV, a SEC document containing information about compensation, services, and disciplinary history. You can search by firm name to find the Form ADV at SEC.gov. State authorities regulate smaller firms, but you can check on those firms at the same site. You can check on brokers regulated by FINRA by using FINRA BrokerCheck®.[31] The advisor should be able to provide you with the disclosure form called Form ADV Part II or its state equivalent. An advisor should be compliant with FINRA, SEC, and state regulatory agencies.

Interviewing Potential Candidates

Regardless of the financial advisor's qualifications, experience, credentials, licenses, and reputation, your prescreening and background checks can only go so far. You also need to talk with each potential candidate. You can initially talk with each over the phone, which should take about 15–20 minutes per candidate, and save your face-to-face meetings with several finalists to determine if they're a good fit. Your personal comfort level is very important, and partly takes the advisor's communication skills into account.

What questions should you ask? Although the questions could vary depending on your needs, they should typically focus mainly on the advisor's background, services, compensation (fees and costs), approach to financial planning and investing, and regulatory compliance. NAPFA provides a comprehensive check-list of questions to ask.[32] Remember, you want to find someone whose offerings and personality suit your needs. For the telephone interview, here are some sample questions to help cross-check and clarify information that you've already learned from your search, as well as some questions to give you a sense of how you feel about the advisor.

1. What financial planning experience, licenses, credentials, or other certifications do you have?

2. What services do you or your firm provide?

3. What is the profile of your typical or preferred client?

4. How do you charge for your services and how much?

5. What approach do you take to financial planning?

6. Are you held to fiduciary standards at all times?

7. Have you or your firm ever been cited by a professional or regulatory governing body for disciplinary reasons?

Once you have conducted your telephone interviews, review your notes and select several candidates for face-to-face interviews, and make the appointments. A financial advisor usually will not charge you for an initial visit to discuss becoming a potential client. Advisors may ask you to complete a questionnaire before the appointment. If not covered by a questionnaire, at the beginning of the interview, you should provide a brief description of your personal situation and what you want to gain from working with an advisor. During these interviews, you can clarify any lingering questions from the telephone interviews and then ask some tough questions. These will help you learn about an advisor's communication skills and whether you understand the information provided. To maintain control of the interview, you should have a list of questions in writing. This list can keep you on track and help prevent the financial advisor from taking over and making a sales pitch. Here are some useful questions to ask:[33]

1. Who is your ideal client?

2. Would I be working only with you or with a team?

3. How will you help me reach my financial goals?

4. What happens to my account if something happens to you?

5. How frequently will you communicate with me and in what form?

6. What approach do you take to investing?

7. Will you provide me with a personal investment policy statement (IPS) and a plan for carrying it out?

8. What method will you use to measure performance of my portfolio?

9. Will you provide a written agreement detailing the agreed-upon services and costs?

10. Do you think you would be a good advisor to me? If so, why?

Finally, before leaving, ask the advisor for several references along with telephone numbers and email addresses from existing clients who have profiles similar to your own. You should also request a sample financial plan. Afterwards, you should contact the references and review the financial plan. If you need further clarification or forgot to ask some questions, you can contact the advisor. After the meeting, note whether the advisor expressed an interest in you by asking questions to understand your goals, financial background, beliefs about money, and the like. Similar to buying a car, you don't want to get a dud as an advisor. Key factors of a successful advisory relationship are trust, understanding, and open communication.

Selecting the Right Advisor

Although no bulletproof method exists for hiring an expert advisor, Carlos Sera, a RIA, provides some personal insights.[34] Don't hire an advisor:

- Who doesn't have a full-time passion for the business,

- Who hasn't personally advised clients through at least one full stock market cycle,

- Without a valid easy-to-explain investment methodology,

- Who provides conflicted advice,

- With a narrow focus,

- Who tries to be all things to all people,

- Who will invest less than 40% of your money in the stock market, and

- Who can't see you within two weeks of your initial appointment request.

You are probably aware of the phrase "The customer is always right," which Harry Gordon Selfridge, the founder of Selfridge's department store in London, coined in 1909. From a financial advisor's perspective, clients should come first but they are not always right. For example, a client may want the financial advisor to take some action that is not in the client's best interest. The best financial advisors don't always do what the client asks. A financial professional should not simply be an order taker and assist a client in committing financial suicide. You should seek a financial advisor who has the courage to tell you no when taking an action is likely to be inappropriate and have detrimental results.[35]

Finding the right advisor can benefit you in many ways. Although advisors are not immune from making mistakes, they can often help you avoid making them. Good advisors can also help you recognize your behavioral biases and steer you away from investment traps. The additional time and effort you devote to finding the right advisor can far outweigh the immediate gratification of making a quick decision.

USING A ROBO-ADVISOR

Traditionally, investors could either self-direct their investments or use a financial advisor. Now technology offers the option of receiving online advice through a *robo-advisor*, which is an automated financial advice tool offering a relatively low-cost way of providing portfolio solutions for individuals' financial needs. These digital platforms ask questions about an investor's risk tolerance, investment horizon, and other preferences then use algorithms to generate recommendations using these inputs. These Internet-based investment advisory services are aimed at small investors and could help fill an "advice gap" for investors who want to avoid high upfront fees for financial advice.

Less comprehensive robo-advisors basically offer advice on asset allocations and rebalancing, which the investor must implement elsewhere. More comprehensive robo-advisors offer discretionary investment services that can conduct security transactions and an investment program for an investor. Most robo-advisors have little or no investment minimums. Investment vehicles used or recommended by robo-advisors include mutual funds and exchange-traded funds (ETFs). Some firms such as Vanguard even offer hybrid services that pair robo-advice with on-call professional advisors.

Robo-advisors have both proponents and critics. Proponents contend that robo-advisors provide personal financial advice, minimize costs, are free from conflicts of interest, act in the client's best interests, and meet the standards of care for fiduciary investments. By contrast, some critics maintain that robo-advisors generally do not achieve any of these alleged benefits.[36] According to the SEC and FINRA, robo-advisors may result in investment recommendations that are based on incorrect assumptions, incomplete information, or circumstances not relevant to an individual investor.[37]

Despite their low cost, ease of use, and broad access, robo-advisors involve risks and limitations that you should understand before using them. Using robo-advisors requires a certain amount of faith in the technology. How investors using this new digital platform react to an extended bear market is still untested. Moreover, a computer advisor can't do all the things that a human financial advisor can such as providing a holistic look at your total wealth. Whether you should replace your human advisor with a computer solution depends on many factors such as your financial circumstances, reaction to risk, and comfort level.[38]

LESSONS LEARNED

Financial decision-making, especially investing, can be difficult. The investment landscape is cluttered with traps intended for gullible investors. To avoid these financial landmines, you need to acquire knowledge, pay attention to detail, and develop a healthy sense of skepticism. Because many perpetrators of investment traps roam the landscape, the more prepared you are, the better you can sidestep a trap that could damage your financial future.

Although some people can handle the associated complexities largely on their own, others require the help of financial professionals and robo-advisors. Knowledgeable and ethical financial advisors can also help you avoid such traps. Although most financial advisors are ethical, you want to avoid those who do not have your best interests in mind. This requires due diligence. They are wolves in sheep's clothing so beware. The bottom line is that most people can probably benefit from the services of a good, low-cost investment advisor. Yet, those with small portfolios, say less than $250,000, may have difficulty finding an expert advisor.

Regardless of the path taken, recognizing and avoiding common investing mistakes, behavioral biases, and investment traps can have a tremendous impact on investment success. Many investors are unaware of these traps or how easily they can be influenced by others or by their own biases. Although avoiding all financial hazards and biases is unrealistic, mitigating them is not. You first need to know about these pitfalls if you are going to deal with them. To do so you need to keep an open mind and avoid the *bias blind-spots*, which result from the inability to recognize that you are likely to suffer from similar cognitive, emotional, and social biases that plague others. Still, merely being aware of your biases is very seldom effective in combating them. Next, you need to develop and execute a plan for changing your behavior when making decisions. That is, you need to take action. As William G. Hammer, Jr., author of *The 7 Secrets of Extraordinary Investors*, notes, "Being an extraordinary investor is not just about knowing what to do, but doing what you know."[39] The following chapters provide guidelines on helping you achieve such changes. As Mark Twain once said, "The secret of getting ahead is getting started."

In summary, here are some key learning points from this chapter:

- Strive to become financially literate.

- Don't kid yourself about how much you think you know about financial planning and investing.

- Don't be afraid to ask for help in managing your financial matters, including your investments.

- Consider using a qualified financial advisor, especially if you are an inexperienced investor.

- Use an advisor who is a fiduciary and has a legal duty to act in your best interests.

- Be aware of different fee structures and select a financial advisor whose fee structure best fits your specific circumstances.

- Carefully investigate robo-advisers before using them.

- Educate yourself to guard against making investing mistakes, becoming a victim to psychological influences and behavioral biases, and falling into investment traps.

- Take personal responsibility for your investment actions.

QUESTIONS

1. List several reasons why someone might need a financial advisor.

2. Identify four types of financial advisors.

3. Explain the differences between fee-only and fee-based compensation.

4. Distinguish between suitability and fiduciary standards.

5. Discuss the steps in finding the right financial advisor.

6. Distinguish among the CFP, ChFC, CPA/PFS, and CFA designations.

7. Discuss how individual investors might benefit by using robo-advisors.

NOTES

1. Lipper, A. M. (2014). Current investment traps. *Inside Investing*, January 28, pp. 1 – 9. Retrieved from http://blogs.cfainstiute.org/insideinvesting/2014/01/28/current-investment-traps

2. Shefrin, H. (2007). *Behavioral corporate finance. Decisions that create value*. New York, NY: McGraw-Hill/Irwin.

3. Wikipedia. (2015). *Financial literacy*. Retrieved from http://en.wikipedia.org/wiki/Financial_literacy

4. Goodkind, N. (2014). A lack of financial education is costing the U.S. billions if not more. *Yahoo Finance*, February 5. Retrieved from http://finance.yahoo.com/blogs/daily-ticker/a-lack-of-financial-education-is-costing-the-u-s–billions-if-not-more–heidi-moore-135631985.html

5. Sera, C. (2015). *Financial tales*. North Charleston, SC: CreateSpace.

6. Princeton Survey Research Associates International. (2013). *Financial planning profiles of American households: The 2013 household financial planning survey and index*. Retrieved from http://www.cfp.net/docs/public-policy/2013-fin-planning-profiles-of-amer-households.pdf

7. Kinniry, F. M., Jr., Jaconetti, C. M., DiJoseph, M. A., & Zilbering, Y. (2014, March). Putting a value on your value: Quantifying vanguard advisor's alpha. *Vanguard Research*, pp. 2 – 28. Retrieved from http://www.vanguard.com/pdf/ISGQVAA.pdf

8. Statman, M. (2000). The 93.6% question of financial advisors. *Journal of Investing*, 9(1), 16–20.

9. How to choose a financial planner. (2008, December 17). *The Wall Street Journal*, 1 – 3. Retrieved from http://guides.wsj.com/personal-finance/managing-your-money/how-to-choose-a-financial-planner/tab/print/

10. Anspach, D. (2015). *7 step process to find the best financial advisor*. Retrieved from http://moneyover55.about.com/od/findingqualifiedadvisors/tp/bestfinancialadvisor.htm

11. Anspach, D. (2015). *6 ways financial advisors charge fees*. Retrieved from http://moneyover55.about.com/od/findingqualifiedadvisors/a/finadvisorfees.htm

12. Anspach, D. (2015). Are independent financial advisors unbiased? Retrieved from http://moneyover55.about.com/od/findingqualifiedadvisors/a/Are-Independent-Financial-Advisors-Unbiased.htm

13. Fuhrmann, R. C. (2011). Choosing a financial advisor: Suitability vs. fiduciary standards. *Investopedia*, November 17, pp. 1–4. Retrieved from http:www.investopedia.com/articles/professionaleducation/11/suitability-fiduciary-standards.asp

14. Skinner, L. (2016). Figuring out fiduciary now comes the hard part. *Investment News*, May 6. Retrieved from http://www.investmentnews.

com/article/20160509/FEATURE/160509939/the-dol-fiduciary-rule-will-forever-change-financial-advice-and-the

15. Dzombak, D. (2016). IRA vs 401k: which is better for you? *The Motley Fool*. Retrieved from http://www.fool.com/retirement/ira-vs-401k-which-is-better-for-you.aspx

16. Menickella, B. (2016). How the DOL's fiduciary rule will impact your retirement accounts. *Forbes*, June 6. Retrieved from http://www.forbes.com/sites/brianmenickella/2016/06/06/how-the-dols-fiduciary-rule-will-impact-your-retirement-accounts/#3dfd111d2ab5

17. Sera, C. (2015). *Financial tales* (p. 139.). North Charleston, SC: CreateSpace.

18. Hellmich, N. (2014). How to find the right financial adviser. *USA Today*, September 19. Retrieved from http://usat.ly/1mfZdqU

19. Hawkins, K. (2015). The cost and consequences of bad investment advice. *Investopedia*. Retrieved from http://www.investopedia.com/articles/pf/08/bad-investment-advice.asp

20. Marte, J. (2015).Obama backs new rules for retirement advice. *The Washington Post*, February 24, p. A11.

21. Council of Economic Advisors. (2015, February). The effects of conflicted advice on retirement savings. Retrieved from http://www.whitehouse.gov/sites/default/files/docs/cea_coi_report_final.pdf

22. Horovitz, B. (2016). How to shop for a money manager. *The Washington Post*, Business, March 27, pp. G1, G4.

23. Kahneman, D. (2011). *Thinking, fast and slow*. New York, NY: Farrar, Straus and Giroux.

24. Illán, I. M. (2015). *How to hire (or fire) your financial advisor: Ten simple questions to guide decision making*. Bloomington, IN: iUniverse. Other useful sources are *"How to find your financial advisor."* Retrieved from http://www.napfa.org/HowtoFindAnAdvisor.asp and Anspach, D. *7 step process to find the best financial advisor*. Retrieved from http://moneyover55.about.com/od/findingqualifiedadvisors/tp/bestfinancialadvisor.htm

25. Anspach, D. 5 search engines to use to find the right financial advisor. Retrieved from http://moneyover55.about.com/od/findingqualifiedadvisors/tp/findingadvisors.htm

26. NAPFA. *Pursuit of a financial advisor – Field guide*. Retrieved from http://www.napfa.org/UserFiles/File/PursuitofaFinancialAdvisorField Guidev14.pdf

27. Cussen, M. P. A guide to financial designations. *Investopedia*. Retrieved from http://www.investopedia.com/articles/financialcareers/07/ different_designations.asp

28. FINRA. (2016). Professional qualifications. Retrieved from http:// www.finra.org/Investors/ToolsCalculators/ProfessionalDesignations

29. CFP Board. (2015). Disciplined individuals by state. Retrieved from http://www.cfp.net/about-cfp-board/ethics-enforcement/disciplined-indi- viduals-by-state

30. Cussen, M. P. (2013). Becoming a registered investment advisor. *Investopedia*, April 10. Retrieved from http://www.investopedia.com/ articles/professionals/041013/becoming-registered-investment-advisor.asp

31. FINFA BrokerCheck®. (2015). Retrieved from http://www.finra.org/ Investors/ToolsCalculators/BrokerCheck/index.htm

32. NAPFA. (2015). How to choose a financial planner — Tough ques- tions to ask. Retrieved from https://www.napfa.org/UserFiles/File/ Tough_Questions_To_Ask%281%29.pdf

33. Shin, L. (2013). 10 questions to ask when choosing a financial advi- sor. *Forbes*, May 9. Retrieved from http://www.forbes.com/sites/laura- shin/2013/05/09/10-questions-to-ask-when-choosing-a-financial-advisor/ 2/. Hebeler, H. K. (2014). 25 questions for a potential financial advisor. *MarketWatch*, June 19. Retrieved from http://www.marketwatch.com/ story/25-questions-for-a-potential-financial-adviser-2014-06-19. Carson, R. (2014). 10 tough questions you need to ask your financial advisor. *CNBC*. October 16. Retrieved from http://www.cnbc.com/id/102066973

34. Sera, C. (2015). *Financial tales* (pp. 133–136). North Charleston, SC: CreateSpace.

35. Ritholtz, B. (2016). Say 'Yes' to the Financial adviser who'll tell you 'No'. *The Washington Post*, May 29, pp. G1, G4.

36. Fein, M. L. (2015). *Robo-advisors: A closer look*. Social science research network, June 30. Retrieved from http://ssrn.com/abstract= 2658701 or http://dx.doi.org/10.2139/ssrn.2658701

37. U.S. Securities and Exchange Commission. (2015). *Investor alert: Automated investment tools*. Office of Investor Education and Advocacy

and Financial Industry Regulatory Authority, Inc., May 8. Retrieved from https://www.sec.gov/oiea/investor-alerts-bulletins/autolisting-toolshtm.html

38. Weisser, C. (2016). The rise of the robo-adviser. *Consumer Reports*, September, pp. 44–49.

39. Hammer, W. G., Jr. (2012). *The 7 secrets of extraordinary investors* (p. 189). New York, NY: Morgan James Publishing.

2

COMMON INVESTING MISTAKES:
ROUND ONE

I'm only rich because I know when I'm wrong ... I basically have survived by recognizing my mistakes.
                              George Soros, Business magnate
                                              and investor

According to an ancient Latin proverb, "errare humanum est, perseverare autem diabolicum." Although you might not have much knowledge of Latin, you probably are familiar with the meaning of the first part of this proverb, "to err is human." Everyone makes mistakes, and investors are no exception. However, if you didn't make mistakes, you would never learn from making them.

Many factors cause errors in action, opinion, or judgment, including poor reasoning, carelessness, emotion, and insufficient knowledge. The fact that investing mistakes are so common is not surprising given the available amount of faulty advice and irrational decision-making. In fact, studies show that individual investors don't behave rationally, despite economic theory suggesting they should.[1] Not surprisingly, most investors have made decisions that they would like to go back and change.

Despite the truth underlying the first part of the Latin phrase, you probably are unfamiliar with the second part, which means "to persevere [in erring] however [is] of the devil." Making a mistake the first time is much more understandable than engaging in repeat offenses. Alexander Pope, the English poet in *An Essay on Criticism*, once wrote "To err is human; to forgive, divine." Forgiving mistakes is a nice gesture, but recognizing and avoiding investing errors is certainly divine. By doing so, you can simultaneously reduce your chances of losses and increase your odds of achieving your goals. After all, shouldn't that be why you invest in the first place?

Most investors realize that investing is not for amateurs or the faint of heart. In fact, self-directed investors usually underperform the market as a result of making investing mistakes, being prone to behavioral biases, and falling into investment traps. The list of investing mistakes is long. You should be aware that a strong bull market tends to hide investor mistakes, but a bear market reveals them. A *bull market* refers to a market that is on the rise, whereas a *bear market* is one that is in decline. The naming of these markets stems from how each animal attacks its victims. A bull drives its horns up into the air, whereas a bear swipes its paws downward upon its prey.[2]

As you would suspect, beginning or rookie investors are typically prone to making more errors than more seasoned or sophisticated investors who have learned from experience not to repeat their mistakes. Working with highly competent and experienced investment professionals should reduce the frequency of such blunders. Shelby Foote, an American historian and novelist, notes, "I think making mistakes and discovering them for yourself is of great value, but to have someone else to point out your mistakes is a shortcut of the process." That is, you can learn from someone else's mistakes. However, financial advisors and other investment professionals are not immune to making mistakes. Unless you realize that you live in a "buyer beware" society, you can easily get hurt. You need to assume personal responsibility for your financial success, and your best defense against making investing mistakes is knowledge. You need to be a proactive learner.

Chapters 2 and 3 identify and explain 15 common investing mistakes and provide advice on how to avoid them.[3] This list is not exhaustive, but it does provide a good starting point to highlight frequent blunders that many investors, including some financial professionals, make. These mistakes illustrate that investors are often their own worst enemy. The final section summarizes key lessons learned from the chapter.

INVESTING PREMATURELY

A common investing mistake is that individuals often neglect to start or continue an investment program. They may fail to start because of a lack of knowledge or trepidation of entering the market, or fail to continue because of a poor investment experience. Generally speaking, the sooner you start investing, the more time you have for your investments to grow. Before you start investing, you should consider saving for an emergency fund of at least a couple of months of expenses and paying off high interest debt such as credit cards. However, if you have retirement savings plan sponsored by an employer with an employer match, you want to take advantage of that free money as soon as possible while building your savings fund and paying down debt.[4] If you have a retirement plan available to you but you are not taking advantage of it, stop procrastinating and start investing.

NOT HAVING AN INVESTMENT PLAN

Recall the story about Alice and the Cheshire cat at the beginning of Chapter 1. If you don't know where you're going, you will probably end up somewhere else. You will fail to achieve your goals unless you take that first step — getting started. You may have hesitated to start investing because you are too busy or the time isn't right or you view investing as too risky, too complicated, and too time-consuming. However, the time to start investing is now, so that your investments have longer to grow. A Chinese proverb states "The best time to plant a tree was 20 years ago. The next best time is today." Regardless of whether you manage your own money or work with an advisor, you should have an investment plan.

"Do-it-yourself" investors often fail miserably over the long term because they are prone to making investment mistakes. However, having a proper investment plan should dramatically improve your odds of long-term success. Simply setting up an investment plan isn't enough to succeed. You must also have the discipline to carry out that plan. Sticking to your investing strategy whether you are winning or losing requires considerable persistence. You are unlikely to stick to your plan unless it fits your personality and you truly believe in it. Following a well-conceived investment plan can help you achieve your goals by generating income and/or capital gains, enhancing your future wealth, strengthening your investment portfolio, and saving on taxes. You should keep in mind that contrary to popular belief, *you* control your investment success, not the market.

HAVING TOO SHORT A TIME HORIZON

Although investors typically have short-, medium-, and long-term goals, they often focus on the short term and place too little attention on the long term. The reasons are many, but often involve strong psychological forces. For instance, people often suffer from *present bias*, which is the tendency to over-value immediate rewards at the expense of long-term intentions. This trait can have big repercussions later in life. The short-term compulsive self wants what it wants and doesn't want to be bothered by anything else. Many people are reactive and focus on the short term because they're right up against it. As noted author Robert Kiyosaki observes, "People don't like the idea of thinking long term. Many are desperately seeking short-term answers because they have money problems to be solved today." Thus, today takes precedence over tomorrow.

The tendency to yield to short-run temptations can overwhelm rational long-run planning. Focusing on the long term requires more discipline than succumbing to short-term needs and desires. Investing for the long run often requires some short-term pain for long-term gain. One of life's lessons is that temporary happiness isn't worth the long-term pain. That is, you don't want to give up what you want most for what you want now. Successful long-term investors avoid knee-jerk reactions based on fear or short-term impulses.

An Example with a 401(k) Plan

Let's look at an example with a *401(k) plan*, which is a qualified plan established by employers to enable eligible employees to make salary deferral (salary reduction) contributions in which earnings accrue on a tax-deferred basis. A 401(k) retirement plan has a long-term focus. Yet, some individuals might be tempted to dip into this account for some short-term purposes such as a vacation or renovation project. With rare exceptions, all 401(k) withdrawals are taxable as ordinary income. An additional 10% early distribution penalty tax is assessed if you have not reached at least age 59½ when you take your distribution. You also lose all the potential future investment growth of that retirement plan money. Furthermore, because annual limits exist to the amount you can contribute to a 401(k) plan, you can't make up for a previous withdrawal later, even when you are on more solid financial ground. As a result, the perceived convenience of making 401(k) early withdrawals for nonurgent expenses is likely to be a costly mistake.

Let's examine further the issue of focusing on the short term. According to Howard Schultz, chairman and chief executive officer of Starbucks, "We live in an age where everything is based on the short term." Placing too much attention on the short term extends to business organizations. For example, survey evidence shows that public companies face increasing pressure from financial markets to maximize short-term results. Despite the substantial benefits of focusing on the long term, the shadow of short-termism has continued to advance. Investors also face such pressure. Focusing on the short term emphasizes the wrong kind of performance for the typical individual investor. You need to look past short-term chatter and focus on the factors that drive long-term performance.

To fight the tyranny of short-termism and to get out of the short-term focus trap, you need to shift their emphasis to the future. This is often easier said than done, but making your long-term goals part of your daily actions is likely to lead to success. You can't build a long-term future based on short-term thinking.

A Retirement Example

Let's now use an example involving retirement. Accumulating sufficient funds for retirement takes time. Although you can't control how markets perform, you can determine when you start saving for retirement and how much you save. When you're young, retirement is in the distant future and often out of sight and out of mind. The later you start saving and planning for retirement, the less likely you are to live comfortably when you retire. Both the amount invested and the return on investment influence your wealth accumulation. Even if you are planning to retire at age 70, your life expectancy is likely to be 15–20 years beyond that. According to Fidelity Investments, 55% of Americans are in danger of not fully covering even estimated essential expenses such as housing, health care, and food in retirement.[5]

When planning for your financial future, you should consider *longevity risk*, which is the chance that you will live longer than expected. You can learn a lesson from those who are already retired. When retirees are asked what they would do differently, one of their biggest regrets is not saving enough, especially when they were young. Some of the best retirement advice is to start saving as early as possible, save consistently over time, and avoid taking loans and early withdrawals from retirement accounts.

Taking the Long View

Focusing on a long time horizon has several benefits. First, it gives money time to grow and you can unleash the power of compounding. An old investment saying is that time in the market is more important than timing the market. The power of compound interest is critical in retirement, especially for that part of your portfolio in low-risk investments. For instance, $10,000 compounded annually at 5% grows to about $16,289 in 10 years but to $70,400 in 40 years. Despite this, in real terms, a dollar received in the future is likely to lose some of its purchasing power due to inflation. You should not forget about inflation. You should focus on the *real return*. The term *real return* refers to the inflation-adjusted rate of return on an investment, not the *nominal return*, which is the rate of return before taking inflation into account. For example, if the return on an investment is 8% during the year and the inflation rate is 3%, the real rate of return is 5%. The bottom line is that money grows over time through compounding.

Second, focusing on a long-time horizon enables you to take greater risks to achieve higher returns. A year of high market volatility is generally less of a concern over the long term. According to the *Ibbotson SBBI 2015 Classic Yearbook*, stocks outperform other asset classes such as bonds and cash (Treasury bills) over time. Yet, on average investors lose money in stocks almost three calendar years each decade. Over a 20- or 30-year time horizon, such market movements would be merely blips on the radar screen. Nonetheless, time can also be an enemy. If a market downturn occurs close to your planned retirement date, you may have to reconsider your retirement plans. However, investors with an extended time horizon are more likely to follow their investment plan and less likely to let emotions rule their behaviors. Therefore, if you find yourself concentrating too much on the short term, you need to refocus.

On the flip side, if your investment strategy focuses only on the long term, you might never live to enjoy the benefits. Life is almost always shorter than you would like it to be. As such, you need to create that delicate balance between living well today and living well in the future.

TAKING TOO LITTLE OR TOO MUCH RISK

Investing requires taking some level of risk in exchange for potential reward. However, the riskiness among investments varies widely. Investments range from conservative, insured investments, such as money market funds (MMFs) and certificates of deposit (CDs) issued by a bank, to highly risky investments such as hedge funds, private equity, commodities, derivatives, and collectibles. Unless you have specialized knowledge and skills, the most risky investments should be left to professional investors because such investments tend to be the most complicated. Investing involves risk but not knowing what you are doing is a greater risk. A common investing mistake is taking either too little or too much risk. Hence, you want a portfolio consistent with your risk tolerance and future financial needs.

Taking Too Little Risk

Investors take on risk to achieve investment returns that will meet their financial goals. Being too conservative and keeping too much money in cash negatively affect returns over time. If you are concerned with building wealth over the long term rather than preserving it, you should consider riskier investments. Why?

Investors expect to be rewarded for taking on risky investments and potentially losing money. However, as with most things, exceptions exist. Although stocks with their higher level of risk historically provide higher returns than bonds and cash equivalents over the long run, this doesn't necessary occur over the short term.[6] Furthermore, some investors do not have the temperament to assume higher degrees of risk. As Peter Lynch, an American businessman and stock investor, remarks, "Everyone has the brainpower to make money in stocks. Not everyone has the stomach. If you are susceptible to selling everything in a panic, you ought to avoid stocks and mutual funds altogether."

Types of Risk

Investors face many types of risk and should recognize the risks they are taking. Below are some major risks that you are likely to encounter.[7]

- *Market risk*, also known as *systematic risk*, is the possibility for investors to experience losses due to factors that affect the overall performance of the financial markets. Such factors include a major natural disaster and macroeconomic factors such as changes in interest rates, recessions, and political turmoil. Investors can partially mitigate market risk by having a long-term investment horizon combined with an active asset allocation strategy.

- *Unsystematic risk*, also called *specific risk* or *diversifiable risk*, is the risk that relates to a particular company or industry, but is not correlated with market returns. Examples of unsystematic risk include a catastrophe such as a major oil spill, poor management, and a large product failure resulting in falling asset prices. Proper diversification can nearly eliminate unsystematic risk.

- *Inflation risk*, also called *purchasing power risk*, is the chance that inflation will erode an asset's value or income. Inflation

risk reflects the uncertainty over the future real value after inflation. Higher prices lower the purchasing power of your investments. If your investment returns don't exceed inflation, you
are losing purchasing power. Treasury inflation protected securities offer a good hedge of inflation. Investing in a broad commodities index may also offer a partial hedge, but an
investment in real estate investment trusts (REITs) offers a
much weaker one. However, some common notions about inflation hedges are ill-conceived. For instance, although many
investors view gold as a good way to protect against unexpected
price hikes, gold is a poor hedge against inflation due to its volatility, opportunity cost, storage needs, and other logistical
complexities of gold ownership.[8]

- *Interest rate risk* is the risk that arises for bond owners from
  fluctuating interest rates. Such changes usually affect fixed-rate
  bonds inversely. That is, bonds tend to rise in value when interest rates fall, and they fall in value when interest rates rise.
  Interest rates also affect economic activity and borrowing costs.
  Investors can reduce interest rate risk by diversifying (e.g.,
  investing in fixed-income securities with different durations) or
  hedging (e.g., through an interest rate swap).[9] *Duration* is a
  measure of the sensitivity of the price of a fixed-income investment to a change in interest rates. An *interest rate swap* is a
  financial derivative instrument in which two parties agree to
  exchange interest rate cash flows, based on a specified notional
  amount from a fixed rate to a floating rate (or vice versa) or
  from one floating rate to another.

- *Default risk* is the possibility that a bond issuer will fail to repay
  principal and interest in a timely manner. Bonds issued by the
  federal government are generally immune from default because
  the government can print more money if needed. By contrast,
  bonds issued by corporations are more likely to suffer default

because companies can run into financial difficulties or go bankrupt. Municipalities can also default, but this is less common. To lessen the impact of default risk, lenders often charge rates of return that correspond to the issuer's level of default risk. The higher the risk, the higher is the required return, and vice versa. Investors can reduce default risk not only by diversifying their bond portfolio but also by selecting debt issues with higher credit ratings provided by nationally recognized statistical rating organizations (NRSROs) such as Standard & Poor's, Moody's Investor Service, and Fitch Ratings. By contrast, buying low-quality, high-yield junk bonds increases your default risk in relation to investment grade bonds. *Junk bonds* are fixed-income instruments that carry a credit rating of BB or lower by Standard & Poor's or Ba or below by Moody's.

- *Liquidity risk* is the possibility that an investor may be unable to buy or sell an investment in a timely manner to prevent a loss. Investments differ greatly in their liquidity. For example, most publicly traded equity and bonds are fairly liquid but occasionally even the biggest stocks can suffer from illiquidity during times of crisis. Many alternative investments such as real estate, private equity, hedge funds, and collectibles tend to be less liquid.

These risks represent only a few of the potential risks that investors face. After reviewing these risks, you might discover that your risk tolerance is lower than you expected or that you might have to accept more risk to meet your financial goals. According to Robert Arnott, the founder and chairman of Research Affiliates, "In investing, what is comfortable is rarely profitable." At times, you may need either to step out of your comfort zone to realize needed gains or to lower your financial goals. Once you understand the different types of investment risk, you can mitigate and minimize risk with various portfolio management tools.

Taking Too Much Risk

On the other hand, some investors make the mistake of taking on more risk than necessary. This mistake can occur in several ways. For example, they take a large investment exposure in one security or sector. Such a portfolio is likely to be subject to large gyrations in performance if the market moves against such a concentrated position. Concentrating in one or a few investments could be out of the investor's comfort zone. In this instance, too much risk results from having too little diversification.

Others investors use excess leverage, which can also lead to large variations in investment performance. In the 2014 Berkshire Hathaway Shareholder Letter, Warren Buffett, Chairman, Berkshire Hathaway, comments:

> *Investors, of course, can, by their own behavior make stock ownership highly risky. And many do. Active trading, attempts to "time" market movements, inadequate diversification, the payment of high and unnecessary fees to managers and advisors, and the use of borrowed money can destroy the decent returns that a life-long owner of equities would otherwise enjoy. Indeed, borrowed money has no place in the investor's tool kit.[10]*

Leverage involves using various financial instruments, such as options and futures, borrowed capital, such as margin, and leveraged exchange-traded funds (ETFs) to increase an investment's potential return. Individuals also commonly use leverage in real estate transactions when they take out a mortgage to buy a house. Let's look at an example of each.

- *Call options*: Some investors use call options for speculative purposes. A *call option* is an agreement that gives an investor the right, but not the obligation, to buy a stock, bond, commodity, or other instrument at a specified price (known as the *exercise* or *strike price*) within a specific time period. Thus, a call option gives the holder the right to call in, or buy, an asset. The call buyer pays the call writer an *option premium* to buy the option. The call buyer realizes a gain if the underlying asset increases sufficiently above the exercise price to not only cover the option premium paid to the call writer but also to provide a profit. When option buyers use option contracts for speculative purposes, they are basically betting on the price movement of the underlying asset such as a stock. The call buyer gains exposure to a stock for a relatively small price. Although call options can provide substantial gains if a stock rises, they can also lead to 100% losses if the call option expires worthless as a result of a decline in the underlying stock price. Thus, options contracts used for speculative purposes are highly risky because they involve a high degree of leverage.

The call writer can also be taking on a high level of risk by selling calls on stocks not owned, which is called a *naked call*. Thus, if the stock prices increases above the exercise price, termed being *in the money*, the call buyer will exercise the right to buy 100 shares of the stock. The call writer, who is obligated to deliver 100 shares of the stock to the call buyer, would have to enter the market, buy the stock at the market price, and deliver it to the call buyer. A less risky strategy would be to use call options to generate income through a *covered call* strategy. With a covered call strategy, the call writer owns an underlying stock but sells a call option, collects the option premium, and hopes the option expires worthless. Although this strategy generates additional income for the investor, it can also limit profit potential if the underlying stock price rises sharply.[11]

- *Margin*: Investors can also engage in *margin buying*, which refers to buying securities with cash borrowed from a broker, using other securities as collateral. Essentially, you are getting a loan from your brokerage firm, which allows you to buy more stock than you normally could. Margin buying is a double-edged sword: it can either magnify any profit you make on the securities or it can exaggerate your losses. Thus, if the investment doesn't go as expected, you could face a large debt obligation. Buying on margin involves various other costs and drawbacks such as paying interest on your loan and carefully monitoring your positions. You are also required to maintain a minimum account balance. If you fail to do so, your broker can force you to deposit more funds or sell stock to pay down your loan. You could end up selling your stock used as collateral when its price has declined even though you may still believe in the stock's long-term prospects. New or inexperienced investors should rarely buy on margin because of the risks involved.

- *Mortgages*: As the subprime mortgage crisis of 2007–2010 shows, excessive leverage can have devastating effects. The housing boom of the mid-2000s coupled with low interest rates led many lenders to offer home loans to borrowers who previously would have had difficulty getting mortgages. Rapidly rising housing prices both contributed to and facilitated the expansion of mortgage credit. When the real estate bubble burst, many borrowers could not make payments on their subprime mortgages. The sharp increase in high-risk mortgages that went into default beginning in 2007 contributed to the most severe recession in decades.[12]

- *Leveraged ETFs*: Unlike a traditional ETF, a leveraged ETF uses financial derivatives and debt to amplify the returns of an underlying index. Introduced in 2005, these funds have a non-traditional return structure because they try to maintain a constant amount of leverage during the investment time frame, such as a 2:1 or 3:1 ratio. Thus, leveraged ETFs create the potential for an investor to earn 2% or 3% for every 1% change in the underlying index. This magnified exposure requires only a fraction of the capital. However, this investment involves many risks, ranging from basic risks associated with leverage to complex risks associated with compounding returns on a daily basis. Consequently, inexperienced investors should avoid using leveraged ETFs.[13]

HAVING IMPROPER DIVERSIFICATION

Another frequent investing error involves the level of portfolio diversification. *Diversification* is a risk management strategy that mixes a wide variety of investments within a portfolio. The concept of diversification is not new. In fact, the Bible mentions diversification in the book of Ecclesiastes (11:2), written in about 935 BC: "But divide your investments among many places, for you do not know what risks might lie ahead." Proper diversification is a fundamental principle of successful long-term investing.

How Diversification Works

Diversification reduces investment risk by relying on the lack of a tight positive association among the assets' returns. As Judith Ward, a senior financial planner with T. Rowe Price, notes:

> *Diversifying broadly across and within asset classes is not a guarantee that you won't lose money, but investors should maintain a diversified strategy that reflects their long-term goals and risk tolerance and that they can stick with during periods of short-term volatility, rather than bailing out of stocks and going to cash.*[14]

Following a more diversified approach doesn't eliminate all risk, but it does reduce the risk of all of your assets being affected in a similar fashion. For example, let's look at a portfolio consisting of stocks, bonds, and cash instruments such as Treasury bills. Over long periods of time, stocks outperform bonds and Treasury bills but these other diversification building blocks provide steady income and usually help to reduce volatility. Thus, the positive performance of some investments neutralizes the negative performance of others. As Russ Wiles notes, "Think of these as an anchor. They will slow your boat during balmy weather but keep it from crashing into the rocks during a storm."[15] As a result, a diversified portfolio yields higher returns, on average, while offering lower risk than any individual investment contained within the portfolio. Although diversification does not provide a guarantee against loss, this strategy is a time-tested way to help you achieve your long-range financial goals. A well-diversified portfolio is a key way of reducing unsystematic risk.

An Example of Risk Reduction

Here's an example that illustrates the importance of risk reduction outside of an investment portfolio: Let's suppose conjoined twins decide to cross the street and are hit by a bus. Because the twins move in tandem, whatever happens to one of the twins also happens to the other. That is, they both bear the same risk, which in this case is being hit by a bus. However, if they are separated, they don't have to move together or even be in the same location. Although one might be hit by a bus, the other might be safely drinking espresso in a coffeehouse.

A similar situation occurs when the returns between two stocks do not move perfectly together. If the returns have perfect positive correlation, expressed as +1, an increase or decrease in the returns of one stock always predicts the same directional change for the second stock. Correlation does not imply that one variable (e.g., returns on a stock) causes or influences the other variable (e.g., returns on another asset), but simply shows that the variables have a positive, zero, or negative relation with one another. As long as the returns between the two stocks are not perfectly positively correlated, the risk of the portfolio, as measured by the standard deviation of its returns, decreases. *Standard deviation* is a statistical measure that is used to quantify the amount of variation or dispersion of a set of data values such as returns.

One of the criticisms of modern portfolio theory for individual investors is that optimizing with volatility as a risk measure is not behaviorally justified. The implication that deviations away from the expected return, both positive and negative, add to risk does not reflect how individuals either do, or should, think about risk. Investors rarely state that getting more than they expect feels like a risk.

Achieving the Right Level of Diversification

Investors, like Goldilocks in the story of Goldilocks and the three bears, should strive for something that is "just right" for them. That is, they should attempt to find a balance and achieve a well-diversified portfolio. Unfortunately, no one standardized solution for allocating assets is right for all investors. Because no universally optimal asset allocation exists, each investor requires a tailor-made solution to achieve the right balance between risk and return. Allocating to different asset classes serves as a starting point for diversifying a portfolio. Selecting a portfolio's target asset allocation involves a trade-off between risk and return. In general terms, an *asset class* is a group of securities that exhibits similar characteristics, behaves similarly in the marketplace, and is subject to the same laws and regulations. Thus, various asset classes contain substantially different investments that are not highly correlated with each other. However, during market corrections, asset classes tend to become more correlated, resulting in muting the benefits of diversification and necessitating a downside protection strategy that goes beyond traditional diversification.

Many ways are available to designate asset classes. For example, traditional asset classes typically include equities (stocks), fixed-income (bonds), and cash equivalents (money market instruments). You can also diversify within each asset class. With stocks, for example, you can also allocate by: (1) geography and type of security such as domestic equities and foreign stocks;

(2) market capitalization, which is the market value of its total stock outstanding, such as mega cap (greater than $200 billion), large cap ($10–$200 billion), mid cap ($2–$10 billion), and small cap ($300 million to $2 billion) for U.S. stocks; (3) style such as value, growth, aggressive growth, blend, and growth and income; (4) market sectors or industries; and (5) industry groupings such as consumer staples and consumer durables. With bonds, you can allocate in various ways such as by geography (domestic and foreign), type (corporate, government and agency, municipal, and mortgage backed), maturity (short-, mid- or long-term), and credit rating (investment grade and noninvestment grade).

Alternative Investments

One way to provide greater diversification is to include exposure to some alternative asset classes in your portfolio. Generally speaking, an *alternative asset class* or *alternative investment* is any investment beyond the traditional stocks, bonds, and cash equivalents. Another view of alternatives is using different strategies, such as short selling or leverage, with traditional investments. Alternative asset classes include a wide range of possibilities from real estate, hedge funds, private equity, and commodities, to collectibles such art, antiques, toys, stamps, coins, comic books, and classic cars. Although some of these alternatives such as hedge funds are only available to more sophisticated investors called *accredited investors*, others are well within the reach of other types of investors. Although alternative investments are not appropriate for everyone, they provide additional opportunities if they meet an investor's objectives and risk tolerance. Those with greater income and wealth often have higher risk tolerance levels, which make alternative investments more attractive.

Although alternative investments can provide diversification, their investment risks may be understated because of the complex and irregular methods used to value them. For example, valuing alternative investments, such as private equity, hedge funds, and nonpublicly traded real estate, is based on estimates and appraisal values of illiquid assets instead of daily public market transactions for traditional asset classes. As a result, reported returns can become a smoothed version of the true realized returns and, thus, can bias the evaluation of the asset's performance. The main consequence of artificially smoothing an investment's returns, which is a phenomenon called *return smoothing*, is that it appears to lessen an investment's risk.

Underdiversification

Many individual investors underdiversify. They think they can maximize returns by taking a large investment exposure in a single security or investment. For example, some investors devote a large portion of their portfolios to their own company's shares, which can compound their suffering if the company does poorly. When the market moves a concentrated position, the results can be disastrous. You've probably heard of the saying "Don't put all of your eggs in one basket." If you do and you drop the basket, you're likely to lose most, if not all, of your eggs. This concept also applies to investments. If your portfolio has concentrated exposure to a particular type of asset that incurs a loss, your entire portfolio suffers. As William Berger notes, "A correction takes place to determine which investments are the tennis balls and which are the eggs. You want to own the things that bounce, as in tennis balls, and not in eggs."

Research shows that the level of underdiversification is greater among younger, low-income, less-educated, and less sophisticated investors.[16] These investors prefer familiar stocks and exhibit overconfidence. Individual investors tend to hold undiversified stock portfolios by overweighting stocks of their employers and investing in companies close to where they live. This results in unnecessary levels of idiosyncratic, and thus uncompensated, risk.[17] *Idiosyncratic risk*, which is quite similar to unsystematic risk, is the risk specific to an asset or a small group of assets. Such risk can be substantially mitigated or eliminated from a portfolio by using adequate diversification. Idiosyncratic risk accounts for most of the variation in the risk of an individual stock over time.

Although underdiversification is costly to many investors, some successful investors underdiversify by following a focused portfolio strategy. Billionaire investor Warren Buffett states that "diversification is protection against ignorance. It makes little sense if you know what you are doing." According to Buffet, studying a few industries in great depth and using that knowledge to profit on those industries is more profitable than diversifying a portfolio across a broad array of sectors so that gains from certain sectors offset losses from others. Although Buffett's view has merit for highly knowledgeable and experienced investors, beginners[18] and less experienced investors should consider the merits of proper diversification. Whatever investment strategy that you follow, you should be sure that you know what you are doing.

Overdiversification

In contrast, some investors and their financial advisors overdiversify. The main problem with overdiversifying is that having too many individual stock positions can lead to extensive due diligence, a complicated tax situation, and performance that simply mimics a stock index. Overdiversifying can also lead to *diworsification*, which is the process of adding investments to a portfolio in such a way that actually worsens the risk-return trade-off.[19] Financial advisors could be motivated to over-diversifying your investment portfolio because of job security and personal financial gain. Here are some signs of overdiversification:[20]

- Owning too many mutual funds within any single investment style category, which leads to overlapping holdings.

- Excessive use of multimanager investments such as a *fund of funds*, which is an investment strategy of holding a portfolio of other investment funds rather than investing directly in stocks, bonds, or other securities.

- Owning an excessive number of individual stock positions.

- Owning privately held "non-traded" investments that are not fundamentally different from the publicly traded ones you already own.

In conclusion, diversification is like eating chocolate: it's good but only in moderation. Investment professionals typically agree that diversification is a prudent strategy to adopt to help achieve long-term goals. Properly diversifying your portfolio provides more consistent overall portfolio performance. Of course, instead of investing in individual stocks, bonds, and other assets, you can invest in pooled investments such as mutual funds or ETFs to gain the benefits of diversification with relatively low transaction and search costs and let professional managers handle the investments. However, diversification does not ensure a profit or guarantee against loss. It can reduce unsystematic risk, but it can't eliminate all risk. Rather than diversifying too much or too little, you want to achieve a well-balanced portfolio that is right for you.

Strategies for Diversification

Your desired level of portfolio diversification is related to factors such as your investment goals, risk tolerance, and level of expected returns. The number of asset classes needed to achieve your desired level of portfolio diversification depends on the correlation or association between the asset classes that make up your investment universe. As the degree of correlation decreases, the potential for diversification increases, resulting in the need for fewer asset classes to achieve your desired level of diversification. Nonetheless, you should allocate to all major sectors and generally avoid allocating more than 5–10% to any one investment. Because asset correlations are not static, you may need to change allocations and replace some of the assets in your portfolio.

FAILING TO REVIEW AND REBALANCE INVESTMENTS REGULARLY

Constructing an investment portfolio that matches your needs is not a one-time proposition. You can't just sit back and ignore it. Similar to owning an automobile, a portfolio requires regular monitoring and maintenance to continue functioning properly. Market fluctuations are always a part of investing. Over time, *portfolio drift* occurs because a portfolio's investments produce different returns, so that the proportion of assets in each asset class changes relative to the target asset allocation. Thus, a carefully constructed portfolio will start to look quite different as time passes. Keeping each asset within the range specified in an investment plan requires rebalancing. *Rebalancing* is the process of realigning the weightings of a portfolio of assets. It involves periodically buying or selling assets in a portfolio to maintain the original desired level of asset allocation. Rebalancing keeps your portfolio well-balanced and diversified.

The main goal of a rebalancing strategy is to minimize risk relative to a target asset allocation, not to maximize returns. Why? Without rebalancing, a portfolio drifts from its target asset allocation as the weight of higher return, higher risk assets increases. Consequently, asset classes are overweighted at market peaks and underweighted at market lows, which is likely to lead to poor performance over time. For example, if the stock market increases dramatically, the value of the equities in the portfolio is also likely to increase and move the asset allocation for equities beyond the maximum percentage set forth in the investment plan. Without rebalancing, investors tend to ride well-performing assets higher. In up markets, stocks will take over if left unattended for too long. Substantial declines in the stock market have the opposite effect on the equity portion of the portfolio. Without rebalancing, investors are likely to incur larger losses in the event of a sharp decline. Thus, rebalancing does not guarantee an investor's goals will be met. Still, rebalancing is a smart decision because it maintains a portfolio's original risk-return characteristics more closely than with a never-rebalanced portfolio.

Rebalancing forces you to take profits from investments that have increased and put money in investments that have merit but haven't gone up. That is, rebalancing helps investors to potentially take advantage of market declines by investing at more attractive prices. It also smooths investment returns. You can also use rebalancing to readjust the weighting of each asset class to reflect changes in your investment strategy or risk tolerance resulting in a revised asset allocation. Thus, rebalancing helps you maintain a level of risk that you find more comfortable and gives you another opportunity to review your portfolio.[21]

Strategies for Rebalancing

Although rebalancing the mix of assets in your portfolio is a good idea, the question remains, how should you go about doing this? Similar to asset allocation, no universally optimal rebalancing strategy exists. To avoid the procrastination often associated with rebalancing, some investors set deadlines or rules. Several main options are available to investors: (1) time-only, (2) threshold-only, and (3) time-and-threshold. With a *time-only strategy*, rebalancing occurs periodically, such as every month, quarter, or year, regardless of how much portfolio drift has occurred from its target. With a *threshold-only strategy*, rebalancing occurs when the portfolio's asset allocation drifts from the target asset allocation by a predetermined minimum rebalancing threshold such as 1%, 5%, or 10%. Finally, a *time-and-threshold strategy* calls for rebalancing the portfolio on a scheduled basis, but only if the portfolio's asset allocation has drifted from its target asset allocation by a specified minimum rebalancing threshold.

A rebalancing strategy involves a trade-off between risk and return. Each strategy involves costs such as any applicable taxes, transaction costs to execute and process the trades, and time and labor costs to compute the rebalancing amount. What rebalancing strategy is best? A study conducted by Vanguard concludes: "... monitoring frequencies (such as annual or semiannual) and reasonable allocation thresholds (variations of 5% or so) is likely to provide sufficient risk control relative to the target asset allocation for most portfolios with broadly diversified stock and bond holdings."[22] Regardless of the approach, rebalancing does not protect against loss in a declining market.

Challenges to Investors

For many investors, rebalancing can be difficult because it involves a contrarian action: selling some assets in the best performing asset classes and buying more of the worst-performing asset classes. That is, rebalancing forces you to sell some of your hot assets and reinvest the proceeds in laggards. Taking such action seems counterintuitive to some investors, especially given the uncertainty about the future. For example, investors are reluctant to rebalance their portfolios not only when equity markets are in distress, but also during bull markets for equities. During such bull markets some investors fall victim to the belief that somehow the current bull market differs from past markets and will continue to increase indefinitely. As John Templeton, a stock investor, businessman, and philanthropist, once noted, "The four most dangerous words in investing are 'This time, it's different'." Templeton also said that "The time of maximum pessimism is the best time to buy and the time of maximum optimism is the best time to sell." This latter statement is consistent with rebalancing. In essence, the rebalancing process results in selling high and buying low.

If you fail to rebalance your portfolio by increasing its alloca-tion to equities during difficult times, you might miss out on the subsequent equity returns when underperforming assets take off. Further, by failing to rebalance your portfolio by decreasing its allocation to equities during exuberant markets, you might miss out on locking in gains before the market eventually declines. The bottom line is that rebalancing will help you stick to your invest-ing plan regardless of what the market does, which helps to mini-mize the emotional aspects of investing. If you don't have the willpower to rebalance when markets move sharply, then your portfolio is probably too risky. A well-maintained portfolio cer-tainly beats a pocketful of regrets.

BEING INFLUENCED BY EMOTIONS

Let's face it, investors don't always act rationally. A market reflects the combined behavior of many people responding to information, misinformation, and whim. The highly complex, unpredictable, and competitive market environment leads to inves-tors being caught up emotionally. Money is emotional. Emotions and unconscious forces, not fundamental principles, often drive investment decisions. Yet, investors both big and small sometimes get caught up in market euphoria.

You need to get in touch with your inner investor because investing can bring up emotional issues that can impede rational decision-making. Although you can't control outside events and their effects on markets, you can control your own mind and behavior. Thus, self-control is a key to investment success. Unfortunately, many investors find subordinating an impulse is difficult. As a result, submitting to your emotions can be a major killer of investment returns.

As Kevin O'Leary, a Canadian businessman and television per-sonality, notes, "When you're an investor, you can look at the quantitative and qualitative elements of an investment, but there's a third aspect: What you feel in your gut." Recognizing and acknowledging your hidden desires can help you make better choices and ultimately achieve your real goals. A common investing mistake is letting emotions steer your investments. Some investors become enamored with a company and ignore its fundamentals. Getting caught up in the excitement of an investment also provides easy entry for others such as scammers and con artists to take advantage of you. If you let your emotions rule your financial decisions, then you probably need to have a trusted financial advisor handle your investment portfolio.

Research shows that many individual investors are unsophisticated "noise traders" who are subject to fads and psychological biases. A *noise trader* is an investor who makes decisions about buying and selling assets without using fundamental data. As a result, these investors generally have poor timing, follow trends, and over-react to good and bad news. Apart from making less informed investment decisions, they often hold undiversified portfolios and trade actively and speculatively, which leads to poor performance. Such investors tend to buy high and sell low and don't stay with their long-term investment strategy. To them, the process feels fun, more like a game than rational financial planning, until they start losing money.[1]

Greed and Fear

Investors frequently base how much risk they should take on how it makes them feel. They tend to take more risks when they feel comfortable and fewer risks when they don't. As a result, investors generally take more risks when markets are high and less risk when markets are low. This can lead to the common investing mistake of buying high and selling low, especially when their portfolios encounter extreme volatility. That is, many investors get in and out of the market at the wrong times and for the wrong reasons.

Given that a fundamental principle of investing is to buy low and sell high, why do so many investors do the opposite? One reason is that some investors buy high because they focus on near-term returns instead of attempting to achieve their long-term investment goals. Another reason is that investors often engage in a *herd mentality*, which refers to following the crowd and investing in what's popular without concern for valuations or one's individual circumstances. Their focus on short-term returns leads them to focusing on the latest investment craze or fad. Investors are emboldened to buy shares when markets rise but sell them when markets plummet. Buying high generally means overpaying for an investment while selling low means incurring losses. This is a classic example of greed and fear, which are two major emotions driving markets.[23] As James Grant notes, "In almost every walk of life, people buy more at lower prices; in the stock market they seem to buy more at higher prices."

In a famous op-ed piece in the *New York Times* in October 2008, Warren Buffet wrote: "A simple rule dictates my buying: Be fearful when others are greedy, and be greedy when others are fearful." This quote reveals the mind-set of a highly successful investor on how to respond to dramatic market changes. When the market increases, don't be overly aggressive or buy into bubbles, but tone down your emotions. When the market falls, don't run in fear — view this as an opportunity to buy cheaply. Thus, the best time to buy is often when everyone else is selling, but this means having the conviction to go against the crowd. As previously noted, you can't control what happens in financial markets but you can manage your response to whatever the market creates. For many investors, market corrections come when they are least prepared for them. You need to be ready to take advantage of volatility. As Warren Buffett notes, "Look at market fluctuations as your friend rather than your enemy. Profit from folly rather than participate in it."

Investors in the financial markets are aware of the gyrations that can wreak havoc on both a portfolio and the psyche.

Nonetheless, an investor's psyche can overpower rational thinking during times of stress. For example, investors sometimes form emotional attachments to the assets in which they invest. This occurred in the case of dot-com mania in the late 1990s and the more recent oil price bubble when investors were caught up emotionally in the excitement and speculative bubbles. Inevitably, such a euphoric bubble has to burst. You should avoid letting your pride take priority over your pocketbook by holding on to a losing investment.

Fear can have a devastating effect on your long-term financial well-being. Perhaps the greatest risk that investors take is staying out of the market. For example, after the 2008–2009 market meltdown, many investors exited the stock market due to their fears and trauma of a major collapse. For example, the Dow Jones Industrial Average (DJIA) lost half its value in less than a year. As a result, millions of investors saw billions of dollars in assets disappear. They "freaked out" when the market dropped and bought "safe" assets out of fear for the next crisis. By keeping their money in cash and gold, they missed out on the market recovery starting in March 2009. Their "safe" assets not only underperformed the market but also actually lost value. The winners were patient investors who adhered to a buy-and-hold strategy. Hence, by priming your portfolio for a crisis, you are likely to miss out on big gains. Over time, having a balanced portfolio is a better approach than maintaining a safe but fearful portfolio.

Strategies for Handling Emotions

Fortunately, some strategies are available to take at least some of the emotion out of investing.[24] Perhaps the most obvious approach is to create an investment plan containing your goals as well as asset allocations and to stick to your plan. If you have a financial advisor, one of the first steps in that relationship is to develop such a plan, called an investment policy statement (IPS).

This plan serves as a guide to keep you on track when emotions take over your rational side.

Another approach is to use *dollar-cost averaging* (DCA), a strategy in which an investor places a fixed dollar amount into a given investment such as common stock on a regular basis. By following DCA, you can buy more shares when prices are low and fewer shares when prices are high. Thus, DCA reduces the risk of investing a large amount in a single investment at the wrong time. This approach enables you to buy more when the stock slumps and to buy less when the stock is more expensive. Other previously discussed strategies are to diversify and periodically rebalance your portfolio.

Although these strategies can mitigate some risks, they don't matter unless you can keep your emotions in check. Although following your emotions can lead you astray, cognition and emotion can't be totally separated. You need to acknowledge that investing is inherently emotionally charged and understand how emotions might influence your behavior. Additionally, emotions play a role in explaining the repeated occurrences of systemic events such as market-wide asset pricing bubbles and related phenomena, which illustrate how markets may occasionally break down. As Jim Cramer, an American television personality, former hedge fund manager, and best-selling author, comments, "Every once in a while, the market does something so stupid it takes your breath away." Without some emotion and passion about investing, investors couldn't generate the conviction necessary to take the risk of investing. Sticking to sound investment decisions while controlling your emotions and not blindly following market sentiment is important to successful investing and maintaining your long-term strategy.

LESSONS LEARNED

As Yogi Berra, an American professional baseball catcher, manager, and coach, once said: "We made too many wrong mistakes." All investors make mistakes at one point or another during their investing careers. You should understand where you go astray and then correct those mistakes. Average investors view mistakes as bad whereas successful investors see mistakes as an opportunity to learn something new. Making mistakes is part of the learning process, but repeating them is disregarding what you have learned. According to one definition, insanity is doing the same thing over and over again, but expecting different results.

This chapter highlights common investing mistakes and suggests how to avoid them. You can avoid succumbing to various financial transgressions by heeding the following suggestions:

- Begin investing as soon as practical.

- Develop an investment plan, stay with it, and remain disciplined.

- Resist the urge to act all the time and focus on your long-term investment strategy. Investing is a lifelong journey, not a sprint.

- Realize that all investing is subject to risk and understand the various types of risk.

- Don't put all of your investment eggs in the same basket. Spread out your risks by having a low-cost, well-diversified portfolio that suits your risk tolerance and goals.

- Rebalance your portfolio periodically to ensure your asset allocation isn't getting out of whack.

- Get off the emotional roller coaster. Smart investing involves making decisions with a cool head.

- Learn quickly from your mistakes.

QUESTIONS

1. Explain when you should start investing.

2. Discuss the importance of having an investment plan.

3. Discuss the potentially negative effects of focusing on too short a time horizon.

4. Distinguish among the following types of risk: market risk, unsystematic risk, inflation risk, interest rate risk, default risk, and liquidity risk.

5. Explain how diversification can reduce a portfolio's risk.

6. Comment on why periodically rebalancing a portfolio is important.

7. Discuss how emotions can affect investment decisions.

NOTES

1. Barber, B. M., & Odean, T. (2013). The behavior of individual investors. In G. M. Constantinides, M. Harris, & R. M. Stulz (Eds.), *Handbook of the economics of finance* (pp. 1533 – 1570). Amsterdam: Elsevier B. V. Retrieved from http://faculty.haas.berkeley.edu/odean/papers%20current%20versions/behavior%20of%20individual%20investor

2. Investopedia Staff. (2016). Digging deeper into bull and bear markets. *Investopedia*. Retrieved from http://www.investopedia.com/articles/basics/03/100303.asp

3. Lewis, J. (2013). 7 investment traps that could harm your wealth. *Hargreaves Lansdown*, July. Retrieved from http://www.hl.co.uk/news/articles/features/7-investment-traps-that-could-harm-your-wealth. Yoder, J. 7 common investor mistakes. *Investopedia*. Retrieved from http://www.investopedia.com/articles/stocks/07/mistakes.asp. Investopedia Staff. 7 investing mistakes and how to avoid them. *Investopedia*. Retrieved from http://www.investopedia.com/articles/01/121901.asp

4. McWhinnie, E. (2014). 5 rookie investing mistakes to avoid. *USA Today*, May 4. Retrieved from http://www.usatoday.com/story/money/personalfinance/2014/05/04/wall-st-cheat-sheet-5-rookie-investing-mistakes-to-avoid/8634965/

5. Fidelity Investments. How ready is America to retire? Retrieved from https://www.fidelity.com/bin-public/060_www_fidelity_com/documents/picture-of-americas-retirement-readiness.pdf

6. FINRA. (2016). The reality of investment risk. Retrieved from http://www.finra.org/investors/reality-investment-risk

7. Landes, L. (2012). Four risks of investing. *Forbes.com*, June 15. Retrieved from http://www.forbes.com/sites/moneybuilder/2012/06/15/four-risks-of-investing/

8. Swedroe, L. (2012). How to hedge against inflation (Hint: forget gold). *CBS Money Watch*, June 14. Retrieved from http://www.cbsnews.com/media/how-to-hedge-against-inflation-hint-forget-gold/

9. Securities and Exchange Commission. (2013). Interest rate risk — When interest rates go up, prices of fixed-rate bonds fall. SEC Publication No. 151 (6/13). Retrieved from https://www.sec.gov/investor/alerts/ib_interestraterisk.pdf

10. Buffet, W. E. (2014). 2014 Berkshire Hathaway shareholder letter, p. 19. Retrieved from http://www.berkshirehathaway.com/letters/2014ltr.pdf

11. Investopedia Staff (2016). Call option. *Investopedia*. Retrieved from http://www.investopedia.com/terms/c/calloption.asp

12. Duca, J. V. (2013). Subprime mortgage crisis. *Federal Reserve*, November 22. Retrieved from http://www.federalreservehistory.org/Events/DetailView/55

13. Kuepper, J. (2013). 7 mistakes to avoid when trading leveraged ETFs. *Yahoo! Finance*, September 4. Retrieved from http://finance.yahoo.com/news/7-mistakes-avoid-trading-leveraged-130053722.html

14. Price, T. R. Rebalancing can help mitigate market risk. *Investor*, Summer, pp. A5–A7.

15. Wiles, R. (2016). Despite tumult, stock-market tenets stand test of time. *USA Today*, May 14, p. 6B.

16. von Gaudecker, H. -M. (2015). How does household portfolio diversification vary with financial literacy and financial advice? *Journal of Finance*, 70(2), 489–507.

17. Goetzmann, W. N. & Kumar, A. (2008). Equity portfolio diversification. Review of Finance, 12(3), 433–463.

18. Investopedia Staff. (2015). What did Warren Buffett mean when he said, 'Diversification Is Protection Against Ignorance. It Makes Little Sense If You Know What You Are Doing.' *Investopedia*, March 11. Retrieved from http://www.investopedia.com/ask/answers/031115/what-did-warren-buffett-mean-when-he-said-diversification-protection-against-ignorance-it-makes.asp

19. Portfolio Diversification. (2015). *Your complete guide to investing in mutual funds*. Valley Vista Enterprises, LLC. Retrieved from http://www.investing-in-mutual-funds.com/portfolio-diversification.html

20. Allison, D. Top 4 signs of over-diversification. *Investopedia*. Retrieved from http://www.investopedia.com/articles/financial-theory/11/signs-of-over-diversification.asp

21. Bold, A. (2011). Why rebalancing your portfolio is important. *U.S. News and World Report*, March 15. Retrieved from http://money.usnews.com/money/blogs/the-smarter-mutual-fund-investor/2011/03/15/why-rebalancing-your-portfolio-is-important

22. Jaconetti, C. M., Kinniry, F. M., Jr., & Zilbering, Y. (2010). Best practices for portfolio rebalancing. *The Vanguard Group*, July. Retrieved from http://www.vanguard.com/pdf/icrpr.pdf

23. Statman, M. (2015, June 14). How your emotions get in the way of smart investing. *The Wall Street Journal*. Retrieved from http://www.wsj.com/articles/how-your-emotions-get-in-the-way-of-smart-investing-1434046156

24. Zucchi, K. (2010). How to avoid emotional investing. *Investopedia*, June 28. Retrieved from http://www.investopedia.com/articles/basics/10/how-to-avoid-emotional-investing.asp

3

COMMON INVESTING MISTAKES: ROUND TWO

Success does not consist in never making mistakes but in never making the same one a second time.

George Bernard Shaw, Playwright and critic

All investors make mistakes. However, not all investors learn from them. If they do, they can avoid repeating them, become smarter investors, and gain greater financial self-control. As Bill Gates, American business magnate, notes "It's fine to celebrate success but it is more important to heed the lessons of failure." Successful investors focus on the long term, which is difficult in a short-term world, and develop the proper temperament. That is, they learn to keep their emotions in check and tune out the noise.[1] This chapter identifies other common investing mistakes and provides advice on how to avoid them.[2] It concludes by discussing how to develop a financial plan. As Manoj Arosa, author of *From the Rat Race to Financial Freedom*, comments, "Long term thinking and planning enhance short term decision making. Make sure you have a plan of your life in your hand, and that includes the financial plan and your mission."

CHASING INVESTMENT RETURNS AND TRENDS

Related to the emotional side of investing is chasing performance or returns. Chasing investment returns involves switching from a poorly or average performing investment into one that has a strong recent return in hopes that the positive performance continues into the future. Performance chasing is based on the assumption that the past is a good indicator of the future. This behavior is a mistake because it's like driving while looking in the rear-view mirror. Chasing returns or yields is living in the past, not investing for the future, because past returns do not guarantee future performance. Nonetheless, when investors see an asset's price move higher and higher, they often fear missing out on an exciting opportunity. They want to hop on the bandwagon, but generally it's too late. Although many investors take a rear-view-mirror approach to investing, Warren Buffet focuses on what really matters before putting his money into a company — its path ahead.

The phenomenon of chasing returns is well documented. As John Bogle, the founder and retired CEO of The Vanguard Group, observes, "Money flows into most funds after good performance, and goes out when bad performance follows." Despite the empirical evidence that chasing performance typically does not work, this strategy is still popular. However, research shows that return-chasing behavior has a significantly negative impact on the performance or return. A good piece of advice is don't join the herd or follow a fad. In most instances, a buy-and-hold strategy outperforms a performance-chasing strategy.

Drawbacks to Chasing Returns

The strategy of chasing investment returns has several drawbacks. First, "hot" investments usually don't stay hot over long periods. The factors leading to a surge in performance may be nearing their end. Today's top performers might not be so tomorrow. You should heed one of the most common disclaimers in the investment industry: "past performance is no indication of future performance." Second, chasing performance can involve additional fees and expenses as a result of buying and selling, as well as tax implications for impulsively entering and exiting an investment. Taxes eat into the profit of investors who frequently alter their portfolios. Fund-switching strategies make more sense in tax-deferred portfolios such as an individual retirement account (IRA) and 401(k) than in taxable ones. Third, the smart money is often moving out of such investments as the dumb money is pouring in. Every transaction involves a buyer and a seller. Sophisticated investors (smart money) such as institutional investors tend to sell securities when their prices are high to less sophisticated investors (dumb money) such as individual or retail investors. Sophisticated investors largely base their decisions on information, whereas individuals often base their decisions on "noise." *Noise traders* make buy and sell decisions without using fundamental data. They often have poor timing, follow trends, and overreact to good and bad news. Warren Buffett advises turning down the noise when making investment decisions.[3]

Chasing returns is a market timing mistake that usually results in investors buying high and selling low, which is the opposite of good market timing. Logically, the best time to buy is when the price is low. Less sophisticated investors have difficultly following this principle because their emotions lead them into believing chasing performance is a good strategy. They are naturally drawn to top performing assets such as stocks or mutual funds, and consequently chase returns. Mutual funds encourage investors to chase performance by promoting their high performing funds through advertising. Such efforts are more pronounced during periods of uncertainty in financial markets. Fund managers exploit this behavior by preferentially timing fee increases to align with periods of heightened investor demand resulting from stale performance chasing. As a result, investors end up buying investments after they have gone way up and then sell them after they have dropped in price. This is equivalent to "buying on greed" and "selling on fear."

Buying low, however, requires courage, discipline, and independent thinking because it means buying the "losers" or underperforming assets, not the winners. Conversely, simply buying assets that appear to be a bargain may also be a mistake because the company may be worth less now for fundamental reasons. Prudent investors try to identify companies that aren't doing well now but are good investments for the future. Investors should be buying, not selling, in a down market.

Chasing performance is not a good idea because investors typically get burned chasing winners. This "momentum investing" approach might work in some short time frames, but falls short over the long term. By following this strategy, investors are always one step behind the smart money. Choosing investments based on strong recent performance or last year's "winners" is a dangerous game and can be hazardous to your financial health. Even experienced investors have to fight the urge to chase returns. Larry Swedroe, principal and the director of research of Buckingham Asset Management and BAM Advisor Services, notes: "The bottom line is that while performance-chasing seems to be an all-too-human trait, if you're ever tempted by the recent record of a 'hot' fund manager, remember that you cannot buy yesterday's outperformance, only tomorrow's returns."[4]

Strategies to Avoid Chasing Returns

Several options are available to avoid the problems associated with chasing returns. One is to stick with your goal-based investment plan and continue to make regular contributions. Another option is to periodically rebalance your broad-based portfolio to ensure it matches your desired asset allocation. A final tactic is to groom your patience. Despite short-term volatility, good quality investments tend to appreciate given time.

PAYING TOO MUCH IN CHARGES AND TAXES

Although investment performance critically affects your total returns, another factor is the charges and taxes that you pay on returns. As Robert Kiyosaki, a self-help author and financial commentator, notes, "It's not how much money you make, but how much money you keep, how hard it works for you, and how many generations you keep it for." People typically pay close attention to their expenses for housing, transportation, groceries, and even wireless plans, but often have little idea of the charges and taxes associated with their investment accounts. Investors often make the mistake of buying expensive, underperforming private investments such as hedge funds and venture capital as well as high-cost mutual funds or paying too much for advisory services. Even a small increase in these charges can affect your wealth over the long term. Simply put, reducing the amount that you pay in fees or commissions leads to higher net returns.

You should also consider the tax consequences of your investments as a means of improving your returns. For example, municipal bonds, stocks, and tax-advantaged equity mutual funds tend to be appropriate in taxable accounts. By contrast, ordinary bonds, real estate, commodities, and other tax-inefficient holdings are better suited for tax-deferred accounts. You can also use losses on your financial investments to cut taxes. Although you need to be smart about taxes, some investors focus too much on taxes instead of the underlying merits of the investment. They let the "tax tail wag the dog," so to speak. You should avoid making hasty decisions to dodge taxes.

An Example of Mutual Funds

Because charges and taxes differ dramatically among different types of investments, let's narrow our focus by looking at mutual funds and U.S. tax laws. A *mutual fund* is an investment vehicle that pools funds from many investors to buy securities such as stocks, bonds, money market instruments, and similar assets. Mutual funds have many virtues such as not requiring a large up-front investment, being professionally managed, providing good administration, and being easy to buy and sell. Yet, they can be costly to own and might not be tax friendly.

Because mutual fund investors don't write a check to the fund for its services, they often don't realize how much they are paying for their fund unless they are vigilant. Although fees and expenses differ from fund to fund, they can be classified into two broad categories. The first category is *one-time* or *shareholder fees*, which are costs incurred in connection with particular investor transactions. These costs include sales commissions, redemption fees, exchange fees, account fees, and purchase fees. Not all funds charge one-time fees. The second category involves *regular fund operating costs*, which are ongoing annual expenses that all funds charge. The typical practice is for funds to pay their regular and recurring fund-wide operating expenses out of fund assets instead of imposing separate fees and charges on investors, although investors still indirectly pay for them. Such costs include investment advisory fees, marketing and distribution expenses (12b-1), brokerage fees, and custodial, transfer agency, legal, and accountants' fees. These ongoing charges are typically deducted from return figures, which are available in public sources.[5]

Owning mutual funds involves tax implications for investors. In the United States, each shareholder participates proportionally in the gain or loss of the fund. Mutual funds must pass along any realized capital gains that are not offset by capital losses by the end of their accounting year. A *capital gain* is the profit that results from the sale price of a capital asset, such as stocks, bonds, or real estate, where the sales price exceeds its purchase price. By contrast, a *capital loss* is the difference between a capital asset's purchase and selling price, where the sale price is lower than the purchase price. Additionally, fund managers must distribute any income that their securities generate. Although such distributions have tax implications, investors can reduce over taxation in various ways:

- Seek out low turnover funds to reduce the amount of realized capital gains.

- Place tax-inefficient funds in tax deferred accounts such as an IRA and 401(k).

- Place funds in a municipal bond fund, instead of a regular bond fund, for those in a higher tax bracket because income from these funds is usually tax exempt.

- Consider tax-managed funds because these funds use different strategies to limit their taxable distributions.[6]

Strategies for Reining in Charges and Taxes

Several strategies are available to limit charges and taxes. For example, before opening an account or hiring a financial advisor, you should be aware of the potential cost of every investment decision. You want to ensure that you are receiving value for any fee that you are paying.

Another strategy for keeping more of what you earn is to invest in low-cost and tax-efficient funds. You need to be aware that investing in actively managed funds typically costs more than in funds that are passively managed. An *actively managed fund* is one that its managers believe can outperform the market. The opposite of active management is called *passive management*, also known as *indexing*, which means that the portfolios attempt to mirror the components of a market index. Index funds have lower turnover than actively managed funds because the underlying securities rarely change as a result of trying to match a market index. *Investment turnover* refers to the buying and selling, or trading, of securities by a fund manager. Lower fund turnover results in a smaller chance for capital gains on which the investor is responsible for paying taxes as well as lower transaction costs.

Generally speaking, investors face both lower risk-adjusted returns and higher investment costs with actively versus passively managed funds. However, you should always look out for any hidden costs. You should consider index mutual funds and exchange-traded funds (ETFs) that have low expense ratios. An ETF is a marketable security that tracks an index, bonds, a commodity, or a basket of assets like an index fund. Unlike mutual funds, an ETF trades like a common stock on a stock exchange. ETFs don't try to outperform or beat their corresponding index, but attempt to replicate its performance.

A third strategy is to take advantage of tax shelters. State and federal governments offer various options for investors to delay or avoid paying taxes on money used for specific purposes such as retirement, education, and healthcare. You might want to consult a financial professional or tax advisor to learn about taking advantage of these opportunities. In the end, the amount that you keep, not the amount that you pay, is what counts. Successful investors try to reduce or minimize the effect of charges and taxes on their bottom line.

TRADING TOO OFTEN

Trading activity has increased over time. In fact, many investors trade far too much. This increase can be attributed to several factors including improved technology, lower costs, and greater convenience. For example, the presence of TD Ameritrade, Charles Schwab, and other online brokers provide excellent service in the form of low-cost stock trades with first-class research and tools, which facilitate excessive trading. Another factor contributing to overtrading is the failure to exercise financial discipline. Investors, especially men, tend to trade too frequently because they are overconfident.[7] These factors can lead to frequent trading and sometimes impulsive decision-making. Although buying and selling securities can be fun, excitement should not be the main reason most people invest.

One problem associated with frequent trading is the cost. Trading too much and too often can compromise returns due to brokerage commissions and other trading costs, as well as taxes. Investors also need to factor in the cost of their time and potential aggravation. Yet, a "trading paradox" exists. Survey evidence reveals that many investors, especially high net worth individuals, believe that they must trade frequently to do well in the markets, but also believe that they trade too much for their own good.[8]

Another problem of frequent trading is that it can become addictive and some lack the self-control to stop.[9] Too much trading can be hazardous not only to your wealth but also to your health. Frequent trading can result in paying higher tax rates on short-term capital gains and missing out on the opportunity of paying lower rates on long-term capital gains. Real investors, not speculators, give their investments the chance to perform over a period of years, not days or weeks. Following a long-term plan tends to be less costly and less risky, but this takes patience. Consequently, frequent trading isn't appropriate for most individual investors. In fact, many mutual funds have adopted policies intended to discourage shareholders from excessive trading. For example, Vanguard and Fidelity limit frequent trading because excessive transactions can disrupt the management of a fund and increase its costs for *all* shareholders, not just those trading too frequently.

Strategies to Limit Excessive Trading

One strategy to limit trading too frequently is to develop an investment plan containing a suitable asset allocation and then stick with it. Having a plan does not mean that you forget about your investments, no matter how well chosen they may be. Periodically, you need to review your plan and adjust (rebalance) your allocations. For example, if your analysis indicates a change in business fundamentals, poor performance, or an asset becomes overvalued, these warning signs suggest the time is right to sell. Overall, a buy-and-hold approach typically provides the best way for you to earn reliable long-term returns.

To keep investment turnover in check, you also need to keep your excitement and emotions in check. Exercising financial discipline requires applying self-control strategies. For example, you could set financial deadlines for yourself or use other people such as a financial advisor to help you meet your goals. Another approach to limiting active trading is to use a cooling-off period to reflect on decisions. That is, you can wait a few days after making a big financial decision before executing it. According to Warren Buffett, "The most important quality for an investor is temperament, not intellect." You should remain calm and rational during the inevitable boom and bust cycles of financial markets.

Another strategy to avoid excessive trading is to gain greater awareness of your trading by keeping a journal of each buy and sell decision and record your emotions during the time of the transaction. You can then set a limit for your trading. This strategy can help you better understand your market temperament and hopefully change your outlook.[10]

ENGAGING IN MARKET TIMING

The evil twin of trading too much is engaging in market timing. Investors often believe they can strategically "time" the market by accurately predicting when it will rise and fall. The topic of market timing is highly controversial.[11] Although market timing may be possible to some degree, few have the training, experience, and skill to do this successfully over time. Even highly sophisticated investors such as institutional investors are often unsuccessful at market timing. Yet, many individual investors engage in market timing due to overconfidence. Overconfidence can spell disaster for a portfolio's returns. Don't let your ego get in the way of reality. One way to achieve this end is to do a reality check. That is, you can examine your actual level of success as a market timer. Keeping a scorecard should show whether overconfidence in your abilities is warranted. Long-term investors would be better off ignoring short-term market distractions.

An Example: Brexit

Brexit refers to the withdrawal of the United Kingdom from the European Union (EU). On June 23, 2016, a referendum on the issue was held in the United Kingdom. The result of the referendum was to advise the UK Government to begin the process of the United Kingdom leaving the EU. The vote resulted in a wobbly market. Benefiting from this behavior required investors to develop a likely range of future outcomes, identify the most likely outcome, and how one's personal view might differ from the consensus. Next, the investor had to engage in nearly perfect timing. Not surprisingly, very few people had the skill to position themselves for the immediate market sell-off followed by the subsequent snapback rally and new record highs. All of this occurred within about a week. Few investors have the ability to develop an investment strategy in which they can correctly guess what the future holds. For most, doing so dooms them to failure.[12]

Strategies to Avoid Market Timing

Rather than trying to trade in and out in an attempt to time the market, you can ride out ups and downs by taking the long road. Some evidence suggests that market timing does not beat a buy-and-hold strategy over time. Another strategy is to consistently contribute to your investment portfolio. This approach, called DCA, involves buying a fixed dollar amount of a particular investment on a regular schedule, regardless of the share price. You buy more shares when prices are low and fewer shares when prices are high. This approach focuses on accumulating assets on a regular basis, instead of trying to time the market. DCA also takes the emotion and guesswork out of investing. A DCA strategy is better suited for investors with a low risk tolerance and a long-term investment horizon involving volatile investments, such as stocks, ETFs or mutual funds, not bonds or money market funds. However, DCA does not guarantee good returns if your investment continues to fall.[13] Nonetheless, your portfolio's long-term returns should be similar to those of your portfolio's benchmarks or market averages. By avoiding market timing, you may also benefit from the irrational behavior of other market participants.

IGNORING INDEXING

Evidence abundantly demonstrates that most managers and active mutual funds routinely underperform their benchmarks, and hence deliver below-average performance.[14] About two out of three mutual funds underperform the overall market in a typical year.[15] A *benchmark* is a standard against which the performance of a security, mutual fund or investment manager can be measured. Charles D. Ellis, a leading American investment consultant, observes that "The long-term data repeatedly document that investors would benefit by switching from active performance investing to low-cost indexing."[16] Mark Hebner, founder of Index Fund Advisors, Inc., echoes this sentiment by stating "Most people are beaten up by the market, instead of beating the market." Investors shouldn't delude themselves about beating the market, especially over the long term. Short-term luck does not equal long-term skill.

Active Investing

Active mutual funds do not add value, on average, because their risk-adjusted returns net of fees are lower than their benchmark returns. That is, such funds, on average, underperform the indexes by the amount of expenses and transaction costs. Other reasons for the failure to beat their benchmarks include (1) asset bloat due to a fund getting too big; (2) *closet indexing*, which is a portfolio strategy used by some portfolio managers to achieve returns similar to those of their benchmark index, without exactly replicating the index, but charging fees for active management; and (3) over diversification.[17] By contrast, index funds outperform a majority of actively managed funds over long periods of time. Although some managers and individuals beat their benchmarks by a solid margin over time, few do this consistently.

Despite the evidence favoring indexing, many individual investors want to invest with active managers or to develop their portfolio and actively trade. As Warren Buffet comments, "Calling someone who trades actively in the market an investor is like calling someone who repeatedly engages in one-night stands a romantic." Several reasons explain the desire to trade. For example, investors are overconfident in the ability of professional managers or their own ability to generate superior returns. Although this notion is typically misguided, more sophisticated and knowledgeable investors still might prefer to construct their own portfolios over index funds.[18] Compared to active investing, indexing can be rather dull because you're not trying to beat a benchmark or the market. According to George Soros, business magnate, investor, author, and philanthropist, "If investing is entertaining, if you're having fun, you're probably not making any money. Good investing is boring." Paul Samuelson, Nobel Laureate in Economics, offers a similar view: "There is something in people; you might even call it a little bit of a gambling instinct .... I tell people investing should be dull. It shouldn't be exciting. Investing should be more like watching paint dry or watching grass grow. If you want excitement, take $800 and go to Las Vegas."

Passive Investing

Traditional indexing, also known as *passive investing*, is an invest-ment strategy that attempts to mimic the performance of a market index. It emphasizes broad diversification and low portfolio trad-ing activity, which provides an important cost advantage com-pared with active investing. Indexing offers an effective means of owning the market and allows investors to participate in the returns of a basket of stocks, bonds, and other assets. Index funds offer diversification at an affordable price and insulate against guesswork and personal emotion.

Despite its positive attributes, indexing has a downside. The term "passive" probably does a disservice to investors because indexing is not really passive, but provides a viable option to investors. Investors still need to choose the right index or indexes for their portfolios. Index funds also carry all the risks typically associated with the type of asset the fund holds. Investors should expect to receive average performance because index funds are intended to provide returns that closely track their benchmark indexes. Indexing can also work against investors if they ignore investment fundamentals. For example, continuing to place money into sectors regardless of valuation could prove detrimental. However, investors could periodically rebalance their portfolios, which would take valuations into account.[19]

For most investors, index funds remain the best wealth manage-ment choice. Index investing is particularly appropriate for those who do not have the time to study the markets and do much research. In a CNBC interview, Warren Buffet, probably the most successful investor in the 20th century, notes "The best way in my view is to just buy a low-cost index fund and keep buying it regu-larly over time, because you'll be buying into a wonderful indus-try, which in effect is all of American industry .... People ought to sit back and relax and keep accumulating over time."[20]

Strategies for Indexing

A wide range of distinctive investment strategies is available to investors interested in indexing. If you are interested in equity indexing, various index mutual funds and ETFs are available to invest in large, medium, or small companies, "value" or "growth" stocks, and international stocks. For example, popular equity indexes are the Standard & Poor's® 500 Index and SPDR S&P 500 ETF, which is dominated by stocks of large-capitalization "blue chip" companies. A *blue chip* is a nationally recognized, well-established, and financially sound company. Indexed bond and alternative investments are also available.

RELYING ON UNFOUNDED TIPS

Have you ever been tempted to buy a stock or another investment based on a tip from a friend, relative, someone on a financial news program or website? If so, you are not alone. The problem with many of these "hot" tips is that they usually do not pan out. Why would a total stranger or someone on television or in a newsletter offer you such profitable advice, especially for free? You should be wary of sources using sensational headlines touting must-buy investments because blindly following such sources might lead to unwise investment decisions. Scrambling to follow others to buy "hot" assets experiencing large gains in hopes that the trend will continue is a sure way to get burned. If a tip comes from an insider, it might not be unfounded, but you should avoid acting on it because *insider trading* is the illegal practice of using confidential information to gain a personal advantage.

In general, you should avoid following the advice of pundits or talking heads and placing too much attention on the financial media. As Chris Mayer, managing editor of the Mayer's 100x Club and Mayer's Special Situations newsletters, notes, "The problem with the 24/7 media culture we live in is that everybody has to have something to say almost all the time. And yet most of the time, there really isn't anything worth saying."[21] Following the news media often leads investors to follow trends, have poor timing, and overreact to both good and bad news. If something grabs your attention, you should do your research and investigate both the source and the investment. You may also want to seek views from other investors whom you trust, or an unbiased financial advisor. As William Hamilton notes, "The market does not trade upon what everybody knows, but upon what those with the best information can foresee." By the time information has become public, market prices have probably factored in this information. You should avoid the common investing mistake of pursuing the latest media fixation and tune out the noise.

Strategies to Avoid Relying on Unfounded Tips

To help avoid relying on unfounded tips, several courses of action are available. First, you should consider the reliability of the source whether a friend, family member, or the media. Whenever possible you should obtain a second opinion from other investors or unbiased financial advisors. Second, you need to do your homework in order to know what you are buying and why. Doing research is critical to understand the investment. In short, the task is to separate the facts from the noise. Don't simply react — investigate! Successful and seasoned investors gather the facts from several sources, verify the information, and conduct independent analysis to become comfortable with the company.

INVESTING IN SOMETHING YOU DON'T UNDERSTAND

Another common mistake that investors make is failing to understand the kind of product they are buying, whether it's a mutual fund, ETF, or an annuity. This mistake is a recipe for disaster because con artists can more easily take advantage of you when you do not understand what you're buying. Warren Buffet also cautions against investing in businesses you don't understand. Similarly, the famous economist, John Maynard Keynes, observes the following: "As time goes on, I get more and more convinced that the right method of investment is to put fairly large sums into enterprises which one thinks one knows something about and in the management of which one thoroughly believes." Peter Lynch, a noted American businessman and stock investor, notes, "Know what you own, and know why you own it." Peter Lynch also whimsically states, "Never invest in any idea you can't illustrate with a crayon." As a simple guideline, if you can't clearly explain the investment to someone else, you probably don't understand it well enough to invest. To be able to realistically consider the advice of your broker or financial advisor, you need to understand their recommendations.

Strategies for Gaining Understanding about an Investment

Some investments can be very complex. To avoid investing in something that you don't understand requires doing your home-work and research. In financial terms, you need to do your due diligence. If you're buying stock in different companies, you need to thoroughly understand their business models and prospects. Like most investors, you probably would prefer spending your time doing something else. If you're unwilling to exert the effort, then you're probably better off investing in a broadly diversified portfolio consisting of mutual funds or ETFs.

BUYING INITIAL PUBLIC OFFERINGS

Initial public offerings (IPOs) are an intriguing but dangerous part of the market. An IPO is the initial sale of stock by a private company to the public. Sometimes IPOs can provide excellent returns. For example, being an early investor in a stock destined for greatness such as Apple Inc. in 1980, Microsoft Corp. in 1986, or Google Inc. in 2004 would have paid off handsomely. Yet, for every stock whose price skyrockets after an IPO, many more post lackluster performance or even go bankrupt. As with any investment, investors should approach IPOs with caution.

Companies go public for various reasons. For example, smaller, younger companies wanting to raise capital to finance growth and get better rates on debt issue IPOs. Privately owned companies that want to become publicly traded also issue IPOs because trading in the open market provides liquidity for their shares. Another incentive for IPOs is to enable previous investors such as founders, private investors, and venture capital firms, to "cash out" at least a portion of what they've invested. This exit strategy can make early investors rich.

Although some strong companies go public and provide attractive returns to investors, many others leave individual investors on the losing end of the transaction. Many of these companies went public before they were ready. Investors should not assume that IPOs are inherently good investment opportunities, despite being highly touted and publicized. Investing in IPOs can be a mistake because the odds of getting in on a good deal are stacked against the average individual investor.[22]

Today, a firm is not required to have strong financials and a solid history to go public. Limited histories can lead to somewhat mysterious valuations. Although regulatory rules, which are designed to protect IPO investors, provide disclosures about the company and the offering process, many individual investors fail to read or understand them. Instead, they jump in to buy the newest hot IPO as a "once in a lifetime" opportunity in which they can "get in on the ground floor." In reality, individual investors are unlikely to get shares of the IPO allocation for a "hot" IPO. Why? The brokers underwriting the deal typically sell IPO shares to their favored customers, such as investment banks, hedge funds, and institutions including mutual funds or pension funds as well as their best high net worth clients. In other words, one hand washes the other. A few big buyers are easier to find than many small buyers. For small investors, the likelihood of buying early shares in an IPO is practically nonexistent.[23] You're typically excluded from the IPO club unless nobody else wants to buy the shares. By the time you can buy shares, others have typically invested earlier at lower prices. Thus, taking advantage of some of the good opportunities provided by IPOs can be difficult for average investors.

Be careful not to be drawn into the emotional excitement surrounding some IPOs. Considerable hype often surrounds the underwriting process to gain as much attention as possible. Given that demand often outstrips supply, the prices of many IPOs initially soar. Institutional investors try to "flip" or resell hot IPOs stocks during the first few days in order to earn quick profits. Although brokerage firms discourage their individual clients from flipping their shares, no laws prevent flipping. Small investors who believe the hype become excited and often enter the market to buy the stock at inflated prices only to see price declines in the future. Many stocks sell below their offering price within a year and continue to underperform other firms of similar size for several years. Individual investors are often lucky to lose out on buying IPOs at inflated prices.

Another factor that can lead to declining prices of IPO stocks involves the *lock-up period*, which is a legally binding agreement imposed by underwriters on company officials and employees (insiders) not to sell their shares for a specified period ranging from 3 to 24 months. The purpose of the lock-up period is to prevent a flood of shares from hitting the market shortly after the IPO. When the lock-up period expires, insiders typically want to sell their stock at a profit, which leads to excess supply and declining stock prices.[24]

Strategies Involving Initial Public Offerings

To determine whether buying the stock of a new company is a good move, you have several major options: (1) conduct your own analysis, which requires considerable skill, (2) rely on analyst reports of the company, and (3) consult a financial advisor or other investment professional to help you make your decision about whether to invest. An analysis often begins by reviewing the registration document, known as Form S-1, required by the Securities and Exchange Commission (SEC) for all new securities. This document is available on the SEC's website. Other important factors to evaluate include researching the company's pedigree, such as the quality of the leadership, the benefits that the IPO offers the firm, and whether major financial firms such as Goldman Sachs, Morgan Stanley, and JPMorgan are involved in the underwriting. Researching an IPO may help you see past the hype and excitement and is useful in determining an appropriate valuation for the company. You also need to consider how the stock fits into your overall asset allocation strategy.

Another strategy is to avoid betting on any individual stock, either of a new or established company, and instead maintain a diversified portfolio. You should typically avoid early investment in stock of a new company until after the lock-up period. Taking this approach enables you to better judge whether the company has strong fundamentals and gives the market time to determine a price.[25]

Given the lack of history of many IPOs, you should not rush into buying them unless your analysis shows that the company is a good investment and is consistent with your investment plan. Unless you can participate in the initial allocation, you should be very cautious about buying IPOs, especially "hot" IPOs shortly after their issuance. If you do buy stock in new companies, you should typically limit your investment in the stock to a small percentage of your total portfolio. As with any investment, IPOs involve a risk-return trade-off that you need to carefully consider.

DEVELOPING AN INVESTMENT POLICY STATEMENT

Although you can't control the uncertainties surrounding your financial future, you can take action to shape it. After you are in the position to start investing, a powerful step in taking control of your financial future is to develop a financial plan. If you don't feel qualified to do this, you can work with a qualified financial planner or advisor.

Although many ways are available to help overcome common investing mistakes, one of the most important is to have an investment policy statement (IPS). An IPS is a written document that defines how an investment portfolio should be managed. That is, an IPS provides a written set of guidelines for current and future investments. You can think of an IPS as a roadmap to financial freedom. A good financial advisor will help you design a custom investment plan to suit your individual situation. This blueprint contains such details as the circumstances, investment goals, constraints, strategies, and monitoring and rebalancing procedures that govern your investment portfolio. You can download Morningstar's Investment Policy Worksheet as a starting point.[26]

Why Have an IPS?

The most important reasons for having an IPS are that it can help you avoid common investing mistakes and keep your portfolio on track. As Suze Orman, an American author, financial advisor, and television host, notes "No one's ever achieved financial fitness with a January resolution that's abandoned by February." Sometimes bad things happen and markets become unhinged. This is why you should plan ahead for events to avoid emotions taking control of your behavior. Following your emotions is not the basis of sound portfolio management. Recall the Brexit example from the previous chapter, which roiled global markets including currencies. A substantial sell-off occurred and many investors panicked. Such volatility in markets is the common course of events. To avoid emotional reactions, you need to have a plan as well as the self-disciple to stay with it. If you do, you are likely to think more calmly and clearly about your best options before an alarming event occurs.[27]

Questions to Ask When Creating an IPS

Although an IPS can take various forms, it should typically answer the following questions:[28]

- What are your financial or investment goals?

- How much do you intend to invest each period (e.g., month or year)?

- How long do you plan to invest?

- What is your investment philosophy about risk, diversification, trading, costs, and taxes?

- What is your expected rate of return for the portfolio?

- What is your target asset allocation mix?

- What are your allowable assets?

- What are your investment selection criteria for individual securities or mutual funds and ETFs?

- How often will you review your investment plan?

- What benchmarks will you use to determine how your individual investments or overall portfolio are doing?

- When will you rebalance your portfolio?

Steps in Writing an IPS

Answering the above questions forms the basis for creating an IPS, which generally follows these basic steps. An example of an IPS is available on the Bogleheads website.[29]

- *Establish goals*: This step involves developing short-, medium-, and long-term financial goals. As Ralph Seger, the founder of Provident Investment Management, notes, "An investor without investment objectives is like a traveler without a destination." Before you can choose investments to meet a particular goal, you need to have an idea of the targeted amounts and a time frame. Examples of goals include large future expenditures such as buying a house or accumulating funds for a child's college education, or generating sufficient income to maintain your quality of life through retirement.

- *Identify investment constraints*: Creating an IPS also involves considering investment constraints, including your liquidity needs, time horizon, tax considerations, legal and regulatory constraints, and unique needs and preferences. *Liquidity* refers to the ability to turn investment assets into cash quickly without having to make large price concessions to do so. Typically, the longer your time horizon, the more risk and illiquidity you can accept in your portfolio. Besides your overall tax rate, the tax treatment of different investments is also a consideration in portfolio construction. Specific legal or regulatory constraints may apply such as if you have an IRA or a defined contribution plan. Finally, you may have specific preferences or restrictions on which securities and assets to include in your portfolio. For example, ethical preferences could lead to prohibiting invest- ments in securities used by tobacco or firearms producers.

- *Determine a risk profile*: Although investors would like to earn high returns with low risk, this typically does not occur in prac- tice. The risk-return trade-off indicates that you generally have to take more risk to achieve higher returns. Either you or your financial advisor must make sure that the stated risk and return objectives are compatible, not mutually exclusive. Distinguishing between your willingness and ability to take risk (i.e., risk tolerance vs. risk capacity) is also important. *Risk tolerance* refers to the maximum amount of risk that you are willing to accept when making a financial decision.[30] Risk tolerance is based mainly on your attitudes and beliefs about investments, and often changes with your age, capacity to endure price declines, and ability to earn money outside of your investment portfolio. Various demographic and socioeconomic factors also affect risk-taking behavior, including:

o *Gender*: Women tend to be less risk-taking (more conservative) and less prone to overconfidence than men.

o *Marital status*: Single individuals are more likely to make riskier decisions than those who are married.

o *Age*: Younger people are inclined to be more risk-seeking than older individuals. Risk-aversion generally increases with age.

o *Education*: People with higher levels of education have a greater tendency to take risks.[31]

By contrast, *risk capacity* refers to the amount of risk that you can afford to take. It concerns whether, for a given level of risk, your financial situation can withstand the impact of a worst case outcome. However, just because you can afford to take risk doesn't mean that you should.

If your willingness is high but your ability to take on risk is low, the low ability to assume investment risk should prevail. However, if your ability is high but your willingness is low, your advisor may try to educate you about risk and correct any misconceptions that you may have. Nevertheless, an advisor's role is not to change your personality characteristics that contribute to your willingness to take on investment risk. If the advisor tries to do so, this could be a red flag signaling you to seek another advisor. Good advisors generally use the lower of your ability or willingness to bear risk to avoid having a risk level that would make you uncomfortable.

- *Establish an expected rate of return*: Investing involves a level of uncertainty about the future. Forming expectations about the risk and return prospects of asset classes is challenging. According to Seth Klarman, an American billionaire hedge fund manager, "Investors should always keep in mind that the most important metric is not the returns achieved but the returns weighed against the risks incurred. Ultimately, nothing should be more important to investors than the ability to sleep soundly at night."

  Expected returns vary depending on the asset class. An *asset class* is a group of securities that have similar financial characteristics, behave similarly in the marketplace, and are subject to the same laws and regulations. For example, traditional asset classes are equities (stocks), fixed-income (bonds), cash equivalents (money market instruments), and sometimes real estate. You should create multiple "what-if" scenarios so that you can envision what your future might look like under difference scenarios. Your expectations about *capital markets*, which are places where buyers and sellers engage in trading of financial securities, are an important input in formulating a *strategic asset allocation*. In strategic asset allocation, your goals, risk tolerances, and investment constraints are integrated with long-run capital market expectations to establish the percentage allocations or exposures to each asset class included in the IPS. For instance, if your IPS specifies three permissible asset classes, you will need to form expectations about those asset classes to develop a strategic asset allocation. To reach your financial goals, your portfolio will need to increase at a certain rate. As a result, you need to form expectations about what that rate is. Chapter 8 provides some historical guidelines on risk and return for various asset classes.

- *Develop asset allocation guidelines*: Asset allocation involves how you divide your assets among different asset classes.

Experts generally view asset allocation as more important than security selection and market timing in the portfolio construction process because it determines a portfolio's risk and return characteristics. Let's assume a three-asset class portfolio of equities, bonds, and cash equivalents with target asset proportions of 50/40/10. Each asset class has a minimum and maximum deviation from these targets called *holding limits* or *rebalancing thresholds*, say 40% (minimum) and 60% (maximum) for equities. This process attempts to balance risk versus reward by adjusting the percentage of each asset in an investment portfolio according to your goals, risk tolerance, and investment time frame. You may want to avoid certain asset classes because of excessive risk, high expenses, or large tax liabilities.

As with most strategies, no one-size-fits-all asset allocation model exists. Although financial advisors and investment firms often use financial planning software, you should not rely solely on it or some other predetermined plan. For instance, some advisors use a rule of thumb to determine the proportion a person should allocate to stocks in which they subtract the person's age from 100. In other words, if you're 30, you should put 70% of your money into stocks and the remaining 30% into other asset classes. This is a questionable rule of thumb to follow because your personal preferences and circumstances not related to your age could dictate a different allocation.[32]

- *Specify the selection criteria.* Various investment strategies or philosophies are available to implement an investment program. An *investment strategy* is a set of rules, behaviors, or procedures designed to guide the selection of an investment portfolio. These strategies typically involve a trade-off between risk and return. Some common strategies are buy and hold, value investing, growth investing, DCA, and contrarian investing. You should carefully evaluate the pros and cons of each approach and decide which you want to use.

o *Buy and hold* is a passive investment strategy in which an investor buys stocks and holds them for a long period of time, regardless of fluctuations in the market.

o *Value investing* is the strategy of selecting stocks that trade for less than their intrinsic values. *Intrinsic value*, also *called fundamental value*, refers to the value of a stock determined through fundamental analysis without reference to its market value. Value investors actively seek stocks of companies that they believe the market has undervalued.

o *Growth investing* is a strategy whereby investors seek out stocks with good growth potential in the foreseeable future. A *growth stock* is often defined as shares of a company whose earnings are expected to grow at an above-average rate compared to its industry or the overall market.

o *DCA* is a strategy of buying a fixed dollar amount of a particular investment on a regular schedule, regardless of the share price. Using DCA, investors buy more shares when prices are low and fewer shares when prices are high.

o *Contrarian investing* is an investment strategy characterized by buying and selling in contrast to the prevailing sentiment. Contrarian investors believe that certain crowd behavior among investors can lead to exploitable mispricings in securities markets.

- *Develop monitoring and rebalancing procedures*: *Monitoring* involves systematically keeping track of your circumstances, market and economic changes, and the portfolio itself. For example, risk tolerance can change over time, so periodically revisiting the topic is important. An IPS should indicate the frequency of monitoring, the benchmark for comparing portfolio returns, and acceptable deviations from the benchmark. *Rebalancing* involves adjusting the actual portfolio in the current strategic asset allocation because of changes in portfolio holdings. An IPS should specify a timeframe for altering these allocations. For example, let's return to the example in which your IPS specifies holding a minimum of 40% and a maximum of 60% in equities. In this instance, rebalancing would occur when the weight of equities first passes through one of its rebalancing thresholds.

- *Celebrate the achievement of financial milestones*: Many investors get so caught up in their pursuit of financial success that they don't stop and celebrate their milestones and achievements, even small ones. Celebrations help to lock in learning. Pausing to celebrate requires reflection, which reinforces achievement and provides motivation to keep moving forward to accomplish financial goals.

Benefits of Using an IPS

A properly constructed IPS provides many potential benefits. For example, it serves as a foundation for all future investment decisions that you may make and helps to clarify investment strategies. Without having an IPS, people are more likely to alter their investment strategies. The failure to consistently implement an investment plan is a major reason for underperformance. Using an IPS instills a disciplined approach to investing, especially during turbulent markets or exuberant times when you might be tempted to make impromptu revisions to a sound long-term asset allocation policy. Asset allocation is not the sole determinant of portfolio performance, but it is its largest determinant. Sticking to your written plan's guidelines might also keep you from making spontaneous decisions due to emotions.

If you are using a financial advisor, you should insist on having an IPS, as it provides the ground rules of the relationship. Drafting an IPS helps an advisor gain a better sense of what you expect in terms of risk and return. It also helps educate you on realistic outcomes and the importance of following a plan for achieving specific financial goals. Furthermore, conducting a periodic review of your IPS is crucial to keeping you on track. Sometimes you might need to make adjustments to reflect life changing events such as births, deaths, marriage, or divorce.

Creating a formal IPS may seem too complex or complicated for some investors. If so, you can develop a more informal investment plan in which you formulate your goals, set up a plan for achieving each goal, and select the best investments to fulfill your desired asset allocation. Whether you have a formal IPS or simply an investment plan, you should put your plan in writing to help you stick to a sound long-term policy. Although having a written plan may seem unnecessary, it is likely to help you become a more successful investor. In particular, following an IPS can protect you from falling into some investment traps and save you money.

LESSONS LEARNED

The investing process entails many pitfalls. To become a successful investor you need to be aware of possible mistakes, realize whether you're committing them, and know how to avoid them or at least learn from them. Charlie Munger, the vice chairman of Berkshire Hathaway, provides the following useful advice: "Spend each day trying to be a little wiser than you were when you woke up." If you do, you'll make fewer mistakes and better decisions. Having a thoughtful financial plan and sticking with it is perhaps the best step that you can take to avoid committing investing mistakes.

- Avoid chasing returns or buying into bubbles because doing so will cost you considerable money over time.

- Don't engage in a herd mentality.

- Select investments with an eye on reducing expenses and taxes. Take advantage of tax strategies and shelters.

- Avoid overtrading because it often leads to lower returns.

- Don't try to time the market because you are highly unlikely to be successful doing this over time.

- Include index funds or ETFs in your portfolio to achieve low expense ratios, tax efficiency, risk control, and diversification.

- Don't relying on unfounded stock tips and pundits but on reliable research.

- Invest in what you know and what is suitable for you.

- Be careful if you buy shares of an IPO, especially if you are not part of the initial offering, because it can be risky and expensive.

QUESTIONS

1. Explain why chasing investment returns is a bad idea.

2. Identify the two major types of fees and expenses for mutual funds and give several examples in each category.

3. Explain why trading too often is a bad idea.

4. Discuss the pitfalls of market timing.

5. Justify why investors should consider indexing.

6. Explain why investors should avoid relying on unfounded tips.

7. Indicate why you should invest only in what you understand.

8. Discuss why individual investors should be cautious about investing in IPOs.

9. Discuss the importance of an IPS and list its steps.

NOTES

1. The Motley Fool. (2016). *Step 5: Avoid the biggest mistake investors make*. Retrieved from http://www.fool.com/how-to-invest/thirteen-steps/step-5-avoid-the-biggest-mistake-investors-make.aspx

2. Kiplinger (2016). *8 biggest mistakes investors make*. Retrieved from http://www.kiplinger.com/slideshow/investing/T052-S001-biggest-mistakes-investors-make/index.html; Hamm, T. (2015). 20 common investment mistakes and five simple steps to avoid them. *The Simple Dollar*, December 2. Retrieved from http://www.thesimpledollar.com/20-common-investment-mistakes-and-five-simple-steps-to-avoid-them/

3. Pelletier, M. (2013). Copy Buffett and Turn Down the noise when making investing decisions. *Investing*, May 6. Retrieved from http://business.financialpost.com/investing/turning-down-the-noise

4. Swedroe, L. (2014). Why it doesn't pay to chase fund performance. *Moneywatch*, September 23. Retrieved from http://www.cbsnews.com/news/why-it-doesnt-pay-to-chase-mutual-fund-performance/

5. U.S. Securities and Exchange Commission. (2013). *Mutual fund fees and expenses*. January 15. Retrieved from http://www.sec.gov/answers/mffees.htm

6. Morningstar. *Avoiding overtaxation*. Course 104. Mutual Funds and Taxes. Retrieved from http://news.morningstar.com/classroom2/course.asp?docId=2871&page=4&CN=com

7. Barber, B. M. & Odean, T. (2001). Boys will be boys: Gender, overconfidence, and common stock investment. *Quarterly Journal of Economics*, *116*(1), 261 – 292.

8. Barclays Wealth and Ledbury Research. (2011). Risk and *rules – The role of control in financial decision making* (Vol. 13). Barclays Wealth. Retrieved from https://www.investmentphilosophy.com/uploads/cms/risk-and-roles.pdf

9. Sommer, J. (2011). The guilt of trading too much. *The New York Times*, June 4. Retrieved from http://www.nytimes.com/2011/06/05/your-money/05stra.html?_r=0

10. Richards, B. (2015). Problem: Investors are trading too much. CNN, May 4. Retrieved from http://money.cnn.com/2015/05/04/investing/investors-trade-too-much/

11. Block, B. (2016). Market timing fails as a money maker. *Investopedia*. Retrieved from http://www.investopedia.com/articles/trading/07/market_timing.asp

12. Ritholtz, B. (2016). Timeless lessons brought on by Brexit. *The Washington Post*, July 25, pp. G1, G5.

13. NerdWallet. (2014). Why dollar cost averaging is a smart investment strategy. *Nasdaq*, May 19. Retrieved from http://www.nasdaq.com/article/why-dollar-cost-averaging-is-a-smart-investment-strategy-cm354240

14. Cremers, M., Ferreira, M. A., Matos, P., & Starks, L. (2013). The mutual fund industry worldwide: Explicit and closet indexing, fees, and performance. Working Paper. University of Notre Dame. Retrieved from https://editorialexpress.com/cgi-bin/conference/download.cgi?db_name=cicf2013&paper_id=934

15. Bogle, J. C. (2010). *Common sense on mutual funds*. Hoboken, NJ: Wiley.

16. Ellis, J. D. (2014). The rise and fall of performance investing. *Financial Analysts Journal, 70*(4), 14 – 23.

17. Jaffee, C. (2015). 90% of fund managers beat the market — but their shareholders don't. *MarketWatch*, January 21. Retrieved from http://www.marketwatch.com/story/90-of-fund-managers-beat-the-market-but-their-shareholders-dont-2015-01-21?page=2

18. Kennon, J. 3 reasons why some sophisticated investors don't buy index funds. *About Money*. Retrieved from http://beginnersinvest.about.com/od/Index-Funds/fl/3-Reasons-Some-Sophisticated-Investors-Dont-Buy-Index-Funds.htm

19. Zhang, J. J. (2013). The downsides to index investing. *MarketWatch*, June 19. Retrieved from http://www.marketwatch.com/story/the-downsides-to-indexed-investing-2013-06-19

20. Spence, J. (2007). Buffett gives nod to index funds over ETFs. *MarketWatch*, May 7. Retrieved from http://www.marketwatch.com/story/warren-buffett-backs-index-mutual-funds-over-etfs

21. Mayer, C. (2015). Don't chase returns in 2015! *Daily Reckoning*. January 5. Retrieved from http://dailyreckoning.com/dont-chase-returns-2015/

22. Hamilton, B. (2013). 5 reasons investing in an IPO could be a terrible idea. *Business Insider*, October 23. Retrieved from http://www.businessinsider.com/5-myths-about-ipo-investing-2013-10

23. Steiner, S. (2011). Getting in on an initial public offering. *Bankrate*. Retrieved from http://www.bankrate.com/finance/investing/getting-initial-public-offering-1.aspx

24. Investopedia Staff. (2016). IPO basics: Don't just jump in. *Investopedia*. Retrieved from http://www.investopedia.com/university/ipo/ipo2.asp

25. Stalter, K. (2015). Should you buy an IPO? *U.S. News & World Report*, August 10. Retrieved from http://money.usnews.com/money/personal-finance/mutual-funds/articles/2015/08/10/should-you-buy-an-ipo

26. Morningstar. Investment policy statement. *Morningstar*. Retrieved from http://news.morningstar.com/pdfs/Investment_Policy_Worksheet.pdf

27. Ritholtz, B. (2016). Brexit happens. Know your plan, and stick to it. *The Washington Post*, June 26, pp. G1, G5.

28. Spann, S. Creating an investment policy statement. *NAPFA*. Retrieved from http://www.napfa.org/tips_tools/article.asp?CATEGORY_ID=10&TT_ID=264

29. Bogleheads. (2015). Investment policy statement. *Bogleheads*, January 24. Retrieved from http://www.bogleheads.org/wiki/Investment_policy_statement

30. Grable, J. E. (2008). Risk tolerance. In J. J. Xiao (Ed.), *Handbook of consumer finance research* (pp. 3 – 19). New York, NY: Springer.

31. Ricciardi, V., & Rice, D. (2015). Risk perception and risk tolerance. In H. K. Baker & V. Ricciardi (Eds.), *Investor behavior – The psychology of financial planning and investing* (pp. 325 – 245). Hoboken, NJ: Wiley.

32. Investopedia Staff. 5 things to know about asset allocation. *Investopedia*. Retrieved from http://www.investopedia.com/articles/03/032603.asp

4

HOW BEHAVIORAL BIASES CAN HURT YOUR INVESTING

We have met the enemy and he is us.
Walt Kelly, Pogo daily cartoon strip
from Earth Day (1971)

Individual investors tend to do worse than the overall stock market. Why? A major reason is that they have behavioral or psychological biases that affect their ability to act objectively when investing. Yet, people frequently think they are better investors than they actually are. This contradiction reflects a discrepancy between perception and reality. Investors like to believe they can remain unbiased, but they can't because they have built-in "handicaps" that alter their thinking and negatively affect their decision-making.

Even the smartest people make judgment mistakes and have behavioral biases. Investors put their decisions through various filters resulting from their own experience that sometimes make them biased.[1] They can easily become prey to those wanting to take advantage of them because of their own vulnerability and naiveté.

Behavioral biases are classical forms of dysfunctional psychology directly applied to the investment area. Understanding how and why investors make decisions is fascinating and complex because irrationality and bias can lead to making decisions that are difficult to explain in hindsight. Successful investors are masters of personal psychology. Although investors can't control the market, they can exert control over themselves.[2]

This chapter reviews how behavioral biases can lead to errors in investment decision-making. It groups these biases into three major categories: cognitive, emotional, and social. However, few, if any, behavioral biases can be viewed in isolation because they constantly interact with each other. In fact, some biases conflict with others or fall into more than one category. The behavioral biases discussed are a sampling of the ever-growing list of irrational behaviors in the investment realm. The chapter also indicates how to address the complex task of mitigating behavioral biases, which involves changing personal behavior.

THE BEHAVIOR GAP

Investors can suffer from a *behavior gap*, which is the distance between what they should do and what they actually do. Being aware of your biases is only a first step in combating this gap. Mitigating biases requires developing a conscious plan as well as creating and following fundamental investing guidelines. Simply knowing about your biases is insufficient because you also need to change your behavior. Awareness may lead to a small improvement in actions and decisions, but any effect is probably short lived because the stimuli for the biased action have not been changed or removed. As you'll see, changing behavior can be difficult. Anyone who has ever tried to stop smoking or lose weight knows that making such a change is challenging.

The effects of behavioral bias on economic behavior and decision-making can be similar and can lead to questionable decisions and erroneous conclusions. Thus, investors can unknowingly become their own worst enemy. As Jason Zweig, a columnist *for The Wall Street Journal* and author of *Your Money and Your Brain*, notes, "Investing isn't about beating others at their game. It's about controlling yourself at your own game."

TYPES OF BIASES

Controlling your behavior starts by becoming aware of your behavioral biases. A *behavioral bias* is the tendency to think or feel in certain ways that can lead to systematic deviations from a standard of rationality or good judgment. Behavioral bias can result from either internal or external factors. Internal actors include cognitive and emotional biases.[3]

Cognitive Bias

A *cognitive bias* is a type of error in thinking that occurs when people are collecting, processing, and interpreting information. It is a deficiency or limitation in how people think. Such biases can result from attempting to simplify information processing and may or may not be factual. That is, people use mental shortcuts called heuristics to speed up the process of finding a satisfactory solution, rather than an optimal one, and to ease the cognitive load of making a decision. Overcoming cognitive biases requires both recognizing their existence and changing the way of thinking.

Emotional Bias

An *emotional bias* is a distortion in cognition and decision-making due to emotional factors. Unlike cognitive behavioral biases, finding a solution to emotional biases requires great care because they are tied deeply to personal sentiments. Cognitive errors are generally more easily corrected than emotional biases, which are ingrained in a person's emotional psyche. As Warren Buffet notes about investing, "It's an easy game if you can control your emotions."

Social Bias

Psychological influences on investor decision-making extend beyond how investors think and feel. Investors don't make decisions totally based on internal inputs. As social creatures, others influence how someone behaves. Therefore, behavioral bias may also result from external factors called *social bias*. These social influences include not only the media and the Internet but also friends, colleagues, culture, and other factors. For example, one type of social bias is *herd behavior*, which occurs when individuals mimic the actions of a larger group. As a result, investors gravitate to the same or similar investments because many others are investing in them.

DIFFERENT PERSPECTIVES: TRADITIONAL AND BEHAVIORAL

In practice, investors are subject to many behavioral biases. As such, a behavioral finance viewpoint differs markedly from the foundation blocks of traditional or standard finance that are based on the premise of rational agents making unbiased judgments and maximizing their self-interests. Traditional finance theory assumes that investors always behave rationally. That is, investing is considered purely logical. Yet, in practice, investors may sense a tug-of-war between their analytical brains and their emotional selves. Because individual investors don't behave as rationally as economic theory suggests, behavioral finance substitutes normal or real people for rational ones.

Traditional finance also assumes that markets are efficient. An *efficient market* is one where all participants have all pertinent information available at the same time, and where prices respond immediately to all available information. In behavioral finance, markets are not efficient, even though they are difficult to beat. In summary, behavioral finance indicates how people individually and collectively behave, whereas traditional finance indicates how people should act according to theory.[4]

Although the traditional approach to finance provides many useful insights, it offers an incomplete picture of actual, observed behavior. The normative assumptions of traditional finance do not apply to how most investors make decisions or allocate capital. Consequently, normative models can fail because people are sometimes irrational and the models are based on false assumptions. For example, a criticism of modern portfolio theory for individual investors is that optimizing with volatility as a risk measure is not behaviorally justified. The implication that positive or negative deviations away from the expected return add to risk does not reflect how individuals either do, or should, think about risk. Investors rarely believe that getting more than they expect feels like a risk. For example, if an investor expects to earn a portfolio return of 10% but actually earns 12%, the investor is unlikely to view the extra return as involving more risk.

By contrast, behavioral finance applies psychology to financial behavior. It is based on the premise that a wide range of objective and subjective issues influence the decision-making process. Evidence shows that individuals are not always rational when making real life judgments and decisions. They may select a merely satisfactory outcome rather than the optimal outcome. This is known as *satisficing*. However, investors are more likely to do something about most biases they face if they're motivated to do so. Thus, knowing about and taking action to lessen your behavioral biases can help you achieve greater investment success.

COGNITIVE BIASES: HOW INVESTORS THINK

Investors make costly mistakes due to various cognitive biases that affect their decisions.[5] Some cognitive biases are built into the brain and hence subconsciously influence investor behavior. These biases result from either an investor's inability to analyze all information or basing decisions on incomplete information. Cognitive biases can be separated into two broad groups: belief perseverance biases and information processing biases.[6]

Belief Perseverance Biases

Belief perseverance biases stem from an individual's attempts to avoid conflicts between beliefs or opinions and reality. Investors frequently have difficulty modifying existing beliefs when confronted with new, contradictory information. Hence, they experience mental discomfort in having to reconcile these differences known as *cognitive dissonance*.

Cognitive Dissonance

Cognitive dissonance is the discomfort that results when confronted with new information that conflicts with existing beliefs and ideas. People don't like having dissonant thoughts. For example, assume an investor buys a stock based on a recommendation from a market newsletter. Subsequently, the investor receives information that conflicts with the original recommendation. For example, the stock lacks strong fundamentals or has weak growth prospects. To lessen the discomfort caused by the conflicting views, the investor may distort, manipulate or ignore this new information. Basically, the investor is lying to himself. This type of mental gymnastics is commonplace when investors try to justify their behavior when they know they are wrong. This self-deluding behavior suggests that investors fail to learn from their mistakes. Instead, they try to fool themselves into believing something else.[2]

If you are subject to cognitive dissonance, you need to become self-aware of your actions and beliefs and to recognize the conflict between the two. One option is to ask others whom you trust to review the evidence related to your actions and beliefs and suggest an alternative course. Successful investors seek feedback from others and consider its merit when making investment decisions.

Confirmation Bias

A bias related to cognitive dissonance is *confirmation bias*. Although investors like to think they carefully gather and evaluate information before making a decision, they often don't.

Confirmation bias is the tendency to notice, seek out, or evaluate information in a way that supports one's existing thinking and preconceptions and to ignore contradictory information, regardless of its validity. In other words, investors believe what they want to believe. They have a selective memory leading them to choose the memories best served to fuel their established narrative. As such, investors are frequently drawn to information that validates existing beliefs and opinions and dismiss anything negative. For example, an investor buys a stock based on the recommendation of a friend. Later, several stories appear in the news media about the company indicating that its stock is not a good investment but the investor ignores them. This unconscious act can threaten how the investor views the stock and can lead to overconfidence and overweighting an investment in his portfolio.

Investors suffering from confirmation bias also tend to surround themselves with those who have similar views. This *in-group bias* gives them a false sense of security involving their views. Additionally, in-group bias can cause investors to overestimate their abilities and value the group's views at the expense of others who may have better ideas. In summary, when investors make bad decisions, they tend to rationalize them through cognitive dissonance, and then reinforce the decision with confirmation bias. Given such behavior, the fact that the average investor does so poorly is not surprising.

To mitigate confirmation bias, you should actively seek out and carefully consider sources offering different opinions. Trying to find information that disagrees with your current view requires deliberate action in the quest to make better-informed decisions.

Representative Bias

Representative bias, also called the *representativeness heuristic*, is the presumption that once people or events are categorized, they share all the features of other members in that category. This bias causes investors to attach too much importance to a small set of data because they incorrectly believe that it represents the whole picture. When people use categories to make a decision about a person, thing, or event, they are using the representativeness heuristic. This bias is comparable to relying on stereotypes. If something does not fit exactly into a known category, people will approximate with the nearest class available.

Representative bias helps explain the *gambler's fallacy*, which is the tendency to put more weight on previous events under the assumption that they influence future outcomes. This fallacy indicates that if something occurs more often than normal during some period, it will happen less frequently in the future, or vice versa, if something happens less frequently than normal during some period, it will happen more frequently in the future The major drawback of the representativeness heuristic is in assuming that similarity in one aspect leads to similarity in other aspects.[7]

Investors encounter many investment examples of representative bias. For instance, they may assume that goods stocks (i.e., stocks that perform well) come from good companies (i.e., those that are run well). However, evidence shows that good management and subsequent stock performance are unrelated.[8] Representativeness also results in investors labeling an investment as good or bad based on its recent performance. Consequently, they buy stocks after prices have risen expecting those increases to continue and ignore stocks when their prices are below their intrinsic values. Another example is many investors view IPOs that show large initial price increases are good long-term investments. Empirical evidence does not support this belief.[9] A final example is that many investors believe that top performing mutual funds are likely to continue to remain top performers in the future. Despite evidence to the contrary, investors continue to chase performance.[10]

To reduce representative bias, you should consider the true probability that information fits a category. You also need to have a clearly defined analytical process that you test and retest to refine and improve over time to improve decision-making.

A financial advisor can help guide you in developing such an analytical process.

Conservatism Bias

Conservatism bias is the tendency to revise one's beliefs insufficiently when presented with new evidence. This bias causes individuals to overweight initial beliefs and under-react to new information. They also tend to revise their belief insufficiently when presented with new evidence.[11] For example, a client of an investment advisor may cling to his prior forecast of his expected portfolio value at retirement at the expense of acknowledging new information. Consistent with conservatism, evidence shows that investors under-react to corporate events including announcements of earnings, changes in dividends, and stock splits. Due to the conservatism bias, if the signal indicates good news, an investor with conservatism bias would have both a smaller conditional mean of the asset payoff than a rational trader and a larger conditional standard deviation of the asset payoff than a rational trader.[12]

You can reduce conservatism bias by carefully examining new information to determine its value relative to prior beliefs. Another approach is to be more flexible in your thinking and let go of prior beliefs when confronted with credible evidence to the contrary.

Illusion of Control Bias

Illusion of control bias is the tendency to overestimate one's degree of control or influence over external events. Key attributes that influence the illusion of control are task familiarity, information, skill, and active involvement. Despite all of the information and technology available, as well as extensive educational preparation, unexpected events can interfere with investors' plans to control an outcome or an event. Not surprisingly, overconfidence and excessive optimism, which are common emotional biases, can stem from the illusion of control.

Investors like to think that they have more control over their investments than they actually do. Although do-it-yourself investors have control over their asset allocations, security selection, and market timing, they don't have control over the outcomes resulting from these decisions. The illusion of control can lead to excessive trading, especially among online traders, with the accompanying costs and concentrated portfolios. One study finds that the more traders think they are in control, the worse is their actual performance.[13] The illusion of control can also stop investors from learning from their mistakes and being sensitive to feedback.

To lessen the illusion of control, you should stick to a well-crafted investment plan and avoid unnecessary trading. You can also seek the opinion of others and keep records of trades to see if you are successful at controlling investment outcomes. Once you realize your control in markets and investments is illusory, you can begin practicing flexibility and conserve your energy for those matters over which you can exert influence.

Hindsight Bias

Hindsight bias is the tendency to see past events as having been predictable and reasonable to expect before they occurred. With the benefit of hindsight, the "correct" choice at the time of the decision seems obvious later, but it really was not at the time. This bias, also known as the "knew-it-all-along effect," is difficult to eradicate because it is fundamental to the human experience. A problem with hindsight bias is that someone actually didn't know it all along, but simply thought that he did. For example, the United States experienced a housing bubble in which housing prices peaked in early 2006 and then started to decline in 2006 and 2007. After the bubble burst, many investors said "I knew that would happen" but failed to exit the real estate market before it was too late.

Investors afflicted with hindsight bias may be overconfident in the certainty of their judgments or forecasts. This bias can also lead to a false sense of security when making investment decisions, which can lead to excessive risk-taking. Additionally, hindsight bias can get in the way of learning from experiences because it involves the distortion of past events.

One way to deal with this cognitive fault is to admit to being susceptible to this bias. You can keep a diary of the basic numbers and thought processes of your investment decisions. Revisiting your investment decisions and forcing yourself to face the information available at the time of the decision, instead of the information available now, can help you understand the chain of events. Another approach is to consider and explain how outcomes that didn't happen could have happened, which may counteract the usual inclination to discard information that doesn't fit your narrative.[14]

Information Processing Biases

Information processing biases involve errors in how people think when processing information regarding financial decisions. Investors regularly process information by using mental shortcuts, also called *heuristics* or *rules of thumb*, to reduce the amount and complexity of information requiring analysis. These shortcuts allow the brain to generate estimates before fully digesting all the available information, which speeds up and simplifies the decision-making process. Thus, heuristics focus on certain aspects of a decision but not on others. Despite the functional aspects of using heuristics, they can lead to systematic and predictable mistakes. Using heuristics can also result in outcomes that differ from what conventional wisdom predicts.

Anchoring and Adjustment Bias
An anchored ship does not stray too far from its tethering point. Likewise, investors prefer to stick close to the references with which they feel most comfortable. *Anchoring bias*, also called the *relativity trap*, is the tendency to rely too heavily on a single piece of information when making decisions. The theory of anchoring

indicates a propensity to associate a decision with a reference point. Investors frequently consider a past event, decision, price, or trend as an anchor or reference. Based on this anchoring, they make estimates using some initial value and then adjust that number up or down.

Let's examine several examples. One instance is when investors latch on to market prices as anchors. This practice is dangerous because prices are simply the latest estimate of value and could be overvalued or undervalued. Investors may fixate on the price at which they bought a stock and largely ignore other salient information. They tend to keep losing investments by waiting for the investment to break even at the original purchase price, which anchors the value of their investment. This anchor can unduly influence the final decision to sell, causing investors to miss out on putting invested funds to better use.

Another example is when investors are attracted to a stock that has fallen considerably from its previous or all-time high. By anchoring on the stock's high price, they now believe the stock represents an investment opportunity. If the stock's declining price results from overall market sentiment and not to deterioration in business fundamentals, these investors made the right decision. On the other hand, if the price decline results from worsening fundamentals such as declining earnings, cash flow, or dividends, they are likely to suffer losses after buying the stock.

Several remedies are available for dealing with anchoring bias. First, you can consider a wide range of investment choices and not focus on a specific reference point of information when making a decision. Second, you can focus on fundamentals, not just price. That is, don't worry about the artificial anchoring point of a buying price. Third, you need to remain flexible in your thinking, be open to new sources of information, and determine how such information affects your original forecast or opinion. Fourth, you can choose an anchor that is something predictive, such as income streams in the form of dividends, which provides a barometer of a company's financial health. Finally, you can discuss an investment with trusted individuals and even take a "devil's advocate" role in evaluating it to help avoid anchoring to a nonpredictive element of the investment. A *devil's advocate* argues against a cause or position, not as a committed opponent but simply for the sake of argument or to determine the validity of the cause or position.

Mental Accounting

Mental accounting is the tendency to treat one sum of money differently from another equal-sized sum based on how the money is categorized. This behavioral bias occurs when people put their money into separate categories or mental accounts based on the source of the money or the intent of the account. They treat some dollars differently from other dollars and take different risks with money depending on its source. For example, people may view money earned from a job differently from money obtained from capital gains or an inheritance. They consider money earned from working as more valuable than money gotten from other sources. This sometimes translates into them having money that they are more willing to lose because it came from a different source. Another example is viewing income and capital gains received from an investment separately, rather than as parts of the same total return. Mental accounting can affect how a person spends or invests money. Consequently, mental biases lead to reaching conclusions about value inconsistently and irrationally.[15]

Let's take another example. Assume you recently earned profits from selling a stock. You keep the capital or principal in a separate mental account from recent profits, which could lead to viewing these profits as disposable. By doing so, you are more inclined to take greater risks with gains from a profitable trade by buying higher risk stocks. Why? You view the profits as "playing with house money," a gambling expression meaning you're risking money you've already won from "the house," which in this situation is the market. The notion that capital gains are "free money" or "money you can afford to lose" is a purely mental creation. Yet, you are willing to risk the profits because whether you win or lose, you incorrectly assume that you are no worse off than when you started because you still have your initial capital. In other words, you view your money (capital) differently from house money (trading profits). This psychological phenomenon is economically irrational because money is money regardless of its origin or intended use. A dollar in your right pocket is worth the same as a dollar in your left pocket.

How can you avoid this all too human mental accounting fallacy? One approach is to focus on the big picture of your entire portfolio. You should treat all investments as if they are part of the same portfolio instead of in separate "buckets" or mental accounts. Then you can examine the overall contribution of the various accounts to the portfolio's overall return and deploy capital appropriately. Taking these steps should help you avoid making financial mistakes due to mental accounting.[16]

Framing Bias

Framing bias is the tendency to behave differently depending on how a situation is presented or framed. In other words, framing bias deals with the fact that people tend to answer a question differently depending on how it is asked or presented. As an example, showing an investor a single outcome for a portfolio tends to produce lower levels of risk aversion than showing the outcomes of individual investments in the portfolio.[17] This situation illustrates *narrow framing*. Investors suffer from narrow framing if they make investment decisions without considering the context of their total portfolios. They only evaluate a few factors that may affect their investment, rather than looking at the whole picture. Displaying fund performance as growth in value or yield affects perceived risk and return and preferences for the fund.[18]

Let's illustrate how framing results in terms of probabilities of success (winning) or failure (losing) alters the preference for an option. Assume you have 50/50 odds of either winning $8 or $32 and a 50/50 chance of losing $8 or $32. Rationally, you should feel good about either option in the first example because you win money and bad about losing money in the second example. Despite this, research evidence shows that subjects reported feeling dissatisfied when they won $8 because they didn't win $32. Similarly, they felt slightly positive when they lost $8 because they avoided losing $32, despite still losing money. Hence, they felt good about losing $8 because the gamble was framed in terms of losses and they felt bad about winning $8 because the gamble was framed in terms of gains.

Despite the malleable minds of investors, you can lessen framing effects by trying to see through the frame, or rather, to look at things more objectively. This task is difficult given that others are frequently trying to "nudge" you into a certain direction or decision through the way they present information. For instance, mutual funds try to nudge you into their high performing funds by advertising and presenting them in a positive way. Another way to avoid framing bias is to focus on total returns and risk instead of on gains or loses.

Availability Bias

Availability bias is the tendency to give a greater weight to easily recalled and recent information over information that is less recallable or harder to understand. This bias prevents investors from considering other potential and relevant information. They may readily recall information in the media and corporate releases and from advertising. As a result, investors with this mindset may be attracted to mutual funds that do the most advertising, instead of doing independent research to identify potentially better funds to meet their investment goals. Selecting investments based on how easily their memories are retrieved and categorized could lead to suboptimal results. If investors have a narrow range of experience, availability bias can lead to concentrated portfolios and increased risk. To mitigate availability bias, you can develop an IPS and construct an appropriate portfolio based on your own diligent research.

Outcome Bias

Outcome bias is the tendency to judge a decision by its eventual outcome without regard to how the past events developed. Investors sometimes judge the efficacy of a decision based primarily on how things turn out and rarely examine the conditions that existed at the time of the decision. For example, an investor may buy a stock because a colleague realized a large return by investing in that stock. The investor doesn't examine that factors that resulted in his colleague's success, such as the state of the overall economy, which may have changed when the investor bought the stock. A problem with outcome bias is that it leads investors to repeat poor decision-making based on outcomes rather than on the process used to obtain the outcome. Outcome bias can also limit returns if investors are unaware of this behavior.

To overcome outcome bias, you should not focus on a single factor when investing, in this case, the outcome. Instead, you should understand the factors leading to the results, examine the process that led to that outcome, and use a longer period for your analysis. You should also make your decision based on the information you have at the time. Some useful questions to focus on the process as a whole include the following:

- What factors led to making the decision?

- What information was and wasn't available at that point?

- Was the information obtainable?

- Was a better process available in making the decision?[19]

Recency Bias

Recency bias is the tendency to use recent experience as the baseline for what will happen in the future. In other words, investors think that trends and patterns observed in the recent past will continue in the future. This bias can lead investors to make incorrect conclusions that ultimately lead to faulty decisions about how the stock market or an investment behaves. For example, if a company has exceeded earnings expectations for the past four quarters, investors with recency and pattern-seeking bias are likely to expect the trend will continue.

Although investors manage to make decisions that feel right at the time, such investments end up hurting them in the end. To illustrate, assume that the market has been relatively calm for several years, which could lead investors to forgetting about the market's overall riskiness over time. Another example is when investors select mutual funds based solely on their recent performance. Recency bias combined with the hope for higher prices during bull markets clouds their decision-making process. Unfortunately, "hope" is an ineffective investment strategy. Those who suffer from recency bias may also be subject to illusion of control, representativeness, and outcome bias.[20]

For example, during a bull market, recent experience indicates that the market has been climbing higher, so investors believe this pattern will continue. This situation occurred during the bull market for real estate in the United States between 2003 and 2007. Consequently, investors continue buying, often at inflated prices, and chasing performance. Eventually, the market declines, causing fear among retail investors who engage in "panic selling" and place their money in cash or low-yielding investments. Similarly, when the market is down, recency bias indicates that the market isn't going to increase, so many individual investors stay out of the market entirely. Eventually the market increases.[21] Their notoriously short-term memories lead buyers to engage at the top and sellers to exit at the bottom.[22] To mitigate recency bias, you need to take the long view and consider as many factors as possible such as the market going both up and down.

Limited Attention Bias

Investors face a multitude of different asset classes as potential investments. Within each asset class, thousands of choices are available. Because individual investors don't have the time or the desire to research each, they fail to incorporate all relevant information or take notice of something crucial when making decisions. Hence, they suffer from *limited attention bias*.[23] Such investors may consider only investments such as stocks or mutual funds that come to their attention through financial media, websites, or other sources. They are prone to certain attention-grabbing events such as news about a stock, abnormal trading volume, and extreme returns. These investors tend to be net buyers after these events.[24] However, the increase in investor attention generates purchases and leads to higher prices. Given their limited knowledge, investors overlook, neglect, or misinterpret the available information. Consequently, they make satisfactory decisions instead of optimal ones.

To overcome limited attention bias, you should expand your research and evaluation of investments beyond well-known or highly publicized securities. You should also resist the temptation of letting media noise influence your decisions. Instead, you should use multiple sources to identify potential investments and avoid being swayed by a single source such as the media.

Familiarity Bias

Investors face a countless number of possible investments both at home and abroad. Trying to analyze the expected return and risk of each investment is impossible, so what do they generally do? A popular Wall Street adage is to "invest in what you know." Hence, many investors invest in familiar securities. To some, having money invested in a familiar business provides comfort. Others invest in familiar investments for such behavioral reasons as overconfidence, patriotism, and social identification.[25] However, investing in "what you know" can lead investors down the wrong path. Investing in the familiar can also lead to underestimating an investment's risk. When investors underestimate risk, they don't take steps to mitigate it, such as diversifying, and usually end up taking too much risk. They forego higher returns and lower risks available from greater diversification and hence hold suboptimal portfolios.[26]

Familiarity bias occurs when investors prefer familiar investments despite the seemingly obvious gains from diversification. They prefer local assets with which they are more familiar (*local bias*) as well portfolios tilted toward domestic securities (*home bias*). Familiarity bias could manifest itself in several ways such as overinvesting in an employer's stock or being concentrated in assets in one's home country.

To overcome familiarity bias, you need to cast a wider net and expand your portfolio allocation decisions to gain wider diversification and risk reduction. For example, investing in both home and international markets helps to avoid familiarity bias and reduce volatility. You can also discuss different investing strategies with your financial advisor and then consider employing the appropriate strategies for meeting your financial goals.

EMOTIONAL BIASES: HOW INVESTORS FEEL

Despite the best of intentions, investors can't be Spock-like in their lack of emotion. Humans have emotional biases that inevitably lead to poor investment decision-making. For example, even after working with a financial advisor to create an IPS based on risk tolerance and objectives, some investors are eager to abandon their plan when markets become turbulent. Because they can't remain disciplined during such volatile times, they react emotionally, which generally leads to making the wrong decision. Consequently, they buy on greed in up markets and sell on fear in down markets. The inability to manage emotions helps to explain why so many investors fail to earn satisfactory returns over time.

As Benjamin Graham, the father of value investing, once noted: "Individuals who cannot master their emotions are ill-suited to profit from the investment process." Not surprisingly, the really great investors follow strict investment disciplines to reduce the impact of their emotions.

Emotional biases result in taking action based on feelings rather than fact. Emotional biases influence how individuals see or frame information and make decisions. Such biases are more spontaneous than deliberate. Making decisions for emotional reasons carries a price in the form of higher costs or lower returns. Consequently, emotional biases have a tremendous impact on investment success. Although escaping the influence of emotions on investment decision-making is admittedly difficult, you can lessen these biases through awareness and taking a reflective approach to investing. Below are some major emotional influences and suggestions for dealing with them.[27]

Loss-Aversion Bias

Many investors exhibit *loss aversion*, which refers to the tendency to prefer avoiding losses to acquiring gains. In short, investors have difficulty coming to terms with losses. The expression "losses loom larger than gains" summarizes this bias. Additionally, investors remember declines in their investment portfolios more vividly than gains, even when the gains are greater. One problem with loss aversion is that the fear of loss leads to withdrawing capital at the worst possible time or "panic selling." *Panic selling* occurs when an investor wants to get out of an investment with little regard to the price. Wide-scale panic selling of an investment matters because it causes a sharp decline in prices.

Loss aversion is also a behavioral condition in which people feel the pain of loss more than the joy of gains. For example, if you lose $1000 versus gain $1000 on an investment, the pain that you experience from the loss is not the same as the satisfaction that you receive from the gain. The pain of losing is psychologically about twice as powerful as the pleasure of an equivalent gain. Basically, people are "hardwired" to try to hold on to what they have. Investors are willing to undertake higher risk and go to potentially irrational lengths to avoid losses, but they become risk averse in the case of gains.

Another factor contributing to loss aversion is the *sunk cost fallacy*. A *sunk cost* is a cost that has already been incurred and cannot be recovered. Investors should disregard sunk costs when making the decision to continue investing in an ongoing project because they can't recover the cost. A sunk cost is similar to spilled milk. Having spilled the milk, you can't do anything about it except clean it up. Yet, the inability to ignore sunk costs causes investors to fail to evaluate an investment on its own merits. Sunk costs may also cause investors to hold on to a losing stock despite deteriorating business fundamentals.

Loss-aversion bias also results in the *disposition effect*, which relates to the tendency of selling assets too soon whose price has increased (winners), while keeping assets too long whose price has dropped (losers). Two strong emotions – pride and regret – play a key role in the predisposition of investors to sell winners too early and ride losers too long. Because people want to feel good about themselves, they seek pride and avoid regret when making decisions. Selling a winner is a good feeling, indicating that the original purchase was a good decision. However, investors tend to sell a winning stock quickly to ensure collecting the gain only to see the stock continue to rise in price after the sale. Similarly, attempts to avoid regret lead investors to do financially stupid things. If the stock price declines after the purchase, they are reluctant to realize losses in order to avoid admitting that they were wrong. By not selling the position and locking in a loss, they don't have to deal with regret. Investors sell winners too early and a losing position too late to avoid the regret of losing gains or losing the original cost basis, affecting their port-folio returns.[28]

Investors appear predisposed to "get-evenitis,"[29] which is also called the *breakeven effect*. This "waiting to get even" behavior involves waiting to sell a loser until it gets back to its original cost basis. Clinging to losers involves two major costs. First, the investment could continue to decrease in price, resulting in fur-ther losses. Second, investors incur an opportunity cost by not putting investment dollars to better use. The strong preference for selling winners and keeping losers is also harmful to inves-tors because it can not only increase the capital gains from taxes they pay but also can reduce returns even before taxes. Because investors who have lost money want to make up their losses, they may take bets that they otherwise wouldn't have taken. In over words, get-evenitis leads investors to taking risks to avoid taking a loss.

One approach to dealing with loss aversion is to consider the merits of each investment by performing a thorough fundamental analysis. *Fundamental analysis* is a method of evaluating a secu-rity in an attempt to measure its intrinsic value by examining related economic, financial, and other qualitative and quantitative factors. Ask yourself, would you buy this investment today? If the answer is "no," then why are you holding it? This awareness can create an impetus to sell a losing investment and buy one with bet-ter prospects. You have to overcome the mental anguish of recog-nizing losses. Consequently, you should not go into an investment without an exit strategy. Following the advice of "cut your losses and let your profits run" enables you to engage in disciplined investment management that can generate higher returns. Another approach is to talk with your advisor about market expectations and how to manage emotions, especially during market down-turns. A third approach is to set up and follow preestablished guidelines for when to sell a winner or loser, and stick to them no matter how you feel in the moment.

Regret Aversion Bias

Regret aversion is the indecision and failure to take action due to fear of bad outcomes. Investors suffering from regret aversion bias do not take a necessary action because of the regret of a previous failure. This bias stems from the desire to avoid feeling responsible for a poor result. Regret aversion bias is associated with risk aversion because regret-averse investors sometimes fear not buying the right assets or buying the wrong assets. They want to avoid the emotional pain related to making poor decisions. For example, investors who suffered recent losses might become too conservative in order to avoid the pain associated with additional loses. They may develop a habit of investing in short-term bonds to avoid the greater volatility of investing in the stock market. By staying in low risk investments, their portfolios have limited upside potential. However, if stocks declined to where bargains are available, regret aversion could prevent them from breaking their bond-buying habit to take advantage of high-potential stocks. If investors suffer from regret aversion bias, they may also invest in familiar investments or follow the heard.

To avoid regret aversion, you should realize that not making a decision is a choice to maintain the *status quo* and current portfolio holdings. You must develop the discipline to stick to your investment plan, especially during declining markets, in order to reach your long-term goals and periodically rebalance your portfolio.

Self-Control Bias

Self-control bias is the failure to pursue long-term goals because of a lack of self-discipline in the short run. Investors may try to make up the shortfall by assuming too much risk. This behavior is both counterproductive to achieving long-term financial goals and hazardous to your wealth.

Self-control bias may lead to several ineffective investment behaviors. First, people may spend more today at the expense of saving for tomorrow. Investors with self-control bias suffer from *short-termism* due to their tendency to avoid investments necessary for the future because they don't want to sacrifice short-term benefits. Consequently, their saving consumption patterns are frequently suboptimal. This immediate gratification mindset reflects a *current moment bias* in which people want to live as well as possible today but pay for it later. The level of credit card debt in the United States partly reflects this bias.

Second, self-control bias leads to inadequately planning for retirement. Many retirees wish that they had spent less, saved more, and started investing sooner. After becoming aware of their retirement shortfall, they may take more risk in their portfolios to make up for lost time, which can place their retirement security at increased risk. A lack of willpower to consider tomorrow at the expense of today can sabotage retirement plans.

Third, self-control bias may result in asset allocation imbalance. That is, due to a "spend today" mentality, investors may prefer income-producing assets, which may inhibit achieving a level of long-term wealth needed for retirement. Although the benefits associated with self-discipline in investing can be difficult to obtain, the results merit the effort.

To lessen self-control bias, you need to strike a careful balance among short-, medium- and long-term goals, which translates into assessing the appropriate level of saving, investing, and risk-taking. Achieving this balance requires planning. People don't plan to fail, they simply fail to plan. Another remedy is to maintain a proper balance of assets in your portfolio to attain your financial goals. Establishing and following a budget can help deter the propensity to over-consume. A final suggestion is to pay yourself first. That is, set a certain amount of funds aside each period for investment purposes. Taking this step enables you to take advantage of basic financial principles such as such as compounding of interest or dollar cost averaging.

Inertia Biases

In an investments context, inertia bias occurs when investors fail to update their economic conditions despite the presence of potential gains. As with many other biases, inertial biases lead to suboptimal decisions. Two emotionally related inertia biases are status quo bias and the endowment effect. Conservatism bias is another inertia bias previously discussed under cognitive biases.[30]

Status Quo *Bias*

Status quo bias is the tendency to do nothing or maintain a previous decision unless some compelling incentive exists to change. *Status quo* investors prefer to hold the investments they already have based on the unwarranted assumption that another choice will be inferior or make matters worse. By maintaining the current asset allocation, they may forego making value enhancing adjustments and experience changing risk characteristics of their portfolios. *Status quo* bias helps to explain why many individuals tend to defer savings for retirement or postpone opening and making contributions to a retirement account. After entering a retirement plan, investors may not actively manage or monitor their accounts, but instead maintain the *status quo*. Remaining comfortable or complacent with an existing portfolio could lead to an inappropriate risk-return profile over time. For example, if stocks or other assets in a portfolio increase dramatically, this could result in greater risk without rebalancing.

Many people prefer things to remain about the same for two reasons. First, they don't want to make a decision because this might imply that the previous decision, such as buying an asset, was a poor one. This situation is especially true after an investment's price has fallen. The default choice is sometimes the do-nothing option. However, keeping the current state of affairs is actually making a decision. Second, investors won't face any consequences of making a bad decision by not making a change. This reasoning is also flawed because maintaining the *status quo* might not be the best choice.

Investors with *status quo* bias may suffer from related biases. For example, *negativity bias* makes them place more weight on negative impacts than benefits. Investors tend to pay more attention to bad news on account of their *selective attention*. That is, they perceive negative news as more important or profound than positive news. The mind generally reacts more quickly, strongly, and persistently to bad things than it does to equivalent good things. So investors have difficulty seeing the benefits of a change because they are too fearful of the negative impacts.[31] They tend to place more emphasis on the effects of risk than on the possibility of reward. Investors may also suffer from *inattention bias*, which refers to the tendency for beliefs to endure once formed. Changing these biases requires strong motivation or incentives.

To resist *status quo* and related biases, you should implement a disciplined investment strategy based on a portfolio approach, which requires education about risk and return and proper asset allocation. For example, you should match your level of risk tolerance with a predetermined asset allocation. You also need to periodically reexamine your investment plan, which could provide the impetus to take action due to changing conditions and constraints or new opportunities. Another way to mitigate *status quo* bias involves rebalancing a portfolio at least annually. This action helps to ensure that your risk tolerance profile matches the asset allocation throughout the life of a long-term portfolio. Although an active asset allocation provides less upside gains during bull markets, it lessens downside risk during bear markets. You can also have a knowledgeable friend, colleague, or financial advisor play devil's advocate by pointing out potential benefits of changing the *status quo* of your investments. Obtaining a different perspective could be enlightening and help foster change. However, if you ultimately decide to take the "do-nothing" path, you should be confident that it will lead to accomplishing your goals.

Endowment Effect

The *endowment effect* is the tendency for investors to overvalue assets that they already hold over those that they do not. Investors can cling to assets, whether bought or inherited, because of familiarity, comfort, or emotional attachment. For example, someone who inherits shares of a stock may refuse to sell them despite the shares being inconsistent with the individual's risk tolerance or investment goals or having a negative impact on a portfolio's diversification. Another example of the endowment effect is when an investor continues to hold a stock despite evidence that others in its sector are better investments. This bias leads to holding on to an asset for too long and possibly losing money in the process.

To deal with the endowment effect, you need to determine whether the current asset allocation is appropriate. That is, you should analyze whether keeping a security or other asset negatively affects your overall asset allocation. If so, you should replace it with another asset to bring your asset allocation within the limits specified by your investment plan. To counter the endowment effect for inherited securities, ask yourself the following question: If you received cash as part of an inheritance, what portion would you allocate to buy the inherited security? If your answer is little or none, this awareness could provide an incentive for selling the inherited security.

Self-Deception Biases

Investors are prone to self-deception. *Self-deception biases* examine how mistakes that arise from people's desire for a positive self-image affect their reasoning and decision-making. Although having a positive self-image can be beneficial, it can also lead to negative investment decisions. The most common of the self-deception biases is overconfidence. Two other biases — self-attribution bias and excessive optimism — represent either side of overconfidence.[30]

Overconfidence Bias

Overconfidence bias is an excessive belief in one's own judgments and abilities. Overconfident investors believe that they know more than they actually do. In other words, they have a subconscious faith in what they think they know and rely too much on their own judgment due to feelings of superiority. This belief stems from the feeling that they have more or better information or they are better at interpreting information. Accordingly, overconfident investors usually overestimate their abilities and ignore the actual risk involved in a decision. In short, overconfident investors are victims of the "ego" or "superiority trap."[32]

Overconfidence bias generally arises from the desire for a positive self-image. For instance, both individual and professional investors tend to overestimate their level of financial sophistication and the accuracy of their predictions. This level of overconfidence can lead to a false sense of security when making investment decisions. Additionally, overconfident investors may engage in excessive trading, hold under-diversified portfolios, and underestimate the downside while over-estimating the upside potential of their investments.

Several factors contribute to overconfidence when investing. One factor, called the *illusion of knowledge*, is when someone's knowledge or understanding is rather shallow. As Stephen Hawking, an English theoretical physicist and cosmologist notes, "The greatest enemy of knowledge is not ignorance, it is the illusion of knowledge." Many investors think they know or understand something, but they really don't. As such, self-proclaimed experts are more vulnerable to the illusion of knowledge. Furthermore, evidence suggests that searching the web reinforces an illusion of knowledge. Investors begin to confuse what's online with what's in their heads, giving them an exaggerated sense of their own intelligence. Also, doing searches on one topic inflates their sense of how well they understand other unrelated topics.[33]

Besides the illusion of knowledge, many individual investors also believe they are better than the experts and can beat the market or pick winning stocks. Yet, they are unlikely to have better information, experience, intuition, or analytical powers than investment professionals, especially institutional investors. The market is littered with investors who have lost a fortune because they believed they were better than the rest. The odds overwhelmingly favor institutional investors. This type of *self-deception bias* leads to suboptimal decisions on the part of investors resulting in such negative consequences as engaging in excessive trading, taking too much risk, paying too much in commissions and taxes, having less diversified portfolios, and experiencing lower returns. In short, overconfident and frequent traders are basically paying fees to lose money.

Investors who fall into the ego or superiority trap are easy prey for the true experts who can and do exploit them. Overconfident investors also tend to be slow in combining additional information about any decision-making situation because they are confident in their initial decisions. The level of overconfidence can relate to the degree of past successes, length of professional experience, and amount of education.

Self-Attribution Bias

Self-attribution bias, also called *self-serving bias*, is the tendency to attribute successes to one's own choices (*self-enhancing bias*) and to blame failures on the impact of others and external factors (*self-protecting bias*). In other words, investors credit themselves for the "good stuff" that happens and blame others for the "bad stuff." They want to maintain high self-esteem and feel good about themselves. This behavioral pattern influences them to exaggerate their abilities and ignore their mistakes. As previously noted, individual investors tend to take credit for successful investments and blame their failures on external factors such as the market or their financial advisor. Conversely, as investors make more decisions, they begin to learn their true ability at investing. Prior experience and performance can help moderate the extent of biased self-attribution.

Excessive Optimism

Although excessive optimism and overconfidence are related, they represent two distinct behavioral biases. *Excessive optimism* involves a belief that future events are more likely to be positive than is realistic. Investors frequently make bold forecasts due to their optimism. Their optimistic assumptions may lead to rather dramatic reversions when met with reality. Not surprisingly, excessive optimism contributes to market bubbles, as excessively optimistic investors believe that the market will continue to rise.

To overcome overconfidence and its related biases, you need to recognize the signs of overconfidence such as attributing a few short-term "wins" to superior knowledge, ability or skill, bragging about short-term investment performance, trading too much, and taking excessive risk. When these signs become visible, you need to apply the brakes. Trading less, especially in taxable accounts, and diversifying your portfolio should also help to curb overconfident behavior. Additionally, you should carefully examine your assumptions and conduct adequate research before undertaking an investment. Keeping detailed records of trades and the motivation for each can enable you to identify personal mistakes and successes relative to the strategy used. Developing accountability mechanisms such as seeking constructive feedback from others can help you become aware of overconfidence bias. You also need to keep an open mind about other opinions and seek alternative viewpoints when making an investment decision.

SOCIAL BIASES: ATTRIBUTIONAL ERRORS

A third group of biases involves social influences. Social interactions influence investor emotions and affect their investment decisions. Investors learn by interacting with others such as friends, colleagues, and financial advisors. Both the media and Internet play a role in influencing investment decisions. For example, the media relate facts and provide opinions about various markets and investments.

However, the information provided tends to be in sound bites rather than in-depth analysis. The media are biased, favoring optimism to sell products from advertisers and attract viewers or readership. The media typically focus on specific stories for long periods of time, which can contribute to exuberance or dismay surrounding the investment. The interactive nature of the Internet creates a social environment where investors can exchange ideas through chat rooms, message boards, blogs, and newsgroups.[34] Perhaps the most common social bias is herding behavior.

Herding Behavior

Herding refers to the tendency to flock together, especially under conditions of uncertainty. Herding behavior in investing occurs for several reasons. First, some investors feel powerful social pressure to fit in and conform, which is known as the *conformity effect*. For example, many members of the Jewish community invested in Bernie Madoff's Ponzi scheme because others in their community were doing so. Given the sociable nature of most people, they want to be part of the group, so following the group is an ideal way of becoming a member. Those engaging in herding behavior may ignore conflicting information in favor of acting as other investors do. This unconscious bias can provide reassurance and comfort. Although investors may feel better when investing with the crowd, this investment strategy is unlikely to lead to superior long-term performance. Additionally, investors feel that a large group is unlikely to be wrong. Novice investors are particularly susceptible to herding because they may believe that others know more than they do, so following the crowd makes sense to them.[35]

Having a herd mentality leads investors to buy when the market is high and sell when the market is low. Greed and fear are the underlying emotions that create this behavior. Such behavior is exactly the opposite of the common investment mantra to "buy low/sell high." As Warren Buffett notes, "You want to be greedy when others are fearful. You want to be fearful when others are greedy. It's that simple."

Investors don't want to be left out of a winning stock. So without much research or homework, they start buying it because they think everyone else is, not because of underlying fundamentals of the company that issues the stock. They are going along with what everyone else is doing and going with the flow of the crowd. Their irrational exuberance leads them to buy a stock at increasingly higher prices. This is the *bandwagon effect*. Eventually the stock starts to decrease when market participants realize it is overpriced and a sell-off occurs. Those who bought the stock for irrational reasons begin to regret their purchases and fear losing their money so they start selling.[36] This type of "groupthink" results in an irrational or dysfunctional decision-making outcome. Herding behavior also contributes to stock market and other bubbles, when market participants drive prices above their value relative to some valuation system.

Several approaches are available for dealing with herding behavior. Although you might not want to be left out of a market trend, you should question the views of the herd. To avoid the lure of crowd psychology, you should resist following the herd or jumping on the bandwagon by doing your own research and homework before investing in any security. You may also want to consider taking a contrarian approach in which you do the opposite of what everyone else is doing. By using such an approach you can capitalize on what others may overlook. However, you should base your decisions on the fundamentals, not optimism. To avoid groupthink, you should incorporate a devil's advocate into your decision-making process such as a knowledgeable friend or financial advisor.[37]

OVERCOMING BEHAVIORAL BIASES

No easy fixes exist for many of the behavioral biases that affect investors. Merely learning about such biases does not eliminate them. Overcoming psychological biases involves three issues. First, you should be aware that trying to change a bias in isolation ignores the complexity of human behavior. Many simultaneous effects influence behavior — some are internal (cognitive and emotional biases) and others are external (social biases). These multiple factors interact. Attempting to understand and change behavior by addressing a list of biases one by one in isolation fails to account for this complexity.

Second, some psychological biases have a flip side that is beneficial. For example, the tendency to weigh losses more heavily than gains could be a beneficial trait. If investors place too much emphasis on potential gains versus potential losses, they could risk experiencing losses that jeopardize achieving their long-term goals. Another example is by earmarking money for retirement, investors could avoid frivolously spending it.

Third, some behavioral biases conflict with and are related to others. For example, some investors may overestimate their abilities to pick "winners" while blindly following the actions or advice of others.

Given these caveats, here are some general suggestions on how to mitigate psychological traps.

- *Understand and avoid behavioral biases*: Although avoiding behavioral biases on a subconscious level is difficult, you should begin by making a conscious effort to identify your biases and understand their effects on your investing behavior. These biases are cognitive, emotional, and social. Distinguishing between these three groups is appropriate when discussing the reasons you may fall victim to these errors and when reviewing their impact on your investment policy and asset allocation strategy. The challenge is to learn why such biases occur so often.

- *Develop an investment plan*: Once you understand the nature of your biases, you can develop an investment plan or IPS setting forth your objectives and constraints, risk tolerance, asset allocation, and performance benchmarks. You can even tailor your asset allocation to suit your psychological tendencies. For example, if you tend to bail out of investments in the face of losses, you might consider having less exposure to volatile investments in your portfolio.

- *Establish quantitative investment criteria*: Quantitative investment criteria serve as guidelines to help monitor your decisions and to protect against your own biases. Following objective strategies and trading rules can help you avoid investing based on emotions, rumors, and other behavioral biases in order to achieve your investing goals.

- *Follow fundamental investing principles*: These basic principles include investing for the long-term, providing adequate portfolio diversification, and periodically reviewing and rebalancing your portfolio.

LESSONS LEARNED

Everyone has behavioral biases that creep into their mindsets and lead them to make similar mistakes that can undermine investing success. Combining different behavioral biases can create a dangerous cocktail and drinking it can lead to some dumb behavior. Although avoiding or completing eliminating detrimental biases is difficult, you can take steps to reduce their harmful effects. Highly effective investors have learned that success repeatedly comes from reining in emotions and overcoming their behavioral biases. They are proactive learners, patient, focused, disciplined, and have a well-defined investment strategy that they stick to in good times and bad.[38] Consequently, successful investors try to avoid making the same mistakes common to new investors.

By mitigating behavioral biases, you can more readily reach impartial decisions based on available data and logical processes.

You can emulate successful investors by learning to overcome your cognitive biases, overriding your emotions, and resisting social influences. Here are some key "takeaways" from this chapter.

- Don't be your own worst enemy when investing.

- Be aware of your behavioral blind-spots and be realistic with yourself.

- Resist the urge to believe that you are better than others in the market.

- Seek competent advice to bring you back to reality before acting on your behavioral biases.

- Don't focus too much on a single piece of information when making decisions.

- Trade less and invest more.

- Don't chase performance.

- Avoid investing based on emotions.

- Steer clear of the stampeding herd when investing. Just because many others may be moving in and out of the market does not mean this is the right move for you.

- Do your homework before following any trend.

- Stick with your investment plan and rebalance periodically.

- Don't fall in love with a stock or other investment. It does not know you own it.

QUESTIONS

1. Distinguish among cognitive, emotional, and social biases.

2. Explain how behavioral and traditional finance differ.

3. Distinguish between belief perseverance and information processing biases.

4. Identify three cognitive biases and indicate the investment implications of each.

5. Identify three emotional biases and ways to mitigate each.

6. Explain the investment implications of herding behavior and how to lessen this social bias.

7. Explain several steps for mitigating psychological traps.

8. Analyze your own behavior as an investor.

NOTES

1. Parker, T. Behavioral bias — Cognitive vs. emotional bias in investing. *Investopedia*. Retrieved from http://www.investopedia.com/articles/investing/051613/behavioral-bias-cognitive-vs-emotional-bias-investing.asp

2. Housel, M. (2013). Why you never learn from your investment mistakes. *The Motley Fool*, May 30. Retrieved from http://www.fool.com/investing/general/2013/05/30/why-you-never-learn-from-your-investment-mistakes.aspx

3. Pompian, M. M. (2013). Investor behavior: Cognitive vs. emotional biases. *Morningstar Advisor*, March 31. Retrieved from http://www.morningstar.com/advisor/t/72323448/investor-behavior-cognitive-vs-emotional-biases.htm?&si

4. Statman, M. (2014). Behavioral finance: Finance with normal people. *Borsa Istanbul Review*, 14(2), 65–73. Retrieved from http://www.sciencedirect.com/science/article/pii/S2214845014000143

5. Todd. (2013). 12 cognitive biases that endanger investors. *Minyanville*, January 13. Retrieved from le.com/special-features/random-thoughts/articles/12-Cognitive-Biases-that-Endanger-Investors/1/17/2013/id/47441?page=full

6. Pompian, M. M. (2012). *Behavioral finance and wealth management: How to build optimal portfolios that account for investor biases* (2nd ed.). Hoboken, NJ: Wiley.

7. Liphart, J. (2014). Representativeness heuristic: Understanding decision making bias. *Udemy*, May 20. Retrieved from https://blog.udemy.com/representativeness-heuristic/

8. Taffler, R. J. (2010). The representativeness heuristic. In H. K. Baker & J. R. Nofsinger (Eds.), *Behavioral finance: Investors, corporations, and markets* (pp. 259–276). Hoboken, NJ: Wiley.

9. Wasik, J. (2013). Why IPOs are unlikely to produce long-term gains. *Reuters*, November 4. Retrieved from http://www.reuters.com/article/us-column-wasik-ipo-idUSBRE9A30SD20131104

10. Stenner, T. (2014). Why chasing performance is a costly (and futile) pursuit. *The Globe and Mail*, November 7. Retrieved from http://www.theglobeandmail.com/globe-investor/investment-ideas/this-is-the-cost-of-chasing-performance/article21478240/. Swedroe, L. (2014). Why it doesn't pay to chase fund performance. *MoneyWatch*, September 23. Retrieved from http://www.cbsnews.com/news/why-it-doesnt-pay-to-chase-mutual-fund-performance/

11. Pompian, M. M. (2016). Conservatism bias: Why some clients won't change their minds. *MorningstarAdvisor*, June 23. Retrieved from http://www.morningstar.com/advisor/t/115727940/conservatism-bias-why-some-clients-won-t-change-their-minds.htm?&ps=9

12. Luo, G. Y. (2014). *Asset price response to new information: The effects of conservatism bias and representativeness heuristic*. New York, NY: Springer.

13. Fenton-O'Creevy, M., Nicholson, N., Soane, E., & Willman, P. (2003). Trading on illusions: Unrealistic perceptions of control and trading performance. *Journal of Occupational and Organizational Psychology*, 76(1), 53–68.

14. Roese, N. J. (2012, September 6). *'I Knew It All Along...Didn't I?' – Understanding hindsight bias*. Association for Psychological Science. Retrieved from http://www.psychologicalscience.org/index.php/news/releases/i-knew-it-all-along-didnt-i-understanding-hindsight-bias.html

15. Gray, W., Vogel, J., & Folke, D. (2014). Mental accounting and your money. *Alpha Architect*, September 4. Retrieved from http://blog.alphaarchitect.com/2014/09/04/behavioral-bias-bingo-mental-accounting/#gs.=HbSBkQ.

16. Cross, J. (2013). 8 examples of 'mental accounting' and how to avoid them. *The College Investor*, August 2. Retrieved from http://thecollegeinvestor.com/8748/examples-of-mental-accounting/

17. Steul, M. (2006). Does the faming of investment portfolios influence risk-taking behavior? Some experimental results. *Journal of Economic Psychology*, 27(4), 557–570.

18. Diacon, S., & Hasseldine, J. (2007). Framing effects and risk perception: The effect of prior performance presentation format on investment fund choice. *Journal of Economic Psychology*, 28(1), 31–52.

19. Interaction Design Foundation. (2015). *Outcome bias – Not all outcomes are created equal. Interaction-Design.org*, December 2. Retrieved from https://www.interaction-design.org/literature/article/outcome-bias-not-all-outcomes-are-created-equal

20. Pompian, M. M. (2012). Recency bias linked with other pitfalls. *MorningstarAdvisor*, June 21. Retrieved from http://www.morningstar.com/advisor/t/58050848/recency-bias-linked-with-other-pitfalls.htm

21. Richards, C. (2012). Tomorrow's market probably won't look anything like today. *Bucks.blog*, February 13. Retrieved from http://bucks.blogs.nytimes.com/2012/02/13/tomorrows-market-probably-wont-look-anything-like-today/

22. Maurer, T. (2015). When it comes to investing, rely on long-term wisdom. *CNBC*, July 28. Retrieved from http://www.cnbc.com/2015/07/28/when-it-comes-to-investing-rely-on-long-term-wisdom.html

23. Lim, S. S., & Teoh, S. H. (2010). Limited attention. In H. K. Baker & J. R. Nofsinger (Eds.), *Behavioral finance: Investors, corporations, and markets* (pp. 295–312). Hoboken, NJ: Wiley.

24. Barber, B. & Odean, T. (2009). All that glitters: The effect of attention and news on the buying behavior of individual and institutional investors. *Review of Financial Studies*, 21(2), 785–818.

25. Foad, H. (2010). Familiarity bias. In H. K. Baker, & J. R. Nofsinger (Eds.), *Behavioral finance: Investors, corporations, and markets* (pp. 277–294). Hoboken, NJ: Wiley.

26. Nofsinger, J. 2008. Familiarity bias part I: What is it? *PsychologyToday*, July 25. Retrieved from https://www.psychologytoday.com/blog/mind-my-money/200807/familiarity-bias-part-i-what-is-it

27. Amjaroen, K. (2014). 5 emotional biases undermining your investing success. *The Motley Fool*, August 12. Retrieved from http://www.fool.com/investing/general/2014/08/12/5-emotional-biases-that-undermine-your-investing-s.aspx

28. Parker, T. (2013). 4 behavioral biases and how to avoid them. *Investopedia*, May 8. Retrieved from http://www.investopedia.com/articles/investing/050813/4-behavioral-biases-and-how-avoid-them.asp

29. Shefrin, H. (2000). *Beyond greed and fear: Understanding behavioral finance and the psychology of investing*. Boston, MA: Harvard Business School Press.

30. Dowling, M., & Lucey, B. (2010). Other Behavioral Biases." In H. Kent Baker and John R. Nofsinger (Eds.), *Behavioral finance: Investors, corporations, and markets* (pp. 313–330). Hoboken, NJ: Wiley.

31. Dvorsky, G. (2013). The 12 cognitive biases that prevent you from being rational. *io9.com*, January 9. Retrieved from http://io9.gizmodo.com/5974468/the-most-common-cognitive-biases-that-prevent-you-from-being-rational

32. Belsky, G., & Gilovich, T. (1999). *Why smart people make big money mistakes and how to correct them*. New York, NY: Simon & Schuster.

33. Fisher, M., Goddu, M. K., & Keil, F. C. (2015). Searching for explanations: How the internet inflates estimates of internal knowledge. *Journal of Experimental Psychology: General, 144*(3), 674–687.

34. Baker, H. K., & Nofsinger, J. R. (2002). Psychological biases of investors. *Financial Services Review, 11*(Summer), 97–116.

35. Phung, A. Behavioral finance: Key concepts – Herd behavior. *Investopedia*. http://www.investopedia.com/university/behavioral_finance/behavioral8.asp

36. Johnston, K. Evidence of the bandwagon effect in the stock market. *Zachs*. Retrieved from http://finance.zacks.com/evidence-bandwagon-effect-stock-market-7130.html

37. Smith, A. K. (2015, April). 4 ways to beat your investing biases. *Kiplinger's Personal Finance*. Retrieved from http://www.kiplinger.com/article/investing/T031-C023-S002-ways-to-beat-your-investing-biases.html

38. Martins, A. T. (2016). 15 characteristics of highly successful investors. *InvestorGuide.com*. Retrieved from http://www.investorguide.com/article/6679/15-characteristics-of-highly-successful-investors/

5

TRAP 1: BECOMING A VICTIM OF PYRAMID AND PONZI SCHEMES

Corruption, embezzlement, fraud, these are all characteristics which exist everywhere. It is regrettably the way human nature functions, whether we like it or not. What successful economies do is keep it to a minimum. No one has ever eliminated any of that stuff.

Alan Greenspan, American economist and former chairman of the U.S. Federal Reserve

Have you ever been subjected to an investment fraudster's sales pitch or received unsolicited calls? If not, you probably know someone who has. History has seen countless investment frauds, scams, cons, schemes, and swindles. Although many fall victim to fraudsters, some are more susceptible to being duped than others.

Who do you picture as prime targets of investment fraud? A common stereotype is an elderly person, perhaps a widow, who has less wealth, education, and financial know-how than the general public. Perhaps this person is also isolated and gullible. Based on a study conducted by the American Association of Retired Persons (AARP), fraud victims do tend to be older, on average, than the general population. However, unlike the stereotype, those most likely to be victims of investment fraud are college educated men with above average income and financial knowledge. Such targets are less upset by the prospect of losing money, so they're more likely to be open to new ideas and to attend events that include a sales pitch. Furthermore, possible victims tend to be optimistic and self-reliant in making financial decisions. Additionally, those who have received windfall insurance in the wake of the death of a spouse are also prime targets for con artists.[1]

In *Outsmarting the Scam Artists*, Doug Shadel notes that people with more assets are the most likely to be scammed.[2] Why? Consider the legendary criminal Willie Sutton, who, when asked by Federal Bureau of Investigation (FBI) agents why he robbed banks, allegedly replied "Because that's where the money is." Likewise, people of means are also prime targets for investment scams because they have money.

Do any of the above characteristics apply to you? If so, you need to be especially vigilant for fraudsters. If you enjoy taking risks, this can lead to overconfidence when investing. You might decide that you can "afford" a risky investment when you really can't. You might also choose to invest in riskier assets and schemes and end up overextending yourself. Having a high risk tolerance could make you more vulnerable to investment scammers. Your penchant for risk and the lure of high returns could lead to trouble.

Before discussing other common investment traps, let's examine the most severe trap: investment fraud. *Investment fraud* is any scheme or deceptive practice relating to investments that convince investors to make decisions based on false information. Such frauds are perpetuated by what some call "financial serial killers"[3] and often result in losses and violate securities laws. In his book *Swindling Billions: An Extraordinary History of the Great Money Fraudsters*, Kari Nars estimates that fraud victims around the world have lost hundreds of billions of dollars in the last decade to investment fraud.[4]

This chapter begins by explaining why people fall for investment fraud and then discusses how to avoid fraud and recognize some warning signs. Next, the chapter focuses on two major types of investment fraud — Ponzi schemes and pyramid schemes — and provides an extended example of each. The chapter closes with a warning about how easily someone can be duped by skilled fraudsters and then recounts the lessons learned from this chapter.

WHY PEOPLE FALL FOR INVESTMENT FRAUD

Don't assume that you are immune to investment fraud because of your education, background, or business savvy. Even highly successful, financially intelligent people fall prey to investment frauds. As discussed later involving Madoff's Ponzi scheme, his notorious investment scandal fooled thousands of individuals, including celebrities, as well as financial institutions and universities. Anyone with money is at risk of investment fraud. Fraudsters are students of human nature and use persuasive techniques that they tailor to the victim's psychological profile. If you are victimized, don't hesitate to report an investment fraud, even if you're embarrassed or fearful. No one likes to admit that they have been duped, especially sophisticated investors. Con artists are aware of such sensitivities that often prevent or delay victims from reporting the scam to authorities and use this failing to their advantage.

A recent study funded by AARP Fraud Watch and the Financial Industry Regulatory Authority's (FINRA) Education Foundations and conducted by psychologists at Stanford University provides insights on understanding how fraud works.[5] Financial fraudsters repeatedly attempt to get their victims into a heightened emotional state whereby they suspend rational thinking to convince them to hand over their money. Seniors are particularly vulnerable to the effects of heightened emotions on decision-making.

People fall for investment scams for many reasons including the following:[6]

- *People are gullible*: Those who have a tendency to trust easily are especially vulnerable because they tend to believe what people tell them. They think that everything really is what it appears to be. When they get a fact that doesn't exactly fit in the puzzle, they tend to force it to fit. Fraudsters prey on this trusting nature.

- *People are sometimes irrational*: Everyone occasionally makes quick, irrational decisions. Those who tend to be impulsive, driven by emotion, or non-reflective are particularly susceptible to becoming victims of investment fraud. Fraudsters frequently stress the need for fast action to avoid missing out on a "once in a lifetime investment opportunity." This tactic is highly effective on those who act impulsively.

- *People are attracted to financial gain*: The lure of "get-rich-quick" schemes flames the innate desire to become financially better off. Most schemes promise that participants can obtain a high rate of return with little risk, skill, effort, or time. Realistic gains are one thing, but when an investment looks too good to be true, it probably is.

- *People are uncertain about the financial environment*: When people feel uncertain about financial decisions, they often turn to others who appear or proclaim to be experts, and to groups with which they share some kind of connection, such as religious or ethnic communities and professional groups. People often have difficulty saying no to experts or members of affinity groups of which they are a part because these individuals trust that they are being steered in the right direction. Those who promote affinity scams often are or pretend to be members of said groups.

- *People are overly optimistic*: Those who suffer from "optimism bias" are more likely to be hoodwinked than others. *Optimism bias* refers to the tendency to overestimate the likelihood that good things will happen and underestimate the potential for unpleasant events. Fraudsters play to this tendency by making good things happen initially reinforcing an investor's decision.

For example, they ask investors to make a small initial investment that pays off in order to lure them into making larger investments later. Fraudsters also accentuate the positive by either downplaying or avoiding the possibility of bad things occurring as a result of an investment.

- *People want to feel special*: People have a psychological need to feel special. Fraudsters play upon this need by convincing investors that they are part of an "exclusive club" and are being given special access to an investment opportunity. This ploy is called the *illusion of inclusion*. The perceived scarcity of the number of people involved in the investment makes the target feel special and more likely to invest.

- *People are more vulnerable when they believe they are knowledgeable*: Although this sounds counter-intuitive, those who have some experience in investing or believe they are experts are more susceptible to investment fraud than others. They think they know more than they actually do or that they're too smart to fall for a scam. This psychological bias is the *illusion of knowledge* discussed in Chapter 4.

- *People tend to trust authority and credentials*: People often place their trust in authority, whether this is a respected institution or an individual holding a status position. As a result, scam artists send fraudulent emails that appear to be from trusted organizations such as banks and brokerage firms. Additionally, they create fake diplomas and credentials, pretending to have a certain level of knowledge or competence that they do not.

HOW TO AVOID INVESTMENT FRAUD

How can you avoid becoming prey to investment fraud? You need to remain in charge of your investment decisions and to do so in an educated manner. Too many investors trust unscrupulous individuals and outright con artists to make financial decisions for them. Taking the following actions can help lessen the chances of falling prey to scams:[7]

- *Ask questions*: Perhaps the best advice when making any investment is to ask questions not only about the investment, but also about the salesperson and his company. For example, some questions that you might ask about an investment are the following:
  - ○ Is this investment product registered with the Securities and Exchange Commission (SEC) and my state securities agency?

  - ○ Does this investment match my investment goals?

  - ○ How will this investment make money?

  - ○ What are the total fees to buy, maintain, and sell this investment?

  - ○ How liquid is this investment?

  - ○ What specific risks are associated with this investment?

  - ○ Who will provide me with a copy and explain the prospectus or offering circular?

  The SEC offers examples of guidelines to consider before investing.[8]

- *Research before investing*: Fraudsters expect you to do little, if any investigation, before investing. They want you to fall for their pitch and believe that they have already done all of the research for you. Before investing your hard-earned money, you should check out the background of anyone with whom you might be doing business. You need to be wary of anyone who suggests putting your money into something you don't understand. An investment also has to be consistent with your goals and risk tolerance. An investment that is right for you will make sense because you understand it and feel comfortable with the degree of risk involved.

- *Know the salesperson or financial advisor*: You should check out the person touting the investment before you invest, even if you know the person socially. For example, you should verify licenses and check out a person's disciplinary history. You should also be wary of those who prey on your fears and tout investments with unrealistic returns and little or no risk. Fear and greed can cloud your judgment and leave you worse off financially. Beware of the "halo" effect. The *halo effect* is the tendency for an impression created in one area to influence opinion in another area. This bias based on an overall impression of a person colors your judgment of that person's character. Thus, you should avoid judging an investment by how a person looks or sounds because these qualities have no bearing on the soundness of an investment opportunity. Swindlers want to appear polished and professional to create the impression that you can trust them.

- *Be watchful of unsolicited offers*: You should regard unsolicited sales offers with the utmost caution and skepticism, especially when they promise unusually high rates of return, quick profits, and "once in a lifetime" opportunities. Also, you should avoid being rushed and say no to anyone pressuring you to make an immediate decision. You should not make an investment until you have received written material about the company and the investment and have taken the time to carefully review it. If the solicitation is by telephone, you should hang up if you're not interested or feel pressured to make a quick decision. To reduce the number of sales pitches you receive, use the Federal Trade Commission's National Do Not Call Registry.

- *Be constantly vigilant*: You should avoid making an investment and then sitting by the sidelines for the results. Instead, you need to monitor your investments by keeping track of their progress. You should insist on regular written reports and be skeptical of excessive trading. If you have trouble retrieving your principal or cash out of profits, you need to find out why.

- *Know what to look for*: If you understand little about the world of investments, you should take the time to educate yourself or talk to a qualified but uninvolved party about the investment. By making yourself knowledgeable about different types of fraud and signs of any impending problems, you can reduce the chances of being deceived.

- *Avoid making decisions when emotions are high*: The worst time to make an important financial decision is whenever your emotions are in control. Scammers are aware of this behavior and know how to use your emotions against you. To avoid being scammed or falling victim to an investment fraud, you need to manage your emotions around financial decisions.

RED FLAGS FOR INVESTMENT FRAUD

Scam artists use an arsenal of tricks to separate you from your hard-earned money. Here are some red flags that may signal potential problems with a product or security, including investment fraud:[9]

- *Investments with high guaranteed returns with little or no risk*: Claims of huge gains with almost no risk are illusions or "phantom riches" for unsuspecting investors, despite the efforts of fraudsters to convince you otherwise. All investments carry some degree of risk. Fraudsters dangle the prospects of easy money in front of you to entice you to buy. You should be suspect of such guarantees to avoid being scammed.

- *Once-in-a-lifetime deals*: Scam artists use the tactic of "Don't miss this opportunity — get in now!" to pressure you into making a quick decision. You should resist the pressure to invest quickly. Instead, take the time you need to investigate any investment opportunity and get independent third-party advice.

- *Everyone is buying*: You should beware of pitches stressing how "other savvy investors have invested, so you should, too." Just because the salesperson claims that others have bought a product or security does not mean that it is a good investment or right for you. A variation on this theme is the claim that your friends are investing, so why shouldn't you? This approach relies on the trust you place in your friends, which might be misplaced because your friends could be wrong or the salesperson could be lying.

- *Pressure to buy quickly*: Scam artists often create a false sense of urgency by claiming limited supply. They want you to buy quickly so that you won't have time to figure out their game. No reputable investment professional should push you to make a quick decision. Thus, you should steer clear of a pushy salesperson. Be sure to research both the investment and the individual selling it before seriously considering investing.

- *Overly consistent returns*: Although not applicable to all investments, you should be suspicious of investments, such as common stocks or equity mutual funds, providing consistently stable returns regardless of market conditions. Returns generally vary over time due to market volatility.

- *Insider or confidential information*: *Insider trading* is the illegal practice of trading to one's own advantage through having access to nonpublic (confidential) information. Most jurisdictions around the world have rules against insider trading. In various countries such as the United States, trading based on insider information is illegal. Anyone indicating that the trading is based on insider or confidential information is potentially placing you at risk.

- *Free seminar and meal*: Another tactic that fraudsters use to attract investors is offering a free seminar with the promise to educate those attending about investing strategies or managing money in retirement. The real purpose of such seminars is often to lure new clients and to sell investment products or services. Fraudsters rely on the concept of reciprocity. That is, if they do a small favor for you, such as providing an expensive lunch or dinner, you are more likely to do them a big favor in return and buy what they are selling. Although you might not get a hard sales pitch during the seminar, you can expect high-pressure tactics during follow-up contacts from the person selling the investment.

- *Unregistered products and salespeople*: Anyone offering to sell you an investment should be registered and licensed. You should research the background of the individuals and firms wanting to sell you investment products by searching the SEC's Investment Adviser Public Disclosure online database and FINRA's BrokerCheck online database, and contacting your state securities regulator.

- *Avoiding questions*: If the person selling you the investment doesn't answer your questions directly, they're probably trying to keep you from seeing the truth. A legitimate investment adviser has nothing to hide and willingly responds to your queries.

- *Overly complex investments and strategies*: Legitimate professionals can explain what they are doing and strive to make sure that you fully understand the investment product, any associated fees, and why it is appropriate for you. If you don't understand the investment, it probably isn't right for you.

TYPES OF INVESTMENT FRAUD

Investment fraud comes in all types and varieties. This chapter discusses pyramid and Ponzi schemes, followed by other types of investment fraud in Chapter 6. Pyramid and Ponzi schemes share many similar characteristics in that devious scammers target unsuspecting individuals by promising them extraordinary returns. But with little or no legitimate earnings, these schemes require a consistent flow of money from new investors to continue. The schemes eventually collapse when recruiting new investors becomes difficult or when many investors want to cash out. Some people use the terms interchangeably or classify a Ponzi scheme as a type of pyramid scheme. However, one point to keep in mind is that unlike some pyramid schemes, Ponzi schemes are always illegal.

Pyramid Schemes

Multilevel or *network marketing* is a strategy used by some direct sales companies to encourage their existing distributors to recruit new distributors. Distributors earn commissions not only by making retail sales and but also from retail sales made by others whom they recruit. Examples of well-known legal multilevel marketing (MLM) companies include Amway, Herbalife, Mary Kay Cosmetics, and Oriflame.

MLM programs often spend large amounts on advertising and promotion. In an MLM program, representatives typically get paid for products or services that both they and the distributors in their *downline* (i.e., participants they recruit) sell to others. However, some MLM programs are pyramid schemes. A *pyramid scheme* is a type of fraud in which participants profit almost exclusively through recruiting others to participate in the program, rather than by supplying any real investment. The scheme cannot continue forever because only a finite number of people can join the program.

The SEC provides the following warnings about the hallmarks of illegal pyramid schemes:[10]

- *No genuine product or service*: MLM programs involve selling an actual product or service to people who are not in the program. You should be cautious if no underlying product or service is being sold to others, or if what is being sold is speculative or appears inappropriately priced.

- *Promises of high returns in a short period*: You should be wary of pitches for high returns and fast cash in an MLM program because they could mean that the money used to payout commissions is from new recruits rather than product revenues.

- *Easy money or passive income*: You should be apprehensive of being offered compensation in exchange for performing little work, as you rarely get something for nothing.

- *No demonstrated revenue from retail sales*: You should request to see documents including financial statements audited by a certified public accountant (CPA) indicating that the MLM company generates revenue from selling its products or services to people outside the program.

- *Buy-in required*: You should be wary of an MLM program that requires you to pay a buy-in to participate in the program.

- *Complex commission structure*: You should be aware of how you will be compensated. Commissions should be based on products or services sold to those outside the program. You should be able to easily understand the commission structure.

- *Emphasis on recruiting*: You should be cautious if a program mainly focuses on recruiting others to join the program for a fee.

Ponzi Schemes

A *Ponzi scheme* is a form of investment fraud that involves the payment of purported returns to existing investors from funds contributed by new investors. Ponzi scheme organizers solicit new investors by promising to invest funds in opportunities claimed to generate high returns with little or no risk. The basic framework of a Ponzi scheme can be applied and reapplied in many different contexts. The scheme revolves around the process of paying old investors with the money received from new investors. The central method involves hooking a few investors who are willing to get in early on a promising venture. Ponzi scheme organizers frequently use the latest innovation, technology, or product to entice investors and promise high returns. Potential investors are often less skeptical of an investment opportunity when assessing something novel, new, or "cutting-edge."

Eventually, the second rung of investors will need its payout. The money from a newly recruited third rung of investors can pay off the second rung and deliver more returns to the first rung. But as the cycle goes on, it gets more complicated. Earlier rungs of investors will get suspicious if they don't continue to see returns. New investors will have to be paid back their initial investment, and the schemer will have to appease them with regular returns. This means that new investors must be added to the Ponzi scheme continuously in order to pay all the previous investors.

Carlo Ponzi — Swindler Extraordinaire

The Northern Italian Carlo (Charles) Ponzi arrived in Boston aboard the S. S. Vancouver in November 1903, having gambled away his savings during the Atlantic crossing. In a later interview, he told *The New York Times* "I landed in this country with $2.50 in cash and $1 million in hopes, and those hopes never left me."[11]

In 1920, Ponzi duped thousands of investors by promising massive returns on international reply coupons, which could be purchased in one country and redeemed for postage stamps in another. Ponzi promised a return of 50% in 45 days — equivalent to an annual profit of 360%! The profit was to be made on the difference in prices between countries. Curious parties began examining the accounts because sufficient international reply coupons were unavailable for his investment plan to function. In fact, Ponzi was repaying investors with newer investors' money, pocketing much of it himself.

Ponzi claimed to have elaborate networks of agents throughout Europe who were making bulk purchases of postal reply coupons on his behalf. In the United States, Ponzi asserted that he worked his financial wizardry to turn those piles of paper coupons into larger piles of greenbacks. When pressed for details on how he achieved this transformation, Ponzi explained that he had to keep such information secret for competitive reasons.

Of course, no network of agents existed, and Ponzi did not expend any effort to corner the market on postal reply coupons. A final audit of his company's assets after his business ended revealed $61 worth of the coupons. Ponzi took in $20 million in a few months, equal to about $222 million in current dollar values.[12]

Ponzi's extravagant lifestyle strained his personal finances. He bought a 12-room mansion in Lexington, Massachusetts, which boasted some features quite unusual in those days: air-conditioning and a heated swimming pool. Investors gradually started wondering how Ponzi became a multimillionaire.

The tide turned quickly against Ponzi. In July 1920, *The Boston Post* started to publish a series of sensational disclosures about Ponzi's life. For example, one disclosure was that he had not invested any money into his company. Another disclosure was that more than 160 million postal reply coupons needed to be in circulation to cover the multimillion dollar investments made into Ponzi's company. Yet, the U.S. postal service reported that the actual figure was only 27,000 coupons. *The Boston Post's* revelations caused a run on Ponzi's scheme — people wanted their money back. The newspaper also disclosed that the "financial wizard" had a jail sentence in Canada for forging checks and had served another term in a federal prison in Atlanta for smuggling five Italians from Canada into the United States.

In August 1920, *The Boston Post* reported that Ponzi was hopelessly insolvent. Later that month federal agents raided his office and found no signs of any postal reply coupons. In the federal trial in November 1920, Ponzi admitted his guilt and was sentenced to five years in prison.

The SEC lists the following common red flags of Ponzi schemes:[13]

- *High returns with low risk*: All investments involve risk with those yielding higher returns typically having more risk. You should be cautious of almost any "guaranteed" investment opportunity.

- *Highly consistent returns*: Prices of various investment vehicles such as stocks and bonds display volatility, especially those offering potentially high returns. Relatively few investments generate regular, positive returns, regardless of overall market conditions.

- *Unregistered investments*: Ponzi schemes mainly involve investments that have not been registered with either the SEC or state regulators. The importance of registration is that it provides investors with access to useful information about the company's management, products, services, and finances.

- *Unlicensed sellers*: According to Federal and state securities laws, investment professionals and their firms need to be licensed or registered. Most Ponzi schemes involve unlicensed individuals or unregistered firms.

- *Secretive and/or complex strategies*: Ponzi scheme promoters often are unwilling to provide sufficient details of the investment to preserve secrecy. They might also indicate that their strategies are too complex for average investors to understand. You should avoid investments for which you can't get sufficient information or don't understand the information that your receive.

- *Issues with paperwork*: Those perpetrating Ponzi schemes often do not provide sufficient written documentation. Account statements containing errors and inconsistencies might signal that funds are not being invested as promised.

- *Problems receiving payments*: You should be suspicious if you do not receive a payment or have problems cashing out your investment. Ponzi scheme promoters encourage participants to "roll over" investments and sometimes promise even higher returns on the amount rolled over.

How Pyramid and Ponzi Schemes Differ

Pyramid and Ponzi schemes are closely related because they both involve paying longer-standing members with money from new participants, instead of actual profits from investing or selling products to the public. These schemes are self-sustaining as long as cash outflows can be matched by monetary inflows. The basic difference arises in the type of products that schemers offer their clients.

The SEC lists some common differences between pyramid and Ponzi schemes:[14]

Characteristic	Pyramid Scheme	Ponzi Scheme
Typical "hook"	Participants earn high profits by making one payment and finding others to become distributors of a product. The scheme usually doesn't involve a genuine product. The purported product may not exist or it may be "sold" only to other people who also become distributors.	Participants earn high investment returns by taking little or no risk by simply handing over their money. Often the investment doesn't exist or the promoter actually invests only a small percentage of incoming funds.
Payments	Participants must pay a one-time or recurring participation fee and recruit new distributors to receive payments.	Participants do not have to recruit others to receive payments.
Interaction with the original promoter	Sometimes none. New participants may enter the pyramid scheme at different levels.	The promoter generally interacts directly with all participants.
How the scheme works	The promoter uses funds from new participants to pay recruiting commissions to earlier participants.	The promoter uses funds from new investors to pay purported returns to earlier investors.
Collapse	Fast. Each level requires an exponential increase in the number of participants.	Slow. Collapse may be relatively slow if existing participants reinvest money.

Pyramid and Ponzi schemes were common in Eastern Europe after the collapse of the Soviet bloc and communism because few regulatory agencies monitored and regulated these adolescent markets. People who had spent their whole lives under communism and poverty were particularly susceptible to schemes that promised large, quick payoffs. Anyone who idealized capitalism should have been wary of swindlers promising interest rates of 30% a month. Pyramid scams seem like equalizers or opportunities for ordinary citizens, but such prospects are a cleverly crafted illusion.[15]

Examples of Investment Fraud

Now that you have some background about investment fraud, here are two examples that highlight investment frauds in Western countries. The first example of investment fraud involves WinCapita, a Finnish Internet-based investment pyramid scheme. The next example is the Madoff case, which is the biggest Ponzi scheme in history. It occurred on Wall Street under the eyes of the SEC, the world's most powerful financial regulator.

THE WINCAPITA PYRAMID SCHEME

The Finnish WinCapita started in 2003 as a private gambling club under the name of GiiClub. Originally, the alleged purpose of the club was to generate profits for its investors using a betting system for international horse racing. Every member chipped in a sum of their choice, ranging from hundreds to tens of thousands of euros, and then accumulated profits on that amount. Over time, the club changed its activities to currency speculation and its name to WinClub, and eventually productized its operating scheme and changed its name to the now infamous WinCapita. WinCapita presented itself as an invitation-only foreign exchange investment club.

It promised annual profits of between 260% and 400%, with the help of investment software called FxTrader signals system.

All operations of WinCapita took place on the Internet, and the investors used the WinCapita website to manage their investment. The website could only be accessed with a personal user name and password. It provided general information and news about the club and showed investors how the value of their investment had developed over time. A British Internet payment service called Moneybookers handled money transfers in and out of the club. WinCapita had an account with Moneybookers, and investors could transfer their money by using another account with the same service.

The website and the account with Moneybookers were the entire scope of WinCapita's operations. When investors withdrew money from the scheme, it was paid out of the same account where they paid their invested funds. The actual trading or operations generated no new funds at any point during the scheme's existence. The virtual profits shown on the WinCapita website were completely artificial, and had no link to any real-world investment assets.[16]

WinCapita based its entire investment philosophy on the FxTrader software, which supposedly showed buying signals for EUR/USD in real time, as well as displaying a meter intended to indicate when the next buy/sell signal would approach. Hannu Kailajärvi, the founder and mastermind of the club, developed the software, which was his "meaningful" attempt at economic alchemy. He had no experience in currency trading or economics but he did have some background in software programming and was an "amazing number cruncher."

WinCapita operated by selling the licenses for the software and under a complicated and absurd scheme the members were then given access to the club's profits. WinCapita dressed up these profits as returns from trading in accordance with the software's signal, when in fact they were just redistributions of members' payments.

The original idea behind the software was that both the club and its members could use the signals in their currency speculation. Later evidence surfaced that the club's members were misled into believing that FxTrader signals were showing real time foreign exchange trades made by the club. The belief was further reinforced as the "profits" paid out matched the "profits" that would have been generated by trading in accordance with the signals.

Details about the club's operations were often described as business secrets, and WinCapita did not provide the club members with much information about its actual activities. Members could follow the profits their investments had earned, but WinCapita did not inform them about the specific transactions or trades that generated these profits.

Admission into this private "investment club" required receiving a recommendation of several sales agents, known as sponsors, and making a minimum initial investment of €3000, supposedly the software license payment. The club essentially operated as a classic MLM scheme: existing members who had purchased the FxTrader software license could endorse the club in their social networks and become sponsors. The opportunity of becoming a sponsor was valuable because sponsors received payments for attracting new club members. A sponsor attracting five new members would receive 20% of all of their profits in perpetuity.

These bonus-driven sponsors were highly motivated to endorse the club to new members and targeted mainly unsophisticated investors. Most of WinCapita's members came from nonacademic backgrounds and were in lower middle class professions such as farmers, firefighters, policemen, pensioners, small rural entrepreneurs, and civil servants. The biggest concentrations of WinCapita members were in rural areas. Using aggressive and persuasive marketing techniques, sales agents would first present potential investors with marketing materials that promised unrealistic returns. When met with disbelief, they would assert their claims using personal bank statements with five digit profits or new cars bought with profits from the club. This word-of-mouth marketing approach was the club's only way of acquiring new members because WinCapita prohibited existing members from disclosing any information to the public without the club's written permission. Surprisingly, nobody seemed to view such a restriction as odd. Perhaps members thought that the "secret formula" should not be made public because it was so valuable. According to Kari Nars, the author of *Swindling Billions: An Extraordinary History of Great Money Fraudsters*, the sales approach created a psychologically infectious picture: "The mumbo jumbo of banks' investment managers, with their offers of a measly one or two percent deposit interest, did not catch on when a brother, friend, cousin or a colleague had boasted about his 100 percent profits."[4]

The marketing material presented by the sponsors claimed that during a two-year period, WinClub managed to achieve about 5% in weekly profits in its foreign exchange trading, which translates into 260% a year. The material also contained a profit forecast for 12 months, indicating that an initial investment of €10,000 was expected to grow, assuming regular reinvestments, to the sum of €53,257, amounting to an annual profit of 433%. The marketing material also stated the "Foreign exchange trading is quite sustainable in relation to global economic disturbances." Anyone with the slightest knowledge of economics, foreign exchange or historical bank scandals would know this statement was deceitful. Kailajärvi later destroyed all the records and web content, so police estimates are based on witness testimonies and copies of material and printouts collected from investors. The club did not want public attention and its rules explicitly forbid members from distributing information about the club through websites, news groups, web forums, mass emails, or other forms of public media.

The club's website presented even more confusing material. A VIP member (i.e., the purchaser of a €3000 license) would trade in four different categories, labeled A, B, C, and X. The rules on category X are puzzling: the balance on the member's X-category account would define the maximum investment percentage into the trading operation. The exact investment percentage would be calculated every 13 weeks according to the following formula: $P = Z + (C/20,000)$, where P = new investment percentage, Z = previous investment percentage, and C = balance of the X-category account. As Nars notes, "The formula looks completely nonsensical, a pure bluff, and it is hard to see that anything sensible could be calculated on that basis."[4]

WinCapita first came to public attention in September 2007 when an investigative TV journalist made a news story of the club and raised doubts about its profit mechanism, speculating that it may function like a Ponzi or pyramid scheme. Paradoxically, many investors mention in their interrogation that the media coverage strengthened their faith in the club, which could result from overconfidence. The club continued its operation without any visible reaction from the authorities, and investors concluded that the authorities must have investigated the club and found its operations legitimate.[17]

Based on the police investigation, all club activities from the early GiiClub's gambling to WinClub's currency speculations resulted in heavy losses. Thus, as the size of the club grew and Kailajärvi's bets were not generating profits, he started using payments from the club's members to payout the promised monthly profits. Finally, in March 2008, with the club's bank balance just one monthly payout round away from becoming insolvent, Kailajärvi transferred €80,000 from the club's account to his personal account and €25,000 to his girlfriend's account, and they fled the country together. As he fled, Kailajärvi shut down WinCapita's website, leaving investors completely unaware of what would happen to their investments. Moneybrokers had also locked WinCapita's bank account just a couple of days after Kailajärvi fled Finland. On October 12, 2008, after nearly nine months in hiding, the Finnish police arrested Kailajärvi in southern Sweden and held him for more than a year before his trial. Kailajärvi destroyed the club's records and website during the escape, and investors could not withdraw any money from the club after the website was taken down.

The main reason WinCapita could operate so long without inter-ference was that the Finnish authorities had difficulty obtaining any information on its operations. Because of the sponsoring system, no public information was available about the club. As long as no one had suffered any losses, the police had no imminent cause to investi-gate. The authorities could not access many potential sources of information located abroad unless clear evidence of a crime existed. When WinCapita ended, its shell company was in Panama, its bank account was in the United Kingdom, and the website was on a web server in Luxemburg.

Between 2005 and 2008, WinCapita collected about €100 mil-lion from more than 10,000 investors. About 80% of the investors were males and the average age was 46 years. About 78% of the investors were between 30 and 60 years old. Of the investors, 12.8% had only mandatory basic education, 49.3% had upper secondary education, and 37.9% had higher education in the form of a university or polytechnic degree. According to Statistics Finland StatFin database, the corresponding percentages among over 20-year-old Finns in 2007 were 31.0%, 40.6%, and 28.3%, respectively. These statistics indicate that WinCapita investors were more educated than average Finnish adults.[18]

With estimated damages at more than €41 million, WinCapita is probably the largest fraud in Finnish history. Besides the finan-cial losses, the collapse of the club also destroyed personal rela-tionships between sponsors and their sponsored investors.

In December 2011, the District Court of Vantaa found Kailajärvi guilty of aggravated fraud and sentenced him to four years in prison. In February 2013, the Court of Appeal of Helsinki also found him guilty of a money collection offense, increasing his prison sentence to five years.

WinCapita is an example of an investment fraud in the form of a pyramid scheme. Participants should have identified this operation as an obvious scam because annual returns of 260−400% cannot be achieved without excessive risk taking. Hence, this case also involves the investment trap of making unrealistic return expectations. This "money-making machine" presented itself as an invitation-only foreign exchange trading club. Although foreign exchange trading is a zero-sum game in which someone's gain is always another's loss, WinCapita promised excessive returns without any rational basis. WinCapita targeted financially unsophisticated but otherwise educated investors because they could be easily fooled by deceitful materials. WinCapita also demonstrates the destructive nature of greed. As the late Erich Fromm, a German social psychologist, notes: "Greed is a bottomless pit which exhausts the person in an endless effort to satisfy the need without ever reaching satisfaction."

Trap Judgment

The following chart shows the various types of investment traps discussed in this book. A large star depicts the major investment trap illustrated by a specific example, whereas a small star represents a lesser prominent investment trap that also occurred.

WinCapita's Pyramid Scheme

Becoming a victim of investment fraud

Misrepresenting risky products as safe

Making unrealistic return expectations

Falling for mutual fund traps

Overpaying for products and services

Investing in complex products

Engaging in gambling disguised as investing

Relying on unsupported promises

THE MADOFF PONZI SCHEME

Bernard (Bernie) L. Madoff started his brokerage firm in 1960 and grew it into one of the largest on Wall Street. While doing so, he began investing money as a favor to family and friends, but was not licensed to do so. Over a period of 50 years, these side investments became an investment fund that mushroomed into a $50 billion Ponzi scheme. Thousands of wealthy clients, philanthropic organizations, and middle-class people whose pension funds found their way into Madoff's investment fund lost their entire life savings.

Madoff's fund is a classic example of a Ponzi scheme: the firm paid first investors from money invested by later investors. However, unlike many other Ponzi schemes, Madoff did not promise to deliver high returns, but vowed to deliver consistent returns regardless of the performance of financial markets. To most people, Madoff could not be a get-rich-scam because he was offering a return of 10–20% each year, which is within the realm of possibility. Madoff appealed to the Jewish mentality of prudence, especially financial prudence and conservatism. He was antirisk. He would tell prospective investors "I'm not hitting the ball out of the park every year. Not me, I'm not a hotshot. If you invest with me, you'll get consistent, less-than average returns — but you'll get them every year." Madoff reported strikingly consistent returns, especially during market downturns.

Marco Avellaneda, who was working for the French hedge fund Capital Fund Management in 2004, recalls a business trip to Geneva to visit a potential client and tell them about his new fund. The potential investor was unimpressed:

> We are not interested in investing with you. Your fund is too young, and we do not really understand what you do. We are very conservative here and we invest only in people with a stellar track record and in the top managers.
>
> I see that you are interested in options investments. The only fund with options that we invest in is Bernard Madoff. Madoff is a wizard. He uses a strategy of buying put options in the Standard and Poor's 500 Index and selling calls. Then, he buys stocks which he carefully selects.

This mixture produces very stable returns and is one of the best strategies that we know with options, and the only one that we would invest in …. If you can find out what he does, or do something similar, you will be very successful. Half of Geneva's asset management companies are invested with Madoff.

Madoff's reputation obviously had reached a European capital market in 2004. When asked about his ability to deliver such smooth returns, Madoff would emphasize how his strategy's use of options and futures helped "cushion" the returns against market volatility. When followed with a question on how such extensive and expensive hedging did not reduce returns and cause him to trail stock market returns, he explained that good stock-picking and market timing enabled him to make up for the cost of hedges. Madoff did not charge management fees because he claimed that the fees received on the trading deals via his broker-age activities were sufficient. He told his clients that he was letting them share in the benefits of his expertise in securities valuation.

In terms of professionalism, the scheme was also unique. Typically, Ponzi schemes are based in businesses that don't exist. Yet, at least part of Madoff's business was real and involved a complex brokerage operation requiring strong technological and financial savvy to run. As Madoff confessed in his guilty plea, the investment business was not real and he had not traded since the early 1990s. Thus, Madoff fabricated all of the returns since the 1990s in a typical Ponzi manner. That is, he used capital from new investors to provide returns to old ones.

A feature typical of a classic Ponzi scheme is that Madoff kept the detailed investment strategy secret, a typical feature of a classic Ponzi scheme. According to him, a small team, isolated from the larger and more open brokerage operation, ran the investment operations because they were supposedly too complicated for out-siders to understand. This was a lie.

Over time, Madoff built a strong reputation for his funds. He initially gave only a few privileged investors the opportunity to invest in them. Investors had to be invited to join and could be thrown out at will. They spread the word to others, giving the impression that Madoff's skills were magical. Madoff typically refused to meet directly with clients, playing "hard to get" and building a sort of mysterious, myth-like aura.

Madoff had been a prominent member of the securities industry throughout his career. He served as vice chairman of the National Association of Securities Dealers and chairman of its New York region. He was also a member of the NASDAQ Stock Market's board of governors and its executive committee and chaired its trading committee. Madoff owned residences in New York, the Hamptons, Palm Beach, and Cap d'Antibes in southern France, and had other notable assets including jewelry worth $2.6 million and a 50% share in a private jet worth $12 million. However, he did not boast about his financial success. Madoff was quiet yet charismatic. He exhibited a strong sense of family, loyalty, and honesty, and did not drink alcohol. Elderly clients treated him as a son, peers treated him like a brother, and younger clients treated him like a friendly uncle.

As Madoff developed a strong but fraudulent track record, he eventually hit the "sweet spot" for any investment fund: his fund attracted the interest of large hedge fund managers. Thereafter, the key to Madoff's sales strategy was to market his investment fund to feeder hedge funds (i.e., funds of funds). A *feeder hedge fund* is a hedge fund that feeds its clients' investments into other investment funds rather than investing directly in stocks, bonds, options and other securities. The consistent returns of Madoff appealed to these hedge funds and their clients.

In retrospect, both financial regulators and Madoff's investors ignored several clear warning signs of Madoff's scheme. For example, outside analysts had raised concerns about Madoff's firm for years. In May 2000, Harry Markopolos, a financial analyst and hedge fund manager, tried unsuccessfully to simulate Madoff's returns. He even alerted the SEC that the returns produced by Madoff were mathematically impossible, but the SEC decided not to take any action. A major red flag noted by Markopolos was that Madoff reported being down only three months out of an 87-month period. The S&P 500, over the same period, had been down 28 months. In later testimony before Congress, Markopolos concluded "That would be equivalent to a major league baseball player batting 0.966 and no one suspecting that this player was cheating."

In 2003 and 2004, after receiving two more complaints alleging that Madoff operated a Ponzi scheme, the SEC finally decided to investigate. Madoff reminded the investigators that he had served as NASDAQ chairman for three years, had several times provided expert opinions to the SEC on complicated financial issues, and claimed he was on a short list of people under consideration to be the next SEC chairman. The last issue was a lie. The size of Madoff's multi-billion dollar fund surprised SEC investigators. They eventually caught him in several obvious lies and contradictory statements. When questioned about not being a licensed investment adviser, Madoff stated that he had less than 15 clients, the threshold required for licensing, which was another lie. The SEC believed Madoff and closed the case without additional follow-up.

In 2005, Markopolos published a memo entitled "The World's Largest Hedge Fund Is a Fraud," describing in detail 30 red flags related to Madoff's investment business. Madoff's auditor and several other hedge fund professionals started to raise their concerns after the memo, but still regulators took no decisive action.

A once-in-a-generation financial crisis in 2007–2008 served as the impetus to unravel Madoff's scheme. As the general market downturn accelerated, investors desperately in need of capital started withdrawing funds. In December 2008, clients tried to withdraw as much as $7 billion from Madoff's firm. Following this mass withdrawal, Madoff started frantically reviewing his contact network in search of emergency financing as he realized that his Ponzi scheme was close to collapsing. With investors wanting to avoid any kind of risky holdings, Madoff failed to gather sufficient funds to keep the scam running and had no other choice but to recognize that the end had come. On December 10, 2008, he confessed to his sons, who had spent almost all their professional lives working for their father's investment company, that his investment scheme was "one big lie." Madoff's sons then reported him to the police. On December 11, 2008, the SEC made an announcement titled "SEC Charges Bernard L. Madoff for Multi-Billion Dollar Ponzi Scheme."

> *Washington, D.C., Dec. 11, 2008 — The Securities and Exchange Commission today charged Bernard L. Madoff and his investment firm, Bernard L. Madoff Investment Securities LLC, with securities fraud for a multi-billion dollar Ponzi scheme that he perpetrated on advisory clients of his firm. The SEC is seeking emergency relief for investors, including an asset freeze and the appointment of a receiver for the firm.*
>
> *The SEC's complaint, filed in federal court in Manhattan, alleges that Madoff yesterday informed two senior employees that his investment advisory business was a fraud. Madoff told these employees that he was "finished," that he had "absolutely nothing," that "it's all just one big lie," and that it was "basically, a giant Ponzi scheme." The senior employees understood him to be saying that he had for years been paying returns to certain investors out of the principal received from other, different investors. Madoff admitted in this conversation that the firm was insolvent and had been for years, and that he estimated the losses from this fraud were at least $50 billion.*

No one has been able to prove when exactly Madoff began stealing from investors. Madoff himself has made contradictory claims about when the crime began. He told CNNMoney in an interview that it all started in 1987, but he later said the scheme began in 1992.

In March 2009, Madoff pled guilty to being the mastermind behind the largest Ponzi scheme ever. He confessed to 11 federal crimes. The prosecutors estimated the size of the fraud to be $64.8 billion. The authorities sentenced Madoff to 150 years in prison. A substantial amount of the reported $50 billion in losses, which soon rose to $65 billion in newspaper headlines, was paper profit. Madoff had received $36 billion from investors and paid out approximately $18 billion, which meant $18 billion was missing. The difference between the invested $36 billion Madoff received and the $65 billion reported by the media consisted of unclaimed profits from 20% annual fund increases. But even the $18 billion loss made the Madoff case the most notorious Ponzi scheme in history. The largest financial losers included the feeder funds such as Fairfield Greenwich Advisors (one of the earliest of the so-called feeder fund managers, $7.5 billion) and Banco Santander (Spain's largest bank, $2.9 billion), nonprofit organizations such as New York University ($24 million), and individuals including Carl Shapiro (a long-time friend of Madoff and Boston philanthropist, $500 million) and Zsa Zsa Gabor (actress, $10 million).

In March 2009 Madoff made a statement to the U.S. District Court in New York admitting his fraud:

> *As I engaged in my fraud, I knew what I was doing was wrong, indeed criminal. When I began the Ponzi scheme I believed it would end shortly and I would be able to extricate myself and my clients from the scheme. However, this proved difficult, and ultimately impossible, and as the years went by I realized that my arrest and this day would inevitably come. I am painfully aware that I have deeply hurt many, many people, including the members of my family, my closest friends, business associates and the thousands of clients who gave me*

*their money. I cannot adequately express how sorry I
am for what I have done. I am here today to accept
responsibility for my crimes by pleading guilty and, with
this plea allocution, explain the means by which I carried
out and concealed my fraud.*

*The essence of my scheme was that I represented to cli-
ents and prospective clients who wished to open investment advisory and individual trading accounts with me
that I would invest their money in shares of common
stock, options and other securities of large well-known
corporations, and upon request, would return to them
their profits and principal. Those representations were
false because for many years up and until I was arrested
on December 11, 2008, I never invested those funds in
the securities, as I had promised. Instead, those funds
were deposited in a bank account at Chase Manhattan
Bank. When clients wished to receive the profits they
believed they had earned with me or to redeem their
principal, I used the money in the Chase Manhattan
bank account that belonged to them or other clients to
pay the requested funds. The victims of my scheme
included individuals, charitable organizations, trusts, pension funds and hedge funds.*[19]

Besides its magnitude, what makes the Madoff case so interesting is its level of sophistication. Madoff could attract investors without having to falsely market returns for the fund
because investors could withdraw money from the alleged fund
and enjoy good returns at any point. Investors flocked to him,
so he did not have to actively promote the fund. Even investment professionals, who are supposed to understand custody
and reporting issues, were drawn to Madoff's reputation and
supposed success. Only massive withdrawals during the financial
crisis led to discovering the fraud. Madoff claimed that his

investment strategy combined with stock-picking and timing enabled steady returns in all market conditions. Thus, he was guilty of not only perpetrating one of the greatest investment frauds in history, but also misrepresenting a risky product as safe because the product (fund) itself did not exist. Many investors can be seduced by the belief that they have found a low-risk way of performing surprisingly well. But surprisingly good investment performance always involves risk.

Trap Judgment

Madoff's Ponzi Scheme

Becoming a victim of investment fraud

Misrepresenting risky products as safe

Making unrealistic return expectations

Falling for mutual fund traps

Overpaying for products and services

Investing in complex products

Engaging in gambling disguised as investing

Relying on unsupported promises

AFTER THE TIDE

Some estimate that Madoff's fraudulent "hedge fund" might have continued had the stock markets not collapsed in 2008. With the crash, investors suddenly wanted their money back and Madoff did not have it. He was not alone. *Forbes* estimated that in the six-year span from 2008 to 2013, Madoff's scheme was only one of more than 500 Ponzi schemes in the United States that collectively involved more than $50 billion. On average, the authorities uncovered or busted a Ponzi scheme every four days in that six-year period. In 2008 and 2009, at least 157 Ponzi schemes collapsed, involving nearly $40 billion in investor funds. A comparison of these losses to the annual gross domestic product (GDP) of world countries provides some alarming statistics. For example, the $50 billion uncovered in Ponzi schemes between 2008 and 2013 would rank in the top 75 countries in the world by GDP.[20] The uncovered cases included the top three Ponzi schemes in history: Madoff's scheme ranked first with an estimated $17 billion in investor losses, followed by R. Allen Stanford's scheme with an estimated $7 billion in losses and the $3.6 billion Ponzi scheme of Thomas Petters.

Allen Stanford was the chairman of Stanford Financial Group, an offshore bank based in Antigua. He orchestrated a 20-year fraud by selling certificates of deposit (CDs), pocketing some of the proceeds, and using the rest to invest in dubious real estate deals, his own business ventures, and cricket tournaments. Some 28,000 investors, which was 10 times the number of direct investors in the Madoff case, bought CDs from Stanford International Bank. Stanford's U.S. sales force had promised the investors that the CDs were at least as safe as instruments from a U.S. bank. But a jury later found most of the clients' money financed Stanford's lavish lifestyle instead of the high-grade securities and real estate as promised. The government prosecuted Stanford and several of his top executives. Stanford is serving a 110-year sentence at a federal penitentiary in Florida.[21]

Thomas Petters, a Minnesota businessman, sold promissory notes through his wholesale brokerage firm Petters Co. Inc. (PCI), offering stunning returns of 15–20%. The company offered financing on the niche business known as *diverting*. Instead of using funds provided by investors to PCI to buy merchandise to be resold to retailers at a profit, Petters and his co-conspirators diverted the funds for other purposes including making payments to investors, called *lulling payments*, paying off those who assisted in the fraud scheme, funding businesses owned or controlled by Petters, and financing his extravagant lifestyle. Investors believed PCI was dealing in electronics and consumer goods, but

PCI bought and sold no real merchandise and hence generated no real profits. Petters operated a scam. According to prosecutors, Petters defrauded investors in part to finance his lavish lifestyle, which included luxury homes, fancy cars, several yachts, and a private jet. Federal authorities convicted Petters of fraud charges in 2009 and he is serving a 50-year prison sentence.[22]

LESSONS LEARNED

Unfortunately, many investors still haven't learned the lessons that highly publicized pyramid and Ponzi schemes should have taught. As Warren Buffet notes, "Only when the tide goes out do you discover who's been swimming naked." Such scams are more prevalent than most realize, and many investors simply abide by the notion that "it won't happen to me." Yet, these age-old scams still work to cheat victims of their hard-earned savings. Even sophisticated investors are sometimes unable to recognize that a seemingly appealing investment opportunity is really a scam. Today, investors face an array of increasingly complex and confusing scams. The fight against fraud continues because creative con artists are constantly developing new ways to fleece the public. However, all is not lost. Being aware of the following lessons might help you avoid becoming prey to investment fraud:

- Understand that people fall for investment scams due to gullibility, irrationality, greed, and being overly optimistic or overconfident among other reasons.

- Avoid investment fraud by asking questions, conducting research, knowing the salesperson, being watchful of unsolicited offers, being vigilant, understanding the investment, and controlling your emotions.

- Recognize the signs or red flags of investment fraud such as investments guaranteeing high returns with little risk, once-in-a-lifetime deals, pressure to buy quickly, and overly consistent returns.

Your best line of defense against investment fraud is education and awareness. By understanding why people fall for scams and how to avoid them, you can reduce the risk of becoming a victim.

QUESTIONS

1. Define investment fraud.

2. List several reasons people fall for investment fraud.

3. Identify actions investors can take to avoid investment fraud.

4. Identify several red flags of investment fraud.

5. Compare and contrast a pyramid scheme with a Ponzi scheme.

6. Discuss WinCapita's pyramid scheme and Madoff's Ponzi scheme.

NOTES

1. Pak, K., & Shandel, D. (2011). *AARP Foundation National Fraud Victim Study*. AARP Foundation, Washington, DC. Retrieved from http://assets.aarp.org/rgcenter/econ/fraud-victims-11.pdf

2. Shadel, D. (2012). *Outsmarting the scam artists — How to protect yourself from the most clever cons*. Hoboken, NJ: Wiley.

3. Ajamie, T., & Kelley, B. (2010). *Financial serial killers: Inside the world of wall street money hustlers, swindlers, and con men*. New York, NY: Skyhorse Publishing.

4. Nars, K. (2009). Swindling billions: An extraordinary history of the great money fraudsters. London: Marshall Cavendish Business.

5. FINRA. (2016). *Emotions increase susceptibility to fraud in older adults: Research from Stanford, FINRA Foundation and AARP*. News Release, May 6. Retrieved from https://www.finra.org/newsroom/2016/emotions-increase-susceptibility-fraud-older-adults-stanford-finra-foundation-and-aarp

6. Frick, B. (2011). Why we fall for scams. *Kiplinger.com*, May. Retrieved from http://www.kiplinger.com/article/investing/T031-C000-S002-why-we-fall-for-scams.html; Geronikos, A. (2012). 6 reasons people fall for scams. *MoneyTalks News*, December 26. Retrieved from http://www.moneytalksnews.com/6-reasons-smart-people-fall-for-scams/. Ajamie, T., & Kelly, B. (2014). Why smart people fall for investment scams. *Forbes.com*, October 20. Retrieved from http://www.forbes.com/sites/nextavenue/2014/10/20/why-smart-people-fall-for-investment-scams/

7. U.S. Securities and Exchange Commission. What you can do to avoid investment fraud. *Investor.gov*. Retrieved from http://investor.gov/investing-basics/avoiding-fraud/what-you-can-do-avoid-investment-fraud. Financial Education Clearinghouse. *Avoiding Investment Fraud*. Washington State Department of Financial Institutions. Retrieved from http://dfi.wa.gov/financial-education/information/avoiding-investment-fraud

8. U.S. Securities and Exchange Commission. *Ask questions*. Office of Investor Education and Advocacy. Retrieved from http://investor.gov/sites/default/files/sec-questions-investors-should-ask.pdf.

9. U.S. Securities and Exchange Commission. What you can do to avoid investment fraud. *Investor.gov*. Retrieved from http://investor.gov/investing-basics/avoiding-fraud/what-you-can-do-avoid-investment-fraud. U.S. Securities and Exchange Commission. (2015). *Investor alert for seniors: Five red flags of investment fraud,* June 15. Retrieved from http://www.sec.gov/oiea/investor-alerts-bulletins/ia_5redflags.html. Red Flags of Fraud. *FINRA*. Retrieved from http://www.finra.org/investors/red-flags-fraud.

10. U.S. Securities and Exchange Commission. (2013, October 1). *Beware of pyramid schemes posing as multi-level marketing programs.* Retrieved from http://www.sec.gov/enforce/investor-alerts-bulletins/investoralertsia_pyramidhtm.html

11. Darby, M. (1998). In Ponzi we trust. *Smithsonian Magazine*, December. Retrieved from http://www.smithsonianmag.com/people-places/in-ponzi-we-trust-64016168/?no-ist

12. Burnsed, B. The greatest financial scandals. *Bloomberg Business*. Retrieved from http://www.bloomberg.com/ss/09/03/0311_madoff/1.htm

13. U.S. Securities and Exchange Commission. (2013, October 9). *Ponzi schemes*. Retrieved from http://www.sec.gov/answers/ponzi.htm

14. U.S. Securities and Exchange Commission. *Ponzi Schemes.* Retrieved from http://www.sec.gov/answers/ponzi.htm

15. Staff Reporter. (1997). Eastern Europe's wild capitalism. *The New York Times*, February 18. Retrieved from http://www.nytimes.com/1997/02/18/opinion/eastern-europe-s-wild-capitalism.html

16. Rantala, V. (2015, March 16). *How do investment ideas spread through social interaction? Evidence from a Ponzi scheme.* Aalto University School of Business. Retrieved from http://papers.ssrn.com/sol3/papers.cfm?abstract_id=2579847

17. Rantala, V. (2015, November 12). *How do investment ideas spread through social interaction? Evidence from a Ponzi scheme.* Working Paper. Aalto University, School of Business. Retrieved from http://bus.miami.edu/umbfc/_common/files/paper-2015/How%20Do%20Investment%20Ideas%20Spread_PhD.pdf

18. Rantala, V. (2015, November 12). How do investment ideas spread through social interaction? Evidence from a Ponzi scheme. Working Paper. Aalto University, School of Business. Retrieved from http://bus.miami.edu/umbfc/_common/files/paper-2015/How%20Do%20Investment%20Ideas%20Spread_PhD.pdf

19. United States of America v. Bernard L. Madoff. (2009). Statement of guilt. Retrieved from http://www.justice.gov/usao/nys/madoff/madoff-hearing031209.pdf

20. Maglich, J. (2014). A Ponzi pandemic: 500 + Ponzi Schemes totaling $50 + billion in 'Madoff Era'. *Forbes*, February 12. Retrieved from http://www.forbes.com/sites/jordanmaglich/2014/02/12/a-ponzi-pandemic-500-ponzi-schemes-totaling-50-billion-in-madoff-era/

21. Cohn, S. (2014). *Five years after Stanford scandal, many victims still penniless.* CNBC, February 15. Retrieved from http://www.cnbc.com/id/101418516

22. CNBC. (2012). American greed: Generous with other people's money. *CNBC*, October 11. Retrieved from http://www.cnbc.com/id/100000111

6

TRAP 2: BEING DECEIVED BY OTHER INVESTMENT FRAUDS

The illiterate of the 21st century will not be those who cannot read and write but those who cannot learn, unlearn and relearn.

> Herbert Gerjuoy, *quoted in Alvin Toffler's* Future Shock *(1970)*

Investment fraud lures investors into making decisions based on false or misleading information. Although unsophisticated investors are particularly vulnerable because they cannot adequately evaluate risk or afford to lose money, no one is immune from clever con artists. Yet, even smart people may be unable to recognize a con immediately. Investment fraud is pervasive and covers a wide range of illegal activities that involve deceiving investors or manipulating financial markets.

Chapter 5 provided a discussion of two common scams: pyramid and Ponzi schemes. Both typically attempt to entice investors by promising high rates of return with little or no risk of loss. The perpetrators of these scams use money collected from new victims to pay the high rates of return promised to earlier investors. These payouts give the impression of a legitimate, money-making enterprise behind the fraudster's story, but in reality investors are the main or only source of funding. Such schemes eventually implode because they are unsustainable. Despite this, both pyramid and Ponzi schemes are like an addictive drug because once someone enters into one, getting out in time is psychologically difficult.

This chapter discusses a wide range of other investment frauds, but these are only the proverbial "tip of the iceberg." Each one is designed to take your money, and often times different types of frauds overlap. Several cases illustrate these scams. Scrutinizing how people have been swindled in the past can give you an idea of the elements of investment scams. Learning from the mistakes of others can help you avoid making the same mistakes yourself. Being able to spot an investment scam can not only protect you and your money, but also put you in charge of your own investment success.

ADVANCE-FEE SCHEMES

An advance-fee scheme is a rising type of fraud. Victims advance relatively small amounts of money, hoping to realize much larger gains from an investment opportunity — hence its name "advanced fee." To participate in an investment opportunity, victims must first send funds to cover processing fees, taxes, commissions, or incidental expenses that will supposedly be repaid later. After they advance the funds, the perpetrators take the money and never deliver on the investment. Gains don't materialize because no legitimate underlying investment actually exists.

A well-known example of advance-fee fraud is a Nigerian scheme, also known as a "419 fraud." In this fraud, someone who pretends to be a government official or businessperson promises high profits for help moving money out of the country. The fraudster only requires a small advance payment to obtain the large sum of money. In actuality, the money does not exist, and the victim sending the advance eventually ends up with nothing but a loss.

Sometimes scammers ask for bank account details to help them transfer money and use this information to steal funds. These schemes violate section 419 of the Nigerian criminal code, which explains the label "419 fraud."[1]

In a report published by Ultrascan in 2014, losses from Nigerian scams totaled $12.7 billion in 2013. Ultrascan is an international research organization based in Amsterdam with more than 3200 experts in 69 countries. Ultrascan suggests that, contrary to widely held beliefs, high achieving professionals are more likely to be defrauded than poorly educated or financially desperate people.[2] Ultrascan indicates the presence of more than 800,000 organized perpetrators around the world, and that number is growing by 5% annually. Roughly 85,000 perpetrators come from the "Nigerian Diaspora," residing across 69 different countries.

The "419 Scam"

The following message is a real example of a 419 scam, including grammatical errors. The scams often contain spelling and grammatical errors because the perpetrators want to convey the impression that they are poorly educated individuals who need your help.[3] The message promises the recipient a share in a large sum of money in exchange for allowing the funds to be transferred into a person's bank account. However, this sum of money does not actually exist. You should never send money or give credit card details, online account details, or copies of personal documents to anyone you don't know or trust, and you should especially never give this information via email.[4]

Solicitation Inquiry

I am Mr. X an Auditor in AMALGERMATED BANK OF SOUTH AFRICA (ABSA). There is an account opened in this bank in 1980 and since 1990 nobody has operated on this account again. After going through some old files in the records, I discovered that if I do not remit this money out urgently it would be forfeited for nothing. No other person knows about this account or anything concerning it, the account has no other beneficiary and my investigation proved to me as well that his company does not know anything about this account and the amount involved is 10 million United States Dollars (USD$ 10 million). I am only contacting you as a foreigner because this money cannot be approved to a local bank here, but can only be approved to any foreign account because the money is in U.S. dollars and the former owner of the account is Mr. X is a foreigner too. I know that this message will come to you as a surprise as we don't know ourselves before. Send also your private telephone and fax number including the full details of the account to be used for the deposit. I want us to meet face to face or sign a binding agreement to bind us together so that you can receive this money into a foreign account or any account of your choice where the fund will be safe. And I will fly to your country for withdrawal and sharing and other investments. At the conclusion of this business, you will be given 25% of the total amount, 70% will be for me, and while 5% will be for expenses both parties might have incurred during the process of transferring.

Besides the 419 fraud, advance-fee frauds appear in many other forms. Variants of this fraud type most often try to fool investors with official-sounding websites and email addresses. Besides the aforementioned warning signs, red flags involving advance-fee frauds include requests to act quickly as well as claiming an exclusive opportunity.[5]

Lottery Scams

A *lottery scam* is a type of advance-fee fraud that begins with an unexpected email notification, phone call, or mailing telling the recipients about their winning a fictitious gift or cash prize in a lottery. In a lottery scam, you are instructed to keep the notice secret and to contact someone who claims to be an official at the lottery company. After contacting this person, you are asked to supply personal information and copies of official documents, such as a passport, as proof of identity. The fraudsters can then use this information to steal your identity. Once you have provided your personal information, the fraudsters will ask you to pay various fees such as taxes, legal, or banking fees so that they can release your winnings. This scam is merely a trick and you never receive any lottery payments.

If you fall for this scam, you are now likely to be a target for other frauds. Why? Fraudsters frequently share details about people they have successfully targeted or approached, using different identities to commit further frauds. If you have already fallen victim to fraudsters, you are particularly vulnerable to *fraud recovery fraud*. This fraud occurs when fraudsters contact those who have already lost money through fraud and claim to be law enforcement officers or lawyers. They advise the victim that they can help them recover their lost money, but request a fee.[6] Official lottery operators and law enforcement officers do not ask for fees.

One of the most common fake lottery scams on the Internet is the Microsoft lottery. In this scam, perpetrators send emails congratulating targets for winning the Microsoft lottery. These emails are usually sent in the name of Bill Gates to take advantage of name recognition and lend credibility to the scam. The emails indicate that you should click on an attachment to claim your prize. After clicking on the file, you discover that it isn't a congratulatory message, but malware that downloads onto your computer. Typically, these viruses attempt to acquire sensitive information from your computer, a process known as "phishing." Another version of this scam claims that you have won a lottery conducted by Microsoft, and asks you to pay a fee to collect your prize. Still another version urges you to claim the money by replying to the email and providing personal information such as your address and bank account details. When facing this spam email, you should be aware that Microsoft does not run any lotteries. According to the UK National Fraud Intelligence Bureau, the so-called Microsoft lottery is just one of several forms of lottery fraud.[7]

Lottery scams are not limited to emails. In 2014, an Australian woman received a personal message to her Facebook inbox from a Facebook friend who had won a Facebook lottery. The message contained a link to the Facebook page of "Lady Officer Gwen Roberts," the supposed distributor of the funds. The woman had begun communicating with this person and received high pressure messages to transfer funds to a certain U.S. individual, otherwise she would miss out on her win.

The woman planned to send this person the requested amount of money in exchange for receiving a large amount of the lottery win. Luckily, the owner of the travel agency where she attempted to wire transfer the money convinced her to hold off and do some more background checking. Eventually, the Facebook friend who had sent the original message learned that scammers had hacked her Facebook account and sent the message. The woman was saved from any damage, but unfortunately another Australian had already sent the scammers several thousand dollars hoping to receive hundreds of thousands of dollars in return.[8]

Several tips can help spot email and lottery scams:[9]

- *Be suspicious of unexpected notifications*: You can't be a selected as a winner if you have not bought a ticket or completed an application to enter a contest or lottery.

- *Be skeptical of what you see*: Scammers make emails appear to come from a reputable source. A business email address may appear legitimate, but this does not mean that it's safe.

- *Be wary of unexpected emails that contain links or attachments*: You should avoid clicking on links or opening files from unfamiliar email addresses because they may contain a virus.

- *Beware of poor grammar and spelling*: Scam emails often are poorly written and frequently contain typos.

- *Be dubious of offers requesting secrecy*: If they ask you to keep your win a secret, it's likely to be a scam because genuine lotteries thrive on publicity.

If you are a victim of an advance-fee fraud, you should take several actions. First, you should report the fraud to the appropriate investigative agency. If you responded to an unsolicited offer, you should break off all contact with the fraudsters at once. Finally, if you gave the fraudsters your bank account details, you need to alert your bank immediately.

AFFINITY FRAUD

Affinity fraud refers to investment scams that target members of religious, ethnic, cultural, and professional groups. Fraudsters may be members or pretend to be members of the targeted group in order to gain your trust. They may also try to enlist respected leaders or members from the group to spread the word about the scheme. Often those members or leaders become unwitting victims in the fraudulent schemes they help to promote. Resisting an investment tip from someone in your social circle is often difficult, but can be necessary to avoid being scammed. Fraudsters use the Internet to target specific groups through email scams, and affinity frauds are especially problematic because they may remain unknown by outsiders and authorities for a long time because of the tight-knit structure of many targeted groups. Additionally, affinity scams often involve pyramid and Ponzi schemes where scammers use new investor money to pay earlier investors.

Warning signs of affinity frauds include investments that promise spectacular profits or "guaranteed" returns, lack of proper documentation in writing, and pressure to act quickly on these limited investment opportunities. To avoid affinity scams, you need to investigate the investment thoroughly regardless of how trustworthy the person who brings the investment opportunity to your attention seems.[10]

Affinity Fraud Targeting African-American Churchgoers

Ephren Taylor, former chief executive officer (CEO) of City Capital Corporation, operated a Ponzi scheme to swindle more than $16 million from over 400 people, primarily African-American church-goers. Taylor's scheme consisted of two distinct fraudulent offerings. First, he sold promissory notes issued by City Capital and various affiliates, bearing annual interest rates of 12–20%. Taylor told investors that their funds would be used to purchase and support various small businesses that City Capital had identified as good investment opportunities. Second, with the assistance of Wendy Connor, City Capital's chief operating officer, Taylor sold "sweepstakes machines," computers loaded with various games resembling those found at casinos. Taylor assured investors that these machines would generate a return of as much as 300% or more in the first year. To tap into the investors' largest source of available funds, Taylor enticed investors to roll over their retirement portfolios to custodial accounts, which he then handled.

Marketing himself as "The Social Capitalist" who understood the importance of "giving back," Taylor emphasized his status as the youngest black CEO of a public company and the son of a Christian minister. Taylor had authored three books and made public appearances on television programs such as *The Montel Williams Show* and *The Donnie Deutsch Show*. He conducted a multicity "Building Wealth Tour," speaking to church congregations. Taylor also offered investments through Internet presentations called "webinars." Additionally, he set up various websites describing his background, level of success, and socially conscious approach to investing. His promotional materials described the sweepstakes machines as "the brainchild of self-made millionaire Ephren Taylor." They also emphasized the "easy" and "risk-free" profits of the investment, in which "top-earning machines" generated 2400% returns per year, "average" machines returned 300% per year." These alleged returns were supposedly based on City

Capital's "years" of experience with "over 3000 machines." Investors even received a "100% risk-free, money-back" guarantee. The materials also claimed that City Capital would donate a percentage of revenues to charity, which dovetailed with Taylor's overarching sales pitch of "socially conscious" investing.[11]

In reality, City Capital generated hardly any revenue from actual business operations, but was wholly dependent upon a continuous stream of new investors. Instead of actual investments in business operations, Taylor and the other defendants used the fund flows for personal expenses. The offering materials were fraudulent. In truth, City Capital's track record with sweepstakes machines was abysmal, and this operation stayed alive only by conning new investors into the scheme. Taylor and Connor authorized payment of phantom monthly returns to investors starting as early as April 2010.

The tale of Taylor and his affiliates ended during the latter half of 2010 when new investor funds dried up and the entire operation grounded to a halt. In March 2015, the courts sentenced Taylor to 19 years and Connor to five years in federal prison.[12]

Affinity Fraud Targeting the Gay Community

Between 2005 and 2011, George Elia and International Consultants & Investment Group received at least $11 million from investors, of whom a substantial number were members of the gay community in Wilton Manors, Florida. Elia promised investors annual returns as high as 26% and transferred more than $3.5 million of investor funds to two entities he controlled. Elia guaranteed that investor money was safe and that he had high rates of returns from his day trading.

Most of his clients became aware of Elia through word-of-mouth referrals. Elia typically met and pitched to prospective investors over meals at expensive restaurants, and many of his investors were related to each other or friends. An associate introduced Elia to numerous gay investors who lived in the same Wilton Manors condominium development.

Besides promotion from those close to potential investors, Elia gained trust among his victims by assuring investors of high returns using falsified and misleading statements. For example, when an investor queried him about his investment track record, Elia replied by email on March 2, 2010: "To respond to your question, for the last ten years the lowest [return] was 16% and the highest was 26%. This year I believe will be in the range of 18–20%." The statement was false. Instead of pooling the funds and investing them, Elia paid phony returns using additional investor funds, and misappropriated more than $2.5 million in investor funds for himself. Elia used these millions to, among other things, pay his and his wife's personal expenses. He also paid more than $2 million to an associate who referred investors to him.[13]

Elia's scheme began to unravel in mid-2011, when he was unable to meet redemption requests by a growing number of investors. Word that Elia was not honoring investment requests circulated among the close-knit group of investors, which led to the collapse of the scheme. According to the U.S. Attorney's office, about 50 victims lost around $10 million in Elia's fraud. In June 2013, the courts sentenced Elia to 12 years in federal prison.[14]

HIGH-YIELD INVESTMENT FRAUDS

High-yield investment programs (HYIPs) are unregistered investment vehicles promising very high returns at little or no risk to investors. These programs might involve various forms of investments such as securities, commodities, real estate, and precious metals. The unlicensed individuals who perpetrate these frauds contact victims by telephone, email, or in person. These offers are typically unsolicited.

Some of these scams use the term prime bank program. *Prime* is a generic term that describes legitimate financial institutions that issue investments. Fraudsters often claim false affiliations with such organizations to trick prospective investors. Promoters of prime bank investment schemes often promise high-yield, tax-free returns to enable the "little guy" to participate in what they claim are financial instruments from elite overseas banks usually available only to very wealthy investors. Offenders may also trick investors into believing that they are participating in an innovative investment program.

Several warning signs should alert investors about fraudulent HYIPs. One sign is guaranteeing investment opportunities that are "too good to be true." Other red flags might include fictitious financial instruments, sophisticated and official-sounding language, extreme secrecy, claims of exclusive investment opportunity, and inordinate complexity surrounding the investments.[15]

Pathway to Prosperity

Between 2007 and 2009, Nicholas Smirnov, also known as Nicoloy Smirnow, Alexander Judizcev, Nicholas Kachura, and Jeff Prozorowiczm engaged in an international Ponzi scheme that resulted in losses of $70 million to more than 40,000 investors in over 120 countries. U.S. residents in 48 states lost money in the scheme. Smirnov's scam, which he operated through his *Pathway to Prosperity* website, was a classic example of a fraudulent HYIP.

Pathway to Prosperity (P-2-P) was a "long-term 'private' retirement Club," or so the P-2-P's Internet site claimed. P-2-P purported to afford the average person the opportunity to take advantage of investment vehicles accessible by only the very rich. P-2-P distributed no prospectus, offering circular or private placement memoranda. The website provided little information to prospective investors. Smirnov created the false appearance of a sophisticated and legitimate international financier to gain investors' confidence and to establish the illusion of honesty. He also denied any connection between P-2-P and the so-called HYIPs.

Smirnov described HYIPs as taking money from one investor to pay another, a practice he described as "highly illegal." As Smirnov asserted on his website, "It is fairly simple to do, as they set the percentages in such a way that there is enough to pay the next guy and run for periods of up to a year! This is NOT a H.Y.I.P. site. We do NOT believe in them!" He warned investors to "stay away" from HYIPs "at all cost."[16]

Smirnov offered investors a choice of 7, 15, 30, and 60-day plans. At the daily interest rates promised by Smirnov, a 7-day plan supposedly earned an annual return of more than 500%, and a 60-day plan supposedly earned more than 700% annually. Although some earlier investors received a substantial return on their investment, most lost everything. P-2-P made few, if any, legitimate investments.[17]

In May 2010, the U.S. Department of Justice (DOJ) announced that Smirnov was charged in 10 criminal complaints. Smirnov's whereabouts remained unknown to authorities until after his arrest in late 2014 in Ontario, Canada. In March 2015, the DOJ requested that Smirnov be extradited from Canada.[18]

ZeekRewards

Between January 2010 and August 2012, Paul Burks, the president of ZeekRewards (collectively "Zeek"), operated an Internet Ponzi scheme that took in more than $850 million from U.S. citizens. The number of victims, which authorities estimate tops a million, likely earns Zeek the infamous distinction as the largest Ponzi scheme in history. For the sake of comparison, the number of investors in Bernard Madoff's Ponzi scheme, the largest in history by investor losses, was "only" in the thousands.[19]

ZeekRewards was a classic example of a HYIP Ponzi scheme. It guaranteed that investors would earn a return of 125% on their investment by claiming that they were collectively allowed to share 50% of Zeek's daily net profits. The daily "award" was usually

1.5% of the individual's investment. Besides the "Retail Profit Pool," investors could also participate in the "Matrix," which was a form of a multilevel marketing plan that rewarded investors for each "downline" investor within that investor's Matrix. The Matrix consisted of a 2 × 5 pyramid, and each person added to an investor's Matrix qualified that investor to receive a bonus.

Besides promising excessive returns, Burks and his co-fraudsters used other ways to actively promote Zeek to current and potential investors. For example, they made false representations of Zeek's success in weekly conference calls referred to as "Red Carpet Events." They also used various media such as print media, including websites, emails, and journals, to make false and misleading statements about Zeek's success to recruit victim investors.[20] In reality, about 98% of all incoming funds came from victim investors. Zeek used these funds to make payments to earlier investors. Burks and his closest affiliates received hefty sums for their involvement in this Ponzi scheme.

In August 2012, the SEC announced an emergency asset freeze to halt the operations of ZeekRewards, which was on the verge of collapse.[21] At that time, the scammers fraudulently represented to their victims that their investments were collectively worth $2.8 billion. In reality, Burks and his co-fraudsters had only $320 million available to pay out to investors.

The DOJ charged Burks with mail, wire, and tax fraud. He relinquished his interest in Zeek and its associated companies and paid a $4 million penalty in 2012 when the SEC's emergency asset freeze took place.

INTERNET AND SOCIAL MEDIA FRAUDS

Internet and social media frauds come in many forms, but each variant exploits the fact that the Internet allows someone to reach a mass audience without spending much time or money. Scammers use persuasive techniques to paint enticing pictures of different investments through unsolicited emails. For example, fraudsters may use the Internet to spread misinformation to artificially inflate a stock's value before selling in a "pump-and-dump" scheme. Others promise high-yield returns through various "alternative" investments or by investing in offshore markets. Still others use the Internet to recruit people to sell illegal or inappropriate investments. Scammers continue to take advantage of technology to lure unsuspecting investors into various schemes. Promoters of fraudulent Internet investment schemes often use social media platforms, online investment newsletters, online bulletin boards and chat rooms, spam mail, or online dating sites ("romance scams") to attract victims. Warning signs include unsolicited offers or tips by anonymous or unknown people and seemingly inordinate hype of an investment opportunity.[22]

Wall Street Capital Funding

Over the course of their long careers but especially during 2009 and 2010, Philip Cardwell, Roy Campbell, and Aaron Hume disseminated fraudulent information about a series of sham energy companies. Through Wall Street Capital Funding LLC (WSCF), which Cardwell and Campbell owned, the trio created and distributed promotional material including a fictitious oil-exploration-and-development company known as PrimeGen Energy Corp.

PrimeGen (PGNE), which was purportedly headquartered in New Jersey, supposedly had operations in Russia generating many millions of dollars in revenues. PrimeGen, however, was a complete scam. Its corporate headquarters was a rented mailbox, its phone line was unattended, and its web page was generated by copying the source code from another company's website. The trio used the same promotion formula for Caliber Energy, Inc., which was also a scam.

The promotional materials of WSCF took the form of "investment opinions," which were sent as mass emails to as many as

50 million addresses at once. The promotional materials typically expressed positive opinions about the companies in question, even though the trio had no reasonable basis for their views. The materials also fraudulently and misleadingly created the appearance of an independent basis for their statements about the promoted companies. The mass emails during December 2009 had headlines such as the following: "Revenues for PGNE to soar with newest 42 Well project/First Oil Well ALONE projected to generate $71.7 Million per year/When PGNE explodes will you be there to enjoy the ride?" or "Revenues for PGNE to soar with newest 42 well project/PrimeGen's successful drilling efforts continue, making it an ideal opportunity/Finally a Small Cap Company worth looking at!"

In late 2011, the authorities banned the trio for life from engaging in any promotional, trading, or other activities concerning micro-stocks. Additionally, Cardwell and Campbell both paid a fine of $125,000 and Hume a fine of $50,000.[23]

Porter Stansberry's Monthly Newsletter

Porter Stansberry is an American financial publisher and author who founded Stansberry & Associates Investment Research in 1999. Stansberry is also famous for his ominous videos — "The End of America" and "The End of Barack Obama." In 2003, the SEC brought a case against Stansberry stating that he, Agora Inc., and Pirate Investor LLC — the firms he controlled — engaged in an ongoing scheme to defraud public investors by disseminating false information in several Internet newsletters.

Through various publications, Stansberry claimed to have inside information about certain public companies and offered to sell the inside information to newsletter subscribers for a fee of $1000, which even if true, would be insider trading. The newsletters, including PirateInvestor.com, claimed to be "a service featuring independent, original and thoughtful research into the process of wealth creation." In total, subscribers paid Stansberry's firm more than $1 million for this alleged inside information. Instead of benefiting from this information, the subscribers failed to receive the promised profits as this information turned out to be false.[24] In 2007, a U.S. District Court ordered Stansberry and his investment firm Pirate Investor to pay $1.5 million in restitution and civil penalties.

The case of Stansberry raised a public debate at the time of his trial. Many media outlets spoke out in support of Stansberry due to the relevance of the case to First Amendment rights. They claimed that a guilty verdict was a major threat to the free dissemination of news about the financial markets and specific investment opportunities, and could lead to a situation that would be contrary to the spirit of the system of a free and independent press. Some media outlets also stated that this verdict could result in situations where any financial commentator who passes bad information in good faith could be sued. The court rejected Stansberry's First Amendment defense, saying "Stansberry's conduct undoubtedly involved deliberate fraud, making statements that he knew to be false."[25]

PUMP-AND-DUMP SCHEMES

A *pump-and-dump scheme* is an illegal practice that attempts to artificially boost a stock's price with false, misleading, or exaggerated statements about the underlying company. If the fraudsters succeed in pumping up the stock price, they seek to profit from the inflated stock price by dumping their holdings of the stock. Pump-and-dump schemes often occur on the Internet and involve microcap stocks whose prices are more likely to move based on false or misleading information. The term *microcap stock* refers to stocks of public companies in the United States with a relatively small market capitalization, roughly $50 million to $300 million. Red flags concerning such schemes include claims of inside or unique market information and requests to act quickly.[26]

Stratton Oakmont

The notorious tale of Stratton Oakmont began in 1989 when Jordan Belfort founded the firm with Danny Porush. During the 1990s, Stratton Oakmont grew to be the largest over-the-counter (OTC) firm in the United States. Stratton Oakmont participated in numerous pump-and-dump schemes causing massive losses to investors.

Two years after Stratton Oakmont closed in 1996, the FBI arrested Belfort and Porush. In 2003, they were both convicted on charges of money laundering and securities fraud, each receiving a four-year prison sentence. The courts also ordered Belfort to pay more than $110 million in restitution to his victims. By 2014, he had paid around $12 million of this debt.

The tale of Belfort and Stratton Oakmont became well-known to the public in the movie *The Wolf of Wall Street*, which premiered in December 2013. Belfort also captured his tale in his own memoirs, *The Wolf of Wall Street* and *Catching the Wolf of Wall Street*.[27]

Langbar International

The pump-and-dump scheme of Langbar International, which until 2005 went by the name Crown Corporation Limited, was one of the biggest and most audacious frauds in UK history. Crown Corporation, which listed on the Alternative Investment Market in London Stock Exchange during 2003, was purportedly buying companies that were not meeting their economic potentials and then improving them to sell at a profit. After its debut on the Alternative Investment Market, the company made a series of official stock exchange announcements claiming, for example, that it had won more than $600 million in contracts in Argentina for construction and waste management. On another occasion, Crown reported that it was investing in a gold mine and Russian gas groups.

Instead of any actual business actions taking place, Crown traded back and forth fake contracts and bogus certificates of deposit (CDs).

Soon Crown claimed to have cash reserves of $633 million, which it supposedly held on deposit at Banco do Brasil in Sao Paulo.

Despite the company's claims of massive cash reserves and prosperous foreign projects, investors remained wary until Stuart Pearson, head of Langbar Capital, stepped in as the CEO of Crown. The share price of Crown, which now had changed its name to Langbar International, rose with Pearson's declarations to the market that the funds had been released from Brazil. However, soon after this, the London Stock Exchange suspended trading of Langbar's stock, when various parties questioned the company's value. Shortly after the suspension, the company collapsed and investors faced estimated losses of up to £100 million.

The aftermath of Crown and Langbar International went on for years until the investigation ended in June 2011. The only person convicted was Stuart Pearson, who at the time of the collapse had been with the company for only six months. Pearson faced a one-year sentence. Behind the scenes, many claim that Pearson was little more than a patsy, and that the true mastermind behind this elaborate fraud was Avi Arad, the head of Lambert Financial Investments. Whether or not this is true remains unclear because Arad died from a heart attack in 2008 during the fraud investigation.[28,29]

MICROCAP FRAUDS

Microcap frauds are investment scams related to *microcap stocks*, which are low-priced stocks issued by the smallest companies. These microcap stocks are typically traded in the *OTC market*, which is a market without a central physical location. Instead, market participants trade with one another through various communication modes including the telephone, email, and proprietary electronic trading systems. This off-exchange trading occurs directly between two parties without any supervision of the exchange. As publicly available information about and liquidity of microcap stocks is often scarce, fraudsters can more easily spread false information and manipulate stock prices. Many microcap frauds include pump-and-dump schemes. Warning signs of microcap frauds include unsolicited stock recommendation or heavy stock promotion, no real business operations, unexplained increases in stock price or trading volume, and frequent change in the company name or type of business.[30]

Operation Shell-Expel, operated by the SEC Enforcement Division's Office of Market Intelligence, uses technology to scour the OTC market and identify dormant companies ripe for abuse. Since this operation started in 2012, it has resulted in trading suspensions of more than 800 microcap stocks, which comprise more than 8% of the OTC market. A round of trading suspensions occurred in March 2015 when the SEC announced it had suspended trading in 128 inactive penny stock companies to ensure they don't become a source for microcap frauds.

Once suspended from trading, a stock can't be relisted unless the company provides updated financial information to prove that it is operational. These requirements are rarely fulfilled, and thus the trading suspensions are essentially rendering the shell companies worthless and thus useless to fraudsters.[31]

Gregg Mulholland's Microcap Frauds

Gregg Mulholland, who has dual citizenship in the United States and Canada, was involved in several microcap frauds between 2008 and 2015. The first SEC complaint against Mulholland was filed in 2011 for fraudulent pump-and-dump manipulation of a sports drink company "Rudy Nutrition" founded by Daniel "Rudy" Ruettiger. Ruettiger was a former Notre Dame football player depicted in the 1993 film *Rudy*. The SEC alleged that investors received false and misleading statements about the company. For example, a promotional mailer sent to potential investors falsely claimed that in "a major southwest test, Rudy outsold Gatorade 2 to 1!" Another promotional email also falsely boasted that in "several blind taste tests, Rudy outperformed Gatorade and Powerade by 2:1." Meanwhile, the scheme's promoters engaged in manipulative trading to artificially inflate the price of Rudy Nutrition stock while selling unregistered shares to investors. The SEC suspended trading and later revoked registration of the stock in late 2008. Rudy Nutrition is no longer in business.[32]

Mulholland initiated the pump of Rudy Nutrition in March 2008 by sending out two different mailers to more than two million U.S. households. The mailers told prospective investors that Rudy Nutrition had "partnership agreements" with two large soft drink distributors: Canteen Franchise Group and Vistar Corporation. These were false statements. During March 2008, Rudy Nutrition also issued press releases about supposed agreements between Canteen and Vistar with a headline "Rudy Nutrition Signs National Vending Distribution with Vistar Corporation." The press releases were materially false. Mulholland also filmed two Internet videos purporting to provide advice on a website called PirateStockTV. com. In less than a month, the price of Rudy Nutrition stock climbed from $0.25 a share to $1.05 a share. At that point, the members of the scheme sold millions of shares on the market.

In June 2015, the SEC charged Mulholland with illegally selling more than 83 million penny stock shares that he secretly obtained through at least 10 different offshore front companies. *Penny stocks* are shares of small companies that trade at low prices per share. According to the SEC, Mulholland controlled at least 84% of the shares of Vision Plasma Systems Inc. before dumping them to the market and making a profit of at least $21 million.[33]

In July 2015, the authorities charged Mulholland in yet another microcap fraud involving CYNK Technology, a penny stock company that briefly rose from $15 million to $6 billion in value despite having no revenue. The SEC said that the main orchestrator in this scam was Philip Thomas Kueber, who filed a false and misleading registration statement for the company and then enlisted a small group of "straw shareholders" and "sham CEOs" to conceal his control of the company's nonrestricted shares.

From CYNK Technology and other schemes in which he was involved, Mulholland made about $300 million in profits, which he laundered through at least five offshore law firms. Mulholland, who was arrested in June 2015, faces several fraud charges in the United States. U.S. Attorney Currie stated that:

> *As charged in the criminal complaint, Mulholland used an elaborate offshore corporate structure built on lies and deceit to defraud U.S. investors in publicly-traded companies and profited to the tune of $300 million. He concealed his leadership role in this fraudulent network, which included stock promoters, lawyers, and broker-dealers, by using aliases and sham companies, and fled the United States when his secretly-owned brokerage firm was indicted last summer.[34]*

PRE-IPO INVESTMENT SCAMS

An initial public offering (IPO) is the first sale of stock by a company to the public. *Underwriting* is the process by which investment bankers raise investment capital from investors on behalf of corporations that are issuing securities. IPOs only happen once for each company, so sellers often tout them as "once in a lifetime" opportunities. IPOs often attract a throng of investors because the stock prices of these firms sometimes soar above their offering prices. Thus, flipping a hot IPO stock in the first few days can provide an opportunity to earn a quick profit, but brokerage firms strongly discourage such behavior. Although some IPOs soar high and keep rising, many others end up selling for below their offering prices within a few months. For average investors, the chances of getting early shares of a hot IPO are slim, unless they have some special association with the underwriter. If they do get shares, this is probably because nobody else wants them.[35]

Pre-IPO investment scams fraudulently purport to offer investors the opportunity to buy pre-IPO shares of companies. Offering pre-IPO shares is neither illegal nor uncommon, but unregistered offerings may violate securities laws unless they meet a registration exemption. Investors should look for the following red flags concerning pre-IPO investment scams: difficulty of obtaining information about the offering, an unregistered offering, and unsolicited promotional contact of the offering.[36]

Pre-IPO Shares of Facebook

In 2011, Allen Weintraub contacted both Kodak and Dallas-based AMR, parent company of American Airlines, with separate purchase offers. The Kodak offer was for $1.3 billion, which represented roughly a 70% premium over the level where Kodak stock was trading. The SEC sued Allen Weintraub and his Florida-based company, Sterling Global Holdings, alleging that he had violated the Securities Exchange Act of 1934 by giving the impression that he was a serious bidder when, in fact, he had no assets or access to the huge sums of money those deals would require. Weintraub had filed for personal bankruptcy in April 2007. The SEC said Weintraub has a sizable rap sheet, with convictions in Florida in 1992, 1998, and 2008 for fraud and grand larceny.

In February 2012, Weintraub defrauded investors by selling worthless shares that he claimed to be pre-IPO shares of Facebook. Weintraub used an alias, various entities, and a website to perpetrate his scheme. He steered potential investors seeking to purchase pre-IPO stock of Facebook to the website of Private Stock Transfer Inc. by posting a response on www.quora.com. In that post, Weintraub claimed that he had purchased Facebook stock from Private Stock Transfer Inc. When victims went to the website and sought information on buying Facebook stock, Weintraub represented that Private Stock Transfer Inc. had thousands of Facebook shares available for purchase. He directed victims to buy shares described as "Facebook Inc. by and through PST Investment III, Inc. Class A shares on a one for one conversion basis." PST

Investment III Inc. was another company associated with Weintraub. After the victims sent payment to Weintraub's bank accounts, he issued stock certificates for PST Investment III shares that would convert to Facebook shares on a one-for-one basis once Facebook went public. In reality, neither Weintraub nor Private Stock Transfer Inc. had any Facebook shares. In 2014, the authorities sentenced Weintraub to more than nine years in prison for charges of fraud. The authorities also ordered him to pay restitution to his victims and forfeit more than $140,000.[37,38]

Pre-IPO Share Ponzi Scheme

Between 2001 and 2009, Randy Cho defrauded more than 50 investors of about $8 million. Cho assured investors that these funds would be used to invest in shares of specific well-known companies in anticipation of expected IPOs. These companies included Centerpoint, AOL/Time Warner, Google, Facebook, and Rosetta Stone. Cho claimed to have access to sell stock in these companies, which he offered as part of a "friends and family" investment pool. He told investors that he had worked at Goldman Sachs, still had an account with and made his investments through Goldman Sachs, and/or that Goldman Sachs still considered him a preferred client. These statements were false, as Cho neither worked with nor had an account at Goldman Sachs. Instead of actually investing any money in pre-IPO shares, Cho used the funds for his personal expenses. He also used some of the funds to repay previous investors to keep his Ponzi scheme running.

Besides defrauding individual investors, Cho also managed to fool the tax authorities by failing to report about $4.8 million of additional income between 2004 and 2007, resulting in an underpayment of $1.5 million in federal income taxes. In January 2013, the authorities sentenced Cho to 12 years in prison when he was found guilty of charges of wire and tax fraud. The authorities ordered him to pay $8 million in restitution to investors and $1.5 million to the Internal Revenue Service (IRS).[39,40]

PRIME BANK INVESTMENT FRAUDS

As previously mentioned, *prime bank programs* are a type of HYIP promising excessive returns with little or no risk. What is common for every prime bank investment is that the investment does not exist and is a scam. The sellers frequently tell potential investors that they have special access to programs that otherwise would be reserved for top financiers on Wall Street or in London, Geneva or other world financial centers. The sellers also tell investors that profits of 100% or more are possible with little risk. The promoters of these schemes have demonstrated remarkable audacity, advertising in national newspapers such as *USA Today* and the *Wall Street Journal*.[41]

Prime bank programs often claim that investors' funds will be used to buy and trade prime bank instruments that are allegedly guaranteed by well-known organizations such as the World Bank, International Monetary Fund, or central banks. They are promoted using complex, sophisticated, and official-sounding terms. Warning signs around prime bank programs include secrecy or even requirements of nondisclosure agreements and claims of an exclusive investment opportunity.[42]

Prime Bank Investment Scheme

Between 2012 and 2013, Fotios Geivelis and Bernard Butts defrauded almost $4 million from nearly 50 investors in a prime bank investment scam. Geivelis, who acted through his purported financial services firm Worldwide Funding III Limited, and Butts, a Miami-based attorney, lured investors by promising enormous returns of $8.7 million in 15–45 business days on an initial investment between $60,000 and $90,000. Investments were transferred to Butts' attorney trust account for the benefit of Worldwide Funding. Geivelis and Worldwide Funding were to use the investors' funds to pay banking charges to lease Standby Letters of Credit (SBLC) in the amount of €10 million from a banking group in Europe. Geivelis and Worldwide were to leverage the SBLC to invest in a securities trading program that was to generate a rate of return of about 14% a week for approximately 42 weeks.

Instead of buying any nonexisting prime bank instruments, Geivelis and Butts each took about 45% of the nearly $4 million and paid the remaining 10% to the sales agents whom they used to promote their scam. In September 2013, the SEC announced charges and an emergency asset freeze against the scammers.[43]

In June 2014, an agreement between the SEC and Butts forced Butts and associated entities to pay more than $3.8 million to settle claims over the alleged involvement in the investment scheme. Butts didn't admit or deny any allegations in the SEC's suit. On the other hand, Geivelis pled guilty and received a five-year prison sentence in August 2014. Assistant U.S. Attorney Leo Dillon told the sentencing judge that the case involved "an enormous worldwide fraud" with victims in the United States, Germany, Switzerland, Hong Kong, Japan, and Australia.[44]

PROMISSORY NOTES

A *promissory note* is a form of debt that companies sometimes use to raise money. Promissory notes typically contain all the terms pertaining to the indebtedness by the issuer or maker to the note's payee, such as the amount, interest rate, and maturity date. When correctly used, promissory notes are legitimate financial instruments, but they are often fraudulently exploited in investment scams. Typically, promissory note scams promote high, guaranteed returns that are backed by collateral. Although promissory notes can be legitimate and worthwhile investments, individual investors should bear in mind that promoters generally sell promissory notes to sophisticated and institutional buyers, who can do their own research on the company issuing the notes to determine whether the notes are a good deal.[45,46]

Success Trade Securities

Between 2009 and 2013, Fuad Ahmed, the CEO and the President of Success Trade Securities, orchestrated a fraudulent sale of promissory notes and created a Ponzi scheme costing its victims more than $19 million. The majority of the victims were current and former National Football League and National Basketball Association players. The promissory notes of Success Trade Securities, which Ahmed sold to at least 65 investors, were promised to return annually between 12.5% and 26.0%. In reality, Ahmed converted investor funds and used them for his personal expenses and to repay earlier investors to keep the Ponzi scheme afloat.

Besides promising excessive returns, Ahmed sought to persuade investors by misrepresenting and omitting material facts. For example, he created the false impression that his businesses were thriving and about to be listed on a European stock exchange. In reality, his company had lost money in 13 of the last 14 years. In April 2013, the Financial Industry Regulatory Authority (FINRA) issued a complaint against Success Trade Securities and Ahmed charging fraud in the sales of promissory notes. FINRA also filed a temporary cease and desist order to immediately halt their activities, to which Ahmed and his firm consented. In June 2014, FINRA ordered Ahmed and his firm to pay $13.7 million in restitution to the victims of their fraud.[47]

Medical Capital Holdings

Between 2003 and 2009, Medical Capital Holdings (MedCap) raised $2.2 billion from 20,000 investors by selling promissory notes with the pledge that the money would be spent on the company's accounts to fund its medical device business. Estimates of the total investor losses from the scheme range from $800 million to $1.1 billion. By the time the SEC sued MedCap for fraud in July 2009, the firm had more than $543 million in phony receivables on its books and had lost $316 million on various loans. Meanwhile, the company had collected $323 million in fees for managing money-losing loans.

The SEC also uncovered the makings of a massive Ponzi scheme at MedCap. The scam ultimately became one of largest alleged Ponzi schemes in the history of Orange County, California. According to the SEC, MedCap was selling receivables at a markup among the funds it controlled and using money from newer investors to pay investors in the older funds. According to the SEC, MedCap also spent $4.5 million on a 118-foot yacht called the Home Stretch and another $18.1 million on an unreleased movie.[48]

The promissory note Ponzi scheme of MedCap had unpleasant ramifications for several well-known financial corporations. For example, in February 2013, Bank of New York Mellon, the world's largest custodial bank, agreed to pay $114 million to settle claims over its role as trustee for debt issued by MedCap. Investors accused the bank of failing to properly review MedCap's dealings before letting the company use investors' money, breaching its fiduciary and contractual obligations to those investors. In April 2013, Wells Fargo agreed to pay $105 million to settle similar claims. Joseph Lampariello, former MedCap president, pled guilty in May 2012 to a wire fraud charge. His plea agreement was filed under seal and his sentencing has been postponed several times. He faces up to 21 years in federal prison and $49 million in restitution to the victims of the fraud.[49]

COMMODITY POOL FRAUDS

In financial terms, a *commodity* is a raw material or primary agricultural product that can be bought and sold, such as copper or coffee. A *commodity pool* is an arrangement where an individual or organization collects money from multiple investors and pools it together to invest in commodities and futures. *Futures* are a financial contract to buy or sell an asset, such as a physical commodity or a financial instrument, at a predetermined future date and price. Misconduct related to commodity pool frauds typically occurs in three main forms: (1) misappropriation of pooled funds, (2) misrepresentation of the risk and return profile, and (3) operating without registering.

Commodity pool frauds are closely related to affinity frauds because the fraudsters often promote these pools through different social groups. Besides claims of high returns at little or no risk, warning signs of commodity pool frauds include claims of profiting from current news already known to the public ("As a result of that hurricane, the price of oil futures will increase substantially"), claims of unique information on market trends, and requests for immediate cash payments ("There are only two units left, so I'd sign up today if I were you").[50]

Paul Eustace and Philadelphia Alternative Asset Management

Between 2001 and 2005, Paul Eustace, the former president and founder of Philadelphia Alternative Asset Management, fraudulently operated four commodity pools and caused losses of about $200 million for his investors. The Philadelphia Alternative Asset Fund, Ltd. (Off-Shore Fund), which was based in the Cayman Islands, traded commodity futures and options on U.S. futures exchanges. The Off-Shore Fund also traded foreign currencies and engaged in the *exchange of futures for physicals*, which is a transaction between two parties in which a futures contract on a commodity is exchanged for the actual physical good.

Eustace concealed the losses he incurred by issuing false account statements reflecting high and consistently profitable trading results. He also misappropriated investors' assets and received incentive and management fees through his fraudulent operation of the pools. In 2005, Philadelphia Alternative collapsed, leaving its investors with massive losses. In August 2008, a federal court in Philadelphia ordered Eustace to pay more than $279 million in restitution and a $12 million civil penalty. Eustace was also banned from trading indefinitely.[51]

Mark Bloom and North Hills Management

Between 2002 and 2008, Mark Bloom, the owner of North Hills Management LLC, operated an unregistered commodity pool through which he misappropriated at least $13 million of investors' funds. Bloom used the misappropriated funds to finance his lavish lifestyle. Bloom and his wife maintained multiple apartments in Upper Manhattan, owned beach houses in Florida and New Jersey, as well as several luxury cars and boats.

Bloom and North Hills Management hid their fraudulent behavior by making misrepresentations and material omissions to commodity pool participants and issuing false statements about North Hills. For example, Bloom failed to inform his investors that he had invested about $17 million of North Hills' assets in the fraudulent commodity pool operated by Paul Eustace's Philadelphia Alternative Asset Management. In 2015, the authorities ordered Mark Bloom and North Hills Management to pay a $26 million civil penalty for running a fraudulent commodity pool and misappropriating customer funds. Bloom pled guilty to criminal charges.[52,53]

FOREIGN CURRENCY TRADING FRAUDS

The *foreign exchange market* (FX, forex, or currency market) is a global decentralized market for the trading of currencies by investors and speculators. It is the world's largest market in terms of volume of trading. Large banks and financial institutions are the main participants in this market, thus in terms of the volume of trading, individual investors play a minor role. Although participants trade currencies for many different reasons, individual investors engage in speculative trades and are profit motivated. For instance, consider a situation in which the U.S. dollar is expected to weaken in value relative to the euro. In this situation, a FX trader would sell dollars and buy euros. If the euro strengthens, the purchasing power to buy dollars has now increased. The trader can now buy back more dollars than initially sold, thus making a profit.[54]

Foreign currency trading fraud is an investment scam used to defraud traders by convincing them that they will gain a high profit by FX trading. FX frauds often promise that no bear markets exist with FX. A *bear market* is a market in which prices are falling, encouraging selling. Any current or possible FX investor should keep in mind that the FX market is a zero-sum game, meaning that whatever one trader gains, another loses. Thus, the expected return of currency speculation is zero. Besides claims of no downside risk, red flags around FX trading frauds include claims of unique market information, requests of immediate cash payments, and claims of exclusive investment opportunity.[55]

Russell Cline and Orion International

Between 1998 and 2003, Russell Cline, founder of Orion International, orchestrated an investment scheme in which he fraudulently solicited customers to send funds totaling more than $40 million to participate in a purported foreign currency fund. Cline deceitfully asked customers to purchase illegal off-exchange FX options and futures by misrepresenting the profits and risks involved in FX trading. Cline falsely represented that the Orion Fund had been profitable every month between December 1998 and May 2002 and had either met or exceeded its expected annual earnings by at least 96% in the first four years since its inception. Cline further falsely represented to investors that Orion had a history of earning 8% a month and that "based on trades and the compounding principle, Orion has provided an average return in excess of 150% per year for its members." He claimed through the Orion website that the FX market "mathematically conforms to technical analysis charting and obeys technical rules, which presents the opportunity to trade with minimal risk."[56]

In reality, instead of operating a highly successful FX fund, Cline used more than $16 million of the funds to finance his luxurious lifestyle, and $13 million to repay earlier investors. His purchases included private chartered jets, a river house valued at more than $3 million, seven houses each worth between $500,000 and $1.5 million, and a $500,000 sound system. In May 2003, the U.S. Commodity Futures Trading Commission (CFTC) and the State of Oregon sued Cline and his co-fraudsters, freezing all of Cline's assets. In May 2006, Cline pled guilty to mail fraud and money laundering charges and was sentenced to more than eight years in prison. In January 2007, he was ordered to pay more than $33 million in restitution and civil penalties. Total sanctions against Cline, Orion International, and other fraudsters amount to almost $150 million.[57,58]

Refco's Foreign Exchange Fraud

The FX fraud of Refco, once the biggest independent U.S. futures trader, was one of the largest in history. Some estimate Refco's bankruptcy in October 2005 to have cost $2.4 billion for its 17,000 FX trading customers. Refco's short but sad tale as a public company began in August 2005, when it raised more than $500 million in its IPO, valuing the entire company at about $3.5 billion. Refco's strong track record attracted investors. The firm reported an average annual growth of 33% in its earnings over the four years before its IPO.

To the outside world, Refco seemed to vault from one success to another. Behind the scenes the situation was not as attractive. Since 1983 regulators such as the CFTC had punished Refco 140 times for keeping sloppy records, filing false trading reports, inadequately supervising its traders, and other violations.[59] Refco's troubles became public in October 2005 when it announced that Phillip Bennett, its CEO and chairman, had hidden $430 million in bad debts from the company's auditors and investors. Later in October 2005, Refco filed for Chapter 11 to seek protection from its creditors. With about $17 billion in assets and liabilities, it became one of the biggest bankruptcies in U.S. history at that time.

The fraud bought Bennett a stable of high-end sports cars, including seven Ferraris; a $20 million plane; luxury homes and more than $29 million in artwork, including works by Andy Warhol, Robert Rauschenberg, Cy Twombly, and Willem De Kooning. In July 2008, the authorities sentenced Bennett to 16 years in prison. His charges consisted of 20 counts of conspiracy and fraud.[60] Furthermore, in June 2014, the authorities ordered Bennett and two of his ex-colleagues to pay $672 million in restitution to Sphinx Providence and its hedge funds for losses stemming from the fraud.[61]

PRECIOUS METALS FRAUDS

Precious metals refer to a classification of metals that are considered to be rare and/or have a high economic value. Several factors contribute to the higher relative values of these metals such as their rarity, uses in industrial processes, and use as an investment commodity. Precious metals include, but are not limited to, gold, silver, platinum, iridium, rhodium, and palladium. Precious metals offer a glittering temptation for investors seeking to increase their investment returns, but investing in them is far from foolproof. Evidence suggests that having at least some exposure to precious metals tends to improve a portfolio's overall performance.

Although the benefits of adding precious metals to an equity port-folio vary over time, the reduction in risk tends to be larger during restrictive policy periods when the Federal Reserve's monetary policy tightens.[62]

Precious metals frauds try to trick investors by making promises of easy profits from rising prices of precious metals. The fraudsters often offer "financing agreements," which are structured so that investors are only required to pay a small percentage – typically between 15% and 25% – of the total purchase price. Investors are supposed to pay the rest of the price by a loan that the com-pany arranges for them. The fraudsters claim that they will pur-chase precious metals with these funds and store them for the investors in a storage facility or "bank." In reality, the fraudsters use the funds to pay themselves commissions. Warning signs con-cerning precious metals scams include failure to identify the finan-cial institution that will be loaning the rest of the purchase price or the storage facility where the precious metals will be stored, missing documentation that seems necessary, and unsolicited pro-motion contacts from a broker or a sales person.[63]

Hunter Wise Commodities

Between 2011 and 2013, Hunter Wise Commodities, three of its fully owned subsidiaries, and the individuals running the compa-nies, Fred Jager and Harold Martin, Jr., orchestrated a massive precious metals fraud. The fraud was a multilevel marketing scheme in which so-called retail dealers served a sales function for Hunter Wise, soliciting customer accounts. The dealers advertised and claimed that they sold physical metals, including gold, silver, platinum, palladium, and copper, to retail customers on a financed basis, and forwarded customer funds to Hunter Wise, whose iden-tity was not disclosed to the customers.

The dealers claimed to arrange loans for the purchase of physi-cal metals, and told customers their metals would be stored in a secure depository. Customers were then charged exorbitant interest and storage fees. In reality, neither Hunter Wise nor any of its dealers purchased any precious metals or arranged any actual loans. The court order estimated that more than 3200, or greater than 90% of the retail customers, lost money in the fraud. In May 2014, a federal court in Florida ordered Jager, Martin, Hunter Wise Commodities, and its three fully owned subsidiaries to pay more than $108 million in restitution and civil penalties.[64]

Atlantic Bullion & Coin Inc.

Between 2001 and 2012, Ronnie Wilson, owner of Atlantic Bullion & Coin Inc., operated a Ponzi scheme involving $90 million in precious metals. Starting in 2009, as silver prices were booming, Wilson offered investors the opportunity to take advantage of the boom by purchasing silver bars that would then be kept in storage. Instead of buying the massive amounts of silver bullion as he claimed, Wilson used tens of millions of dollars of investors' funds for his and his family's personal and business interests. Atlantic Bullion & Coin Inc. proceeded to collect about $65 million during the three-year period from January 2009 to February 2012, including $33 million alone from January 2011 to February 2012. This should have translated into the purchase of thousands of 100-ounce and 1000-ounce silver bars held in storage for investors. In June 2012, Beattie Ashmore, the court-appointed receiver, discovered that only 85 1000-ounce silver bars had been purchased since 2009 and of that only 64 bars remained.[65]

In June 2012, the authorities sentenced Wilson to almost 20 years in prison for mail fraud. He was also ordered to pay more than $57 million in restitution to his victims for his involvement in the Ponzi scheme. In February 2013, the authorities also ordered Wilson to pay more than $34 million in restitution and civil penalties.[66]

ADDITIONAL WAYS TO AVOID INVESTMENT SCAMS

You should focus your attention on finding sound investments rather than letting "opportunities" find you through contacts by strangers or recommendations from social connections. Before making an investment, you should consider the following actions to avoid being scammed.[67]

- Conduct due diligence by reviewing promotional materials and verifying the accuracy of information.

- Research the company and its filings by using the SEC - EDGAR database.

- Use FINRA BrokerCheck to verify that an investment advisor has the credentials claimed.

- Check out investor alerts and more warning signs from trusted sources such as FINRA and the SEC.

- Confirm that investments are held in a third-party custodian account unrelated to the company making the investment offering.

- Don't rush or feel pressured to make an investment.

LEARNING POINTS

The creative imaginations of scam artists permit almost limitless ways to swindle investors. Despite diligent investigations by various government authorities these illegal activities persist. To protect yourself and avoid becoming a victim, you need to be aware of a wide range of investment frauds and their warning signs. This chapter has discussed a breadth of investment frauds, but many others exist. Below are some key learning points to keep in mind.

- Don't believe everything that a seller is telling you.
- Don't be swayed by the affiliations or credentials of the promoter or by your emotions.

- Take time to conduct your own research on an investment's potential.

- Ask questions and get the facts about any investment before you buy.

- Seek further information about an investment from an unbiased, independent source, and review both the promises and risks.

- Recognize that investment returns are made over time, not overnight.

- Approach any unsolicited investment opportunity with suspicion.

- Don't get sucked in by the hype of IPOs.

- Be skeptical when someone offers you "guaranteed returns," "superior returns" or claims that "everyone is buying it."

- Make sure that you understand what you are buying and all the associated fees.

QUESTIONS

1. Describe the nature of advance-fee schemes.

2. Explain affinity fraud and why it is often successful.

3. Describe microcap frauds and pump-and-dump schemes.

4. Explain the appeal of pre-IPO investment scams to investors.

5. Explain the meaning of a prime bank investment fraud.

6. Discuss why frauds involving promissory notes, commodity pools, foreign currency trading, and precious metals lure victims.

7. Explain why FX trading is a "zero-sum game."

8. Identify some warning signs or red flags of investment frauds.

NOTES

1. Federal Bureau of Investigation. *Common fraud schemes*. Retrieved from https://www.fbi.gov/scams-safety/fraud

2. Ultracan Advanced Global Investigations. (2014, July 23). *419 Advance fee fraud statistics 2013*. Retrieved from http://www.ultrascan-agi.com/public_html/html/pdf_files/Pre-Release-419_Advance_Fee_Fraud_Statistics_2013-July-10-2014-NOT-FINAL-1.pdf

3. Levene, T. (2001). Beware email scam with a deadly sting. *The Guardian*, October 27. Retrieved from http://www.theguardian.com/guardian_jobs_and_money/story/0,,581433,00.html

4. Georgia Department of Law, Consumer Protection Unit. *Nigerian fraud scams*. Retrieved from http://consumer.georgia.gov/consumer-topics/nigerian-fraud-scams

5. U.S. Securities and Exchange Commission (SEC). *Advance fee frauds*. Retrieved from http://investor.gov/investing-basics/avoiding-fraud/types-fraud/advance-fee-fraud

6. ActionFraud. *Lottery scams*. National Fraud & Cyber Crime Centre. Retrieved from http://www.actionfraud.police.uk/fraud_protection/lottery_fraud.

7. "The U.K. National Fraud & Cyber Reporting Centre warns that 'Microsoft lottery' is a scam. (2010). *Actionfraud.police*, August 6. Retrieved from http://www.actionfraud.police.uk/microsoft-lottery-is-a-scam-aug10

8. The Government of Western Australia, Department of Commerce. (2014). Lady officer Gwen Roberts international Facebook lottery scam. *WaScamNet*, February 18. Retrieved from http://www.scamnet.wa.gov.au/scamnet/Types_Of_Scams-Advanced_fee_frauds-Gwen_Roberts_facebook_lottery_scam.htm.

9. Patterson, E. (2013, December 6). Scam email poses as award message from Microsoft. *Better Business Bureau*. Retrieved from http://www.bbb.org/blog/2013/12/scam-email-poses-as-award-message-from-microsoft/

10. U.S. Securities and Exchange Commission (SEC). *Affinity fraud: How to avoid investment scams that target groups*. Retrieved from http://www.sec.gov/investor/pubs/affinity.htm/

11. U.S. Securities and Exchange Commission (SEC). (2012). *Complaint: SEC vs city capital corporation, Ephren W. Taylor, II and Wendy Jean Connor*. Retrieved from http://www.sec.gov/litigation/complaints/2012/comp22330.pdf

12. Menzie, N. (2015). Ephren Taylor sentenced in $16M Ponzi scam that targeted megachurches led by Eddie Long, Joel Osteen. *The Christian Post*, March 17. Retrieved from http://www.christianpost.com/news/breaking-ephren-taylor-sentenced-in-16m-ponzi-scam-that-targeted-megachurches-led-by-eddie-long-joel-osteen-135844/

13. U.S. Securities and Exchange Commission (SEC). (2011). *Litigation release: SEC charges South Florida man with fraud in phony stock-trading funds*. Retrieved from http://www.sec.gov/litigation/litreleases/2012/lr22319.htm

14. Brinkman, P. (2013, June 12). Ponzi schemer George Eli gets 12 years. *South Florida Business Journal*. Retrieved from http://www.bizjournals.com/southflorida/news/2013/06/12/ponzi-schemer-george-elia-gets-12-years.html

15. U.S. Securities and Exchange Commission (SEC). High-yield investment frauds. Retrieved from http://investor.gov/investing-basics/avoiding-fraud/types-fraud/high-yield-investment-programs

16. Southern District of Illinois. (2010, May 28). *Criminal complaint: United States of America v. Nicholas A. Smirnov, a/k/a Nicoloy Smirnow, Alexander Judizcev, Nicholas Kachura, and Jeff Prozorowiczm*. Retrieved from http://www.justice.gov/sites/default/files/usao-sdil/legacy/2014/12/10/r_Compaint.pdf

17. Office of the U.S. Attorney, Southern District of Illinois. (2010, May 28). *News release: Resident of the Philippines charged by criminal complaint with numerous fraud offenses*. Retrieved from http://www.justice.gov/sites/default/files/usao-sdil/legacy/2014/12/10/Smirnow%20Press%20Release.pdf

18. United States Attorney, Southern District of Illinois. (2010, May 28). *Affidavit in support of criminal complaint: United States v. Nicholas A. Smirnov*. Retrieved from http://www.justice.gov/usao-sdil/victim-witness-assistance/smirnow

19. Maglich, J. (2012). Feds halt alleged $600 million zeekrewards Ponzi scheme: How it happened and what's next?" *Forbes*, August 18. Retrieved from http://www.forbes.com/sites/jordanmaglich/2012/08/18/

feds-halt-alleged-600-million-zeekrewards-ponzi-scheme-how-it-happened-and-whats-next/

20. Department of Justice, U.S. Attorney's Office, Western District of North Carolina. (2014, October 24). *ZeekRewards president indicted on federal charges for operating $850 million internet Ponzi scheme.* Retrieved from http://www.justice.gov/usao-wdnc/pr/zeekrewards-president-indicted-federal-charges-operating-850-million-internet-ponzi

21. U.S. Securities and Exchange Commission (SEC). (2012, August 17). *Complaint: SEC shuts down $600 million online pyramid and Ponzi scheme.* Retrieved from http://www.sec.gov/News/PressRelease/Detail/PressRelease/1365171483920

22. U.S. Securities and Exchange Commission (SEC). *Internet social media frauds.* Retrieved from http://investor.gov/investing-basics/avoiding-fraud/types-fraud/internet-social-media-fraud

23. U.S. Securities and Exchange Commission (SEC). (2011, October 14). *Litigation release: SEC v. Wall Street capital funding* LLC, Philip Cardwell, Roy Campbell, and Aaron Hume. Retrieved from https://www.sec.gov/litigation/litreleases/2011/lr22125.htm

24. United States District Court for the District of Maryland, Baltimore Division. (2003, November 14). *Amended complaint: SEC v. Agora, Inc., Pirate Investor, LLC and Frank Porter Stansberry.* Retrieved from https://www.sec.gov/litigation/complaints/comp18090.htm

25. United States District Court for the District of Maryland, Baltimore Division. (2003, November 13). *SEC v. Agora, Inc., Pirate Investor, LLC and Frank Porter Stansberry.* Retrieved from http://www.sec.gov/litigation/complaints/comp18090.htm

26. U.S. Securities and Exchange Commission (SEC). *Internet Social Media Frauds.* Retrieved from http://investor.gov/investing-basics/avoiding-fraud/types-fraud

27. Kolhatkar, S. (2013). Jordan Belfort, the real wolf of Wall Street. *BloombergBusiness*, November 7. Retrieved from http://www.bloomberg.com/news/articles/2013-11-07/jordan-belfort-the-real-wolf-of-wall-street

28. Bowers, S. (2011). Langbar international: The greatest stock market heist of all? *The Guardian*, June 24. Retrieved from http://www.theguardian.com/business/2011/jun/24/langbar-international-fraud-history

29. Mason, R. (2011). Langbar chief Stuart Pearson jailed over 'Grand Scale' aim fraud. *The Telegraph*, June 21. Retrieved from http://www. telegraph.co.uk/finance/financial-crime/8587952/Langbar-chief-Stuart-Pearson-jailed-over-grand-scale-AIM-fraud.html

30. U.S. Securities and Exchange Commission (SEC). *Microcap fraud.* Retrieved from http://www.sec.gov/spotlight/microcap-fraud.shtml

31. U.S. Securities and Exchange Commission (SEC). (2015, March 2). *Press release: SEC suspends trading in 128 dormant shell companies to put them out of reach of microcap fraudsters.* Retrieved from http:// www.sec.gov/news/pressrelease/2015-44.html

32. U.S. Securities and Exchange Commission (SEC). (2011, December 16). *Complaint: SEC charges Daniel 'Rudy' Ruettiger and 12 others in scheme to pump stock in sports drink company.* Retrieved from https:// www.sec.gov/news/press/2011/2011-268.htm

33. U.S. Securities and Exchange Commission (SEC). (2015, June 23). *Press release: SEC charges microcap promoter with illegally selling penny stock shares.* Retrieved from http://www.sec.gov/news/pressrelease/2015-129.html

34. The FBI, New York Field Office. (2015, June 23). *Press release: Secret owner of offshore brokerage firm arrested for alleged leadership role in a $300 million securities fraud and money laundering scheme.* Retrieved from https://www.fbi.gov/newyork/press-releases/2015/secret-owner-of-offshore-brokerage-firm-arrested-for-alleged-leadership-role-in-a-300-million-securities-fraud-and-money-laundering-scheme

35. Investopedia Staff. *IPO basics. Investopedia.* Retrieved from http:// www.investopedia.com/university/ipo/ipo.asp

36. U.S. Securities and Exchange Commission (SEC). *Pre IPO frauds.* Retrieved from http://investor.gov/investing-basics/avoiding-fraud/types-fraud/pre-ipo-investment-scams

37. Daneman, M. (2011). SEC sues man who said he wanted to buy American, Kodak. *USA Today,* May 5. Retrieved from http://usatoday30.usatoday.com/money/companies/management/2011-05-05-sec-american-kodak-bids_n.htm

38. *WPBF 25 News.* (2014). Allen Weintraub: Bounton beach man gets prison in Facebook stock fraud. *WPBF West Palm Beach,* April 28. Retrieved from http://www.wpbf.com/news/allen-weintraub-boynton-beach-man-gets-prison-in-facebook-stock-fraud/25692210

39. U.S. Securities and Exchange Commission (SEC). (2010, September 17). *SEC litigation release: SEC v. Randy M. Cho, district court enters judgment order setting disgorgement, prejudgment interest and a civil penalty against Randy M. Cho.* Retrieved from http://www.sec.gov/litigation/litreleases/2010/lr21654.htm

40. Singer, B. (2013). Ponzi fraudster gets 12 years in prison. *Forbes,* January 23. Retrieved from http://www.forbes.com/sites/billsinger/2013/01/23/ponzi-fraudster-gets-12-years-in-prison/

41. U.S. Securities and Exchange Commission (SEC). *How prime bank frauds work.* Retrieved from https://www.sec.gov/divisions/enforce/primebank/howtheywork.shtml

42. U.S. Securities and Exchange Commission (SEC). *Prime bank investments.* Retrieved from http://investor.gov/investing-basics/avoiding-fraud/types-fraud/prime-bank-investments

43. U.S. Securities and Exchange Commission (SEC). (2013, September 9). *Press release: SEC halts Florida-based prime bank investment scheme.* Retrieved from http://www.sec.gov/News/PressRelease/Detail/PressRelease/1370539799436

44. Mandak, J. (2014). Florida man gets 5 years in Pa. Loan Scam Case. *The Washington Times,* August 14. Retrieved from http://www.washingtontimes.com/news/2014/aug/14/florida-man-faces-loan-scam-sentence-in-pittsburgh/

45. U.S. Securities and Exchange Commission (SEC). *Promissory notes.* Retrieved from http://investor.gov/investing-basics/avoiding-fraud/types-fraud/promissory-notes

46. The Financial Industry Regulatory Authority (FINRA). (2014, July 14). *Investor alerts: Promissory notes can be less than promised.* Retrieved from http://www.finra.org/investors/alerts/promissory-notes-can-be-less-promised

47. The Financial Industry Regulatory Authority (FINRA). (2014, June 25). *News release: Ordered to pay $13.7 million in restitution; majority of defrauded investors were NFL and NBA players.* Retrieved from http://www.finra.org/newsroom/2014/finra-hearing-panel-expels-success-trade-securities-and-bars-ceo-fuad-ahmed-fraudulent

48. Hargett, M., & Caruso, P. C. (2010, May 8). *Medical capital fraud: How did it happen?"* Retrieved from http://www.investorprotection.com/blog/2010/05/08/medical-capital-fraud-how-did-it-happen/

49. AllGov California. (2013, May 6). *Wells Fargo 'Denies All Allegations' but pays $105 million in medical capital holdings fraud case.* Retrieved from http://www.allgov.com/USA/ca/news/where-is-the-money-going/wells-fargo-denies-all-allegations-but-pays-105-million-in-medical-capital-holdings-fraud-case-130506?news=849935

50. U.S. Commodity Futures Trading Commission (CFTC). *Commodity pool fraud.* Retrieved from http://www.cftc.gov/ConsumerProtection/FraudAwarenessPrevention/CFTCFraudAdvisories/fraudadv_commoditypool

51. U.S. Commodity Futures Trading Commission (CFTC). (2008, August 19). *Press release: Hedge fund trader Paul Eustace and Philadelphia Alternative Asset Management Co. Ordered to pay more than $279 million to defrauded customers and more than $20 million in civil monetary penalties in CFTC action.* Retrieved from http://www.cftc.gov/PressRoom/PressReleases/pr5531-08

52. United States District Court, Southern District of New York. (2009, May 24). *U.S. Commodity Futures Trading Commission v. Mark Evan Bloom and North Hills Management,* LLC. Retrieved from http://www.cftc.gov/ucm/groups/public/@lrenforcementactions/documents/legal-pleading/enfbloomcomplaint02252009.pdf

53. Stockbroker Fraud Blog. (2015, March 7). *District court imposes $26m commodity pool fraud penalty.* Retrieved from http://www.stock-brokerfraudblog.com/2015/03/district_court_imposes_26_comm.html

54. Cavallaro, M. The Forex market: Who trades currency and why. *Investopedia.* Retrieved from http://www.investopedia.com/articles/forex/11/who-trades-forex-and-why.asp

55. U.S. Commodity Futures Trading Commission (CFTC). *Foreign currency trading (Forex) fraud.* Retrieved from http://www.cftc.gov/ConsumerProtection/FraudAwarenessPrevention/CFTCFraudAdvisories/fraudadv_forex

56. United States District Court, District of Oregon. (2006, December 19). *The US commodity futures trading commission and state of Oregon Ex Rel Cory Streisinger, Director of the Department of Consumer and Business Services vs. Orion International, Inc., Russell B. Cline, April Duffy, Bangone Vorachiht, and Nancy Hoyt.* Retrieved from http://www.cftc.gov/ucm/groups/public/@lrenforcementactions/documents/legalpleading/enfclineorder.pdf

57. U. S. Commodity Futures Trading Commission (CFTC). (2007, January 11). *Press release: U.S. district court for the district of Oregon enters final order against mastermind of multimillion dollar fraudulent foreign currency (Forex) scam.* Retrieved from http://www.cftc.gov/PressRoom/PressReleases/pr5274-07/

58. Grant, J. (2007). Fraudster fined $33 m for biggest US retail foreign exchange scam. *Financial Times,* January 12. Retrieved from http://www.ft.com/intl/cms/s/0/8069ecf0-a1e1-11db-8bc1-0000779e2340.html#axzz3o0Wj3rhG

59. Robinson, E. (2006). Refco's collapse reveals decades of quarrels with regulators. *Bloomberg*, January 5. Retrieved from http://www.bloomberg.com/apps/news?pid=newsarchive&sid=a50aqPG7x7qo

60. Nasaw, D. (2008). Refco chief sentenced to 16 years. *The Guardian,* July 3. Retrieved from http://www.theguardian.com/business/2008/jul/03/refco.fraud

61. Van Voris, B. (2014).Ex-refco executives hit with $672 million court judgment. *BloombergBusiness*, June 2. Retrieved from http://www.bloomberg.com/news/articles/2014-06-02/ex-refco-executives-hit-with-672-million-court-judgment

62. Conover, C. M., Jensen, G. R., Johnson, R. R., & Mercer, J. M. (2009). Can precious metals make your portfolio shine? *Journal of Investing*, 18(1), 75–86. Retrieved from https://www.researchgate.net/publication/228478827_Can_Precious_Metals_Make_Your_Portfolio_Shine

63. U.S. Commodity Futures Trading Commission (CFTC). *Precious metals fraud.* Retrieved from http://www.cftc.gov/ConsumerProtection/FraudAwarenessPrevention/CFTCFraudAdvisories/fraudadv_preciousmetals

64. U.S. Commodity Futures Trading Commission (CFTC). (2014, May 22). *Release: CFTC wins fraud trial against Hunter Wise related precious metals firms and their owners.* Retrieved from http://www.cftc.gov/PressRoom/PressReleases/pr6935-14

65. Maglich, J. (2012). A Ponzi Schemer parts with his silver. *Forbes,* September 17. Retrieved from http://www.forbes.com/sites/jordanmaglich/2012/09/17/a-ponzi-schemer-parts-with-his-silver/

66. U.S. Commodity Futures Trading Commission (CFTC). (2013, February 28). *Release: CFTC settles charges against Ronnie Gene*

Wilson of South Carolina and his company, Atlantic Bullion and Coin, for Operating a Multi-Million Dollar Silver Bullion Ponzi Scheme. Retrieved from http://www.cftc.gov/PressRoom/PressReleases/pr6524-13

67. Rains, J. (2013). *5 sure-fire signs of an investment scam. WiseBread,* July 9. Retrieved from http://www.wisebread.com/5-sure-fire-signs-of-an-investment-scam

7

TRAP 3: MISREPRESENTING RISKY PRODUCTS AS SAFE

Within the investment industry, there is a tendency to over promise, and provide false guarantees about how an investment product will perform.

Code of Ethics and Standards of Professional
Conduct, The CFA Institute

Although Bernie Madoff vowed to deliver consistent returns regardless of the performance of market conditions, the "fund" was actually an investment fraud in the form of a Ponzi scheme. He preyed on unsuspecting investors by pretending to provide a solution to risk-averse investors. A key lesson learned from the Madoff case is that investments that appear too good to be true typically don't deliver.

Many investors are attracted to investments promising stable returns. This desire helps explain why so many "stable returns," "capital guaranteed," and "low volatility" products are available in financial markets. Although these descriptions may accurately describe some products, less scrupulous individuals or firms may misrepresent risky products as safe. *Misrepresentation* is a misstatement of the facts, giving a false or misleading account of the product's nature. It is deceptive and untrue. For example, suppose that a stockbroker misrepresents an investment or fails to disclose vital information about it. A misrepresentation does not have to be intentionally false to create liability. A statement made with conscious ignorance or a reckless disregard for the truth can create liability. To prove misrepresentation you will probably need to show that (1) you lost money on the investment due to the misrepresentation or omission, (2) the broker misrepresented the security or omitted information about it, and (3) you relied on the advice of your broker, advisor, or financial planner.

Sometimes the riskiness of an investment product can be misrepresented. Although no perfect definitions or measurements of risk are available, risk varies among different investments. A good way to think about risk, especially for inexperienced investors, is in terms of the odds that a given investment or portfolio will fail to achieve the expected return, and the magnitude by which it will miss that target. Investors should consider both the likelihood and the magnitude of bad outcomes.[1] A *low-risk investment* is one that has a small chance of loss but none of the potential losses are devastating. Low-risk investments typically offer modest or meager returns without much upside potential. Furthermore, inflation can erode the purchasing power of money kept in low-risk investments. Examples of low-risk investments include U.S. Treasury securities, saving bonds, certificates of deposit, savings accounts, and money market mutual funds (MMFs).[2]

In contrast, a *high risk investment* has either a large chance of loss of capital or underperformance or a relatively large chance of a devastating loss. High risk investments usually have a high potential reward but large gains are not guaranteed. Examples of high risk investments include investments in initial public offerings, venture capital, penny stocks, emerging markets, rental houses, collectibles, and precious metals. Although tempting, novice investors should typically avoid such investments and focus on more pedestrian options.[3] However, more experienced investors who seek higher returns must be willing and able to accept higher investment risk and the possibility of losing money. As Robert Arnott, an American entrepreneur, investor, editor, and writer, notes, "In investing, what is comfortable is rarely profitable." In most cases, you can't have your cake and eat it too. Investments always involve trade-offs.

This chapter examines several cases when a supposedly low-risk investment turns out to be high risk, including mortgage-backed securities, preference shares, MMFs with floating rate notes (FRNs), and Minibonds. Misrepresenting risky projects as safe occurs in many settings. Therefore, the chapter presents examples from several countries — the United States, Spain, Finland, and Hong Kong — and offers advice on how to avoid falling into this investment trap.

MORTGAGE-BACKED SECURITIES

When the technology market crashed in 2000, many investors shifted their attention from the stock market to housing. Further fueling the housing bubble, cheap money was available for new loans in the wake of the economic recession. The Federal Reserve or simply the Fed, which is the central banking system of the United States, stimulated the struggling U.S. economy by cutting interest rates to historically low levels. The Fed and banks praised the housing market for helping to create wealth and provide a secured asset that people could borrow money against.

Mortgage-backed securities helped to finance the expansion of household debt. A *mortgage-back security* (MBS) is a type of asset-backed security that is secured by a mortgage or collection of mortgages. The mortgages are sold to a group that securitizes, or packages, the loans together into a security that investors can buy. For example, these loans are pooled by governmental (the Government National Mortgage Association or Ginnie Mae), quasi-governmental (the Federal National Mortgage Association or Fannie Mae), the Federal Home Loan Mortgage Corporation (Freddie Mac), or private entities (banks and other financial institutions). These pools of mortgage loans are then issued as securities through a process called *securitization* that represents claims on the principal and interest payments made by borrowers. Many types of MBS, besides the most basic types, entitle the holder to a pro-rata share (or proportionate allocation) of all principal and interest payments. These include collateralized mortgage obligations and mortgage derivatives, which may be designed to protect investors from or expose investors to various types of risk.[4]

Investors sought out these securitized and seemingly low-risk products because they appeared to provide good returns in a world of low interest rates. Low interest rates created an incentive for U.S. and international banks, hedge funds, and other investors to search for riskier assets that offered higher returns. Also, the government-sponsored mortgage finance companies — Fannie Mae and Freddie Mac — bought some of these existing mortgages.

As part of the U.S. housing boom between 2002 and 2007, the amount of MBS greatly increased. Some lenders extended mortgages to those who couldn't qualify for traditional loans because of a weak credit history or other factors ("No Income, No Job"). These are called subprime loans. *Subprime* refers to the credit quality of particular borrowers, who have weakened credit histories and a greater risk of loan default than prime borrowers. After being granted, these subprime loans were passed to large financial institutions that packaged and securitized them to form MBS. These MBS were supposedly of low risk because the large number of loans would average out any big losses to their holders. This worked well as long as the loans were uncorrelated and defaulted randomly with respect to each other. Consequently, most MBS received the highest credit ratings. Although the large banks argued that the property markets in different American cities would rise and fall independently of one another (i.e., prices would be uncorrelated), this was not the case. Starting in 2006, the United States suffered a nationwide house-price slump. As housing prices declined, major global financial institutions that had borrowed and invested heavily in MBS reported substantial losses.

When the U.S. housing market turned, a chain reaction exposed frailties in the global financial system. Pooling and other clever financial engineering did not provide investors with the protections promised. MBS slumped in value, if they had value at all. Uncertainty over who was holding the toxic assets caused the interbank credit markets to dry up. Many financial institutions suffered losses they couldn't bear and were either forced into bankruptcy or government bailout. As a result, credit taps were closed to individuals and businesses and the world faced its most severe economic downturn since the Great Depression.[5]

Bear Stearns, then the fifth-largest U.S. investment bank, was heavily involved in packaging and reselling subprime MBS. It had a reputation as an aggressive trading bank willing to take risks. *Fortune* magazine listed the firm as one of the most respected securities firms in 2005 through 2007. Throughout its history, Bear Stearns was both innovative and creative, which at times caused it to take some risky positions. The firm's management tended to focus on immediate opportunistic returns with little long-term strategic planning. Bear Stearns was heavily involved in securitization and issued large amounts of asset-backed securities (ABS). Despite the evidence of weaknesses in the mortgage market, Bear Stearns increased its exposure in 2006 and 2007 to gain market share.[6] As discussed shortly, Bear Stearns failed in 2008 as part of the global financial crisis and recession and was subsequently sold to JPMorgan Chase.

Washington Mutual was one of the most active retail mortgage lenders. Washington Mutual, Inc. (WaMu) was a savings bank holding company and former owner of Washington Mutual Bank, which was the largest U.S. savings and loan association until its collapse in 2008. Kerry Killinger, President and CEO of WaMu, sought to build WaMu into the "Walmart of Banking." In 2003, Killinger stated: "We hope to do to this industry what Walmart did to theirs, Starbucks did to theirs, Costco did to theirs and Lowe's-Home Depot did to their industry. And I think if we've done our job, five years from now you're not going to call us a bank."[7]

During Killinger's tenure, WaMu pressed sales agents to pump out loans while disregarding borrowers' incomes and assets. WaMu gave mortgage brokers handsome commissions for selling the riskiest loans, which carried higher fees, bolstering profits, and ultimately the compensation of the bank's executives. WaMu pressured appraisers to provide inflated property values that made loans appear less risky, enabling Wall Street to bundle them more easily to sell to investors. WaMu embraced so-called adjustable rate mortgages (ARMs), that enticed borrowers with a selection of low initial rates and allowed them to decide how much to pay each month. An *adjustable rate mortgage* is a mortgage on which the interest rate is fixed for a period at the beginning, called the "initial rate period," but after that, it periodically adjusts based on movements of an underlying benchmark interest rate. For WaMu, ARMs were especially attractive because they carried higher fees than other loans and allowed WaMu to book profits on interest payments that borrowers deferred. Because WaMu was selling many of its loans to investors, it did not worry about defaults because by the time the loans went bad, they were often already in other hands.

Bear Stearns and WaMu took home loans made by retail banks and mortgage brokers all over the country, and sold them to investors in the United States and around the globe. Many of the loans were subprime. Because subprime borrowers have weak credit, make small down payments, or both, they are likely to have difficulty maintaining the repayment schedule if the economy worsens. When many such homebuyers defaulted on their mortgages as the U.S. property bubble burst, the linked securities turned into bad debt. Securities that had been rated AAA but were based on faulty underlying mortgages turned out to be junk. This caused billion-dollar losses at banks, which had to write down the value of their investments. Also, MBS investors lost massive amounts of money because borrowers could not make their mortgage payments.

In March 2008, Bear Stearns signed a merger agreement with JPMorgan Chase & Co. in a stock swap worth $2 a share, less than 7% of Bear Stearns' market value just two days earlier. JPMorgan bought the company to prevent it from collapsing based on a deal facilitated with a $29 billion loan from the Federal Reserve. In September 2008, Washington Mutual filed for Chapter 11 bankruptcy. JPMorgan Chase acquired the banking operations of WaMu.

Later, investigators examined the practices of JPMorgan, Washington Mutual, and Bear Stearns related to the sale and issuance of residential mortgage-backed securities (RMBS) between 2005 and 2008. On November 19, 2013, the DOJ, along with federal and state partners, announced a $13 billion settlement with JPMorgan — the largest settlement with a single entity in American history — to resolve federal and state civil claims arising from the packaging, marketing, sale, and issuance of RMBS by JPMorgan, Washington Mutual, and Bear Stearns before January 1, 2009. As part of the settlement, JPMorgan acknowledged it made serious misrepresentations to the public, including the investing public, about numerous RMBS transactions.

The settlement included a statement of facts in which JPMorgan acknowledged that it regularly represented to RMBS investors that the mortgage loans in various securities complied with underwriting guidelines. In the United States, *mortgage underwriting* is the process a lender uses to determine if the risk of offering a mortgage loan to a particular borrower under certain parameters is acceptable. Contrary to those representations, on various occasions, JPMorgan employees knew that the loans in question did not comply with those guidelines and were not otherwise appropriate for securitization. Nonetheless, they allowed the loans to be securitized — and those securities to be sold — without disclosing this information to investors. This conduct, along with similar conduct by other banks that bundled toxic loans into securities and misled investors who purchased those securities, contributed to the financial crisis of 2007 – 2009. The settlement did not absolve JPMorgan or its employees from facing any possible civil charges or criminal prosecution. After the settlement, bank executives emphasized that they had not admitted to any specific violation of the law.

On September 19, 2014, a federal judge said that JPMorgan must face a class action lawsuit by investors who claimed that the bank misled them about the credit quality of the home loans behind the $10 billion of MBS it sold before the financial crisis. The lawsuit stated that JPMorgan misled prospective investors about the underlying, appraisals and credit quality of the home loans underlying the mortgage-backed certificates. By the time the litigation began in March 2009, six months after Lehman Brothers Holdings Inc. failed, the certificates were worth at most 62 cents on the dollar.[8]

In this case, banks and other financial institutions misrepresented MBS as being safe. Financial institutions also engaged in fraudulent behavior when packaging, marketing, selling, and issuing MBS. Institutions also sold these complex structured products to those in the investing public who were unable to assess the credit risk of such securities. Investors looking for stable returns ended up holding risky securities whose values fell massively when the U.S. housing boom ended.

Trap Judgment

Mortgage-Backed Securities

Becoming a victim of investment fraud

Misrepresenting risky products as safe

Making unrealistic excessive return expectations

Falling for mutual fund traps

Overpaying for products and services

Investing in complex products

Engaging in gambling disguised as investing

Relying on unsupported promises

PREFERENCE SHARES

Preference shares, also called *preferred stock*, offer holders a higher claim to a company's assets and earnings than common stockholders. For instance, preference shares allow an investor to own a stake of the issuing company with a condition that whenever the company decides to pay dividends, the holders of the preference shares will be the first to be paid. In return for this higher priority of claims, those holding preference shares usually do not have voting rights. Preference shares typically pay a fixed rate dividend, given the company generates sufficient earnings to pay them out as dividends. Preference shares are often less liquid than common stock and may be callable and contain other firm-specific restrictions or qualifications. These differences affect share valuation by making them more complex. Traditionally, the major buyers of preference shares were institutional and other professional investors rather than *retail investors*, who are individual investors who buy and sell securities for their personal accounts and not for another company or organization.

At the end of the 1990s, Spanish banks created a "mastermind/bulletproof idea" on how to strengthen their capital structures with much needed equity in a cost-effective manner. They actively sold preference shares as an investment alternative to their every-day clients. As Carmen Munoz, a senior director at Fitch Ratings in Spain, notes: "The sale of subordinated debt and preference shares through banks' branch networks (to retail clients) has been common practice in Spain for some time." In practice, this meant advising pensioners, school teachers, and others in towns and communities throughout Spain to invest their savings in these rela-tively complex securities.

Banks followed the questionable strategy of selling preference shares to their clients or customers. In doing so, banks misused their positions of trust. In small towns, where Spanish banks mainly sold these products, the banks and their employees tradi-tionally had strong, even family-like, ties with their clients. In some instances, banks opened accounts with deposits as gifts for newborns and held festivities where bankers and town residents could dine and party together.

The bankers described the products as risk-free or as "sure things" and personally guaranteed that investors wouldn't lose their money. They also reassured clients with promises of excellent liquidity and indicated that holders of preference shares, as well as subordinated debt, could easily sell these products if they needed cash. *Subordinated debt* is debt that ranks after other debts if a company falls into liquidation or bankruptcy. Bankers neither informed their customers that returns were not guaranteed nor that the state Deposit Guarantee Fund would not cover losses.

Professional financial advisors and managers of the retail branches advised their retail clients to invest in a complex, high-yield financial instrument designed for institutional and professional investors. Moreover, a substantial majority of these retail clients were elderly and financially illiterate. According to a report by the Consumers and Users Organization, 80% of those affected were more than 65 years old. Further, these individuals placed strong trust in the bank repre-sentatives. In fact, many individuals who invested in preference shares thought they were making ordinary deposits in the bank.[9]

The situation seemed relatively good from 1999 until 2008. The owners of preference shares received the promised high yields and asked few questions while the banks enjoyed cheap equity financing. Many bank employees actually believed that they were selling a good product.

Spain's major banks and savings banks (cajas de ahorro) sold around €31 billion worth of preferential shares. Managers instructed banking staff to pressure customers, who for the most part had no idea of the nature of these financial products, to buy these shares. Banks used sales incentives schemes to encourage the banking staff to sell these riskier hybrid products instead of normal savings accounts. The questionable practices included the following:

- Providing misleading information about the riskiness of the product.

- Aggressively selling these products to their existing retail customers.

- Claiming that these products are "guaranteed" or similar to "safe" banking deposits.

- Providing unsuitable advice to purchase these products.[9]

As the Spanish real estate bubble burst in 2008, investors worldwide began to shun the low-quality debt of Spanish banks. Banks not in good financial shape found themselves needing increasingly larger amounts of capital. Their solution wasn't to fix the fundamentals of their business; instead, banks chose to improve their balance sheets with a familiar and proven strategy — selling more preference shares to their retail clients. The issue peaked in 2008 and 2009 with Spanish banks selling more than €12 billion worth of preference shares. When more sophisticated investors turned their backs on the banks, these banks turned to their loyal depositors to bail them out. Given the absence of transparency and the lack of financial literacy of their clients, this situation was bound to have dire consequences.

With bank fundamentals in poor shape, the bailout from clients was only a temporary fix. As preference shareholders started to realize the problems associated with their shares, many tried to sell their holdings. However, the liquidity of these shares evaporated with increasingly smaller daily volume of preference shares. Spain's dismal economy generated this situation. As the financial situation of these savings banks deteriorated, consumers found that they were facing substantial losses of their capital. Recapitalization of the savings banks resulted in converting preferred shares into ordinary shares. Eventually, preference shareholders received an offer to convert their holdings to common stocks resulting in 70–80% losses on their initial investments.

In summary, Spanish banks clearly engaged in inappropriate practices resulting in many clients filing claims and engaging in mass protests. Spanish banks sold preference shares to about 710,000 customers and their families. The Spanish financial consumer association (ADICAE) reported receiving more than 30,000 complaints about the case. Eventually, some banks issued public apologies. For example, Chairman Jose Maria Castellano and CEO Cesar Gonzalez-Bueno of NCG Banco stated: "We apologize for having sold preferred shares among individual clients that didn't have sufficient financial know-how, causing them such serious problems." Prime Minister Mariano Rajoy told parliament on June 27, 2012, that banks "acted wrongly" on preferred shares. Luis de Guindos, Minister of Economy and Competitiveness told a parliamentary committee that the notes should never have been sold to retail customers.[10]

In this case, banks misrepresented preference shares as being safe. They sold a complex product to investors who did not understand its nature. Banks also engaged in fraudulent behavior by selling shares to those who relied on them to provide adequate information for decision-making purposes. Financially illiterate customers thought they had made a low-risk bank deposit, but later realized that they had preference shares whose values plummeted.

Trap Judgment

Preference shares

Becoming a victim of investment fraud

Misrepresenting risky products as safe

Making unrealistic return expectations

Falling for mutual fund traps

Overpaying for products and services

Investing in complex products

Engaging in gambling disguised as investing

Relying on unsupported promises

MONEY MARKET FUNDS WITH FLOATING RATE NOTES

A MMF is an open-ended mutual fund that invests in short-term (i.e., less than one year) debt securities representing high quality, liquid debt, and monetary instruments. MMF shareholders rely upon the credit quality, liquidity, diversification, transparency, and sound management of the portfolio — not on a government or private guarantee — to lessen investment risks.

MMFs try to limit exposure to losses due to credit, market, and liquidity risks. *Credit risk* refers to the risk that an issuer of any type of debt might fail to make required payments. *Market risk* is the risk that an investment's value might decrease in response to general market and economic conditions or events such as recessions, political turmoil, or changes in interest rates. *Liquidity risk* is the risk stemming from an investment's inability to be traded quickly enough in the market to prevent or minimize a loss. By reducing such risk exposures, MMFs typically offer a safe place to invest easily accessible, cash-equivalent assets and represent low-risk, low-return investments.

In the United States, MMFs emerged in the 1970s when the regulation of the Federal Reserve Board capped the interest that banks could pay on deposits at a level below market yields. The main objective of MMFs is to maintain a stable value of $1 per share while offering money market yields to investors. Although interest rate regulation ended in 1986, the market for MMFs continued to grow. In June 2014, MMFs managed assets were worth €3.2 trillion worldwide. The U.S. market accounts for 58% and Europe constitutes 28% of the global money market assets. This figure represents 13% of the entire mutual fund industry (€25 trillion).[11]

Net asset value (NAV) is a mutual fund's value determined by deducting the fund's liabilities from the market value of all of its shares and then dividing by the number of issued shares. Before the credit crunch in 2007 – 2008, many considered MMFs one of the safest places to put cash. A *credit crunch*, also called a *credit squeeze* or *credit crisis*, refers to a reduction in the general availability of loans or credit or a sudden tightening of the conditions required to obtain a loan from a bank.[12] Although many investors view MMFs to be as safe as bank deposits while providing a higher yield, this characterization is not necessarily accurate. MMFs are investments offering no guarantees. The collapse of Lehman Brothers in September 2008 led to an investor run on the U.S. MMFs. The outflows accelerated when the Reserve Primary Fund, a large MMF, announced it had *broken the buck*, which means that the fund's mark-to-market value deviated from its constant NAV by more than 0.5 cents and the fund's shares had to be re-priced to less than a dollar ("buck"). *Mark to market* is a measure of the fair value of accounts that can change over time. To restore investor confidence, the U.S. Treasury announced a program that guaranteed the share price of $1 for MMFs.

In Europe, the MMF industry consists of two market segments. In one segment, funds based on a constant net asset valuation (CNAV or constant NAV) have a 57% market share. In the other segment, funds using variable net asset valuation (VNAV or variable NAV) account for 43% of the market. Income in CNAV funds is accrued daily and usually is treated as a capital gain reflected in an increased NAV.

Despite the structural differences between the euro area and U.S. markets, MMFs from an investor's perspective are a financial service that offers money market returns while reducing risk through portfolio diversification. Those offering MMFs, such as mutual funds, brokerage firms, and banks, market them to customers looking for a secure investment alternative. The events that took place especially during the second half of 2008 substantially reduced the market values of some MMFs. Banks and others, faced a new challenge in marketing their MMFs.

Let's examine what happened to two MMFs in Finland, the Nordea Euro MMF and Nordea Pro Euro MMF. In 2006, Nordea Bank had about 10 million customers, 1400 branch offices, and a leading banking position with 5.2 million e-customers. At the end of 2006, the company was the largest Finnish mutual fund company with a market share of 31.6% and 921,963 investors. The company had increased its market share from 23.8%.

The target market for Nordea Euro MMF was savers and investors who were seeking an easy way to invest in fixed-income securities and wanted a stable yield higher than a fixed-term deposit can offer. The fund's investment policy stated that "even relatively cautious investors can invest a substantial proportion of their assets in this fund." Investors needed no prior knowledge or experience on fixed-income markets. By contrast, the Nordea Pro Euro MMF was specially designed for institutional investors, given its higher minimum investment and lower administration fee percentage. The target market for this fund consisted of investors who were looking for a stable yield higher than that of fixed-term deposits. Both funds used variable net asset valuation.

Nordea MMFs invested mainly in euro-denominated floating rate notes (FRNs or "floaters"), other bonds with a short duration, and money market instruments issued by companies within the EU area. A *floating rate note* is an unsecured debt issue with an interest rate that is reset at specified intervals according to a predetermined formula. For example, FRNs often have quarterly coupons, meaning they pay interest every three months.

Fixed-coupon bonds are subject to *interest rate risk*, which is the risk that an investment's value will change due to a change in the absolute level of interest rates. An inverse relation exists between bonds and interest rates — that is, as interest rates rise, the prices of fixed-income instruments such as bonds might fall. The reason is straightforward: when interest rates increase, new issues come to market with higher yields than older securities, making those older ones worth less. Hence, their prices go down.[13]

The duration for FRNs was set to three to six months, while the maturity was allowed to be over a year. *Duration* is an approximate measure of a bond's price sensitivity to changes in interest rates. It is an important measure in bond markets. A fixed-coupon bond with higher duration carries more (interest rate) risk than a bond with lower duration. FRNs carry little interest rate risk, as their duration is only months, and their price shows very low sensitivity to changes in market rates. When market rates rise, the expected coupons of a FRN increase in line with the increase in forward rates, which means its price remains constant. FRNs differ from fixed rate bonds, whose prices decline when market rates rise. As FRNs are almost immune to interest rate risk, they are considered conservative investments for investors who believe market rates will increase.

The minimization of interest rate sensitivity causes some investors to make the mistake of thinking that FRN's are substitutes for money market accounts or other high-quality short-term investments. However, they entail substantial credit risk. Given the investment policies of the two Nordea's MMFs, interest rate risk related to the funds was low, but risk related to changes in credit risk premiums was high. For many years, analysts estimated the credit risk exposure as very low because the issuers of FRNs had high credit ratings. Since Nordea's funds invested only in Euro-denominated paper, they were not exposed to *currency risk*, which is a form of risk that arises from the change in price of one currency against another. Although Nordea's MMFs performed well, they had high exposure to changes in credit risk premiums because the portfolios included a substantial proportion of securities with long maturity (FRNs). The floating rate protected funds against changes in general interest rates but not against changes in risk premiums.

Nordea's MMFs attracted considerable attention among investors. At the end of 2007, investors had invested €5 billion into the two funds: Euro Money Market and Pro Euro Money Market. This represented 25% of the total fund assets (€20 billion) of Nordea.

During fall 2008, the risk premiums for bonds issued by banks skyrocketed, causing the value of bonds to fall. Increased risk premiums also caused the value of FRNs to fall. **Figure 7.1** shows the price development of Nordea's MMFs from January 2007 to April 2009. The value of Pro Euro MMF declined 16% from the peak in August 2008 to the bottom in April 2009. The corresponding decline for Euro MMF was a shocking 13%.

Frightened by the value decrease, investors began to redeem their holdings from Nordea's MMFs. Even worse, the funds had to liquidate their assets at bargain prices to cover these redemptions, deepening their losses. As **Figure 7.2** shows, many investors left the funds by redeeming their fund shares: 9400 investors left the Euro MMFs (a 26% decrease in the number of investors) in September 2008 through April 2009. Correspondingly, 1700 investors left the Pro Euro MMF (a 36% decrease). In terms of assets under management (AUM), Nordea lost €2 billion in just half a year.

The Finnish Securities Complaint Board (FSCB) received many complaints and inquiries about the performance of MMFs. According to Satu Kouvolainen, secretary of the FSCB, "The customers had ordered a time deposit, but their money has ended up in a money market fund."[14] The FSCB examined the brochures used in marketing MMFs and found that many brochures stated that the fund was a good alternative for a bank deposit. The Finnish Financial Supervisory Authority (Finnish FSA) conducted its own investigation in 2009 into mutual fund brochures and

Figure 7.1: The Development of the Value of the Euro Money Market Fund and Pro Euro Money Market Fund: January 2007 to April 2009

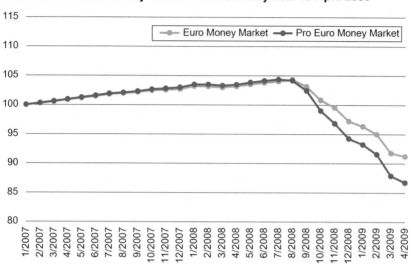

Source: Monthly Mutual Fund Reports January 2007 to April 2009 (The Finnish Association of Mutual Funds, www.sijoitustutkimus.fi). Notes: This figure shows the initial rise and dramatic decline beginning in August 2008 in the value of both the Euro Money Market Fund and Pro Euro Money Market Fund.

found that all the brochures failed to describe truthfully the funds' investment policies and risks. Some of these were MMFs that marketed themselves as substitutes for bank deposits. In a follow-up investigation in 2010, the Finnish FSA reported that the information content of fund prospectuses had improved. It also referred to the new European level guidelines on a common definition for MMFs by the Committee of European Securities Regulators. As of July 2011, European MMFs must provide investors with appropriate information on the fund's risk and reward profile to enable investors to identify any specific risks linked to the investment strategy of the fund.[15]

Nordea acted more quickly. It shut down its MMFs that had been hit hard by the financial crisis in May 2009 and divided the funds into two new MMFs. One fund had low-risk and low expected return, whereas the other had higher risk and higher expected return. Investors received shares of the two new funds

Figure 7.2: The Number of Investors in Two Nordea's MMFs

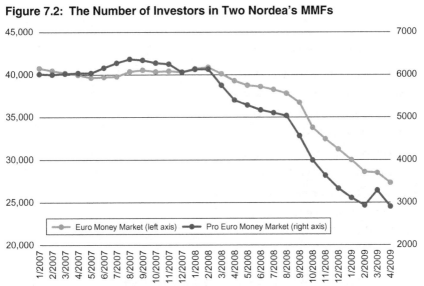

Source: Monthly Mutual Fund Reports January 2007 to April 2009 (The Finnish Association of Mutual Funds, www.sijoitustutkimus.fi). *Notes*: This figure shows how the number of investors in the Euro Money Market Fund decreased from 36,000 in September 2008 to 27,000 in April 2009. Correspondingly, the number of investors in the Pro Euro Money Market Fund decreased from 4600 in September 2008 to 2900 in April 2009.

with respect to their holdings in the funds that were closed. After 12 months, the low-risk fund had an annual realized return of 1.2%. Meanwhile, credit risk fears lessened and the higher risk fund had an annual realized return of 10.4%.

Nordea clearly downplayed some vital aspects of risks in its MMFs, specifically the large proportion of FRNs in the portfolios. They misrepresented a product as safe by marketing its MMFs as a good alternative for a bank deposit. Most investors probably failed to understand that MMFs could be exposed to credit risk. This view can be concluded from the massive outflows from the funds in autumn 2008 when the values of FRNs began falling reflecting increased credit risk. Nordea sold complex products to untrained investors who did not understand that MMFs may invest so much in FRNs whose values decrease as risk premiums skyrocket.

Trap Judgment

Money Market Funds with Floating Rate Notes

Becoming a victim of investment fraud

Misrepresenting risky products as safe

Making unrealistic return expectations

Falling into mutual fund traps

Overpaying for products and services

Investing in complex products

Engaging in gambling disguised as investing

Relying on unsupported promises

HONG KONG MINIBONDS

An old man in a trembling voice made the following statement during a meeting on September 1, 2010, organized by the Consumer Council of Hong Kong, ChinaStakes:

> *I am illiterate. I have deposited my savings in the bank year after year. When the salesman (at the bank) recommended me the Minibonds as the most suitable financial product for retirement, promising higher interest rate and low risk, I invested HK$500,000, all the money I have saved from decades of manual work.*

In Hong Kong, consumers suffered large losses in 2008 after investing in Minibonds. *Minibond* is a brand name for a series of structured financial notes. Using the term "bond" to describe these products is misleading. The return paid by these structured products was linked to a basket of shares, a stock market index, or the creditworthiness of various publicly listed corporations. Both the return and the consumer's original investment depended on the ability of the issuing investment bank to make the payments due under the structured product. Lehman Brothers was the investment bank.

Minibonds typically promised a coupon of 5% or more, far higher than fixed deposit rates at the time. The name "bond" was intended to inspire confidence, but in reality Minibonds were credit-linked notes assembled using complex derivatives. A *credit linked note* (CLN) is a form of funded *credit derivative*, which is a financial instrument whose value is determined by the default risk of an underlying asset. A CLN is structured as a security with an embedded credit default swap allowing the issuer to transfer a specific credit risk to credit investors. The issuer has no obligation to repay the debt if a specified event occurs. Many customers thought they were making a deposit, only with a higher yield. What they were actually doing was writing insurance against defaults by a portfolio of companies.

In total, more than 43,700 consumers bought HK $20.23 billion (US $2.6 billion) worth of Lehman Brothers structured products through retail banks. When Lehman Brothers collapsed in September 2008, the holders of Minibonds suffered major losses. The issuer behind the Minibonds was Pacific International Finance Limited (PIF), a special purpose entity (SPE) created by Lehman Brothers. A *special purpose entity* is a legal entity to fulfill narrow, specific or temporary objectives. Companies typically use SPEs to isolate the firm from financial risk. Investors paid their initial investments to PIF, which then used the proceeds to buy credit-related instruments, specifically collateralized debt obligations (CDOs), with variable coupon payments. A *collateralized debt obligation* is a type of structured ABS such as mortgages, bonds, and loans. The pooled assets are basically debt obligations that serve as collateral for the CDO. Posting these CDOs as collateral for Minibonds enabled them to initially carry an *AAA rating*, which is the highest possible rating that credit rating agencies assign to an issuer's bonds. Investors would receive an annualized coupon of about 5% quarterly and a proportion of the principal at maturity, depending on various factors explained later. PIF entered into several swap agreements with Lehman Brothers Special Financing Inc. (LBSF), another subsidiary of Lehman Brothers. A *swap* is a derivative in which two counterparties exchange cash flows of one party's financial instrument for those of the other party's financial instrument.

The terms of the swaps between PIF and LBSF indicated that if a credit event related to the reference companies occurs, PIF would transfer the CDOs held as collateral to LBSF and receive in return a redemption payment equal to the market value of the debt obligations of the reference companies. A *credit event* is any sudden and tangible (negative) change in a borrower's credit standing or decline in credit rating. A credit event brings into question the borrower's ability to repay its debt. Credit derivative transactions refer to various standard credit events including bankruptcy, failure to pay, restructuring, repudiation, moratorium, obligation acceleration, and obligation default.[16]

In case of a credit event, PIF would then redeem Minibonds from the investors at a price reflecting the market value of the reference companies' debt obligations. This meant that if a credit event occurred, investors would lose a portion of their principal because the market value of the debt obligations was likely to be less than the initial investment. The amount that investors would recover in the case of a credit event was also adjusted for the market value of the collateral (i.e., the CDOs) and the fair value of the swaps. The fair value of a swap depends on the changes in the price of the underlying asset, which in this case meant interest and exchange rates.

Once a credit event occurred, the bonds stopped accruing interest and investors received no coupon payments. The money received by the issuer from LBSF was not payable to investors until the maturity date of the bonds, which ranged from three to six years. Additionally, PIF reserved the right to call Minibonds prematurely. For example, PIF could call the Minibonds before maturity on the basis of the termination of the swap agreements, which could be caused by events such as the bankruptcy of LBSF. In this case PIF would sell the CDOs used as collateral at the prevalent market prices and use the proceeds to redeem Minibonds from the investors. If the value of the collateral was less than the nominal value of Minibonds, investors would face a loss. This arrangement implicitly exposed investors to the counterparty risk associated with the swaps between PIF and LBSF. Investors had to carry several risks to realize the marketed 5% return: credit risk on the reference companies and the CDOs, market value risk on the CDOs, interest rate and exchange rate risks, and swap counterparty risk to LBSF and Lehman Brothers.

Despite the complex structure of the Minibonds, retail investors were eager to buy them. Unconventional investment products were in great demand in Hong Kong in the early 2000s due to the low yields offered by many traditional investments. Also, sellers offered different promotional gifts such as supermarket vouchers and cameras to induce investors to buy Minibonds. These gifts distracted the investors from the relevant facts and enticed them to invest more than they should have.[17]

Information disclosed to consumers about the products was lengthy and complicated, with prospectuses stretching to more than 200 pages. Banks claimed that their sales processes only provided "information" to consumers about the products and not regulated investment "advice" that the product was suitable for their circumstances.[9]

Problems arose when Lehman Brothers went bankrupt in September 2008. This bankruptcy resulted in terminating the swap agreements between PIF and LBSF. PIF had to sell the collateral at market prices, which were unfavorable for sellers at the time. This situation implied that investors were not going to recover the amount they had initially invested. The bankruptcy of Lehman and the ensuing losses on the Minibonds caused a flurry of complaints filed with the two financial watchdogs in Hong Kong: the Hong Kong Monetary Authority (HKMA), which was *de facto* a central bank, and the Securities and Futures Commission (SFC). At this point, both agencies initiated an investigation on the matter. Besides the complaints, the dissatisfaction with banks resulted in more than 300 people taking to the streets in Hong Kong on multiple occasions because they felt cheated by the financial institutions and demanded government intervention.

By the end of 2008, the two agencies received nearly 30,000 complaints associated with different types of financial products related to Lehman Brothers, including Minibonds. According to the SFC, the most common allegations against the banks that distributed Minibonds included the following:[17]

- Front line staff proactively induced complainants to turn their matured fixed deposits into investments in Lehman related products for higher returns and other incentives such as free shopping coupons.

- Front line staff failed to consider the complainants' risk profile and personal circumstances when selling products, especially in the case of the retired, elderly, less educated and less sophisticated, and risk-averse clients.

- Front line staff neither provided product information such as term sheets and prospectuses nor explained product features and risks when selling the product. Some even misrepresented that the products, especially Minibonds, were risk-free, similar to fixed deposits.

- Front line staff only highlighted the well-known reference entities of Minibonds, emphasizing that the risk of Minibonds was only tied to the credit risk of these reference entities without mentioning the role of and the risk associated with Lehman (Brothers) Holdings.

- Banks did not respond to complainants' inquiries and complaints after the collapse of Lehman Brothers.

Unsophisticated investors could not comprehend the risks associated with the CDOs or Lehman Brothers in the multilayer structure. Although the prospectuses covered these aspects, their technical language prevented most retail investors from correctly understanding the structure and risks of Minibonds. A *prospectus* is a disclosure document that describes a financial security for potential buyers. This shortcoming emphasizes the responsibility of the sales agents to ensure investors have a clear understanding of these issues.

In 2009, the banks involved in selling Minibonds made a deal with the SFC and HKMA to pay back 60% of the investments to the 29,000 eligible investors. The recovery rate was 70% for investors over 65 years of age. The banks, including blue-chip lenders Bank of East Asia Ltd. and Bank of China (Hong Kong), spent about HK $6.3 billion to buy back Minibonds.[18] In 2011 these recovery rates were increased ranging from 70% to 96.5% depending on the collateral value of the series.[19] The difference in the recovery rates between the Minibond series caused much uproar, resulting in protests outside the banks' and regulators' offices even years after the bankruptcy of Lehman Brothers.

The supposedly "low-risk" Minibonds generated huge losses for individual investors after Lehman's bankruptcy. Banks sold these risky "bonds" to unwary investors as an alternative to bank deposits. Considering all the associated risks, banks severely misled investors marketing Minibonds as a safe investment. Although the prospectuses mentioned the risks, the product and associated risks were too complex for unsophisticated investors to understand.

Trap Judgment

Hong Kong Minibonds

Becoming a victim of investment fraud

Misrepresenting risky products as safe

Making unrealistic excessive return expectations

Falling for mutual fund traps

Overpaying for products and services

Investing in complex products

Engaging in gambling disguised as investing

Relying on unsupported promises

LESSONS LEARNED

Misrepresenting risky products as safe can be a dangerous and costly investment trap for investors. These case studies provide several lessons for investors. The following advice can help you to avoid becoming yet another victim of this investment trap:

- Don't let anyone talk you into buying a financial product you don't fully understand. You may recall the admonition, "If something sounds too good to be true, it probably is." Although this is good advice, the problem is determining when "good" becomes "too good." To gain greater understanding, you can seek the advice of a neutral and knowledgeable third party.

- Do your due diligence and don't simply rely on those making the claims. You should ask questions and keep a healthy sense of skepticism. If someone makes a questionable claim, ask for evidence. Being inclined to easily trust anyone who is trying to sell you something gives way to vulnerability, if not gullibility, and can be costly.

- Check with relevant regulatory authorities for any complaints or investigations involving those offering the products.

- Don't let greed overcome your good judgment. Although not speaking about investments, Stephen Hawking, an English theoretical physicist, cosmologist, and author, notes: "We are in danger of destroying ourselves by our greed and stupidity." If your internal alarm bell rings, listen to it and find another investment.

- Don't assume that laws in place will automatically protect you from any kind of foul play. You are responsible for checking the true content of the offering.

QUESTIONS

1. Explain how preference shares differ from common (ordinary) shares.

2. Compare the risks of a bond and a bank deposit.

3. Explain the difference between interest rate risk and credit risk.

4. Discuss whether a collateralized debt obligation (CDO) is risk-free if it has the highest credit rating.

5. Compare and contrast MMFs in the United States and Europe.

6. Explain how the collapse of Lehman Brothers resulted in losses of financial products issued in Hong Kong.

NOTES

1. Simpson, S. D. (2012). Low vs. high-risk investments for beginners. *Investopedia*, April 2. Retrieved from http://www.investopedia.com/financial-edge/0512/low-vs.-high-risk-investments-for-beginners.aspx

2. Geffner, M. 7 Low-risk investments with modest returns. Bankrate.com. Retrieved from http://www.bankrate.com/finance/investing/low-risk-investments-with-modest-returns-1.aspx

3. Geffner, M. 9 high-risk investments not for amateurs. Bankrate.com. Retrieved from http://www.bankrate.com/finance/investing/high-risk-investments-not-for-amateurs-1.aspx

4. U.S. Securities and Exchange Commission. *Mortgage-backed securities*. Retrieved from http://www.sec.gov/answers/mortgagesecurities.htm

5. The origins of the financial crisis. (2013). *The Economist*, September 7. Retrieved from http://www.economist.com/news/schoolsbrief/21584534-effects-financial-crisis-are-still-being-felt-five-years-article

6. Ryback, W. (2010). *Case study on Bear Stearns*. Toronto Leadership Centre. Retrieved from http://siteresources.worldbank.org/FINANCIALSECTOR/Resources/02BearStearnsCaseStudy.pdf

7. Goodman, P. S., & Morgenson, G. (2008). Saying yes, WaMu built empire on shaky loans. *The New York Times,* December 28. Retrieved from http://www.nytimes.com/2008/12/28/business/28wamu.html? pagewant

8. Stempel, J. (2014). JPMorgan to face U.S. class action in $10 billion MBS case. *Reuters,* September 30. Retrieved from http://www.reuters. com/article/2014/10/01/us-jpmorgan-mbs-lawsuit-idUSKCN0HP2LU20141001

9. Lindley, D. (2014). Risky business: The case for reform of sales incentives schemes in banks. *Consumers International,* October 21, pp. 1 – 70. Retrieved from http://www.consumersinternational.org/media/1517537/sales-incentive-report_riskybusiness_final2_151014.pdf

10. Penty, C., & Duarte, E. (2012). Spain bank bailout means forcing losses on cooks, pensioners. *Bloomberg Business,* July 12. Retrieved from http://www.bloomberg.com/news/articles/2012-07-11/spanish-bank-bailout-means-forcing-losses-on-cooks-pensioners

11. Mai, H. (2015, February 26). *Money market funds – An economic perspective.* Deutsche Bank Research. Retrieved from https://www.dbresearch.com/PROD/DBR_INTERNET_EN-PROD/PROD0000000000351452/Money+market+funds+–+an+economic +perspective%3A+Matc.PDF

12. Mazen, P. (2008). The credit crunch of 2007 – 2008: A discussion of the background, market reactions, and policy responses. *Federal Reserve Bank of St. Louis Review,* 90(5), 531 – 567. Retrieved from https://research.stlouisfed.org/publications/review/08/09/Mizen.pdf

13. SIFMA (Securities Industry and Financial Markets Association). *Understanding interest-rate risk.* Retrieved from http://www.investinginbonds.com/learnmore.asp?catid=5&subcatid=18&id=178

14. Lampinen, A. (2009). This was supposed to be a secure investment. *Taloussanomat,* May 15.

15. CESR (Committee of European Securities Regulator). *Guidelines on a common definition of European money market funds.* Retrieved from http://www.esma.europa.eu/system/files/10_545.pdf

16. ISDA (International Swap and Derivatives Association). *Credit event definitions.* Retrieved from http://credit-deriv.com/isdadefinitions.htm

17. Godwin, A. (2009). Lehman Minibonds crisis in Hong Kong: Lessons for plain language risk disclosure. *UNSW Law Journal, 32*(2), 486–547.

18. Ng, J. (2009, July 23). Banks to buy back Lehman Minibonds. *The Wall Street Journal,* Retrieved from http://www.wsj.com/articles/ SB124825602525271653

19. The good inside the bad. (2011). *The Economist,* March 31. Retrieved from http://www.economist.com/node/18486397

8

TRAP 4: MAKING UNREALISTIC RETURN EXPECTATIONS

Risk comes from not knowing what you're doing.
Warren Buffett, Chairman and
CEO of Berkshire Hathaway

All investments carry some degree of risk. Stocks, bonds, real estate, mutual funds, exchange-traded funds and other securities and assets can lose value depending on market conditions. John Bogle, the founder and retired CEO of The Vanguard Group, notes, "If you have trouble imagining a 20% loss in the stock market, you shouldn't be in stocks." For example, the financial crisis of 2007–2008 harshly reminded investors of the substantial loss potential of equity investments. In 2008 alone, the S&P Index fell by nearly 40%.

Investors often fail to understand the various risks associated with different investments, which can led to having unrealistic return expectations. For example, a risk that many investors ignore is *inflation risk*, which is the chance that an investment's cash flows won't be worth as much in the future because of changes in purchasing power due to inflation. Even conservative, insured investments, such as CDs issued by a bank or credit union, carry inflation risk.

Sometimes investors and their financial advisors make overly optimistic estimates about the likely performance of certain investments. Optimism and positive thinking are useful in many aspects of life, but having excessive optimism leading to unrealistic expectations can be detrimental when investing. On the other hand, having diminished expectations is also not good for your long-term financial health. What you need are realistic expectations about both returns and their variability (risk) as related to your investment portfolio. Estimating long-term returns is critical when projecting your expected level of income in retirement.

Although no foolproof way exists for making such estimates, a starting point is to understand the history of returns for various asset classes. However, past performance does not necessarily predict future results. In fact, the SEC requires mutual funds to make this statement to investors. Top-performing mutual funds aren't necessarily going to be next year's best performers. Instead, they could have only mediocre or below-average performance the following year. Similar to a weather forecaster, forecasts by finance professionals are not always right, even when using sound models and judgment. If you are going to be surprised by returns different from what you or your financial advisor expect, you'd prefer positive surprises to negative ones.[1]

What rate of return should you expect to receive on an investment? The answer depends on many factors such as the type of investment, market conditions, time period under consideration, and method of calculating returns. Additionally, the risks associated with an investment, either real or perceived, are critically important in determining the rate of return you might earn. Investors typically expect to receive a higher rate of return as they take on more risk. Attaining higher expected returns usually entails assuming higher expected risks and the possibility of greater loss. Although you might be able to earn high returns over a short period due to skill or luck, eventually a market correction occurs and the investment becomes overpriced. You might even be able to beat the market over the long run, but the probability of doing so is slim and you're taking considerable risk in the attempt.

This chapter discusses the risk-return trade-off, differences between traditional and behavioral finance, and provides examples of historical returns based on market data for various asset classes. As previously mentioned, understanding historical return relations among different securities serves as a starting point for forming future return expectations. As Mark Twain reputedly said, "History doesn't repeat itself, but it does rhyme." That is, although the events are not exactly the same, they seem to have a similar ring to them. The chapter also highlights several examples of the investment trap of holding unrealistic return expectations. Successful investors must understand and avoid the hazards of being overly optimistic or pessimistic when forming return expectations.

THE RISK-RETURN TRADE-OFF

You may be familiar with the phrase by Milton Friedman, an American economist who received the 1976 Nobel Memorial Prize in Economic Sciences, "There's no such thing as a free lunch." The saying supposedly originated because many saloons in the United States once provided "free" lunches to their patrons, but required them to buy drinks to get them. This notion also holds in financial markets involving risk and return. That is, you can't expect to get something for nothing. Although something may appear to be free, a cost, no matter how indirect or hidden, typically looms in the background.

What do the terms "return" and "risk" mean? *Return*, or more precisely *total return*, refers to the actual rate of return on an investment over a given period. Total return consists of two parts: (1) income, including interest paid by debt investments, distributions or dividends and (2) capital appreciation, representing the change in an asset's market price. *Expected return* is what an investor expects to earn from an investment in the future.

Financial writers and advisors often reference annual returns of 10% or higher on stocks or equity mutual funds. However, such returns are likely to be an *average return*, which is the same as the *arithmetic return*, over the long run. An *arithmetic return* is simply the sum of all the returns in a series divided by the count of all returns in the series. An average return is usually expressed as a *nominal rate of return*, which is the amount of money generated by an investment before factoring in such items as such as fees, expenses, taxes, and inflation. For instance, a mutual fund's nominal rate of return could be 10%, but after making all adjustments the return would be lower. In fact, average returns are higher than *actual returns*, which are calculated using a different mathematical formula called a *geometric mean*. Without discussing its formula, a *geometric mean* can be described as a compounded growth rate of the returns over time.

An example may help to illustrate the difference between an average return and a geometric return. Assume your investment portfolio of $100,000 doubled to $200,000 in one year. As a result, you earned 100% on the portfolio during the first year. During the second year, the $200,000 portfolio declined to $100,000, which indicates that you sustained a 50% loss, at least on paper. Over the two-year period, the average return on your portfolio was 25%, which is calculated by dividing the sum of your 100% gain and 50% loss by 2 or $(100\% - 50\%)/2 = 25\%$. However, the geometric mean or compounded growth rate of your portfolio was 0%. That is, you started off with $100,000 at the beginning of the first year and ended up with $100,000 at the end of the second, so your portfolio didn't grow. The more volatile the portfolio, the greater will be the difference between the average and actual (geometric) return. In summary, you need to look beyond an investment's average return to get an accurate idea of what your investment actually earns.

Having discussed returns, let's now turn to the other part of the risk/return trade-off — risk. People tend to use the term "risk" rather casually in everyday life. In broad terms, *risk* is the danger that unwanted events might happen or that developments go in an unintended direction. Unexpected events can have harmful consequences to investors. As Niccolo Machiavelli notes in *The Prince,* "All courses of action are risky, so prudence is not in avoiding danger (it's impossible), but calculating risk and acting decisively."

In an investment context, risk has diverse definitions, measurements, and explanations. For our purposes, *risk* refers to the chance that an investment's actual return differs from its expected return. Traditional finance focuses on the quantitative measure of risk, such as the standard deviation of historical returns or average returns of a specific investment. A *standard deviation* is a measure of the dispersion of a set of data such as a stock's returns from its mean or average. A high standard deviation relative to its mean indicates more spread apart data and greater risk. In finance literature, standard deviation refers to *volatility*, which is a statistical measure of the dispersion of returns. Interestingly, traditional finance considers risk as including a return above and below expectations. In practice, investors are more concerned with downside risk, not upside risk. *Downside risk* is the financial risk associated with losses or getting less than expected. That is, downside risk is the risk of the actual return being below the expected return or the uncertainty about the magnitude of that difference. Downside risk includes the possibility of losing some or all of the original investment.

The *risk/return trade-off* is the compromise that an investor faces between risk and return when considering investment decisions. A common misconception is that higher risk equals greater return. What the risk-return trade-off actually means is that higher risk gives the possibility of higher returns. Potential return rises with increased risk, but without any guarantees. **Figure 8.1** illustrates the risk/return trade-off.

Figure 8.1: The Risk-Return Trade-Off

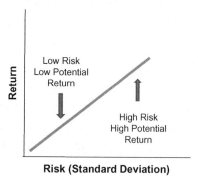

Risk (Standard Deviation)

Notes: This figure shows that higher risk is associated with a greater probability of higher return and lower risk with a greater probability of smaller return. The trade-off between risk and return facing an investor while considering investment decisions is called the risk-return trade-off.

TRADITIONAL VERSUS BEHAVIORAL FINANCE

Traditional finance is based on the notion of "rationality," meaning people are risk-averse. *Rational behavior* refers to a decision-making process in which people make choices that result in the most optimal level of benefit for them. According to this view, people are generally rational "wealth maximizers." Someone who is *risk-averse* prefers lower returns with known risks rather than higher returns with unknown risks. When facing investments having the same expected return with different level of risks, a risk-averse investor would prefer the alternative with the least risk. When the investments have the same risk, a risk-averse investor would prefer the alternative with the higher expected return. In traditional finance, investors value gains and losses equally. This normative view focuses on how people should behave when making investment decisions.

Of course, how people should act versus how they really act often differs. Many examples are available in which emotion and psychology influence people's decisions, causing them to behave in unpredictable or irrational ways. To show this, let's try an

experiment that involves making judgments between two monetary decisions that have prospective losses and gains.[2]

1. Assume that you have $1000 and must choose one of the fol-
   lowing: Choice A: You have a 50% chance of gaining $1000
   and a 50% chance of gaining $0. Choice B: You have a 100%
   chance of gaining $500.

2. Assume that you have $1000 and must choose one of the fol-
   lowing: Choice A: You have a 50% chance of losing $1000
   and 50% of losing $0. Choice B: You have a 100% chance of
   losing $500.

Which would you pick in each situation? The rational choice
would be to select "B" in both situations. In this example, choosing B indicates risk aversion whereas choosing A indicates risk
taking. Risk-averse investors prefer a riskless action to one that is
risky and has an equal or smaller expected value. In situation 1, a
rational investor would pick the sure gain of $500 (Choice B)
rather than A, whose expected outcome is also $500 (0.5 ×
$1.000 + 0.5 × $0 = $500) but is riskier. In situation 2, the sure
loss of $500 and the expected loss (0.50 × −$1000 + 0.5 × $0 =
−$500) are the same, but Choice A is risker because it involves
the possibility of losing $1000.

Evidence shows, however, that an overwhelming majority of
people choose B for situation 1 and A for situation 2, the implication being that people are willing to settle for a reasonable level of
gains despite having a realistic chance of earning more, but are
willing to engage in risk-taking behaviors where they can limit
their losses. In other words, people weight losses more heavily
than an equivalent amount of gains. Traditional finance can't
explain why someone would have a shift in preferences, but
behavioral finance can. As discussed in Chapter 4, a key precept
of *prospect theory* is that people value gains and losses differently
and consequently behave differently than what traditional finance
assumes.

As an alternative to traditional finance, behavioral finance concentrates on how people actually make judgments and decisions in the real world. Investors who inhabit the real world and those who populate academic models are distant cousins. In behavioral finance, risk is multi-faceted and situational in nature. This descriptive approach incorporates psychological risk attributes including one's risk perception. *Risk perception* is the subjective judgment that an investor makes about the characteristics and severity of a risk. Therefore, risk perception incorporates psychological risk attributes. For example, assume a risk-averse investor has one investment with a 50% chance of earning 10% a year and a 50% chance of earning 20% a year, which provides an expected return of 15%, and another investment with a guaranteed return of 15% a year. What would the investor likely to choose? The risk-averse investor would favor the latter investment with the guaranteed return of 15% because it has no uncertainty.

The assumptions underlying behavioral finance differ from those of traditional finance. In behavioral finance, the assumptions of bounded rationality, satisficing, prospect theory, and loss aversion help to explain how individuals act when assessing perceived risk.[3] *Bounded rationality* is the concept that when investors make decisions, their rationality is limited by the information they have, their capacity to evaluate and process the available information, and the amount of time available to make a decision. Under these conditions, individuals can only make *satisficing* choices rather than maximizing or optimizing choices in complex situations. That is, they aim for a satisfactory or adequate result, rather than the optimal solution to potentially avoid a needless expenditure of time, energy, and resources.

Prospect theory is a behavioral economic theory of decision-making under risk used to describe real-life choices, rather than optimal decisions.[2] According to prospect theory, people make decisions based on the potential value of losses and gains rather than the final outcome. Because investors value gains and losses differently, they base decisions on perceived gains rather than perceived losses. If an investor had two equal choices, one expressed in terms of possible gains and the other in possible losses, the investor would select the former despite both choices having the same economic end result.

Prospect theory posits that losses have more emotional impact than an equivalent amount of gains. In contrast, in traditional finance, the amount of utility or satisfaction gained from receiving $50 should be equal to that received from gaining $100 and then losing $50. *Utility* is an economic term referring to the total satisfaction received from consuming a good or service. Both situations result in a net gain of $50. Yet, investors typically view a single gain of $50 more favorably than gaining $100 and then losing $50.

As discussed in Chapter 4, *loss aversion* refers to the tendency to strongly prefer avoiding losses to acquiring gains. Individuals who are loss averse view losses as more painful than the pleasure of an equivalent gain.[4] Because losses are much more powerful psychologically than gains, individuals make investment decisions under uncertainty accordingly. Loss aversion is a type of emotional bias, but this doesn't necessary mean that the bias is a bad thing.

HISTORICAL RETURNS AND RISKS

One way to demonstrate the risk-reward relationship is to assume a so-called "risk-free" investment, which offers a certain return with no variation. U.S. Treasury bills (T-bills) often serve as a proxy for a risk-free investment. An investor can be almost certain to achieve the return. Not surprisingly, the risk-free return is lower compared to riskier investments. If you feel that this return is inadequate, you can potentially increase your expected return by investing in riskier assets. For example, U.S. investment-grade corporate bonds have historically offered higher returns than U.S. Treasury bills with a marginally higher return volatility (i.e., a lower certainty about the realized return in the short run).

Table 8.1 shows the annualized real returns on equities, bonds, and bills over several time periods.[5] The returns are in *real* terms, meaning that they are adjusted for inflation, which eats away purchasing power. Given the volatility of financial markets, especially equities representing ownership in companies, long periods are needed to place risks and returns in a proper perspective. Even over periods as long as 10 or 20 years, "unusual" returns can still occur. For example, during the past decade or so, investors and financial markets have faced many challenges, such as the subprime mortgage crisis, a steep recession, a slow recovery, interest rates close to zero, wars, and terrorism. Between 2000 and 2014, the worldwide annualized real returns on bonds (5.5%) exceeded those on equities (1.8%). Over longer periods, however,

Table 8.1: Annualized Real Returns for Equities, Bonds, and Bills over Different Periods

Asset Class	Location	Annualized Real Returns (%)		
		2000–2014	1965–2014	1900–2014
Equities	World	1.8	5.4	5.2
	The United States	2.4	5.7	6.5
	Europe	1.8	6.0	4.3
	Japan	0.1	4.4	4.1
Bonds	World	5.5	4.3	1.9
	The United States	6.0	3.4	2.0
	Europe	6.6	4.9	1.1
	Japan	3.9	4.4	−0.9
Bills	World	−0.4	0.9	0.9
	The United States	−0.4	0.9	0.9
	Europe	−0.4	0.9	0.9
	Japan	0.1	0.3	−1.9

Source: Adapted from Dimson, Marsh, and Staunton (2015).
Note: This table shows annualized real returns for three asset classes over the periods 2000–2014, 1965–2014, and 1900–2014.

worldwide real annualized returns on equities have been greater than those on bonds and bills. For instance, equities have annualized real returns of 5.2% on a worldwide basis between 1900 and 2014, compared with 1.9% on bonds, and 0.9% on T-bills. These differences can largely be explained by the differing return volatilities for these three asset classes. A tug-of-war constantly occurs between risk (volatility) and return.

Keep in mind that although equities have posted strong annualized real returns over a long time period, they seldom deliver that average in any particular year. Markets go up and down, and the ride is often a bumpy one. For instance, the U.S. stock market experienced periods of high volatility not only in the 2000s and 2010s, but also in the 1910s, 1930s, and 1980s. Despite this fact, many investors extrapolate good short-term performance into the future. That is, they predict trend continuation. In fact, many of the cases in this book try to exploit the tendency to extrapolate past returns by promising consistently high returns based on good historical performance. You need to be wary of someone claiming that a security or financial product will earn an unusually high or even a "normal" return for any given year, or that returns are guaranteed.

As **Table 8.1** shows, returns on various assets can exhibit considerable volatility over time, which makes predicting returns for the next year or other periods difficult. You should keep in mind the observation by Niels Bohr, Nobel laureate in physics: "Prediction is very difficult, especially if it's about the future." However, *mean reversion* suggests that prices and returns eventually move back toward the mean or average over time. For example, periods of high above-average returns tend to be followed by periods when returns revert to the average levels.

Let's use an example of a stock to illustrate how mean reversion may occur. Assume that a stock's price begins to increase abnormally. It eventually attracts investors and traders who decide to go against the crowd. When enough market participants have joined the contrarian side, the stock moves back toward its average price over time.

Value Stocks versus Growth Stocks

Although the risk-return trade-off usually holds among different asset classes, exceptions occur. An example is the well-documented phenomenon of value stocks outperforming their growth-focused counterparts on a risk-adjusted basis. A *value stock* is a stock that tends to trade at a lower price relative to its fundamentals, such as dividends, earnings, and sales. Value stocks usually have a high dividend yield, low price-to-book (PB) ratio, and/or low price-to-earnings (PE) ratio. The *PB ratio* is the share price divided by the book value per share. A *PE ratio* is the market value per share divided by the current year's earnings per share. For example, if the stock sells at $40 per share and its after-tax earnings over the last 12 months have been $4 per share, its P/E ratio is 10 (= $40/$4). Value stocks have generally fallen out of favor and are considered bargain-priced or undervalued by the marketplace. Unpopular value stocks are associated with companies experiencing hard times, operating in mature industries, or facing adverse circumstances. Value investors consider value stocks as bargain-priced compared with their competitors. Hence, value investing is about buying a company for a market price below the intrinsic value of the business.

By contrast, a *growth stock*, also known as a *glamour stock*, refers to shares in a company whose revenues, earnings, or cash flow are expected to grow at an above-average rate relative to the market. A growth stock typically does not pay a dividend and has a high PB ratio and/or high PE ratio.

Although many investment professionals use the terms "value" investing and "growth" investing as opposing ideas, Warren Buffett believes this way of thinking is too simplistic. Buffett states that the two approaches are "joined at the hip" or intimately linked. He views growth as a component when calculating value, whose impact importance ranges from negligible to enormous.[6] Despite some describing Buffett as a "value investor," this might not be an apt description of Buffett today. Value investors typically seek struggling businesses whose shares are selling on the cheap, but that's just not Buffett. He looks for great businesses with excellent management. Some characterize him as a "high-quality investor" who wants to get a good price on what he's buying, but this often is not achievable at bargain-basement prices.[7]

Turning to the numbers, for U.S. companies, over the longest available period (1926–2013), unpopular value stocks have outperformed their more popular glamour counterparts (12.7% vs 9.1%, respectively, based on nominal annual returns). From 1975 to 2013, value premium was positive in 17 countries and negative in six countries. Value strategies yield higher returns because these strategies exploit the suboptimal behavior of the typical investor, not because these strategies are fundamentally riskier. Humphrey Neill, author of *The Art of Contrary Thinking*, notes, "When everyone thinks alike, everyone is likely to be wrong."[8]

A possible explanation for the poor performance of growth stocks is the irrational willingness to hold so-called "hot stocks." A *hot stock* is a stock that rises substantially in a short period of time because buyers greatly outnumber sellers. Investors buy hot stocks in the hope of recognizing the next rising star, but ignore the low probability of this actually happening. That is, some investors get enamored with stocks of fast-growing companies. Jeremy Siegel, author of *Stocks for the Long Run*, calls this the "growth trap." The fixation on growth is a snare because it encourages making bets on the next "big thing," even though the most innovative companies are often not the best place for investors. The trap is that investors pay insufficient attention to the price at which they are paying for this growth.[9] The "growth trap" phenomenon often applies to technology companies and emerging markets.

Diversification Effects

To dampen the risk of an all stock portfolio, investors often add bonds and cash instruments without sacrificing too much return. *Diversification*, which is having different kinds of investments within a portfolio, lowers a portfolio's riskiness so that the positive performance of some investments neutralizes the negative performance of others. However, diversification does not preclude you from incurring losses on your portfolio. What diversification can do is to improve your chances of having a smoother ride or less volatility in your portfolio. Similar to building a house to withstand a storm, preparing a portfolio to withstand market turbulence is important in helping you meet long-term investment goals.

As discussed in Chapter 2, once an overall asset allocation is devised, rebalancing the mix at least once a year is important. Given that stocks have outperformed bonds over the long run, stocks are likely to constitute an increasingly larger portion of a portfolio and lead to higher risk over time unless rebalancing occurs.

For many years, combining the traditional asset classes — publicly traded stocks, bonds, cash, and cash equivalents — did a good job of providing diversification of portfolios. This resulted from having asset classes whose returns were not perfectly positively correlated. That is, reducing the volatility of a portfolio's returns requires combining assets that don't move in the same direction, to the same degree, and at the same time. *Correlation* is a statistical measure of how two variables such as the returns on stocks and bonds are related to one another. Correlation coefficients range from +1 (perfectly positively correlated) to −1 (perfectly negatively correlated). The lower the correlation, the greater is the effect of diversification on risk.[10] Yet, during periods of market distress, the correlation of the returns between traditional "diversifiers" tends to increase, leading to greater risk. Their diversifying effects tend to break down just when you need them most. Moreover, time and broader trends have led to a rise in correlations and hence a reduction in diversification using traditional assets.[11]

ALTERNATIVE ASSETS

The risks associated with traditional asset classes, including the rise in their correlations, have led some investors, especially institutional investors, to include alternative investments as a component of their diversified portfolios. Managers of alternative investment portfolios may use derivatives, leverage, and short securities. A *derivative* is a security with a price that is dependent upon or derived from one or more underlying assets. Examples of derivatives include futures contracts, forward contracts, options, and swaps. *Leverage* is the use of various financial instruments or borrowed capital to increase an investment's potential return. *Short selling* is the practice of selling securities or other financial instruments that are not currently owned and subsequently repurchasing them. Investors engage in short selling based on the belief that a security's price will decline, enabling them to buy back the security at a lower price to make a profit. Because some alternative investments are neither available to nor appropriate for most individual investors, only brief mention is made of these investments. With the possible exception of real estate, alternative investments are typically best suited for more knowledgeable and experienced investors. When investing, you need to recognize the limitations of your skill set and knowledge about different investment types.

The "Big Four"

Opinions vary on what makes an investment "alternative." Collectively, *alternative investments* refer to asset classes outside the traditional stocks, bonds or cash and cash equivalents. Traditional investments include *long-only positions*, meaning buying an asset or security such as a stock with the expectation that the asset will rise in value. The "big four" alternative asset classes are real estate, commodities, hedge funds, and private equity.[12]

1. *Real estate*: Of the "big four" alternatives, real estate is probably most familiar to individual investors. Real estate involves ownership interests in land or structures attached to land. Investors can participate in real estate either directly by owning residential and commercial properties, agricultural land, and

individual mortgages, or indirectly in various structures such as pools of properties or mortgages held by real estate investment trusts (REITs). As an asset class, real estate can provide diversification benefits to an investor's portfolio and a potential inflation hedge because rents and real estate values tend to increase with inflation.

2. *Commodities*: *Commodities* refer to physical assets such as agricultural products, oil and gas, and other raw materials used in production. Buying and selling commodities is usually carried out using derivatives such as futures contracts on exchanges that standardize the quantity and minimum quality of the commodity being traded. Over time, the returns on commodities have been lower than returns on global stocks and bonds, but with higher volatility. However, exposure to commodity markets can provide diversification benefits due to low correlations of commodity returns with those of global equities and bonds as well as an inflation hedge because commodity prices tend to move with inflation.

3. *Hedge funds*: A *hedge fund* is a pooled investment vehicle that uses various strategies to invest in a variety of asset classes. Professional investment managers administer these privately offered funds. Hedge fund managers use many strategies and tools to reduce volatility and risk while attempting to preserve capital and deliver positive returns under all market conditions. Hedge funds are only open to "accredited" or qualified investors including individuals, banks, insurance companies, employee benefit plans, and trusts. Traditionally, the two most commonly cited qualifications for accrediting investors (listed in Rule 501 of Regulation D of the Securities Act of 1933) are either (1) a net worth exceeding $1 million or (2) an annual income exceeding $200,000 ($300,000 if combined with a spouse) for each of the two most recent years. However, the Financial Services Committee and the U.S. House of

Representatives passed H.R. 2187, known as the Fair Investment Opportunities for Professional Experts Act, which incorporates the addition of a knowledge and education-based category of accredited investors by changing and expanding the definition. This bill allows individuals to qualify as accredited investors based on measures of sophistication. For example, these measures include a minimum amount of investments, certain professional credentials, experience investing in exempt offerings, knowledgeable employees of private funds, or by passing an accredited investor examination to qualify as an accredited investor.[13]

4. *Private equity*: *Private equity* is a type of fund that invests in private companies or public companies (leveraged buyout funds) or in early stage companies (venture capital funds). Similar to hedge funds, private equity funds are typically structured as limited partnerships. Over the past several decades, returns on private equity funds have been higher on average than overall stock returns. As with other alternatives, including private equity in portfolios containing traditional assets can provide diversification benefits.

The "big four" alternative asset classes all boomed between 2002 and 2007, but experienced substantial losses during the financial crisis. Other types of alternative investments include tangible collectible assets such as art and antiques, precious metals, fine wines, rare stamps and coins, and sports cards, as well as in intangible assets such as patents.

Characteristics and Benefits

Compared to traditional investments, alternative investments exhibit several common characteristics. For example, the assets or securities held have less liquidity. *Liquidity* is the ability to quickly convert an asset or security into cash with little or no loss in value.

Investing in less liquid assets or securities is more risky than investing in more liquid ones, as investors have greater difficulty getting in and out of such investments.

Alternative investments may also involve relatively high costs of purchase and sale. That is, fee structures for alternative investments differ from those of traditional investments, with higher management fees on average, and often additional performance based incentive fees. Another common characteristic of alternative investments is that limited historical risk and return data may be available. Evaluating the performance of alternative investments can be difficult because of problems associated with determining the current market value of the asset and the complexity of establishing valid benchmarks. Finally, alternative investments often have less regulation and transparency, different legal and tax treatments, and require more specialization by investment managers.

Alternative investments offer several potential benefits. The major motivation for holding alternative investments is that some have a historically low correlation of returns relative to traditional investments, which can reduce an investor's overall portfolio risk. However, the risk characteristics of alternative investments often require using different risk measures than for traditional investments. Although alternatives might provide the attractive risk-adjusted returns that sophisticated investors are seeking, the extra returns are often associated with illiquid investments and the use of leverage. Despite these possible benefits, determining an appropriate portfolio allocation to alternative investments requires careful consideration.

Investing in most alternatives requires specialized knowledge and skills, and as such is probably inappropriate for many, if not most, individual investors. Given that an in-depth discussion of alternative investments is beyond the scope of this book, little additional attention is placed on this topic. This does not mean that nonprofessional investors can't earn satisfactory investment returns, assuming that they avoid making investing mistakes, behavioral biases, and investment traps that litter the investment landscape. In his 2013 "Shareholder Letter," Warren Buffett offers some fundamentals of investing.[14] His first advice is:

> *You don't need to be an expert in order to achieve satisfactory investment returns. But if you aren't, you must recognize your limitations and follow a course certain to work reasonably well. Keep things simple and don't swing for the fences. When promised quick profits, respond with a quick 'no'.*

Buffett continues:

> *The "... know-nothing" investor who both diversifies and keeps his costs minimal is virtually certain to get satisfactory results. Indeed, the unsophisticated investor who is realistic about his shortcomings is likely to obtain better long term results than the knowledgeable professional who is blind to even a single weakness.*

MENTAL SHORTCUTS

Having provided some background about risk and returns and other matters, let's now examine how people make decisions. As discussed in Chapter 4, investors frequently use mental shortcuts to process data and control extreme complexity. These useful rules of thumb, called *heuristics*, help investors reach quick and efficient decisions, but not necessarily optimal ones. Why? By using mental shortcuts, investors process certain details but ignore others to make faster choices. Although heuristics can be helpful in saving time and money in some situations, they can result in poor outcomes or bad decisions in others. For example, one rule of thumb is: "Past performance is the best predictor of future performance, so invest in a mutual fund having the best five-year record."[15] Using past risk-adjusted performance is a popular method to predict mutual fund performance because investors can simply project past outperformance into the future. Although research evidence on the effectiveness of this heuristic varies considerably, chasing "past winners" is an enticing, but questionable, investing strategy.

THE AFFECT HEURISTIC

Although people use many decision-making shortcuts, let's begin by examining the affect heuristic as applied to investors. This heuristic is part of the fast and frugal heuristic toolbox and involves emotional and intuitive variables. The *affect heuristic* is a mental shortcut for making decisions and solving problems in which an emotional response, which is called "affect" in psychology, plays a prominent role. If investors have positive views about a company on one dimension, they tend to apply these positive feelings to other dimensions as well. Investors often fall for this decision-making fallacy when estimating risks and benefits of something. That is, if investors have positive feelings about a company, they are more likely to evaluate the risks related to that company as low and the benefits as high and vice versa.[16]

The affect heuristic can seduce investors into overpaying for growth stocks, especially in rapidly growing and emerging markets. Research reveals the outperformance of value stocks in emerging markets relative to glamour stocks and U.S. value stocks. Because the market often places a high value on growth stocks, investors in growth stocks might also view these stocks as having great worth and are often willing to pay a premium for expected growth. Growth stocks are also typically more expensive than ordinary shares because they are in high demand. Investors can also find many of the best-performing investments in shrinking industries and in slower-growing countries.[9] Yet, they often shun the stocks of the slowest-growing countries, just like out-of-favor value stocks that tend to subsequently outperform. Similar to growth stocks, stocks of fast-growing countries frequently become overheated. Betting on growth alone often does not work because markets have already factored in economic performance.

PROMOTING "GOOD" COMPANIES

Investors often confuse growth companies with growth stocks. A *growth company* is any firm whose business generates substantial positive cash flows or earnings, which increase at much faster rates than the overall economy. A *growth stock* earns a higher rate of return than others with similar risk. Growth stocks are typically from fast-growing companies in dynamic industries with a relatively high profile.

According to the affect heuristic, investors are likely to form positive perceptions of such companies as investments. They can extend the generalization of good characteristics of a growth company to their evaluations of the company as an investment. That is, they tend to view growth companies as having growth stocks. However, a growth company's stock is not always classified as growth stock. In fact, a growth company's stock can be overvalued.

Does the affect heuristic influence others besides individual investors? Empirical evidence shows that professional financial advisors are not immune to the affect heuristic.[17] Financial advisors tend to anticipate higher expected returns from "good" companies when evaluated on general firm-level characteristics such as low leverage, strong management, and good growth prospects compared to "not so good" companies. This result is opposite of what finance theory suggests. According to conventional asset pricing models, any good firm characteristic that is priced by the market is associated with lower, not higher, return expectations. Although blue chip companies, on average, have a relatively low level of risk, and therefore their returns should be expected to be relatively low, investors expect excessive returns from them. *Blue chip companies* are a group of companies having a stable and strong financial track record based on continuous success in their respected field. A stock's long-term return depends not on the actual growth of its earnings, but on the difference between its actual earnings growth and the growth that other investors expect.[9]

A study comparing how returns on companies' stocks differ based on their ranking in *Fortune* magazine's annual list of "America's Most Admired Companies" finds that between 1982 and 2006, stocks of companies ranked in the bottom 10% of the list ("most despised 10%"), outperform stocks of companies ranked in the top 10% ("most admired 10%") (19.7% vs. 15.1% a year).[18] Although the slightly higher volatility of less admired companies partially accounts for the return difference, the higher returns more than compensate for the higher risk. Investors holding stocks of growth companies could receive their reward both in returns and in some sort of "pleasure" or affect associated with holding the stocks, while despised companies reward their owners purely with returns. Affect is not free and owners of admired companies might unknowingly be overpaying for their shares. Good firm-level characteristics are associated with higher valuation multiples and subsequently lower return expectations.

Although financial advisors operating in the best interests of their clients should do their best to prevent their clients from falling for this fallacy, this doesn't always happen. In fact, some financial services providers offer products that further exploit this misconception.

GOOD COMPANIES EQUAL GOOD RETURNS FALLACY

Let's look at the Finnish OP-Pohjola Bank. This bank once offered four rounds of index-linked bonds titled Pohjola World High-Performers. An *index-linked bond* is one in which payment of income on the principal is related to a specific price index. Usually, this feature protects investors by shielding them from changes in the underlying index. The bank offered one subscription round for 2009, 2011, 2012, and 2013. However, these index-linked bonds offered the potential of "equity-like returns" by linking the bonds' payoff to a portfolio of 10 stocks.

The equity portfolios linked to the bonds in each round include some of the world's best-known companies. For example, the 2009 offering is linked to a portfolio consisting of stocks of 10 companies with the best global brands: (1) Royal Dutch Shell, (2) International Business Machines, (3) Google, (4) Visa, (5) Canon, (6) Nike, (7) McDonald's, (8) Microsoft, (9) Coca-Cola, and (10) Sony. The promotional materials explained the choice of these companies as follows:

> *From our standpoint, we see that the 10 companies chosen in our bond will fare better than their smaller and less-known competitors during the turbulent market environment and we expect them to even strengthen their market positions. We believe that the companies we have chosen have a strong profit potential in the case of a highly probable revival of the markets during the loan period.*[19]

Promoting the public brand and fame of a "good" company resulted in individual investors overestimating the likelihood of these companies being good investments. Investors often have some perception of how well-known companies such as Google or Nike previously performed. Although such companies might have generated excellent past returns, the current valuation should reflect all company features. Therefore, any good firm characteristic that is priced by the market is associated with lower, not higher, return expectations. Several academic studies show the outperformance of value stocks relative to glamour stocks.[20]

Trap Judgment

Good Companies = Good Returns

Becoming a victim of investment fraud

Misrepresenting risky products as safe

Making unrealistic return expectations

Falling for mutual fund traps

Overpaying for products and services

Investing in complex products

Engaging in gambling disguised as investing

Relying on unsupported promises

PROMOTING EMERGING MARKETS

A common belief is that economic growth is good for stock returns. Consider the following statement:

> *It is widely believed that economic growth is good for stock returns, and economic growth forecasts are a staple of international asset allocation decisions. Investing in emerging markets with good long-term growth prospects, such as China, is widely viewed as more attractive than investing in countries such as Argentina or the Philippines with prolonged periods of low growth that are expected to persist.*[21]

The financial media have reinforced this long-standing view by paying attention to various economic growth indicators, often combined with linking how changes in these indicators reflect the equity markets. This view has transformed itself into the belief that countries with strong economic growth offer better returns to equity-holders than countries with more stagnant economies.

An example of this misguided idea is the FIM BRIC + mutual fund. The fund emphasizes the economic growth of emerging markets and the return potential that this growth creates for emerging market equities. Fund managers invest at least 80% of their assets in Brazilian, Russian, Indian, and Chinese stock markets.[22] According to the fund's marketing material and website, investors turn to the emerging markets for higher-than-average returns. The fund's market materials offer other subtle hints and implications of strong economic growth as one of the key drivers of good stock returns. The fund's stated strategy is as follows: "The Fund invests in long-term themes, in particular the economic growth of the emerging markets fueled by the growth of their middle class." The fund also states: "The growth story of emerging markets is set to continue for a long time."[23]

Empirical evidence on the link between economic growth and returns to shareholders suggests the opposite. For example, Jay Ritter, a professor at the University of Florida, studies a sample of 19 developed countries for a cross-country correlation between real GDP growth (a proxy for economic growth) and real stock returns between 1900 and 2011. He finds a negative correlation (-0.39) between GDP growth and stock market returns.[24] The same can be observed in developing or emerging countries even though data from such countries are available only since 1988. For 15 developing countries, the correlation between per capita GDP growth and equity returns is negative (-0.41). A notable example is China, where high economic growth of more than 9% on average is combined with low stock returns $(-5.5\%$ a year). China's stock market grew from almost nothing in 1993 to a market value of more than \$10 trillion by mid-2015.[25] Some of the growth in China's aggregate market cap is attributable to the expansion of the number of listed companies, resulting in part from several thousand IPOs, including those of China's four largest state-owned banks. Also, investors are taking on an unreasonable amount of risk for deteriorating economic growth.

A key insight explaining these findings is similar to the logic behind pricing of individual stocks. As Ritter explains, when at the start of the period investors expect a growing economy will help to boost the performance of individual companies, the prices of individual stocks will eventually impound such growth expectations. This leads to higher price-to-earnings (PE) and price-to-dividends multiples assigned by investors to the equity markets. For the companies to justify the new price, which now includes the individual companies' growth expectations driven by general economic growth, they must capitalize on the economic growth and grow both their earnings and dividends per share. Unless they achieve these gains (i.e., earnings and dividends remain on the same level), the realized returns to shareholders will drop due to higher prices paid at the start of the period. Such a situation seems predisposed to earnings disappointments rather than surprises, which is consequently seen in lower returns on equities. This logic is similar to the explanation behind growth stocks underperforming value stocks.

Another explanation of Ritter's findings is that improvements of firm-specific corporate performance, not growth in economy-wide earnings, drive stock returns. The underlying reason is that economy-wide earnings benefit other stakeholders such as customers and workers more than the company's shareholders. Consequently, economic growth of a specific country would be irrelevant to the equity returns exhibited by that country because the driving forces are firm-level indicators, not economy-wide ones. Based on this reasoning, a "growth at all costs" strategy would not seem to favor equity-holders.

Others note that overseas markets help to explain an increasing portion of U.S. corporate earnings. For example, a study conducted for Vanguard finds that the percentage of total U.S. corporate profits derived from direct investment income abroad doubled from 20% in 1999 to 40% in 2008.[26] Multinational firms based in developed markets contribute to emerging market GDP growth in return for higher corporate earnings. Investors should also consider risks in investing in emerging markets. Obviously, companies in developed markets are, on average, less risky.

Emerging markets appeal to investors for several reasons, including their economic growth. The faster growth is typically associated with stronger earnings growth, which many investors associate with higher expected stock returns. This misguided idea of excessive return expectations has been a major sales pitch for emerging market mutual funds. This growth trap seduces investors into overpaying for the equities in emerging markets. History shows that shrinking industries and slower-growing countries offer some of the best-performing investments. Academic studies show a negative link between economic growth and returns to shareholders.[24]

Trap Judgment

Emerging Markets = Good Returns

Becoming a victim of investment fraud

Misrepresenting risky products as safe

Making unrealistic return expectations

Falling for mutual fund traps

Overpaying for products and services

Investing in complex products

Engaging in gambling disguised as investing

Relying on unsupported promises

LESSONS LEARNED

Having unrealistic return expectations is a common investment trap. This is especially true of new or inexperienced investors who enter the market when returns are particularly high. The possibility of missing out on such high returns is simply too much to bear. However, investors, even professionals, are notoriously poor market timers. As Warren Buffet notes:[14]

> *The main danger is that the timid or beginning investor will enter the market at a time of extreme exuberance and then become disillusioned when paper losses occur. (Remember the late Barton Biggs' observation: "A bull market is like sex. It feels best just before it ends.") The antidote to that kind of mistiming is for an investor to accumulate shares over a long period and never to sell when the news is bad and stocks are well off their highs.*

Greed and overoptimism have been the ruin of many investors. You would be wise to heed the warning provided by investment firms that "past performance does not guarantee future results." Considering the following lessons might help you make more intelligent investing decisions:

1. Follow the popular adage of "There's no such thing as a free lunch." The risk-return trade-off indicates that potential return is likely to rise with an increase in risk.

2. Be aware of your personal risk tolerance when choosing investments in your portfolio. Because you can't eliminate all risk, your goal should be to find an appropriate balance that generates sufficient returns but still allows you to sleep at night.

3. Understand how markets behave and risk only what you can tolerate in volatile markets.

4. Diversify your portfolio to help reach your long-range financial goals.

5. Be aware of the trade-offs when diversifying outside of traditional asset classes.

6. Keep in mind what Warren Buffett has said, "Price is what you pay, value is what you get." Intrinsic value of a business stays within a much narrower range than price, which can vary wildly depending on the emotions of investors.

7. Remember that successful investors base their investment decisions on practical and calculated information, not on emotions.

QUESTIONS

1. Explain the risk-return trade-off.

2. Discuss the key tenets of traditional vs. behavioral finance.

3. Explain the differences between value and growth stocks.

4. Explain the "growth trap."

5. Describe how diversification can lower a portfolio's riskiness.

6. Identify the "big four" alternative investments.

7. Discuss the potential advantages and disadvantages of investing in alternative investments.

8. Discuss the affect heuristic.

9. Explain why a good company and a good stock are not necessarily the same.

10. Explain the negative correlation between per capita GDP growth and stock market returns.

NOTES

1. Kahler Financial Group. (2011, May 9). *Pessimistic math and 12% returns*. Retrieved from http://kahlerfinancial.com/financial-awakenings/weekly-column/pessimistic-math-and-12-returns

2. Kahneman, D., & Tversky, A. (1979). Prospect theory: An analysis of decision under risk. *Econometrica, 47*(2), 263 – 291. Retrieved from http://www.princeton.edu/~kahneman/docs/Publications/prospect_theory.pdf

3. Ricciardi, V., & Rice, D. (2014). Risk perception and risk tolerance. In H. K. Baker & V. Ricciardi (Eds.), *Investor behavior – The psychology of financial planning and investing* (pp. 327 – 345). Hoboken, NJ: Wiley.

4. Hastie, R., & Dawes, R. M. (2010). *Rational choice in an uncertain world: The psychology of judgment and decision making*. Thousand Oaks, CA: Sage.

5. Dimson, E., Marsh, P., & Staunton, M. (2015). *Credit Suisse global investment returns yearbook 2015*. Zurich: Credit Suisse AG. Retrieved from http://www.investering.dk/documents/10655/157815/Credit+Suisse/0c0ceeb5-c5af-464d-be00-fb1378cb0412

6. Cardenal, A. (2016). Warren Buffett: Forget about value vs. growth investing. *The Motley Fool*, February 4. Retrieved from http://www.fool.

com/investing/general/2015/02/04/warren-buffett-forget-about-value-vs-growth-invest.aspx

7. Reese, J. P. (2013). Why Warren Buffett is not the world's greatest value investor. *Forbes.com*, December 6. Retrieved from http://www.forbes.com/sites/investor/2013/12/06/why-warren-buffett-is-not-the-worlds-greatest-value-investor/

8. Neill, H. B. (1954). *The art of contrary thinking*. Caldwell, ID: Caxton Press.

9. Siegel, J. J. (2014). *Stocks for the long run* (5th ed.). New York, NY: McGraw-Hill.

10. Wagner, W. H., & Lau, S. C. (1971). The effect of diversification on risk. *Financial Analysts Journal*, 27(6), 48 – 53.

11. ProShare. (2015). *Alternative investments: understanding their role in a portfolio*. Retrieved from http://www.proshares.com/media/documents/alternative_investments.pdf

12. Ilmanen, A. (2011). *Expected returns: An investor's guide to harvesting market rewards*. Hoboken, NJ: Wiley.

13. Goldberg, S. (2016P. Expanding the definition of 'accredited investor.' *Wall Street Daily*, February 25. Retrieved from http://www.wallstreetdaily.com/2016/02/25/accredited-investor-private-equity/

14. Buffett, W. (2014, February 28). 2013 letter – Berkshire Hathaway, Inc. Retrieved from http://www.berkshirehathaway.com/letters/2013ltr.pdf

15. Shefrin, H. (2000). *Beyond greed and fear*. Boston, MA: Harvard Business School Press.

16. Finucane, M. L., Alhakami, A., Slovic, P., & Johnson, S. M. (2000). The affect heuristic in judgment of risks and benefits. *Journal of Behavioral Decision Making*, 13(1), 1 – 17. Retrieved from http://www-abc.mpib-berlin.mpg.de/users/r20/finucane00_the_affect_heuristic.pdf

17. Kaustia, M., Laukkanen, H., & Puttonen, V. (2009). Should good stocks have high prices or high returns? *Financial Analysts Journal*, 65 (3), 55 – 62.

18. Statman, M., Fisher, K. L., & Anginer, D. (2009). Affect in a behavioral asset-pricing model. *Financial Analysts Journal*, 64(2), 20 – 29.

19. The prospectus of *Pohjola world high-performers* ("Pohjola Maailman Menestyjät I/2009"). Retrieved from (in Finnish) https://

www.op.fi/op/henkiloasiakkaat/saastot-ja-sijoitukset/strukturoidut-tuot-teet/pohjola-maailman-menestyjat-i-2009?cid=151019487&srcpl=3

20. Chan, L. K. C., Jegadeesh, N., & Lakonishok, J. (1995). Evaluating the performance of value versus glamour stocks: The impact of selection bias. *Journal of Financial Economics*, *38*(3), 269 – 296. Fama, E. F., & French, K. R. (1998). Value versus growth: The international evidence. *Journal of Finance*, *53*(6), 1975 – 1999. Fabozzi, F. J. Ma, K. C., & Oliphant, B. J. (2008). Sin stock returns. *Journal of Portfolio Management*, *35*(1), 82 – 94.

21. Ritter, J. R. (2005). Economic growth and equity returns. *Pacific-Basin Finance Journal*, *13*(5), 489 – 503. Retrieved from http://bear.warrington.ufl.edu/ritter/pbfj2005.pdf

22. Key Investor Information Document (KIID) of the FIM BRIC + fund. Retrieved from (in Finnish) https://dokumentit.s-pankki.fi/tiedostot/bric_plus_kiid_at https://dokumentit.s-pankki.fi/tiedostot/bric_plus_kiid_fi

23. Marketing material of the FIM BRIC fund. Retrieved from https://www.fim.com/fi/sijoittaminen/fim-rahastot/fim-bric-a/ (in Finnish).

24. Ritter, J. R. (2012). Is economic growth good for investors? *Journal of Applied Corporate Finance*, *24*(3), 8 – 18. Retrieved from http://bear.warrington.ufl.edu/ritter/JACF_2012.pdf

25. Frost, R. (2015). China's stock market value tops $10 trillion for first time. *BloombergBusiness*, June 13. Retrieved from http://www.bloomberg.com/news/articles/2015-06-14/china-s-stock-market-value-exceeds-10-trillion-for-first-time

26. Davis, J. H., Aliaga-Diaz, R., Cole, C. W., & Shanahan, J. (2010). *Investing in emerging markets: Evaluation the allure of rapid economic growth*. Vanguard. Retrieved from http://www.vanguard.com/pdf/icriem.pdf

9

TRAP 5: FALLING FOR MUTUAL FUND TRAPS

The best argument for mutual funds is that they offer safety and diversification. But they don't necessarily offer safety and diversification.

Ron Chernow, American writer,
journalist, historian, and biographer

Investors face a bewildering array of ways to invest their money. However, a highly popular investment vehicle for many investors is a *mutual fund*, which is a type of professionally managed investment fund that pools money from many investors to buy securities. With mutual funds, investors don't have to make decisions about which securities or assets to buy, but instead decide what fund suits them best. Mutual funds are one of the best ways to build wealth over time. The popularity of mutual funds is evident based on the staggering amount of money invested in them. In 2016, total worldwide net assets of mutual funds were $37.2 trillion with $18.1 trillion in the United States.[1]

Selecting the right mutual fund is an important but often a daunting task for individual investors. One reason for this dilemma is the large number of funds available. In 2015, the United States alone had 9521 mutual funds, excluding those primarily investing in other mutual funds.[1] Mutual funds are available for practically every investment strategy, sector, and country or region of the world. In a similar vein, each major economy has specific rules pertaining to the registration, marketing, and sale of funds. For example, all mutual funds marketed to U.S. retail (individual) investors must be registered with the SEC and must abide by the rules set forth under the Investment Company Act of 1940.[2]

This chapter begins by providing some general information about mutual funds, their potential advantages and disadvantages, as well as the various types of funds available. Next, common mistakes and traps associated with investing in mutual funds are discussed. Another topic discussed is the difficulty of predicting fund outperformance, especially those involving actively managed equity mutual funds.

BACKGROUND ON MUTUAL FUNDS

As previously mentioned, a *mutual fund* is a company that brings together money from many people and invests it in stocks, bonds, or other assets. Like many other investments, mutual funds do not guarantee returns and have several distinguishing characteristics. First, investors buy mutual fund shares from the fund itself or through a broker for the fund, not from other investors on a secondary market as with stocks and bonds. Second, the fund stands ready to redeem (buy back) its shares from investors at the end of every business day at its *net asset value* (NAV), a fund's per-share value. Third, mutual funds continuously sell their shares to accommodate new investors. However, some funds might stop selling shares. For example, if a fund becomes too large, sometimes it stops accepting new buyers to keep the fund's size more manageable.

Advantages of Mutual Funds

For many investors, mutual funds offer advantages compared to direct investing in individual assets or securities. As

Ron Chernow, a bestselling and award-winning American author, writes, "Mutual funds give people the sense that they're investing with the big boys and that they're really not at a disadvantage entering the stock market." Below are some potential advantages of mutual funds:

- *Professional management*: Mutual funds offer professional money management in which fund managers make the decisions about when to buy and sell assets.

- *Diversification*: Investing in mutual funds can be less risky than directly buying shares in individual companies due to the wider spread of investments in the portfolio. Mutual fund investors can benefit from increased diversification and risk reduction. However, just because you own a mutual fund doesn't mean you are automatically diversified, as a fund that invests only in a particular industry, region, or sector is still relatively risky.

- *Affordability*: Mutual funds are often the simplest and least expensive way to gain access to different markets and securities. Many mutual funds allow investors to begin with a lower initial payment. By pooling money from different investors, the shareholders may experience savings because they are sharing the costs and benefits from economies of scale, which allow for lower trading costs per dollar of investment.

- *Convenience*: Mutual funds provide a high level of convenience to investors. They are easy to buy and sell and generally have low minimum investments. The fund management company handles buying and selling of assets, as well as collecting any dividends and income, thereby providing service and convenience to investors. Mutual funds also enable some investors to participate in investments that may be available only to larger investors.

- *Liquidity*: Mutual funds permit investors to request that their shares be converted into cash at any time. Mutual funds transact only once per day after calculating the fund's NAV. When selling a mutual fund, access to your cash is available the day after the sale.

- *Dividend reinvestment*: When a fund declares dividends and other interest income, fund participants can use these funds to automatically purchase additional shares in the mutual fund, which helps you grow your investment.

- *Other advantages*: Additional advantages of mutual funds include transparency due to extensive disclosure requirements, daily valuation, flexibility, and regulatory oversight and accountability.

Disadvantages of Mutual Funds

Despite their appeal, some investors may view certain features of mutual funds as disadvantages. Some of these disadvantages also apply to many other investments, not solely to mutual funds.

- *Fees and expenses*: Investors incur costs and fees even when mutual fund returns are negative. The various costs differ from fund to fund but can be classified into two broad categories: one-time shareholder fees and regular fund operating costs. Over time, fees and expenses add up and reduce overall investment returns. Such costs are disclosed in the mutual fund prospectus and are available on the fund's website. A *mutual fund prospectus* is a document detailing the fund's investment objectives and strategies as well as its past performance, managers, and financial information. Some funds, called *load funds*, have a sales charge or load. You can avoid this charge by buying a *no-load mutual fund*, which is a mutual fund in which shares are sold without a commission or sales charge. You buy the shares directly from the investment company, instead of going through a secondary party.

- *Tax inefficiency*: Owning mutual funds can have tax implications for investors. When making decisions, fund managers don't consider investors' personal tax situation, but you should. Due to turnover, redemptions, gains and losses in security holdings throughout the year, investors typically receive distributions from the fund that are an uncontrollable tax event. However, capital gains distributions don't affect retirement plans such as IRAs and 401(k)s. Tax-advantaged vehicles such as Roth IRAs, simplified employee pension (SEP) plans, and 529 accounts provide tax advantages when including mutual funds. A *529 plan* is a tax-advantaged savings plan designed to encourage saving for future college costs. States, state agencies, or educational institutions sponsor 529 plans, which are authorized by Section 529 of the Internal Revenue Code. Index funds are more tax efficient that those following an active investing strategy because they involve less turnover of the fund's investments. Taxes are an issue for U.S. funds, but in many European countries mutual funds are tax free on dividends and capital gains. Investors only pay taxes on capital gains when redeeming fund shares. In other words, mutual funds are tax efficient, not inefficient or even neutral.

- *Management abuses*: Mutual fund managers may engage in excessive turnover and *window dressing*, a strategy used by portfolio managers close to the end of a quarter or year to improve the fund's appearance. For example, they do so by selling stocks with large losses and buying high flying stocks to make the portfolio look better. Thus, investors may be attracted to the fund because it contains high performing stocks.

- *Cash drag*: Mutual funds need to have ample cash reserves to satisfy investor redemptions and to maintain liquidity for purchases. Money sitting around as cash does not "work" for investors and hence affects performance by lowering returns.

- *Poor performance*: Returns on a mutual fund are not guaranteed. Only a small percentage of active portfolio managers consistently beat their market indexes or benchmarks. *Active management* means that the portfolio manager buys and sells investments with the goal of outperforming an investment benchmark index. Given that a fund has limitations on what it can own, this could be a problem if no "good deals" are available within the chosen mandate, especially for funds with a narrow mandate. By contrast, *passive management*, also called *indexing*, involves buying a portfolio of securities designed to track the performance of a benchmark index. Nevertheless, an index fund might suffer from *index risk,* in which the fund's performance might not match that of its benchmark index.

- *Lack of control*: Mutual fund investors neither have any influence over the specific securities or assets that the manager buys and sells nor do they control their timing.

- *Price uncertainty*: Investors do not know the price at which they buy or redeem shares until the fund calculates its NAV after the close of the market. Some claim this characteristic results in poor trade execution. However, others believe that trading at the closing NAV eliminates price fluctuation throughout the day and various arbitrage opportunities that day traders and others practice. *Day trading* involves buying and selling financial instruments within the same trading day, such that all positions are closed before the market closes for the trading day.

Types of Mutual Funds

An appropriate type of mutual fund is available for almost every investing goal and risk tolerance. Here are some major types of funds. Morningstar provides a more extensive classification system for portfolios available for sale in the United States.[3]

- *Money market funds (MMFs)*: MMFs invest in highly liquid, short-term (i.e., less than one year) securities such as Treasury bills, bankers' acceptances, corporate commercial paper, and CDs. As some of the lowest-risk funds available, they typically provide a lower potential return than other types of mutual funds. Thus, long-term investors, such as those participating in employer-sponsored retirement plans, might want to seek other investments than MMFs to provide the capital appreciation needed to meet their financial goals. MMFs are not covered by federal deposit insurance.

- *Fixed-income (bond) funds*: These funds invest in bonds that pay a fixed rate of return. Bond funds generally focus on a particular sector, such as corporate or government bonds, or a broad category, such as investment grade or high-yield (junk) bonds. Investment grade bonds have a relatively low risk of default compared with high-yield bonds. The risks and rewards of bond funds can vary dramatically. Some of the risks associated with bond funds include (1) *credit risk* (the possibility that the issuer might fail to make required payments); (2) *interest rate risk* (the risk that the market value of the bonds decreases when interest rates increase); and (3) *prepayment risk* (the risk that a bond is repaid early and an investor has to find a new place to invest with the risk of lower returns). Bond funds try to have money flowing into the fund on a regular basis, primarily by earning interest. Bond managers accomplish this task by holding bonds within the fund portfolio that mature on a staggered basis to deliver consistent income payments.

- *Equity (stock) funds*: These funds principally invest in stocks and are usually riskier than MMFs and fixed-income funds. Stock mutual funds can be classified in various ways including company size, investment style of the portfolio's holdings, geography, and sector. Size refers to a company's *market capitalization*, which is the market value of a company's outstanding shares. This is calculated by multiplying a company's shares outstanding by the current market price of one share. Common size categories are microcap, small cap, medium cap, large cap, or mega-cap companies. Investment style is reflected in the fund's stock holdings such as growth, value, and income stocks. A *growth stock* is a stock of a company whose revenues and earnings are expected to increase at a faster rate than the average company within the same industry. A *value stock* is the stock of a company that tends to trade at a lower price relative to its fundamentals such as earnings, dividends, and sales and hence is considered undervalued by value investors. An *income stock* pays regular, often steadily increasing dividends, and offers a high yield that may generate the majority of overall returns. Stock funds are also categorized by whether they are domestic or international. A sector equity fund invests solely in businesses that operate in a particular industry or sector of the economy such as industrials, technology, health, and financials.

- *Allocation funds*: Asset-allocation mutual funds come in several varieties. For example, balanced funds provide investors with a portfolio of a fixed or variable mix of the three main asset classes — stocks, bonds and cash equivalents — in a variety of securities. The mix of these securities determines the fund's riskiness, and balanced fund portfolios do not materially change their asset mix. Balanced funds tend to appeal to investors interested in a mixture of safety, income, and modest capital appreciation. Other types of asset-allocation mutual funds, also known as *life-cycle* or *target-date funds*, attempt to provide investors with portfolio structures that address an investor's age, risk tolerance, and investment objectives with an appropriate apportionment of asset classes.

- *Specialty funds*: This category consists of mutual funds that forgo broad diversification and instead concentrate on a certain segment of the economy such as emerging markets, real estate, commodities or socially responsible investing. For example, a socially responsible or ethical fund might invest in companies that support environmental stewardship, human rights, and diversity, and may avoid companies involved in tobacco, alcoholic beverages, gambling, weapons, the military, or nuclear power.

- *Index funds*: These funds attempt to match or track the performance of an index such as the Standard & Poor's 500 Index (S&P 500). However, the performance of an index fund may differ from the actual index's performance because index funds charge management fees, which reduce returns, and the fund's weighting in particular securities may not perfectly match those of the securities in the index. Index funds typically have lower costs than actively managed mutual funds due to low operating expenses and low portfolio turnover.
- *Fund of funds*: A *fund of funds* is a mutual fund that invests in other mutual funds. Although this investment vehicle achieves broad diversification, most have higher fees because shareholders are essentially paying double for an expense that is already included in the expense figures of the underlying funds.

MUTUAL FUND MISTAKES AND TRAPS

Investing in mutual funds requires being aware of some mistakes or traps that can snare unsuspecting investors.[4] Additionally, some conventional wisdom about investing in mutual funds lacks empirical support. For example, investors are often encouraged to buy established mutual funds with experienced portfolio managers that have good long-term track records. Although this might seem like sound advice, recent evidence shows that young actively managed funds tend to outperform their older peers because the new entrants are more aware of the latest techniques. Furthermore, performance tends to deteriorate as funds grow older. Researchers find that funds with three years or less in age actually outperform funds with more than 10 years of history by almost one percentage point annually.[5]

This evidence suggests that investing in younger, rather than older, funds may be less risky. Nonetheless, by taking your time and understanding the nuances about mutual funds, you can avoid some costly mistakes and be successful over the longer haul.

Buying Past Winners

Most mutual funds are actively managed. If you could identify the right fund manager at the right time, this would be a great advantage. However, this is a big "if." Selecting funds that are likely to generate superior risk-adjusted returns in the future (rising stars) is no easy task. Instead, many mutual fund investors buy past winners or focus on Morningstar "stars." That is, they use past performance to predict future performance. The problem with this logic is that it doesn't square with the facts: Only a very small fraction of fund managers can keep up their "superstar" status and beat the indexes beyond very short horizons of one or two quarters. Hot funds, especially those investing in narrow sectors, can quickly go cold, the market can turn, and a superstar fund manager can leave. Thus, attempting to pick funds that consistently outperform others is futile.[6]

The research evidence on the effectiveness of relying on past performance varies considerably based on the time period examined and methodology used. In general, however, studies conclude that the best past performance funds earn back their expenses and transaction costs. The problem is that these funds represent only a small fraction of actively managed mutual funds. Although using past strong risk-adjusted performance to guide investment decisions might work in very short horizons, little consistency in predictive ability exists beyond this horizon. In other words, top-performing funds generally do not continue over long periods to significantly outperform other funds. This outperformance persistence is due to *momentum stocks*, which are stocks that are previous winners. For most investors, buying past winners is not a value enhancing strategy after expenses and fees. As already noted, top performers don't typically stay on top for very long. Thus, this year's top funds can easily become next year's duds. Still, research indicates that investors should avoid poorly performing funds because their performance may persist for many years due to high expenses and fees.[7]

Advertisements, rankings, and ratings often emphasize the strong performance of the past year's top mutual funds. The lure of recent superstar performers attracts investors like moths to a flame, often with similar results — both get burned. Don't be dazzled by last year's high flyers. As Warren Buffet, an investment guru and one of the richest and most respected businessmen in the world, notes, "Investing is like baseball. If you want to score runs, don't study the scoreboard, study the playing field." In other words, a fund's past performance is not as important as you might think.

One reason investors tend to believe that past performance matters more than it does is because they have a cognitive bias called recency bias, which was discussed in Chapter 4. *Recency bias* is the tendency to think that trends and patterns observed in the recent past will continue in the future. Why? Recent events and trends are easier to remember and discern than either events in the distant past or unknown events that will occur in the future. Thus, investors tend to use their recent experience as the baseline for what will happen in the future. Although this bias may work in the short run, it can cause problems when predicting the future in the long term because what happened recently is not the only thing determining what happens to your investments tomorrow. When you take the long view, you realize that many factors influence the performance of mutual funds.[8]

Evidence also indicates a positive relation between advertising and subsequent mutual *fund flows*, which are the aggregate amount that investors put into or withdraw from a fund during a particular period. For example, one study shows that the advertised funds receive about 20% greater flow than do similar

funds that do not advertise. However, although advertising benefits fund companies, it does not benefit investors. After being
advertised, funds tend to underperform the same benchmark
that they beat before being advertised.[9] The SEC typically
requires that performance advertisements contain a disclaimer
that includes a warning that "past performance does not guarantee future results." Yet, individual mutual fund investors tend to
rely on a fund's investment performance track record as the
most important factor when choosing funds. The disclaimer
required by the SEC neither reduces the propensity of investors
to invest in advertised funds nor diminishes their expectations
about funds' future returns.[10]

Evidence also shows that an equity fund's past returns have a
strong positive effect on fund flows. The best-performing funds
attract large inflows, whereas poorly performing funds suffer proportionally smaller outflows. This relation between mutual fund flows
and performance appears to be partly due to investor behavioral
characteristics. That is, individual mutual fund investors use raw
return performance and flock disproportionately to recent winners,
but do not withdraw assets from recent losers. As Ron Chernow
notes, "Mutual fund managers are trapped in this rather deadly
vicious circle: The more successful they are, the more money flows
into their mutual fund. Then, it is more difficult for them to beat the
market average or even to match their own past performance."

Incurring High Fees and Expenses

Another mutual fund trap involves incurring high fees and
expenses without receiving adequate benefits. As Robert Kiyosaki,
an American businessman, investor, and self-help author, notes,
"If you don't like the idea that most of the money spent on lottery
tickets supports government programs, you should know that
most of the earnings from mutual funds support investment advisors' and mutual fund managers' retirement."

Although all mutual funds have costs that eat up returns over-time, index funds are generally less costly to own than actively managed funds. Why? A fund replicating an index is less expensive to run than an active fund that must hire analysts and managers and engage in extensive research to try to outperform the market.

Regarding fees, mutual fund investing is a "buyers beware" situation. Similar types of funds might have very different fees and expenses. To address this issue, you can use websites such as Morningstar.com to see how a fund's expenses compare to other funds in the same category. An *expense ratio* is calculated annually by dividing a fund's operating expenses by the average dollar value of its assets under management (AUM). That is, an expense ratio measures the investment company's cost to operate a mutual fund and hence the cost of owning it. However, the expense ratio does not include the costs of buying or redeeming shares (sales loads), transaction fees, or brokerage charges. As previously noted, a *sales load* is a fee or type of commission paid on a mutual fund. Sales loads can be front-end loads (fees paid when buying the fund) and back-end or deferred loads (fees paid when selling the fund). Sales loads are a raw deal, so avoid them whenever possible. When possible, buy a no-load fund directly from the fund company instead of through a broker where you'd normally have to pay a commission. Chapter 10 provides further discussion of the costs associated with investing in mutual funds.

Overemphasizing Actively Managed Funds

A third trap involves placing too much emphasis on actively managed funds. Conventional wisdom suggests that mutual fund managers have great difficulty trying to "beat the market." In fact, various studies find that roughly 80% of active funds underperform.[11] In other words, the average actively managed fund typically fails to beat the broad indexes over time and hence loses to a low-cost index fund, net of all fees and expenses. Yet, many index funds also underperform their benchmarks largely due to fees and expenses reducing their gross returns.

Should the typical individual investor pay for active fund management? The answer is generally no. However, this response is not always true because some active managers add value for their investors, beating their benchmark indices after all fees and expenses.[12] The challenge, of course, is to identify future superior performing funds, which is extremely difficult to do. Although neither approach — active or passive management — is always superior, index funds such as cheap S&P 500 index funds provide an attractive alternative to capture the broader market at a low cost. Of course, another option is for investors to manage their own portfolios, so long as they have the time and ability.

Holding Closet Indexers

Another mutual fund trap involves holding *closet index funds*, which are funds that claim to actively manage their portfolios but in reality closely emulate a market index and have fees and expenses similar to those of truly active managers. Active fund managers closet index because it's in their best interests, especially when markets are down, as investors do not reward outperformance with higher flows.[13] In some cases, funds become closet indexers as they grow in assets. This fact helps to explain why some superstar managers fail over time. Buyers should be wary of funds charging a fee for active management but whose performance barely varies from the index. Nonetheless, most investors probably don't realize they might have money in a closet index fund because the fund doesn't advertise itself as such. Research shows that closet indexers are doomed to underperform after considering fees and that closet indexing is rife in U.S. active funds.[12]

How can you identify closet indexing? One way to identify and avoid closet index funds is by examining the investment objectives listed in the fund's prospectus to see if it reveals the fund's benchmark, and by inspecting their portfolios. An approach for more quantitatively oriented investors is to calculate and compare the fund's R^2 or $R\text{-}squared$, which measures the extent to which the fund's return is determined by changes in its relevant index/ benchmark. R^2 is also known as the *coefficient of determination* in which R is the correlation coefficient squared. It ranges from 0 to 100. The closer the R^2 is to 100, the more likely the fund manager is a closet indexer.[14] Still another approach is to use a measure called *active share*, which is the percentage of a fund's portfolio that differs from its benchmark. A well-managed index fund will have an active share of 0.[15]

Relying on a Fund's Name

Some investors rely on a fund's name but doing so can be a trap. Mutual fund names can be confusing and not reveal what a fund actually owns. Instead of relying solely on the fund's name, you should "check under the hood" by examining the fund's prospectus to see how its assets are diversified. As already discussed, examining a fund's holdings can also help you spot closet indexers. Some advertisements of funds are misleading and can guide investors down the wrong path. The SEC requires a fund with a name suggesting that the fund focuses on a particular type of investment such as stocks or bonds to invest at least 80% of its assets accordingly. The remaining assets are under the sole discretion of the fund manager and might be vague and wide-ranging.[16] Consequently, a fund can potentially manipulate prospective investors by using names that are attractive but misleading. For instance, instead of labeling itself a small-cap fund, it might be sold under the heading growth fund. In short, you need to know what you own, regardless of what the fund is named.

Failing to Understand the Risks

Like other investments, mutual funds have risks. Investors often don't recognize or understand the various risks that affect the mutual funds they own. The level of risk depends largely on the securities or assets within the fund's portfolio. Taking more risk usually leads to higher returns over time. Because stocks are generally riskier than bonds, equity funds tend to be riskier than fixed-income funds. Specialty funds focusing on certain kinds of investments, such as emerging markets, might try to earn a higher return and hence be subject to greater risk. However, you should avoid overweighting in high-risk, nondiversified funds such as domestic and foreign small-cap growth, emerging markets, and sector funds and in certain high-yield funds.

What types of risk should you consider? *Market risk* and *liquidity risk* can affect all types of investments. *Credit risk* and *interest rate risk* apply to fixed-income securities and thus funds holding these assets. *Country risk* affects foreign investments because a foreign investment's value might decline because of political changes or instability in the country where the investment was issued. Also, funds holding investments denominated in a currency other than their home currency face *currency risk*.

You can assess a fund's level of risk in several ways. One approach is to examine the volatility of returns over time. Funds with greater changes in their returns can be considered more risky because their performance can change by a greater magnitude. Another approach is to examine a fund's prospectus because it details the risks that could affect investors.

Ignoring Taxes

As previously mentioned, owning mutual funds can have tax implications for investors. For example, in the United States, each shareholder participates proportionally in the gain or loss of the fund. Mutual funds must pass along to their shareholders any realized capital gains that are not offset by capital losses by the end of their accounting year. Additionally, fund managers must distribute any income that their securities generate. This "tax-drag" could lessen the desirability of owning mutual funds.

Duplicating Fund Categories

Finally, Investors can engage in inefficient or false diversification by buying two or more funds with the same objectives. For example, having two growth-oriented funds does not provide the risk/reward characteristics of ideal diversification. To avoid duplication, you should represent a fund category with just one fund.

PREDICTING MUTUAL FUND PERFORMANCE

One of the biggest mistakes investors make with mutual funds is being overconfident in their ability to predict the future investment performance of markets and fund managers. Selecting future winners or mutual fund outperformance is extraordinarily difficult. Even mutual fund experts who try to identify mutual funds that they think will beat the market typically experience disastrous results. One reason for this difficulty is that much dissonance exists on what predicts outperformance of actively managed mutual funds. Although one study may show that a specific factor predicts fund outperformance, another reports the opposite. This occurs with expenses and loads, turnover, past performance, mutual fund ratings, activeness, fund and family size, fund governance, and various managerial characteristics.[7]

Most individual investors are likely to have considerable difficulty sorting through the conflicting evidence. As an alternative, many find index investing less complicated but equally or even more rewarding. You are probably better off minimizing your fund's fees and expenses by putting your money in low-cost index funds. As Jim Cramer, an American television personality and bestselling author, notes "I think you'll do as well as most professionals. Most professionals don't beat the market. Let's not overrate my industry. But if you have time, you can be in good mutual funds that have good records."

Having provided some background about mutual funds, let's now turn to several extended examples of actual investment traps.

These traps include a hypothetical track record, fund mergers, fund incubation, and advertising strong historical performance.

HYPOTHETICAL TRACK RECORD

Freedom Fund is one of the three funds offered by a Finnish bou-tique financial services provider, Estlander & Partners. The com-pany established itself in 1991 and the Freedom Fund, its most novel fund, started in 2010. Freedom Fund is a non-UCITS fund with an investment strategy that combines the approaches of Estlander & Partners' two other funds: Global XL and Alpha Trend. The term UCITS stands for "Undertakings for Collective Investment in Transferable Securities." A *UCITS* is a mutual fund based in the European Union, which can be sold to any investor within the European Union under a harmonized regulatory regime. According to the Finnish Financial Supervisory Authority, *non-UCITS funds* are investment funds deviating from the principle of diversification of risk pursuant to the Mutual Funds Act. Although a regular investment fund must have at least 16 different underlying investments, a non-UCITS fund can have fewer investments. Freedom Fund claims that its positions entirely follow these two strat-egies by equally weighting each strategy after adjusting for their risks.

Freedom Fund's hypothetical historical performance was promoted by showing the phenomenal performance of the "program." A hypothetical €1,000 investment in 1991 had steadily grown to approximately €10,000 in 2010.[17] The fund opened to investors in 2010.

As **Figure 9.1** shows, the picture changes when examining the fund's realized returns from actual inception in July 2010. Since its launch to investors, Freedom Fund generated a cumulative 10.5% return by 2015, while the corresponding return for the S&P 500 index is 243%. For further comparison, JPM Global Bond index yielded a cumulative 10.6% return and Newedge CTA index yielded a cumulative 19.7% return in the same period.

Figure 9.1: Freedom Fund's Realized Performance since Inception versus the S&P 500 Index

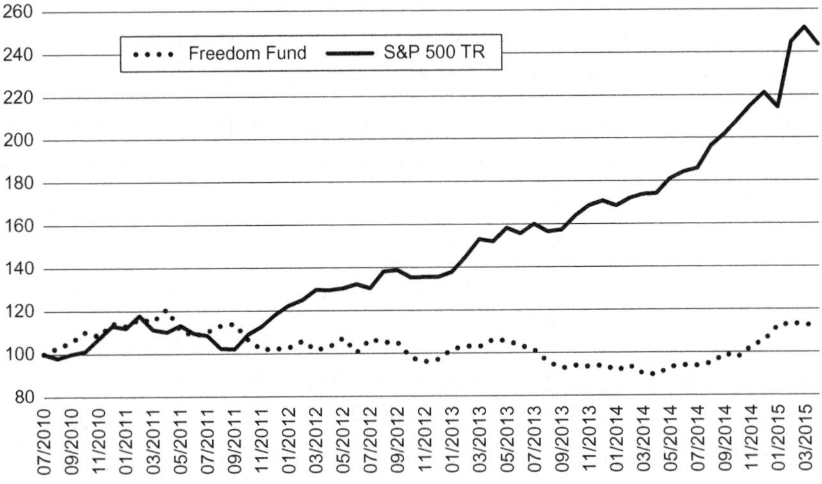

Source: Estlander & Partners monthly reports and Bloomberg. Notes: This figure shows that that Freedom Fund's realized performance generally is clearly less than that of the S&P 500 index. To make comparison easy, both values are set to begin from 100 in July 2010.

Newedge CTA index is a benchmark index for hedge funds. At one point of time (April 2014) the value of Freedom Fund was 10.4% below its value in July 2010.

The true performance clearly paints an entirely different picture of the fund's performance than the claims provided in the fund's marketing material: "Freedom combines two successful key strategies managed by Estlander & Partners; Alpha Trend and Global XL. The underlying investment strategies, which have track records dating back to 1991, have an annualized average net return (after fees) of 12% for over 20 years." Documents deceptively claim that "Freedom could be the right product for you if you are seeking strong returns even in uncertain times." Considering that historical performance is a key driver of fund flows, such marketing choices do not appear to be naïve misunderstandings. The company is also purposely cryptic about the fund's fees, which aren't clearly highlighted to potential investors in the fund summaries.

The activities of Estlander & Partners are particularly troubling. In the United States, only investors who have separately registered with the SEC as sophisticated or wealthy investors can buy hedge fund shares. In Finland, however, anyone who meets the fund's minimum investment requirements can buy such "hedge fund-like" funds as provided by Estlander & Partners. In the case of Freedom Fund, the minimum investment for A-class shares is €1,000, which is not a large sum for a majority of individual investors. As such, despite these clients having enough funds, they might not be sufficiently financially literate to understand the complex nature of such funds. Estlander & Partners does not provide much help either, given the lack of information provided to potential investors.

Freedom Fund is a typical example of how funds can present information in a favorable manner. In this case, the fund presented a simulated trading strategy for a 20-year period to make the fund look more attractive showing a hypothetical graph of returns since 1991 even though the fund began in 2010. The graph generated an image of strong stable returns. This marketing trick exaggerated historical returns and portrayed a strategy that would provide excessive returns in the future. Additionally, the case suggests overpaying because various fees are difficult to trace.

Trap Judgment

Hypothetical Track Record

Becoming a victim of investment fraud

Misrepresenting risky products as safe

Making unrealistic return expectations

Falling for mutual fund traps

Overpaying for products and services

Investing in complex products

Engaging in gambling disguised as investing

Relying on unsupported promises

FUND MERGERS

A widespread phenomenon in the mutual fund industry is survivor-ship bias, which results in overestimating the past returns of mutual funds. *Survivorship bias* is the tendency of mutual fund companies to drop funds because of poor performance or low asset accumula-tion. Mutual fund companies often close losing funds and merge them into other funds to hide poor performance.[18] According to one study, more than 2% of the funds disappear annually from the market due to a merger.[19] As another report notes, "For mutual-fund firms, the best strategy in tough economic times is often to merge funds."[20] Hence, survivorship bias is an important issue to consider when analyzing past performance.

In July 2012, ING Large Cap Growth Portfolio acquired ING American Funds Growth. ING U.S., Inc., managed both funds. This particular case is a classic example of "cleaning up a poor track record." **Figure 9.2** illustrates the performance of ING

Figure 9.2: Performance of the ING Large Cap Growth Portfolio and ING American Funds Growth

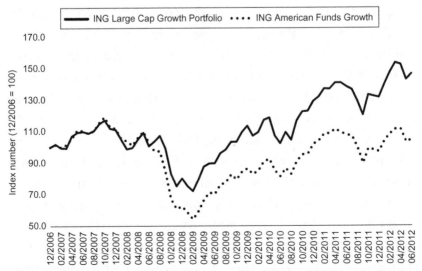

Source: CRSP and Morningstar. *Note*: This figure shows the performance of ING Large Cap Growth Portfolio and ING American Funds Growth over a six-year period.

American Funds Growth (acquired fund) and ING Large Cap Growth Portfolio (acquiring fund) six years before the merger.

Since its inception in December 2006 and until the acquisition of ING American Funds Growth in July 2012, ING Large Cap Growth Portfolio had a cumulative return of 46.5%, while ING American Funds Growth had a cumulative return of 4.8%. For comparison, the S&P 500 had a cumulative return of 8.1% during that period. ING American Funds Growth had performed worse than its benchmarks and especially worse than the star performer ING Large Cap Growth Portfolio.

An interesting matter concerning this fund acquisition is that ING American Funds Growth (acquired fund) was much larger than ING Large Cap Growth Portfolio (acquiring fund). In fact, ING Large Cap Growth Portfolio had only hundreds of thousands of dollars under management until early 2010 and still only $142 million at the time of the acquisition, while ING American Funds Growth had around $2 billion under management during the whole period of December 2006 until July 2012. Figure 9.3 depicts the total net assets of the funds in more detail.

As the previous figures show, ING Large Cap Growth Portfolio is basically ING American Funds Growth dressed in fancier clothes. That is, the assets come from ING American Funds Growth, but the track record used in the latest marketing material is that of ING Large Cap Growth Portfolio. Even though the track record of ING Large Cap Growth Portfolio is impressive and beats those of its benchmarks easily, fund managers achieved the excessive return before acquiring ING American Funds Growth. Figure 9.4 depicts the performance of Voya Large Cap Growth Portfolio and its S&P 500 index after the merger in July 2012.

In May, 2014, ING U.S. Investment Management was rebranded as Voya Investment Management. The large cap growth portfolio fund was relabeled as the Voya Large Cap Growth Portfolio. Voya Large Cap Growth Portfolio performed similarly to its benchmark after the merger. The fund's performance was comparable to that of the S&P 500 during the period

Figure 9.3: The Sizes of ING Large Cap Growth Portfolio and ING American Funds Growth between 2006 and 2015

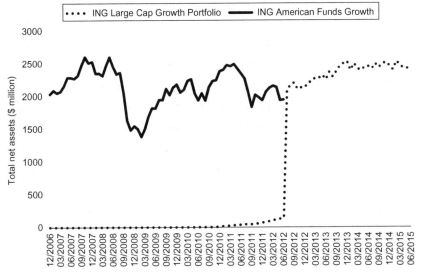

Notes: This figure shows that the acquiring fund (ING Large Cap Growth Portfolio) was considerably larger than the acquired fund (ING American Funds Growth). The funds merged in July 2012. Values are in $ millions.

Figure 9.4: Performance of ING Large Cap Growth Portfolio after the Merger in July 2012 Relative to the S&P 500 Index

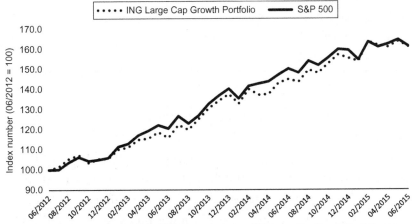

Source: CRSP and Morningstar. *Note*: This figure shows how ING Large Cap Growth Portfolio performed after the merger relative to the S&P 500 index.

when it had a broad asset and customer base. However, the claims that Voya Large Cap Growth Portfolio boasts in its marketing material about its track record since its inception in December 2006 are misleading.

Historical returns are a key factor that investors use to select a mutual fund. Poor performance does not attract cash inflows into a fund. Thus, fund managers use fund mergers to eliminate a fund with a poor track record. Erasing the poor historical performance and only showing the performance of a surviving fund leads to survivorship bias, which exaggerates the fund company's historical returns. Mutual fund mergers require shareholders to do their homework. As an investor, you should be aware when one of your funds merges into another because this result is like buying a whole new fund.

Trap Judgment

Fund Mergers

Becoming a victim of investment fraud

Misrepresenting risky products as safe

Making unrealistic return expectations

Falling for mutual fund traps

Overpaying for products and services

Investing in complex products

Engaging in gambling dressed up as investing

Relying on unsupported promises

FUND INCUBATION

An *incubated* or *limited distribution fund* is a fund that is offered privately when it is first launched. Incubation allows fund managers to keep a fund's size small and to test different investment styles before opening the top-performing funds to the public. The fund company then opens the higher performing funds that survive the incubation period to the investing public.

To better understand the incubation bias, let's analyze a case. Putnam Investments created Putnam Research Fund in October 1995 with about $3 million in net assets. Putnam Investments provided all of the initial capital and inflows from outside investors were minimal until July 1998, when Putnam finally began advertising the fund. This action makes Putnam a so-called incubated fund. Such "lab-grown" funds have become an increasingly common practice in the mutual fund industry. A study of newly created U.S. domestic equity funds from 1996 to 2005 shows that incubated funds represent about 23% of new funds.[21] The funds marketed to investors that eventually grew into full-scale funds are those that beat the market during the incubation period, and the others are usually closed. The industry advocates this practice as a way of identifying the most promising strategies and managers for new mutual funds.

Figure 9.5 shows Putnam Research Fund's performance over the S&P 500 index from October 1995 until August 2015. The fund clearly outperformed the benchmark index until summer 2010. Since then the Putnam Research Fund has been like many other funds: sometimes the fund beats the index and sometimes it underperforms the index. During the incubation period (October 1995–June 1998), Putnam Research Fund outperformed other funds with the same investment objective by 5.3 percentage points a year and the fund's average return was 28% a year. However, critics of the incubation practice contend that the incubation period returns occur under different conditions than for full-grown mutual fund returns. For example, the returns are based on much smaller fund sizes. As such, comparing the returns on incubated and mature mutual funds is inappropriate.

As **Figure 9.6** shows, the overall track record resulted in strong fund inflows. The total net assets of the Putnam Research Fund increased from $700 million in March 1999 to $2.3 billion in December 2001. Yet, the weak performance of the fund quickly changed into fund outflows and the total assets started to

Figure 9.5: Putnam Research Fund's One-Year Moving Average Return over the S&P 500 Index between 1996 and 2015

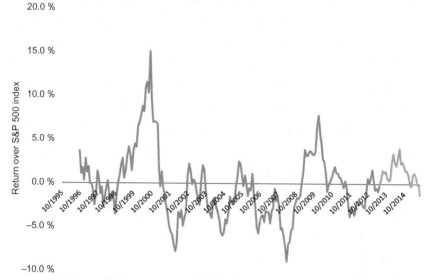

Source: Morningstar. *Note*: This figure shows the under and over performance of Putman Research Fund's one-year moving average return over the S&P 500 index between 1996 and 2015.

Figure 9.6: Total Net Assets of Putnam Research Fund in $ million between 1999 and 2015

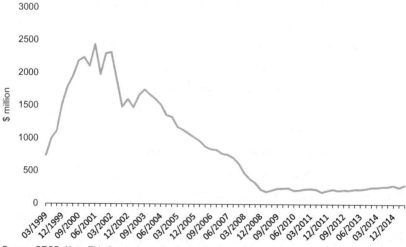

Source: CRSP. *Note*: This figure shows the fluctuation in total net assets of Putman Research Fund between March 1999 and March 2015 in $ million.

decrease. As of June 2015, Putnam Research Fund had total assets of more than $292 million. In recent marketing materials, Putnam shows the value development of $10,000 invested in the fund at inception to $49,471 on June 30, 2015, representing a total cumulative return of 394.71%. The materials state an annual average return rate of the fund as 8.4%. Both of these calculations, however, include the incubation period returns. When calculating these same figures for the period during which investors could actually invest in the fund in July 1998, the fund shows different performance. From July 1998 to August 2015, the fund has produced a total cumulative return of 137.56% and an annual average return of 5.2%. In contrast, the S&P 500 index generated an annual 5.4% return over the same period.

The reasons for incubation are not as noble as they might seem. Because the funds in incubation outperform nonincubated funds, they attract higher net dollar flows when opened to the public. As previously noted, investors emphasize historical fund performance when choosing a mutual fund. The fund company's intentions seem irrelevant as long as the investors are getting a good return. Then what's the problem? One potential result from such a practice is that this outperformance postincubation seems to disappear relative to nonincubated funds as net fund flows increases. In other words, fund companies are probably using the incubation period to create contrived outperformance and not to identify superior managers or strategies. Consequently, the practice of incubation might simply be a strategy for fund companies to develop a strong track record for their fund to attract as high net fund flows as possible once they open the fund to the public. As John C. Bogle writes in *The Battle for the Soul of Capitalism*, "Incubation funds have everything to do with the business of marketing, and nothing to do with business of management."[22]

The SEC has expressed concern about incubator funds in a public response to a private citizen's letter. According to the SEC, "... incubator fund performance should not be included in

a mutual fund's prospectus in the absence of extremely clear disclosure explaining the sponsor's purpose in establishing the incubator fund."[23] One proposition is that wherever a fund reports or
advertises incubation returns, it should include a warning such as,
"These returns were achieved when the fund was very small and
had not been marketed to the general public. It generally is more
difficult for a fund to achieve high returns as it grows."[24]

Because investors tend to focus on historical performance when
making an investment decision, fund management companies use
the incubation practice to trick investors. These companies may
claim that the incubation process produces superior returns but
evidence suggests otherwise. By displaying selected figures on
investment returns, the funds intentionally twist investors' understanding about past returns.

Trap Judgment

Fund Incubation

Becoming a victim of investment fraud

Misrepresenting risky products as safe

Making unrealistic return expectations

Falling for mutual fund traps

Overpaying for products and services

Investing in complex products

Engaging in gambling dressed up as investing

Relying on unsupported promises

ADVERTISING STRONG HISTORICAL PERFORMANCE

Mutual fund companies generally advertise their best-performing
funds.[25] This creates a relatively one-sided image of the company's
offering of mutual funds and directs investor attention toward
past performance reinforcing the habit of selecting mutual funds
with the highest realized returns.

For example, Janus Capital Group highlights the excellent performance of its Contrarian, Growth & Income, Orion, and Adviser Forty funds in an advertisement in 2006. The four funds had received a maximum five stars in the Morningstar fund rating. The Morningstar Rating™ is derived from a weighted-average of the (historical) performance. The top 10% of the funds in each category receive five stars, the next 22.5% receive four stars, the next 35% receive three stars, the next 22.5% receive two stars, and the bottom 10% receive one star.

Janus Growth Investing Is Making a Comeback. At Janus, It Never Went Out of Style.

The growth returns on this page didn't happen because of a market trend. They're the result of a disciplined investing approach that seeks growth in any market. Intensive, fundamental research, refined over 35 years, gives Janus the information edge that has delivered strong performance. See the latest returns below and then ask your financial advisor if Janus funds suit your style.

| | Average Annual Total Returns (%) as of 3/31/06 | | | | | Overall Morningstar |
	One year	Three years	Five years	Ten years	Since inception	Ratings
Janus Contrarian Fund	31.88	35.15	11.64	-	9.61	* * * * *
Janus Growth & Income Fund	20.62	19.11	4.80	12.05	13.79	* * * * *
Janus Orion Fund	34.09	31.81	11.41	-	(1.17)	* * * * *
Janus Adviser Forty Fund	20.64	18.74	5.65	-	13.13	* * * * *

Fund companies naturally want to put "their best foot forward" by advertising their star performers. As previously discussed, research generally shows that past returns do not do a very good job of predicting future returns. For example, one study of mutual fund advertisements in Barron's *Money* magazine finds a significant negative relation between the advertisement of a fund and its subsequent three-year risk-adjusted returns for both equity and fixed-income funds.[26] Another study finds that the amount of money a mutual fund company uses for advertising its funds increases its aggregate inflow when controlling for several other variables known to affect money flows to mutual funds.[27]

As of September 30, 2014, Janus reported that 53% of its complex-wide mutual funds had a four- or five-star Overall Morningstar Rating[TM]. This means that many of its funds had received less than four stars. The company also reported that 48%, 38%, and 58% of the strategies surpassed their respective benchmarks, net of fees, over the one-, three-, and five-year periods, respectively. In other words, roughly half of its funds beat the passive index. Of the four funds advertised in 2006, the Contrarian Fund now had four stars, the Growth & Income Fund had three stars, the Orion (now "Global Select") fund had two stars, and Forty Fund had three stars. All four funds underperformed their respective benchmark index over the five-year period.

A possible explanation for the effectiveness of mutual fund advertising lies in the so-called *availability heuristic*. This heuristic leads people to overweight evidence that comes easily to their mind when making a decision. Just like with other advertised products, selecting a mutual fund that sounds familiar when evaluating various options can benefit the fund. The false confidence and ease of the availability heuristic prompts, distorts attention from more relevant facts causing investors to make decisions quickly on partial information. According to behaviorists, limiting choices makes fund choice easier to solve and enables investors to act.

What does this evidence say about investors? They seemly flock to funds that have performed well in the past and are heavily promoted in advertisements. Of course, this behavior is understandable if mutual fund companies aim to promote these funds on the grounds of superior skills of the fund managers but this does not seem to be the case. Yet, the emphasis on advertising only the top-performing funds does not signal the superior skills of the fund managers, but rather exploits the heuristic of extrapolating from the past returns when selecting a mutual fund in which to invest. Funds that have the highest exposure in advertisements also have higher returns before the advertising period but underperform comparable, nonadvertised funds afterwards.[9]

Ironically, investors' tendency to gravitate toward top-performing funds might lead to diminished subsequent returns. An increase in the AUM of a mutual fund company or an individual mutual fund might provide economies of scale by spreading the overhead costs. It might also result in higher costs in other aspects, such as price impact when trading. Studies find that mutual fund returns are negatively related to increases in their NAVs.[28] This result holds especially for small-cap funds and other funds that invest in illiquid assets. The returns of growth and high-turnover funds also suffer from the increases in their NAVs. These lower returns are mostly due to the increased trading costs associated with the immediate needs of these funds.[29] The interaction among fund performance, advertising, and inflows might result in a self-reinforcing cycle with real-life implications to investors. Yet, advertising does not generally increase inflows to already well-known flagship funds. This result implies that the funds benefiting most from advertising exposure are likely to be those that face diseconomies of scale when new capital enters. Mutual fund advertising thus seems to attract money to the funds whose expected returns decline with this inflow.[30]

The evidence about the advertising habits of mutual fund companies and the way these advertisements shape investor behavior suggests that retail investors should indeed be wary of mutual fund advertising. As investors benefit from the increased knowledge about the funds available, they should try to establish an objective point of view when selecting the appropriate mutual fund for their purposes and resist the tendency to extrapolate past returns into the future.

Fund management companies advertise the strong historical performance of their funds but by doing so they end up exploiting investors. Investors often select past winners, which rarely provide a good indicator of future performance. The returns tend to normalize over time and in some cases inflows of new money might even result in lower than average returns. Advertising only the best-performing funds creates the perception that fund companies only manage well-performing funds. In turn, this encourages investors to have excessive return expectations, which are often misplaced.

Trap Judgment

Advertising Strong Historical Performance

Historical Performance

Becoming a victim of investment fraud

Misrepresenting risky products as safe

Making unrealistic return expectations

Falling for mutual fund traps

Overpaying for products and services

Investing in complex products

Engaging in gambling dressed up as investing

Relying on unsupported promises

LEARNING POINTS

When considering a mutual fund, you should understand both its good and bad points. If the fund's advantages outweigh its disadvantages, the fund might be an investment to consider. The probability of a selecting a good fund to meet your goals increases when you do your homework and avoid the common traps that mutual fund investors face. For investors who lack the time, inclination, or skill to select funds, index funds offer a simple, cheap, and effective alternative. Here are some key learning points from the chapter.

- Know your financial goals and risk tolerance before selecting a fund.

- Match your goals with the fund's investment objective.

- Read the prospectus and make sure the fund company is disciplined and sticks to its stated strategy.

- Determine the role the mutual fund is going to play in the portfolio.

- Identify the risks associated with a specific fund.

- Perform your due diligence before investing in a fund.

- Balance cost, risk, and long-term performance when choosing a fund.

- Avoid chasing stars because yesterday's big winners can become tomorrow's big losers.

- Be realistic about your ability to predict mutual fund outperformance; you might be better off with an index fund instead.

- Be cost conscious and avoid funds with sales charges and high expense ratios and turnover.

- Research the growth of the fund's size, especially asset bloat for a small-cap fund.

- Beware of closet index funds.

- Consider investing in index funds.

QUESTIONS

1. List and discuss several potential advantages and disadvantages of mutual funds.

2. Identify five different types of mutual funds and explain the characteristics of each type.

3. Explain why buying past winners is typically a poor strategy when selecting mutual funds.

4. Discuss the types of fees and charges associated with investing in mutual funds.

5. Compare and contrast actively managed and passively managed mutual funds.

6. Define a closet indexer.

7. Identify three different types of risks that some mutual funds face.

8. Discuss how U.S. mutual funds treat realized gains and losses and income generated from investments for tax purposes.

9. Discuss why predicting mutual fund outperformance is so difficult.

10. Identify and explain three mutual fund traps.

11. Explain the problems of relying on advertisements to select mutual funds.

NOTES

1. Investment Company Institute. (2016). *2016 investment company fact book* (56th ed.). Washington, DC: Investment Company Institute. Retrieved from http://www.icifactbook.org/ch1/16_fb_ch1

2. Brown, M. *How mutual funds differ around the world. Investopedia.* Retrieved from http://www.investopedia.com/articles/mutualfund/08/foreign-mutual-funds.asp

3. Morningstar. (2015, April 30). *The Morningstar category classifications.* Morningstar Methodology Paper. Retrieved from http://corporate.morningstar.com/us/documents/MethodologyDocuments/MethodologyPapers/MorningstarCategory_Classifications.pdf

4. Levitt, A. (2014). The 7 biggest mistakes to avoid when investing in mutual funds. *MutualFunds.com*, September 23. Retrieved from http://mutualfunds.com/education/biggest-mistakes-to-avoid-investing-in-mutual-funds/

5. Pastor, L., Stambaugh, R. F., & Taylor, L. A. (2014, February). *Scale and skill of active management.* NBER Working Paper No. 19891. Retrieved from https://econresearch.uchicago.edu/sites/econresearch.uchicago.edu/files/BFI_2014-03.pdf

6. Portnoy, B. (2014). *The investor's paradox the power of simplicity in a world of overwhelming choice.* New York, NY: Palgrave Macmillan.

7. Morey, M. R. (2016). Predicting mutual fund performance. In H. K. Baker, G. Filbeck, & H. Kiymaz (Eds.), *Mutual funds and exchange-traded funds — Building blocks for investment portfolios* (pp. 349 – 363). Hoboken, NJ: Wiley.

8. Richards, C. (2012). Tomorrow's market probably won't look anything like today. *Bucks — Making the Most of Your Money*, February 13. Retrieved from http://bucks.blogs.nytimes.com/2012/02/13/tomorrows-market-probably-wont-look-anything-like-today/?_r=0

9. Jain, P. C., & Wu, J. S. (2000). Truth in mutual fund advertising: evidence on future performance and fund flows. *Journal of Finance*, 55(2), 937 – 958.

10. Mercer, M., Palmiter, A. R., & Taha, A. E. (2010). Worthless warnings? Testing the effectiveness of disclaimers in mutual fund advertisements. *Journal of Empirical Legal Studies*, 7(3), 429 – 459.

11. Jensen, M. C. (1968). The performance of mutual funds in the period 1945–1964. *Journal of Finance*, 23(2), 389–416. Gruber, M. J. (1996). Another puzzle: The growth in actively managed mutual funds. *Journal of Finance*, 51(3), 783–810. Wermers, R. (2000). Mutual fund performance: an empirical decomposition into stock-picking talent, style, transactions costs, and expenses. *Journal of Finance*, 55(4), 1655–1703.

12. Petajisto, A. (2013). Active share and mutual fund performance. *Financial Analysts Journal*, 69(4), 73 – 93. Retrieved from http://www.cfapubs.org/doi/pdf/10.2469/faj.v69.n4.7

13. Gottesman, A., Morey, M., & Rosenberg, M. (2013). Do active managers of retail mutual funds have an incentive to closet index in down markets? Fund performance and subsequent annual fund flows, 1997 – 2011. *Journal of Investment Consulting*, 14(2), 47 – 58.

Retrieved from http://www.busman.qmul.ac.uk/newsandevents/events/
eventdownloads/bfwgconference2013acceptedpapers/114929.pd

14. Braham, L. (2004). How to spot a closet index fund.
BloombergBusiness, September 5. Retrieved from http://www.bloom-
berg.com/bw/stories/2004-09-05/how-to-spot-a-closet-index-fund

15. Authers, J. (2014). Active fund managers are closet index huggers.
Financial Times, March 12. Retrieved from http://www.ft.com/cms/s/0/
10a5a37c-a96e-11e3-b87c-00144feab7de.html#axzz3kmrrneyo

16. U.S. Securities and Exchange Commission. (2001). *Final rule:
Investment company names*. Retrieved from https://www.sec.gov/rules/
final/ic-24828.htm

17. Estlander & Partners. (2015, August). *Estlander & Partners freedom monthly report*. Retrieved from http://estlanderpartners.com/int/
wp-content/uploads/sites/3/2015/02/Estlander-Partners-Freedom-
Program-August-2015.pdf

18. Jayaraman, N., Khorana A., & Nelling, E. (2002). An analysis of
the determinants and shareholder wealth effects of mutual fund mergers.
Journal of Finance, 57(3), 1521 – 1551. Khorana, A., Tufano, P., &
Wedge, L. (2005). Board structure, mergers, and shareholder wealth: A
study of the mutual fund industry. *Journal of Financial Economics*, 85
(2), 571 – 598.

19. Carhart, M. M., Carpenter, J. N., Lynch, A. M., & Musto, D. K.
(2002). Mutual fund survivorship. *Review of Financial Studies*, 15(5),
1439 – 1463. Retrieved from http://pages.stern.nyu.edu/~alynch/pdfs/
rfs02cclm.pdf

20. Laise, E. (2009, September 2). Fund investors can lose out when
portfolios are merged. *The Wall Street Journal*. Retrieved from http://
www.wsj.com/articles/
SB10001424052970204313604574330203541631532

21. Evans, R. B. (2010). Mutual fund incubation. *Journal of Finance*,
65(4), 1581 – 1611.

22. Bogle, J. C. (2006). *The battle for the soul of capitalism*. New
Haven, CT: Yale University Press.

23. Securities and Exchange Commission. *SEC associate director Jack
W. Murphy's LETTER to Dr. Richard Greene on February 3, 1997*.
Retrieved from https://www.sec.gov/divisions/investment/noaction/1997/
williamgreene020397.pdf

24. Palmiter, A. R., & Taha, A. E. (2009). Star creation: The incubation of mutual funds. *Vanderbilt Law Review*, 62(5), 1487 – 1534.

25. Koehler, J. J., & Mercer, M. (2009). Selection neglect in mutual fund advertisements. *Management Science*, 55(7), 1107 – 1121. Wu, C. (2009). Mutual fund advertisements. *Investment Management and Financial Innovations*, 6(2), 68 – 76. Retrieved from http://businessper-spectives.org/journals_free/imfi/2009/imfi_en_2009_02_Wu.pdf

26. Jones, M. A., Lesseig, V. P., Smythe, T. I., & Taylor, V. A. (2007). Mutual fund advertising: Should investors take notice? *Journal of Financial Services Marketing*, 12(3), 242 – 254.

27. Aydogdu, M., & Wellman, J. W. (2011). The effects of advertising on mutual fund flows: Results from a new database. *Financial Management*, 40(3), 785 – 809.

28. Chen, J., Hong, H., Huang, M., & Kubik, J. D. (2004). Does fund size erode mutual fund performance? The role of liquidity and organization. *American Economic Review*, 94(5), 1276 – 1302. Retrieved from http://www.princeton.edu/~hhong/AER-SIZE.pdf

29. (Sterling) Yan, X. (2008). Liquidity, investment style, and the relation between fund size and fund performance. *Journal of Financial and Quantitative Analysis*, 43(3), 741 – 768. Retrieved from Retrieved from http://business.missouri.edu/yanx/research/JFQA-433-07-Yan.pdf

30. Aydogdu, M., & Wellman, J. W. (2011). The effects of advertising on mutual fund flows: Results from a new database. *Financial Management*, 40(3), 785 – 809.

10

TRAP 6: OVERPAYING FOR PRODUCTS AND SERVICES

One of the funny things about the stock market is that every time one person buys, another sells, and both think they are astute.
William A. Feather, American publisher and author

You are probably familiar with the saying "you get what you pay for." In commercial transactions, the quality of goods and services often increases as the price increases. That is, paying more can mean getting better quality merchandise. Some name brand products are worth the additional costs. In other cases, a higher cost may reflect paying for an expensive label but little else. Similarly, in investing, this aphorism holds true in some cases but not others. Paying more for investment products and services does not necessarily lead to higher performance or returns. For example, an expensive actively managed mutual fund in terms of associated costs may not be any better than an inexpensive index fund in providing better risk-adjusted returns. In fact, the opposite might be true because every additional dollar you pay in fees and expenses reduces your portfolio's net returns dollar-for-dollar. Conversely, the least costly product or service is not necessarily the best one for your needs. Fees and expenses are an important consideration, whether working with a financial advisor, using brokerage services, or investing in different types of investment vehicles, but they should not be the only concern.

No one likes overpaying for something. Yet, investors frequently find themselves in this position. Why? First, figuring out the costs for financial advice, mutual funds, retirement plans, and other products and services can be difficult. Second, many others overpay because of a litany of reasons — inexperience, ignorance, emotions, short-sightedness, lack of planning, and not paying attention. Over time, fees and expenses mount and eat into investment returns. To know the true performance of an investment or portfolio requires calculating returns after accounting for all costs and inflation. Unfortunately, many people have no idea how their investments have really performed.

This chapter discusses the investment trap of overpaying for products and services. Investors face a bewildering array of choices of where to put their money, from traditional to alternative investments, each involving different costs. Although overpaying comes in many forms, this chapter focuses on overpaying for financial services including financial advisors, brokerage services, and various types of investment products such as mutual funds, hedge funds, and fund of funds (FOFs).[1] It also presents several extended examples involving closet indexers and FOFs.

FINANCIAL ADVISORS

Individual investors often overpay for investment advice because of high fees, poor results, or a combination of the two. Although the percentage being charged might not initially appear large, it can take a big bite out of your returns. Moreover, as account balances grow, investors pay an ever-increasing amount in fees because the fees are based on a percentage of assets. Trying to beat or even meet a portfolio's benchmark is extremely difficult when you start out several percentage points in the hole due to various charges. Bad brokers and unscrupulous advisors — often commission-driven advisors — may steer unsuspecting investors into perilous waters. These sharks often have their own best interests in mind and prey on the innocent. If you swim in these hazardous waters, you do so at your own peril.

Beginning in January 2018, a new "fiduciary" rule fully goes into effect in the United States requiring all advisors to put their clients' best interests above their own when managing their retirement accounts. However, this rule only applies to tax-advantaged retirement accounts such as 401(k) plans. Thus, advisors can bypass the rule by limiting their practice to taxable accounts. As discussed in Chapter 1, your interests are best served when your advisor has to adhere to the fiduciary standard.[2] Thus, you should be particularly cautious when dealing with advisors who are not subject to this higher standard.

When dealing with financial advisors, one issue involving their fees is psychological. For example, a typical compensation structure is based on a percentage of assets. Assume that your financial advisor charges you 1% a year of assets under management (AUM). The term *assets under management* refers to the total market value of investments managed by a mutual fund, money management firm, hedge fund, portfolio manager, or other financial services company. Although the percentage of AUM charged may appear small, you should not dismiss it as inconsequential. The actual dollar amount that you are paying could be huge depending on the size of your portfolio and time period. For example, assume a 25-year-old has $25,000 in a retirement account, adds $10,000 to the account annually, and earns a 7% average annual return and plans to retire in 40 years. Paying just 1% in fees could cost this investor more than $590,000 in sacrificed returns over 40 years of saving.[3]

Let's take a look at another example, but for a single year. If an investor has $250,000 under management and the advisor charges 1% of AUM, the fee is $2500. If the advisor invests these funds in an expensive mutual fund charging another 1.5% a year, then a total of 2.5% of your money is consumed by fees. However, the 1.5% comes out of return so the investor is less likely to notice it leaving his or her account. Overall, $6250 in cash is leaving the account. If the investor earns 7% on their $250,000 portfolio, this amounts to $17,500. Thus, the advisor and mutual fund managers are keeping almost 36% of the return, while the investor bears all of the risk.[4] The 2.5% seems much smaller than $6250 because it is given as a percentage. The investor pays these fees regardless of whether the investment gains or loses money.

The difference in fees charged by different types of advisors varies considerably. Recall that Chapter 1 discusses several compensation structures for advisors including fee-only, fee-based, and commission-based. With a fee-only structure, advisors receive a fee for specific services. Fee-based advisors charge fees but may also receive commissions from selling the recommended products. Commission-compensated advisors charge no upfront fees but receive compensation from the products. Good advisors are available in each of these categories, but finding them requires time and effort.

Generally speaking, commission-compensated advisors, such as those of brokerage firms, are the most expensive because they are charging per transaction and not according to the overall relationship. Sometimes charges are hidden in commissions paid by mutual fund companies or insurance companies. In contrast, fee-only and fee-based advisors make their money by maintaining a relationship with the client over time. Before hiring a financial advisor, you should determine not only how the advisor is being compensated, but also what services you will be receiving. Financial planners, advisors, and investment managers often publish such fee structures on their websites or on their Form ADV, or as part of their communications with clients. Professional investment advisors must submit Form ADV to the U.S. SEC specifying the investment style, AUM, and key officers of the firm. The form must be updated annually and be made available as public record for companies managing more than $25 million.

Given the different types of advisors, how much should you pay for financial services? The answer depends on the type of service provider and services received. Given the largely unregulated world of financial planning, fees and commissions vary widely. Because of the difficulty of presenting typical commission-based financial advisor fees, the following discussion focuses solely on fee-only and fee-based financial advisory companies and investment management firms. However, under a commission-based fee structure, taking 3–6% off the top of any fund or annuity you buy is common. The following represents average independent financial advisor fees in the United States for 2016 based on a study by AdvisoryHQ.[5]

- *Average % Fees (Percentage of AUM)*: Less-affluent investors (i.e., those with $100,000 or less in account size) typically pay more than 1.12% in fees a year while clients with about $1,000,000 in invested assets pay around 1%. Although fees on a percentage basis typically decline as the account size increases, they exclude expenses for any mutual, index, or ETFs you may own within your account.

- *Tiered financial advisor fee structure*: Investment management firms often use a tiered "% of AUM" fee structure to encourage investors and high-net-worth clients to invest higher amounts. With a tiered fee structure, investors pay a higher percentage fee on the first tier but a lower percentage on assets managed in subsequent tiers.

- *Average hourly financial planner rates*: These fees range from $120 to $300 an hour based partly on the advisor's location.

- *Average annual retainer financial planning rates*: Besides charging an hourly fee, some advisors charge an annual retainer for specific investing or advisory services, ranging from $6000 to $11,000 a year depending partly on the advisor's location.

- *Average fixed independent financial advisor fees*: Some firms charge only a flat fee based on the amount of assets that are being managed on your behalf. For example, the average fixed financial advisor fees (annual fees per AUM) for 2016 were $7500 for investment amounts from $1 to $499,999 and $11,000 for amounts from $500,000 to $999,999.

ONLINE ADVISORS

To receive professional investment advice, investors traditionally worked with human financial advisors. With advances in technology, you can now use a *robo-advisor*, which is an online financial advisor that uses automation and computer algorithms to help manage your portfolio. An *algorithm* is a specific set of clearly defined instructions aimed to carry out a task or process. Based on how you answer a series of questions involving your risk tolerance, financial goals, time horizon, and other areas, a computer algorithm provides asset allocation and investment recommendations. The robo-advisor can build, monitor, and rebalance your portfolio. The website enables you to see your holdings and the investment performance of each.[6] Some robo-advisors offer tax-loss harvesting for taxable accounts and other services. *Tax-loss harvesting* involves selling investments at a loss and then using that loss to lower or eliminate the taxes you have to pay on gains you made during the year.[7] Other robo-advisors even provide access to dedicated financial advisors, who can provide additional advice or reassurance.

These new digital platforms offer several potential advantages in managing your portfolio. For example, they are easy to use and attract investors who are both comfortable with technology such as Millennials and those who prefer to take a hands-off approach. Most robo-advisors are low-cost and have low account minimums, which is particularly attractive to small investors. For example, Vanguard charges 0.30% of your AUM annually. Thus, with $250,000 under management, you would pay on $750 annually compared with an industry of average of about $2500. Thus, using a robo-adviser instead of a human could result in considerable savings in fees over time. Some digital advisors have higher minimums and more sophisticated investment platforms. Others use low cost, low fee index mutual funds, and ETFs to build portfolios.

Despite these possible benefits, some criticize robo-advisors as gimmicky and overly simplistic. According to one analysis, robo-advisors do not provide comprehensive personal investment advice designed to meet an investor's individual needs. Additionally, their services do not appear to be less costly than many mutual funds that are available online and offer simple asset allocation tools that enable investors to invest directly without using an intermediary. Furthermore, robo-advisors are not free from conflicts of interest and some engage in self-dealing transactions. For example, computer-advisors may use their own investment products and provide services to customers using affiliated brokers, custodians, clearing firms, or other firms from which they receive compensation. Additionally, some neither meet a high standard of care nor act in the client's best interests.[8]

Although robo-advisors currently occupy a small slice of the investment management landscape, the number has grown to several hundred ranging from financial service giants such as Charles Schwab and Vanguard Group to startups including Betterment, Sigfig, and Wealthfront. Just as human financial advisors come in many varieties, so do robo-advisors. Whether a robo-advisor is right for you depends on many factors, including your comfort level using technology, and the features and services that you value most. For example, Wealthfront and Betterment offer inexpensive management fees, a diversified ETF portfolio, and reasonable account minimums. WiseBanyan and Charles Schwab are online advisors with no management fee. Vanguard and Personal Capital combine the lower costs of online investment management with a dedicated financial advisor. This hybrid model fits investors who are fairly self-sufficient but need additional help due to complications in their financial lives. Wealthfront and Personal Capital offer investors with taxable accounts first-rate tax efficiency.[9] Reviews and recommendations of the "best" robo-advisors are available on the web.

BROKERAGE SERVICES

Not surprisingly, the types of brokerage services available and their costs differ greatly depending on the type of broker. *Brokers* are the salespeople who handle your buy and sell orders. Thus, having a brokerage account enables you to buy and sell various investment products. The minimum balance for opening a brokerage account ranges from nothing to thousands of dollars. If your balance falls below a certain amount, your broker may charge you a fee.

The type of account you need depends on the securities you want to hold. Most investors, especially beginners, set up a *cash account* in which they deposit cash to buy investment vehicles such as stocks, bonds, mutual funds, and ETFs or an Individual Retirement Account (IRA) account. More seasoned investors may have a *margin account*, which allows them to borrow from their broker against the cash and securities in their account, or an *option account*, which enables them to trade options. An *option* is a contract that gives the buyer the right, but not the obligation, to buy or sell an underlying asset or instrument at a specified strike or exercise price on a specified date.

Full-Service Brokers

Brokerage services consist of two main types: full-service and discount.[10] A *full-service broker* not only executes trades for clients, but also provides a broad range of services including investment advice, retirement planning, tax assistance, research, and financial products. Examples of full-service brokers include Merrill Lynch Wealth Management and Morgan Stanley Wealth Management. Many full-service brokers also offer in-house products such as mutual funds, ETFs, and insurance. These brokers generally receive a percentage or commission for every sale they make. Thus, their compensation is closely tied to account activity, not to investment performance.

Discount Brokers

A *discount broker* is someone who charges a reduced commission to buy and sell shares for clients and generally does not provide investment advice. Examples of discount brokers include Scottrade, TD Ameritrade, TradeKing, and E*Trade. Many discount brokerage firms offer free research and educational tools to assist you in making better investing decisions. The cost of trades at discount sites depends on various factors such as the size and type of security being bought or sold such as stocks, bonds, options, mutual funds, ETFs, treasuries, and CDs.[11] Many charge additional fees, depending on how you use your account. Additional fees may include large buy or sell orders, stocks selling for less than $1, account maintenance fees, account inactivity fees, and interest if you buy on margin.

Online Trading

Online trading is the act of placing buy and sell orders for financial securities by using a brokerage's Internet-based proprietary trading platforms. It blurs the line between full-service and discount brokers and has changed the industry by lowering costs. Practically all discount brokers offer online service and full-service brokers now also offer online trading options.

Selecting the Right Broker

Which type of brokerage, if any, is right for you? Whether you are considering a full-service firm or a discount operation, no perfect choice exists for every investor. The choice depends on many factors including your personal needs and preferences, the costs versus the benefits of each broker, and the level of services and features offered. Just as you need to check out an advisor, you also need to check the background of all brokers and firms to find an appropriate fit. If you don't want to direct your own investments, then a full-service broker could be the appropriate choice, but will come at a higher cost. Full-service brokers provide the convenience of one-stop shopping for investment and financial management. They can be particularly useful to investors who face complex financial situations and want personalized recommendations and service. Full-service brokers offer more services but can be expensive, generally charging about 1–2% of AUM, plus other fees such as an annual maintenance fee.

For self-directed or do-it-yourself investors, discount brokers are often the better choice. Several reasons favor choosing a discount broker. For example, although discount brokers don't offer the extras, they are more affordable than full-service brokers. You don't have to sacrifice the quality of the trade execution by selecting a discount broker. Also, many discount brokers provide access to research and trading software to help you make informed choices about your investments.[12]

MUTUAL FUNDS

As discussed in Chapter 9, a *mutual fund* pools money from many people and invests it on their behalf according to some particular investment strategy. Each investor owns shares representing a part of the holdings in stocks, bonds, or other assets.

Mutual funds have both advantages and disadvantages compared to direct investing in individual securities or assets. For example, mutual funds are often the simplest and least expensive way to gain access to different markets and securities. Mutual funds also enable some investors to participate in investments that otherwise may be available only to larger investors. Another key advantage is diversification. As John "Jack" Bogle, founder and retired CEO of The Vanguard Groups notes, "Don't look for the needle in the haystack. Just buy the haystack!" Other benefits of mutual funds include professional money management, transparency due to extensive disclosure requirements, daily valuation, liquidity, regulatory oversight and accountability, and ease of comparison. As Warren Buffett notes, "The 'know-nothing' investor who both diversifies and keeps his costs minimal is virtually certain to get satisfactory results." A key to investing in mutual funds is to keep the costs low.

Despite their benefits, mutual funds also have disadvantages. Perhaps the greatest drawback involves various costs that can vary dramatically among funds. Funds pass these costs to investors, diminishing returns. Imagine a race with equally quick horses and talented jockeys, except that one horse has a 100 pound jockey and the other has a much heavier jockey. Which horse is most likely to win? Obviously, the extra weight could affect the outcome of the race. This concept also applies to many types of investments. For example, some mutual funds are saddled with much higher costs than others. High fees and expenses weigh down performance and can make a huge difference over time. Furthermore, taxes can take a big bite out of the returns of some investments outside of tax-sheltered retirement plans. Thus, choosing the right mutual fund is an important decision for individual investors.

Overpaying due to Expenses, Loads, and Other Fees

Mutual funds provide investors with many investment-related services for which investors pay. One way to overpay for mutual funds is by paying overly high expenses, loads, and other fees. Trying to pinpoint the costs associated with investing in mutual funds can be tricky because so many possibilities exist. Mutual fund investors incur two major types of costs: (1) ongoing expenses and (2) loads.[13]

Ongoing Expenses

Ongoing expenses include the following: portfolio management, fund administration, daily fund accounting and pricing, shareholder services including call centers and websites, distribution charges (known as 12b-1 fees), and other operating costs. A fund's *expense ratio* — its annual expenses expressed as a percentage of its assets — includes these expenses. Because expenses are paid from fund assets, investors pay these expenses indirectly.

Over time, average expenses paid by mutual fund investors have fallen considerably. In the United States, average expenses ratios incurred by equity fund investors decreased from 99 basis points in 2000 to 68 basis points in 2015. This decline means that, on average, for every $100 invested, investors paid 31 cents less in expenses in 2015 than in 2000. Correspondingly, the average expense ratios incurred by equity index fund investors decreased from 27 basis points in 2000 to 11 basis points in 2015. A *basis point* is a unit of measure used to describe the percentage change in the value or rate of a financial instrument. One basis point is equal to 1/100th of 1%. The expense ratios for hybrid and bond funds also declined. A *hybrid fund* is a type of mutual fund whose portfolio consists of a mix of stocks and bonds. Between 2000 and 2015, the average hybrid fund expense ratio fell from 89 basis points to 77 basis points, a reduction of 13%. During the same period, the average bond fund expense ratio fell from 76 to 54 basis points. The decrease in average expenses results from such factors as the shift toward no-load funds and funds with below average expense ratios, economies of scale, and competition.[14] Given the downward trend in average expenses, you should expect to pay even lower fees in the future as a mutual fund investor.

Load and No-Load Funds

Mutual funds can be classified into two categories: load and no-load. *Loads* are fees that investors pay at the time of purchase (front-end), when units are redeemed (back-end) usually within a specified time frame, and distribution and marketing costs (level load). The SEC does not limit the size of sales load a fund may charge, but the Financial Industry Regulatory Authority, Inc. (FINRA) does not permit mutual fund sales loads to exceed 8.5%. This percentage is lower if a fund imposes other types of charges. FINRA is a private corporation that acts as a U.S. self-regulatory organization.

Load funds are typically available to those who invest through an investment professional such as a broker or financial advisor. Although mutual funds charge the fee, almost all of the proceeds go to the broker or advisor recommending the fund. Defenders of load funds claim that the charge compensates these intermediaries for their time and expertise in selecting a mutual fund. Over the past few decades, the manner in which fund shareholders compensate financial advisors has changed substantially, moving away from front-end loads toward asset-based fees.

The three major types of load funds are as follows:[15]

- *Front-end load*: A *front-end load* is a one-time sales charge to buy shares of a mutual fund. The sales fee on Class A shares as shown in a fund prospectus is generally around 5%. For example, if you invest $10,000 in a mutual fund charging a 5% front-end load, this amounts to $500 when you buy the fund. Thus, your actual investment after the load is only $9500, not $10,000. You have to earn back the $500 that you paid to the broker just to break even. Some exceptions exist. For example, funds that typically charge front-end load fees often waive load fees on purchases made through defined contribution plans, such as 401(k) plans.

- *Back-end load*: A *back-end load* is a fee paid to sell Class B shares of a mutual fund. The most common type of back-end sales load is the *contingent deferred sales load*. Fund companies charge loads to discourage investors from frequently trading their mutual fund shares. Still, funds with back-end loads could confuse shareholders into thinking they are buying a no-load fund, which is not the case. Funds often assess back-end loads on the beginning value of the investment, but some calculate the charge based on the ending value if the share price falls below the original purchase price. For example, if you invest $10,000 in a mutual fund charging a 5% back-end load and decide to sell it after one year, you would a pay $500 exit fee. Fund companies typically reduce the percentage of the payment for each year you hold the fund. For instance, the redemption fee might be 5% in the first year, 4% in the second year, and so on until the fee is zero. The fund's prospectus discloses the rate at which this fee will decline. If you hold the investment long enough, the fund company will sometimes waive the back-end fee.

- *Level load*: A *level load* is a distribution and marketing cost (12b-1 fee) applied annually on Class C shares as a fixed percentage of a mutual fund's average net assets. This fee is generally paid to intermediaries for selling a fund's shares to the retail public. Unlike front-end and back-end sales charges, a fund's operating expenses include these 12b-1 fees. Regulations cap total 12b-1 fees at 1%.

Some funds do not have loads. A *no-load fund* is a fund that involves no commission or sales charge to buy or redeem. Still, no-load funds may charge fees not considered sales loads. Investors buy shares either directly from a mutual fund company or indirectly through a mutual fund supermarket. A *fund supermarket* is an investment firm or brokerage that offers investors a wide array of mutual funds from different fund families. FINRA allows a mutual fund without any sales charges to have 12b-1 fees up to 0.25% of its average annual assets and still call itself a no-load fund.

Commission-based advisors or brokers are incentivized to recommend load funds, whereas fee-only professionals generally recommend no-load funds. Over time, a shift has occurred toward no-load share classes. This shift can be attributed to do-it-yourself investors, sales growth through defined contribution plans, and sales of no-load share classes through various sales channels that compensate financial professionals with asset-based fees outside of funds.

Why buy no-load versus load funds? For the do-it-yourself investor, the main reasons for buying no-load funds involve cost and performance. By taking the no-load route, your overall investment costs are typically lower. Unlike mutual funds with loads, you also invest the entire amount of your funds with no-load funds. No-load funds also tend to outperform over longer periods. The reported performance numbers of load funds also do not include the load. Consequently, the returns that investors receive from a load fund are actually less than the published returns. Additionally, investors are less likely to feel trapped by buying no-load funds because they can move to another no-load fund without incurring the extra cost.[16] Self-directed investors can find suitable no-load funds through research and asking questions. If they engage an investment professional and use mutual funds as part of their portfolios, they should insist on recommendations involving no-load funds. Burton Malkiel, an American economist and writer, warns that "In no event should you ever buy a load fund." He also states, "There's no point in paying for something if you can get it free."[17]

Given the benefits of no-load funds, why do investors still buy load funds? The answer is simple: Many investors don't know any better. This lack of knowledge can be costly. Loads reduce the investment principal, limit flexibility, and eat up profits. Load funds are typically "sold" whereas no-load funds are "bought." That is, brokers and some financial advisors sell load funds to receive the sales commission in exchange for helping you make decisions and invest your money. You have two choices to avoid loads: either do your own investing or compensate your advisor in some other way. Savvy investors consider all costs of investing and loads are only one of these costs.[18]

Expenses, Loads, and Performance

Expenses are typically measured by the fund's *expense ratio*, which is the percentage of fund assets that pay for operating expenses, management fees, administrative fees, and all other asset-based costs incurred by the fund, except brokerage costs. Some disagreement exists on how expense ratios and loads help to predict fund performance. Considerable research shows a negative relation between both expenses and loads and fund outperformance. That is, funds with low expense ratios tend to outperform other funds. Additionally, funds with no or low loads exhibit consistently better performance than high load funds. Yet, other research indicates that this negative relation is not always the case. Some expenses such as redemption fees and manager incentive fees are beneficial to performance. Redemption fees enhance performance because they reduce redemptions and allow the manager to hold less in cash. Manager incentive fees appear to encourage managers to perform well.[19] The bottom line is that you can find no-load funds that meet your investment goals and have reasonable expense ratios.

Actively Managed versus Index Funds

Expenses, loads, and other fees differ substantially between actively managed mutual funds and index mutual funds. *Actively managed funds* try to outperform their benchmarks and peer-group average. That is, these funds try to beat the market: you're paying a company for the investing skill of its fund managers. By contrast, *index funds* attempt to track the performance of a particular index or market benchmark as closely as possible. The vast majority of ETFs also invest based on an index. The strategy of an index fund is to buy all or a representative sample of the securities in the benchmark. Index funds assets have grown dramatically compared to actively managed funds partly due to having generally lower expense ratios and being more tax-efficient.

The lower expense ratios of index funds result from several factors. First, index funds use a passive or buy-and-hold investment strategy, which reduces trading costs. Because managing an index fund is cheaper, fund fees are much lower. Second, these funds concentrate heavily in "large-cap blend" funds that target U.S. large-cap indexes, especially the S&P 500. Managing portfolios of U.S. large-cap stocks is less expensive than managing portfolios of mid- or small-cap, international, or sector stocks on which actively managed funds focus. Third, the larger average size of index funds compared to actively managed funds helps to reduce fund expense ratios through economies of scale.[14]

Paying more for an actively managed mutual fund would make sense, if these funds consistently outperformed their index-based peers. Yet, evidence shows that such outperformance is rarely the case. When faced with the decision of whether to invest in actively managed versus index funds, the weight of the evidence favors index funds. Although many people can benefit from investment advice, you probably don't need a highly trained professional to tell you to buy an index fund. Even without specialized knowledge of individual stocks, casual investors can benefit by investing in index funds.

Overpaying due to Underperformance

Another way to overpay for mutual funds is by selecting funds that underperform. As previously discussed, "beating the market" is very difficult. In fact, the vast majority of investors, including managers of mutual funds, underperform the market averages. Decades of research show that actively managed funds have generally underperformed their passive counterparts, especially over longer time horizons. According to a recent study of performance after fees, more than 84% of U.S. active funds underperformed the S&P 500® over a recent one-year period and more than 98% of active funds trailed the benchmark over a recent 10-year period. Four out of five active equity funds in Europe failed to beat their benchmark over a recent five-year period, rising to 86% over the past decade.[20]

Do actively managed funds really pay off for investors? The answer is generally no. Yet, despite the evidence, millions of investors continue to trust much of their money with active managers. Several possibilities explain this situation. First, despite the average active manager's inability to beat the indexers, some investors hope to identify potential superior performers. For most investors, this possibility is unlikely and a manifestation of overconfidence in one's own abilities. Others are attracted to the allure of the star manager. However, being able to separate between top-performing managers who are smart and those who are simply lucky is difficult.[21] Secondly, although superior performance is still possible in the short-run, it is very difficult to achieve over the long run. Evidence shows that superior past performance typically does not "persist" for very long, if at all, but that inferior past performance, when caused by high costs and taxes, generally does.

Active fund managers attempt to outperform an index through stock selection and making factor bets, which involve overweighting or underweighting entire sectors, industries, or regions. Most active fund managers do a poor job of selecting securities or making factor bets. Some do a good job but not well enough to compensate for the fund's costs. One of the most influential studies on fees and performance concludes: "While the popular press will no doubt continue to glamorize the best-performing mutual fund managers, the mundane explanations of strategy and investment costs account for almost all of the important predictability in mutual fund returns."[22]

Numerical averages of returns don't convey the full picture because they typically fail to consider various fees and transaction costs. What really matters is how well you do after costs. Therefore, costs play on important role in investment returns. Unlike financial markets, costs are largely controllable. Every dollar paid in fees and trading commissions is simply a dollar less in earning potential returns. Costs can have a major impact on your returns: the lower your costs, the greater your share of an investment's return.

A mutual fund with high costs must perform better than a low-cost fund to generate the same returns. A little difference in costs can result in a very big difference in returns over time. For example, assume that you invested $10,000 in Fund A that produced an 8% annual return after expenses compared with Fund B's 7% annual return after expenses. This 1 percentage point difference adds up. The difference in returns is about $1933 after 10 years, $9924 after 20 years, $24,504 after 30 years, and $61,501 after 40 years.

Let's take another example using the same 1 percentage point difference in return after expenses. If you invested $4000 at the beginning of each of the next 40 years at 7%, you'd have about $854,438 at the end. Yet, by earning an 8% compounded annual return, you'd have $1,119,124 or $264,686 more. They key take-away here is to be aware of the impact that seemingly small costs have on returns, especially over time.

Now, let's return to the expression "you get what you pay for." In the long term, a relatively small percentage of actively managed funds achieve superior returns even after considering their higher fees and expenses. Hence, they offer services worth their costs. Yet, you still would be better off with superior performance coupled with fee-consciousness. In comparison, other funds over-charge for their services and don't provide higher performance commensurate with their costs. The moral of this story is that you need to be careful when investing in mutual funds because you don't necessarily get your money's worth.

Many investors realize that paying more can mean getting less, but others don't. For instance, the increased popularity of index funds and ETFs reflects not only their lower cost but also the fact that the vast majority of active fund managers can't beat the performance of their benchmark indexes over extended periods. By paying less for a mutual fund, you keep more money in your pocket. Although you shouldn't choose an investment solely because it costs less, you should make sure you're not overpaying. Knowing exactly how much you're paying can be difficult because funds don't put the fees all in one place. Consequently, you need to piece together different expenses to determine how much you are paying for the service. This is feasible if you know what you're looking for and where to look. Also, predicting costs is much easier than predicting performance.[23] Your goal should be to get the biggest bang for your investment dollar within your risk class.

CLOSET INDEXING

A recent phenomenon in the mutual fund industry is closet indexing. *Closet indexers* are funds that closely track a benchmark while claiming to be active and charging fees similar to those of truly active managers. You can achieve a similar result by investing directly in a less expensive index fund. Closet indexing in the United States has at times been even more popular than pure indexing. Some speculate that the SEC's decision in 1998 to require all mutual funds to disclose a benchmark index in their prospectus could have acted as an initial trigger for closet indexing.[24]

Closet indexing also occurs outside of the United States. A study of open-end equity mutual funds and ETFs in 32 countries between 2002 and 2010 reports closet indexers manage about 30% of fund assets outside the United States. This percentage represents twice the level of closet indexing that prevails in the United States.[25]

Active fund managers are likely to closet index because doing so is in their best interests. By tracking the index especially during down markets, closet indexers won't be the worst performers, and hence their net flows will be lower than underperforming funds. Although the lower losses in fund flows could still negatively affect the managers' compensation, especially when tied to size of the fund's net assets, the managers are less likely to be fired.[26]

Why should you avoid "closet indexers" when choosing between available mutual funds on the market? Nothing is inherently wrong with a fund tracking an index. The problem is that closet indexers charge higher fees than similar index-tracking passive funds or passive ETFs while trying to hug the benchmark index. Only the positions that stray from the index itself or the fund's active positions can outperform the benchmark index. Consequently, closet indexers are bound to underperform the index in the long run. You should also avoid closet indexers because they tend to be the worst performing active management category.

How can you identify closet indexers? One way to truly measure active managers and in turn closet indexers is by using a metric called *active share*, which is a measure of the percentage of stock holdings in a manager's portfolio that differs from the benchmark index. That is, active share assesses active managers by focusing on how individual stock weights in a portfolio differ from the weights in a benchmark. This measure is intuitively appealing based on the notion that the only way to outperform an index is to be different from it. A perfectly executed index fund would have an active share score of 0. If a fund manager holds more than 50% of the index, then the active share is less than 50%. Anything below an active share of 50% is essentially a combination of an active fund and an index fund. The lower the percentage of active share, the more a fund manager is a closet indexer. For funds with low active share (e.g., below the 60% guideline in the case of U.S. equity mutual funds), active share is a good indicator of a potential closet indexer and, therefore, a potentially expensive investment. Research evidence shows that high active share is more likely to identify a manager's potential to generate high active return and outperform a passive benchmark, even on an after-fee basis.[27]

Putman Investors Fund

Now let's turn to an example of a closet indexer. Launched by Putnam Investments in 1925, Putnam Investors Fund is one of the oldest mutual funds in the business. The fund is a large-cap blend mutual fund, which has most of its holdings in U.S. large-cap equity. The fund claims that its investment objective is as follows: "The fund seeks long-term growth of capital and any increased income that results from this growth."

According to the fund's marketing materials, Putman Investors Fund aims to achieve its investment objective by following three cornerstones in its investment process:

- *"Go-anywhere" approach*: The fund does not rigidly limit itself to a single style. Its manager can invest in growth or value stocks, targeting those that can perform well in different market conditions.

- *Disciplined process*: The fund's manager uses exhaustive fundamental research to identify large U.S. companies whose stock prices do not reflect their long-range prospects.

- *Leading research*: The portfolio manager is supported by Putnam's Global Equity Research Group, whose analysts visit with hundreds of companies each year.

The first look at fund's performance is impressive: $10,000 invested in the fund in 1925 had grown to $28,412,083 by the end of July 2016. This implies 9.17% annual return before any sales charge. The size of the fund was $1.8 billion during summer 2016. Over the 10-year period ending in July, 2016, the annual return of the fund was 5.8% and the cumulative return before sales charges was 76%. This means that $10,000 invested in the fund in 2006 had grown to $17,600 by 2016.[28]

The previous description of the fund's investment philosophy combined with an expense ratio of 1.07% (107 basis points) as of July 31, 2016, suggests an actively managed fund. By comparison, pure index-tracking funds, especially U.S. equity index-trackers, have average expense ratios of 0.10%. As of January, 2014, the fund's Active Share was only 36%.[29] The largest holdings of the fund are Apple, Microsoft, JP Morgan, Johnson & Johnson, and Exxon — big blue chip index companies.

Considering the theory underlying active share, the returns of Putnam Investors Fund relative to the index are not surprising. The fund benchmarks its performance to the S&P 500 index, suggesting it would aim to beat the index in question. During a 10-year period ending in July, 2016, the S&P 500 returned

7.74% annually. An initial investment of $10,000 into the index would have grown to $21,089 while the same investment into the fund would have amounted to $17,600. Putnam Investors Fund receives only one Morningstar "Star" for its 10-year performance, which means that the fund is in the bottom 10% compared to funds in the same category.

In closet indexing, a fund charges an unjustifiably high management fee for passive management. If you want your money to be invested in Apple, Microsoft, and JP Morgan, you should just buy an index fund or ETF that tracks the S&P 500 index. In summary, you should avoid closet indexers because you are overpaying for this type of mutual fund.[30]

Trap Judgment

Closet Indexing

Becoming a victim of investment fraud

Misrepresenting risky products as safe

Making unrealistic return expectations

Falling for mutual fund traps

Overpaying for products and services

Investing in complex products

Engaging in gambling disguised as investing

Relying on unsupported promises

HEDGE FUNDS

According to the SEC, the term "hedge fund" has no legal or official definition. However, a *hedge fund* is commonly described as a pooled investment vehicle that uses various strategies to invest in a variety of asset classes. The fund's goal is typically to earn excess returns relative to the return of a benchmark index, called *alpha*, or to provide a hedge against unforeseen market changes. *Hedging* is a risk management strategy used to reduce the risk of adverse price movements in an asset. Although hedging uses various techniques, it often involves taking equal and opposite positions in two different markets such as cash and futures markets. Despite what its namesake implies, a hedge fund does not necessary hedge against downturns in the markets being traded. Hedge fund industry assets, as of November 2015, stood at just under \$3.2 trillion.[31] By contrast, U.S. mutual funds and ETFs at the end of 2015 amounted to \$15.7 trillion and \$2.1 trillion, respectively. Total worldwide assets invested in regulated open-end funds were \$37.2 trillion.[32]

A hedge fund is typically structured as a limited partnership consisting of the investors (limited partners) who contribute the money and the general partner who manages it according to the fund's strategy. Professional investment managers administer these privately offered funds. Hedge fund managers are typically experienced, highly specialized, and trade only within their area of expertise and competitive advantage.

Hedge funds offer some notable benefits over traditional investment funds. For example, the investment strategies used by hedge funds can potentially generate positive returns in both rising and falling markets. Given that hedge funds may have low correlations with a traditional portfolio of stocks and bonds, including them in a portfolio offers potential diversification benefits. By holding hedge funds in a portfolio, investors can potentially enhance returns and reduce overall portfolio volatility. Hedge funds also have some of the most talented investment managers.

Characteristics of Hedge Funds

Hedge funds are like mutual funds in that both are pooled investment vehicles and can invest in many types of securities. Yet, the similarities largely end here. Hedge funds differ from mutual funds in the following ways:

- *Hedge funds are available only to accredited investors*: Hedge funds are only open to "accredited" or qualified investors such as pension funds, endowments, insurance companies, and employee benefit plans as well as wealthy, sophisticated individual investors. As of February 1, 2016, The Fair Investment Opportunities for Professional Experts Act allows individuals to qualify as accredited investors based on measures of sophistication such as a minimum amount of investments, certain professional credentials, experience investing in exempt offerings, knowledgeable employees of private funds, or by passing an accredited investor examination to qualify as an accredited investor.[33] Essentially, an accredited investor is someone who the SEC deems capable of taking on the economic risk of investing in unregistered securities.[34] Most individuals do not qualify as accredited investors and hence can't invest in hedge funds.

- *Hedge funds are subject to little regulatory oversight*: Hedge funds are lightly regulated but have come under increased regulatory scrutiny as a result of the global financial crisis of 2007–2008. For example, in the United States, the Dodd-Frank Wall Street Reform Act, which passed in July 2010, requires hedge funds with more than $150 million in assets to register with the SEC.

- *Hedge funds use a wide range of investments and strategies*: Hedge funds have wider investment latitude than many other types of pooled investments. Hence, they can engage in more aggressive strategies and positions, such as short selling, trading in derivative instruments such as options and futures, and using leverage (borrowing) to enhance the risk/reward profile of their bets. Using leverage can expose investors to potentially large losses as seen during the financial crisis of 2007–2008.

- *Hedge funds are illiquid*: Hedge fund managers typically place limits on when investors are allowed to withdraw their money. This lock-up period helps managers avoid liquidity problems while capital is put to work in sometimes illiquid investments. Because investor funds can be locked up for several years, investing in a hedge fund is a long-term proposition.

- *Hedge funds offer limited transparency about their strategies and performance data*: Besides providing a broad category group (e.g., directional equity, directional debt, event, global/derivatives, relative value, and multistrategy), hedge fund managers typically don't reveal specifics about their strategies fearing that others might copy their approach. Additionally, hedge funds aren't required to report their performance to others besides their investors, disclose their holdings, or answer questions from shareholders.

- *Hedge funds are subject to high fees and complex incentive structures*: Besides charging a management fee, hedge funds also have a performance or incentive fee. The traditional "2 and 20" fee structure is one in which hedge fund managers charge a flat 2% of total asset value as a management fee and an additional 20% performance fee of any profits earned. The "2 and 20" model is slowly dying. Today, average hedge fund fees are lower and continue to fall because investors demand better returns and funds face the growing demand to compete in a crowded marketplace.[35] Hedge fund investors now generally pay an annual management fee of about 1.5% of assets, along with 17.7% or so of any investment gains.[36]

Overpaying for Underperformance

Many institutional and wealthy individual investors rely on hedge funds to enhance returns and diversify portfolios. Although some top-performing hedge funds are worth their high fees, many investors are rethinking whether the high fees are justified given recent underperformance. Although many hedge funds try to generate positive absolute returns, the actual returns are highly variable over time. Considerable damage occurred to the hedge fund industry between 1998 and 2008 due to negative returns, elevated risk, and high fund mortality rates. According to a research report by Hedge Fund Research, Inc., an investment in an index of equity hedge funds over the five years ending in April 30, 2015, returned 4.38% a year, while the S&P 500 earned 14.31%. By the end of 2015, hedge funds had returned just 2.02%, representing the Preqin AllStrategies Hedge Fund benchmark's worst performance since 2011. However, the benchmark outperformed the S&P 500 for 2015.[31] Meanwhile, Institutional Investor reports that, in 2014 — the sixth straight year of hedge-fund underperformance — the managers of 25 of the largest funds earned $11.62 billion, almost $500 million apiece.[37]

In conclusion, hedge funds vary substantially in terms of investment returns and risk. Overall, accredited individual investors should be cautious before investing in a hedge fund because trying to distinguish in advance the truly talented managers from the merely lucky ones is difficult. Although hedge funds are not for everyone, they can meet the specific investment goals and needs of some investors. For most individual investors, however, investing in hedge funds is not only a bad idea but also unlikely because they don't meet their minimum requirements. In many if not most cases, investors overpay for this investment vehicle.

FUND OF FUNDS

A *fund of funds* is an investment strategy in which a fund invests in other types of funds. This strategy applies to any type of investment fund, from a mutual fund to a private equity fund to a hedge fund. In general, a FOF strategy tries to achieve broad diversification and appropriate asset allocation with investments in different fund categories. FOFs appeal especially to small investors who don't want to invest directly in securities. A drawback is that investors basically pay double for an expense that is already included in the expense figures of the underlying funds. Let's examine a fund of hedge funds and then take an extended example involving a fund of mutual funds.

A fund of hedge funds offers several potential advantages. First, they give investors access to a large number of hedge funds with relatively low minimum investment levels. Many FOFs hold shares in hedge funds, otherwise closed to new investment allowing smaller investors access to the most sought-after managers. Second, FOFs offer diversification across manager styles and asset class. Diversification can potentially increase return potential and decrease risk associated with investing in a single hedge fund. Third, experienced managers of FOFs are likely to have the expertise needed to provide the necessary degree of due diligence and to select successful fund managers. Finally, the manager provides professional oversight of fund operations.

Despite these benefits, FOFs have two major drawbacks: cost and performance. Investors are essentially paying twice for an expense that is already included in the expense figures of the underlying funds. That is, these funds typically charge a fee for their services in addition to the fees charged by the underlying hedge funds. For example, each individual hedge fund might charge a fee of 1–2% of AUM and an incentive fee of 15–25% of profits generated. A fund of hedge funds typically charges its own fees. The SEC adopted a new rule in 2006 requiring that FOFs disclose the expenses and show the additional expense in a fee table.

A key issue facing investors is whether the performance achieved by FOFs offsets the drag from the additional fees. Proponents contend that the manager's information advantage in selecting underlying funds could result in higher risk-adjusted returns that would more than compensate investors for these fees. One study on fees in hedge funds investigates whether the FOF manager adds value for investors. The results show that the average performance of the underlying funds dominates the performance of FOFs, suggesting that any informational advantage does not offset the extra fees.[38]

In summary, funds of hedge funds could be appealing to some investors, especially those interested in the world of hedge fund investing. Many investors have gravitated toward these funds during the past decade. However, given the complexity of hedge funds, inexperienced investors should be leery of hedge funds in general and funds of hedge funds in particular. Such investors especially need to be aware that additional fees cut into their returns, resulting in overpaying for this product.

An Example of a Fund of Mutual Funds

Danske Invest Compass Fund targets long-term value increase through active asset management. The fund invests its assets in mutual funds that invest in international equity markets. The fund may also invest directly in equities and derivatives. Danske suggests that the fund is suitable for investors with a long investment horizon who seek high returns and can tolerate substantial fluctuations or even decreases. The fund is "particularly well-suited for investors who wish to diversify their assets among various equity markets." The fund has no benchmark index.[39] On its fund website, Danske explains that Danske Capital is an international asset manager with offices in Denmark, Sweden, Norway, Finland, and Luxembourg. Danske Capital focuses its resources on selected core investment areas (alpha areas). Carefully selected external managers manage investments in regions where Danske Capital does not have core competencies. Thus, Danske Capital claims to select managers with core expertise and may at any time decide to change managers if deemed beneficial.[40]

A closer look at the fund shows that the portfolio manager has invested only in Danske's own mutual funds. These funds charge their own management fees on top of the 0.5% management fee of Compass Fund (Table 10.1).

Table 10.1: The Holdings of Danske Invest Compass Equity as of August 2016

Holding	Holding %	Sub-funds Management Fee %
Danske Invest European Equity Fund	17.82	1.35
Danske Invest Engros Global Equity	17.23	0.99
Danske Invest North America Equity	9.59	1.50
Danske Invest Nordic Opportunities fee	8.51	1.20 + performance fee
Danske Invest Finnish Equity	4.03	1.90
Danske Invest Finnish Opportunities	3.97	1.50 + performance fee
Danske Invest SICAV — Emerging Frontier	3.32	2.30
Danske Invest SICAV Europe	3.29	1.03
Danske Invest China	3.15	2.80
Weighted average management fee		1.39

Only Danske's own funds may be found in the top holdings of Danske Invest Compass Fund. Even without considering possible performance fees of certain funds, Danske charges 1.39% as management fees from the sub-funds. Investors need to consider this charge instead of looking only at the 0.5% management fee of the Compass Equity Fund. This information may be found from the Key Investor Information Document (KIID) of the Compass fund, which mentions that the ongoing charges from the past 12 months as of summer 2016 were 1.99% instead of 0.50%. Although ongoing changes vary over time, investors can assume that this level existed in the past. This may well explain the somewhat sub-par performance of the fund. Over the 10-year period ending in July 2016, the average annual return of Danske Compass Fund was 3.6%. In the same 10-year period, the Morgan Stanley Capital Index provided an annual 6.3% return.

Trap Judgment

Fund of Funds

Becoming a victim of investment fraud

Misrepresenting risky products as safe

Making unrealistic return expectations

Falling for mutual fund traps

Overpaying for products and services

Investing in complex products

Engaging in gambling disguised as investing

Relying on unsupported promises

LESSONS LEARNED

This chapter examines various ways to avoid overpaying for products and services. One way to pay as little as possible for financial advice is to make some of the decisions on how to invest or to rely on robo-advisors. You can use low-cost providers with online trading. You can also buy index funds and ETFs, which provide a diversified portfolio at low cost. At the other end of the spectrum is a full-service advisor. Not paying high fees leaves you with more money in your pocket for investments offering the same gross return. You should also be cautious about investing in actively managed mutual funds, hedge funds, and FOFs.

- Don't be dazzled by performance but indifferent to costs. The less you pay, the more you keep.

- Be aware that a high-cost fund must perform better than a low-cost fund to generate the same returns.

- Focus on mutual funds that don't charge a load to buy or sell.

- Don't make any investment unless you understand the fees involved.

- Watch the fees and costs on all of your funds, investments, and advisors.

- Be aware that passive funds beat comparable managed funds most of the time.

- Avoid closet indexers.

- Be cautious of investing in hedge funds and FOFs.

- Be aware that ultimately your investment choices depend on such factors as your individual goals, risk tolerance, return expectations, and other constraints.

QUESTIONS

1. Discuss the pros and cons of using a robo-advisor.

2. Compare and contrast full-service, discount, and online brokerage services.

3. Identify the two major costs that investors incur when investing in mutual funds.

4. Distinguish among front-end, back-end, and level loads in mutual funds.

5. Define closet indexing and explain why investors overpay for closet indexers.

6. Identify and explain the key characteristics of hedge funds.

7. Define a FOF and indicate the major advantages and disadvantages of investing in one.

NOTES

1. Securities and Exchange Commission. (2016). *How fees and expenses affect your investment portfolio*. Office of Education and Advocacy. Retrieved from https://www.sec.gov/investor/alerts/ib_fees_expenses.pdf

2. Skinner, L. (2016). Figuring out fiduciary now comes the hard part. *Investment News*, May 6. Retrieved from http://www.investmentnews.

com/article/20160509/FEATURE/160509939/the-dol-fiduciary-rule-will-forever-change-financial-advice-and-the

3. Yochim, D., & Todd, J. How a 1% fee could cost millennials $590,000 in retirement savings. *NerdWallet*. Retrieved from https://www.nerdwallet.com/blog/investing/millennial-retirement-fees-one-percent-half-million-savings-impact/

4. Tuchman, M. (2015). Is your financial advisor overpaid? *Forbes*, September 8. Retrieved from http://www.forbes.com/sites/mitchelltuchman/2015/09/08/is-your-financial-advisor-overpaid/#551609834270

5. AdvisoryHQ. (2016). Financial advisor fees in 2016 | average, hourly, AUM, annual fees. *AdvisoryHQ*, July 20. Retrieved from http://www.advisoryhq.com/articles/financial-advisor-fees-wealth-managers-planners-and-fee-only-advisors/

6. Weisser, C. (2016, September). The rise of the robo-adviser. *Consumer Reports*, pp. 44–49.

7. Yochim, D. (2015). Turning loser investments into a tax break. *Nerdwallet*, December 18. Retrieved from https://www.nerdwallet.com/blog/investing/tax-loss-harvesting-turn-your-loser-investments-into-a-tax-break/

8. Fein, M. L. (2015, June 30). *Robo-advisors: A closer look*. Social Science Research Network. Retrieved from http://ssrn.com/abstract=2658701 or http://dx.doi.org/10.2139/ssrn.2658701

9. O'Shea, A. (2016). Best robo-advisors: 2016 top picks. *Nerdwallet*, March 14. Retrieved from https://www.nerdwallet.com/blog/investing/best-robo-advisors/

10. Rieman, M. (2014). What's the difference between a full-service broker and a discount broker?" *Nerdwallet*, September 26. Retrieved from https://www.nerdwallet.com/blog/investing/full-service-broker-discount-broker/

11. Brokerage Review. (2016). *Best brokerage firms: Top rated online discount stock brokers in 2016*. Retrieved from http://www.brokerage-review.com/stock-brokers/best-brokerage-firms.aspx

12. Jafarzadea, N. (2013). 3 reasons to choose a discount broker. *U.S. News & World Report*, September 23. Retrieved from http://money.usnews.com/money/blogs/my-money/2013/09/23/3-reasons-to-choose-a-discount-broker

13. U.S. Securities and Exchange Commission. (2016). *Mutual fund fees and expenses*. Retrieved from https://www.sec.gov/answers/mffees. htm#salesloads

14. Investment Company Institute. (2016). *2016 investment company fact book*. Retrieved from http://www.icifactbook.org/ch5/16_fb_ch5

15. Smith, D. M. (2016). The economics of mutual funds: Rewards and risks. In H. K. Baker, G. Filbeck, & H. Kiymaz (Eds.), *Mutual funds and exchange-traded funds: Building blocks to wealth* (pp. 21−43). New York, NY: Oxford University Press.

16. Bold, A. (2011). Why investors should avoid load funds. *U.S. New & World Report*, March 1. Retrieved from http://money.usnews.com/ money/blogs/the-smarter-mutual-fund-investor/2011/03/01/why-investors-should-avoid-load-funds

17. Malkiel, B. (2015). *A random walk down wall street: The time-tested strategy for successful investing* (11th ed.). New York, NY: W. W. Norton & Company, Inc.

18. Liston, H. C. (2009). No load mutual funds vs. load mutual funds. *Bankrate.com*, August 14. Retrieved from http://www.bankrate.com/ finance/investing/buying-mutual-funds-load-or-no-load−1.aspx

19. Morey, M. R. (2016). Predicting mutual fund performance. In H. K. Baker, G. Filbeck, & H. Kiymaz (Eds.), *Mutual funds and exchange-traded funds* (pp. 349−363). New York, NY: Oxford University Press.

20. Ung, D., Fernandez, R., & Hahn, B. (2015). *SPIVA® Europe score-card*. S&P Dow Jones Indices. Retrieved from http://us.spindices.com/ documents/spiva/spiva-europe-year-end-2015.pdf

21. Brown, J. (2016). Do actively managed funds really pay off for investors? *U.S. News & World Report*, April 14. Retrieved from http:// money.usnews.com/investing/articles/2016-04-14/do-actively-managed-funds-really-pay-off-for-investors

22. Carhart, M. (1997). On persistence in mutual fund performance. *Journal of Finance*, 52(1), 57−82.

23. About the high cost of mutual funds ... and what you can do about it. *Personalfund.com*. Retrieved from http://www.personalfund.com/ learnmore.html

24. Petajisto, A. (2013). Active share and mutual fund performance. *Financial Analysts Journal*, 69(4), 73−93. Retrieved from http://www. cfapubs.org/doi/pdf/10.2469/faj.v69.n4.7

25. Cremers, M., Ferreira, M., Matos, P., & Starks, L. (2015, January 5). *The mutual fund industry worldwide: Explicit and closet indexing, fees, and performance*. Working Paper. Retrieved from http://papers.ssrn.com/sol3/papers.cfm?abstract_id=1830207

26. Gottesman, A., Morey, M., & Rosenberg, M. (2013). Do active managers of retail mutual funds have an incentive to closet index in down markets? Fund performance and subsequent annual fund flows, 1997 – 2011. *Journal of Investment Consulting, 14*(2), 47 – 58. Retrieved from http://www.busman.qmul.ac.uk/newsandevents/events/eventdownloads/bfwgconference2013acceptedpapers/114929.pd

27. Cremers, K. J. M., & Petajisto, A. (2009). How active is your fund manager? A new measure that predicts performance. *Review of Financial Studies, 22*(9), 3329–3365. Petajisto, A. (2013). Active share and mutual fund performance. *Financial Analysts Journal, 69*(4), 73 – 93. Retrieved from http://www.cfapubs.org/doi/pdf/10.2469/faj.v69.n4.7. Rekenthaler, J. (2014). Active share: What you need to know. *Morningstar Advisor*, May 29. Retrieved from http://www.morningstar.com/advisor/t/92563289/active-share-what-you-need-to-know.htm

28. Putnam Investments. (2016). *Putnam investors fund annual report 7/31/16*. Retrieved from https://www.putnam.com/individual/mutual-funds/funds/53-investors-fund/

29. *Wall Street Journal* (2014, January 17). Is your fund a closet-index fund. Retrieved from http://online.wsj.com/public/resources/documents/st_FUNDS20140117.html

30. Baldwin, W. (2015). Best buys in active funds. *Fortune*, May 6. Retrieved from http://www.forbes.com/sites/baldwin/2015/05/06/best-buys-in-active-funds-2/#655c365d6f3d

31. Bensted, A. (2016). *2016 Preqin global hedge fund report*. Preqin. Retrieved from https://www.preqin.com/docs/samples/2016-Preqin-Global-Hedge-Fund-Report-Sample-Pages.pdf

32. Investment Company Institute. (2016). *2016 investment company fact book* (56th ed.). Retrieved from https://www.ici.org/pdf/2016_fact-book.pdf

33. Goldberg, S. (2016). Expanding the definition of 'Accredited Investor.' *Wall St. Daily*, February 25. Retrieved from http://www.wall-streetdaily.com/2016/02/25/accredited-investor-private-equity/

34. Rosenbaum, E. (2015). Who qualifies as an accredited investor? *CNBC.com*, February 4. Retrieved from http://www.cnbc.com/2015/02/04/who-qualifies-as-an-accredited-investor.html

35. Pasternak, J. (2015). The downward trend in hedge fund fees. *DarcMatter*, June 15. Retrieved from https://www.darcmatter.com/blog/downward-trend-in-hedge-fund-fees/

36. Fletcher, L. (2016, March 30). How to save money on hedge-fund fees. *The Wall Street Journal*. Retrieved from http://blogs.wsj.com/moneybeat/2016/03/30/how-to-save-money-on-hedge-fund-fees/

37. Lowenstein, R. (2015). Hedge funds' conspiracy of mediocrity keeps fees high, returns low. *Fortune*, May 19. Retrieved from http://fortune.com/2015/05/19/hedge-funds-mediocrity/

38. Brown, S., Goetzmann, W., & Liang, B. (2003). *Fees on fees in funds of funds*. NBER Working Paper No. 9464. National Bureau of Economic Research. Retrieved from http://www.nber.org/papers/w9464

39. Danske Invest Compass Equity Fund. *Key Investor Information Document (KIID)*. Retrieved from http://www.danskeinvest.fi/web/show_fund.produkt?p_nId=1527&p_nFundgroup=61&p_nFund=2457

40. Danske Compass Equity. "Manager" section. Retrieved from http://www.danskeinvest.fi/web/show_fund.produkt?p_nId=1527&p_nFundgroup=61&p_nFund=2457

11

TRAP 7: INVESTING IN COMPLEX PRODUCTS

You ought to be able to explain why you're taking the job you're taking, why you're making the investment you're making, or whatever it may be. And if it can't stand applying pencil to paper, you'd better think it through some more. And if you can't write an intelligent answer to those questions, don't do it.

Warren Buffett, Chairman and
CEO of Berkshire Hathaway

Here is some simple but sage advice discussed earlier as a way to avoid a common investing mistake: Never invest in something you don't understand. If you do, you are inviting disappointment. Before making an investment, review your knowledge of it. Do you clearly understand the investment and its value? If you don't, stay away. To remain competitive in rapidly changing financial markets, financial service providers are proactive in offering innovative products to their customers. They often target many of these innovations to individual investors, also called *retail investors*. The amount and complexity of different kinds of investment products available in today's markets can be overwhelming. The complexity of financial products has increased steadily, even after the financial crisis of 2007–2008, and is more prevalent among distributors with a less sophisticated investor base. Additionally, financial complexity increases when competition intensifies.[1]

Investor sophistication has lagged behind the growing complexity of retail financial markets, despite being deluged with more information than ever. For example, on an average day, more than 4000 analyst reports are generated globally, compared to just a few dozen a generation ago.[2] Remaining unsophisticated about investments enables others to take advantage of you. Consequently, they may persuade you to buy investments that are ill-suited for you resulting in your taking inappropriate risk and paying excessive fees.[3]

In 2013 the International Organization of Securities Commissions released a report that set out principles to govern the sale of complex financial products to investors. The report identifies the following as common features of many complex products:[4]

1. Terms, features, or a complex structure that are unlikely to be reasonably understood by an average investor as opposed to more traditional and simpler investment instruments;

2. Difficulty in valuations (i.e., valuations requiring specific skills and/or systems); and

3. A very limited or no secondary market resulting in illiquid products.

The Complex Financial Instruments Unit of the Securities and Exchange Commission (SEC) is devoted to investigating cases involving complicated securities products. This unit devotes more resources to complex products that are being marketed to less sophisticated retail investors. Examples of such products include leveraged and inverse exchange-traded funds, reverse convertibles, alternative mutual funds, and structured notes. For instance, a *structured note* is a derivative with hybrid security features combining payoffs from multiple ordinary securities, typically a stock or bond plus a derivative. Structured notes contain complex payoff structures and opaque pricing.

Annual global sales of retail structured products grew rapidly from 2000 until 2007, when sales peaked at around $600 billion. The demise of Lehman Brothers Holding Co. and its associated default on many structured products had a sobering effect across the structured product market in 2008 resulting in declining sales. By 2015, global sales returned to around $560 billion, driven mostly by demand in Asia.[5]

Some complex financial products require a high level of knowledge to evaluate and assess. Innovative products can be particularly difficult for individual investors to understand, especially when the innovative aspect results from variable maturities, contingent (option-like, nonlinear) payouts, tiered risk exposures, and other complexities. The offering may have a fixed investment term with penalties in case of early withdrawal, which means that the product lacks liquidity. In this case, you may have to sell the product at a heavy discount or be unable to sell it at all. Additionally, the pricing of many financial products may not be transparent for typical investors. This lack of transparency relates to the fact that the "price" may include fees rather than reflect the cost of the product alone. Because many investors can't process large amounts of complex information, having excessive and overly complex disclosures tend to exacerbate matters.[6]

Although the typical investor should avoid investing in overly complex financial products, this may be easier said than done. Earlier chapters discussed various investment products that providers used to lure investors who lacked sufficient understanding of them. For example, financial institutions sold mortgage-backed securities (MBS) to investors who were unable to assess the credit risk of such securities. A long period of low nominal interest rates led to strong demand for new and higher risk assets such as collateralized debt obligations (CDOs) and other structured finance products. Bond issuers obscured the lack of connection between what would prove to be the true credit quality of the underlying collateral and the promised performance of the securities backed by them. Correspondingly, buyers of Hong Kong Minibonds thought they were making a deposit, only with a higher yield. What they were actually doing was writing insurance against defaults by a basket of companies. Despite their name, Minibonds were extremely complex financial products.

This chapter examines three investment vehicles that are inherently complex: (1) long-short equity funds, (2) structured products, and (3) leveraged exchange-traded funds (leveraged ETFs). Despite their complexity, these products attract many investors due to expectations of high returns, even without investors fully understanding the associated costs and risks. However, these featured investment vehicles are only a sampling of complex products.

LONG-SHORT EQUITY FUNDS

Since the early 2000s, some prominent global asset management companies started offering retail investors previously forbidden fruit called long-short equity funds. A *long-short equity fund* is a type of mutual fund that mimics some of the trading strategies typically used by a hedge fund. A *hedge fund* is an alternative investment using pooled funds that may use different strategies in order to earn high returns for their investors, who are typically sophisticated investors. By loosening mutual fund regulation, funds imitating a long-short strategy became available to retail investors and gained increasing popularity. For example, Morningstar lists around 300 different long-short equity mutual fund share classes being offered just in the United States.[7]

Long-short equity funds follow a seemingly straight-forward strategy. The idea is to take long positions in undervalued stocks (buying stocks that are expected to rise in price) and to sell short overvalued stocks (selling stocks that are expected to decline in price). *Short selling* means selling borrowed shares with the expectation that they will decline in value. If the stock's price declines sufficiently, the short investor can earn a profit on the difference between the selling price and the repurchase price, minus the cost of borrowing. Obviously, if a fund manager's forecast on stocks' valuations are correct, such a strategy can earn superior returns compared to a simple long-only strategy. A *long-only strategy* describes an investment strategy that buys assets but does not sell any assets short or employ leverage.

For example, Aberdeen Equity Long-Short Fund "seeks to achieve its objective regardless of market conditions through the purchase and short sale of equity securities of U.S. companies of any size. The Fund's investment team takes long positions in the stocks of companies it believes will increase in value and it sells short the stock of companies it believes will either decline in value or underperform the Fund's long positions."[8] For its allocation in U.S. stocks, Aberdeen Equity Long-Short Equity Fund had 87.14% exposure to long positions and 52.85% exposure to short positions as of August 31, 2016. The *net exposure* is the difference between long and short positions = 87.14% – 52.87% = 34.27%. Such an exposure implies that the fund is not totally neutral to market conditions and that Aberdeen's investment team is betting that the stock market rises in the future.

Most long-short mutual funds follow a more "long-bias" approach in their investing by taking short positions in substantially fewer stocks than in which they have long positions. Thus, the potential for higher returns via higher active return hasn't been the main sales pitch of long-short mutual funds. *Active return* is the difference between a fund's performance and market's return, which is the return generated by the fund manager's "stock picking." However, the marketing materials of essentially all long-short mutual funds stress how their strategy allows achieving equity-like returns with reduced volatility, which is a statement sounding like a financial free-lunch. The following is a typical pitch of the PIMCO EqS Long-Short Fund:

> *The fund has the flexibility to increase or decrease equity market exposure by adjusting its mix of long, short and*

cash positions. It will tend to have more equity market exposure when attractive investment opportunities are plentiful and will take steps to reduce equity market exposure when there is an absence of compelling ideas or when risks appear to outweigh reward.

As Richard Michaud notes, "A long-short strategy is not an economic free-lunch. Increases in active return are generally accompanied by increases in active risk. Claims of superiority often reflect misunderstandings of basic principles of modern finance or the hybrid character of the strategy."[9]

This promise of equity-like returns that reduces volatility essentially implies that long-short mutual funds would have a higher Sharpe ratio than long-only equity funds because they would generate similar returns to the equity markets but with less risk. The *Sharpe ratio*, which is a measure for calculating risk-adjusted return, is the average return earned in excess of the risk-free rate per unit of volatility or total risk, as measured by the portfolio's standard deviation. In other words, the Sharpe ratio describes how much additional return you are receiving for the extra volatility that you endure for holding a riskier asset. You would prefer portfolios with higher Sharpe ratios.

Figure 11.1 compares the performance of the Lipper Long-Short Equity Funds with the S&P 500 Index. In 2008, the stock market experienced considerable losses during the financial crisis and failed to fully recover well until 2012. One might have expected that long-short strategies had performed well during this period because portfolio managers were able to hedge (i.e., reduce equity market exposure), but long-short equity funds typically underperformed relative to the S&P 500 index. The figure shows that long/short equity funds were not immune to the financial crisis: On average, long/short equity fund performance was −16% compared with −18% on the S&P 500 Index. In 2009, the return on the S&P 500 (11%) exceeded that of long/short equity funds

Figure 11.1: Comparison of Lipper Long-Short Equity Funds with the S&P 500 Index

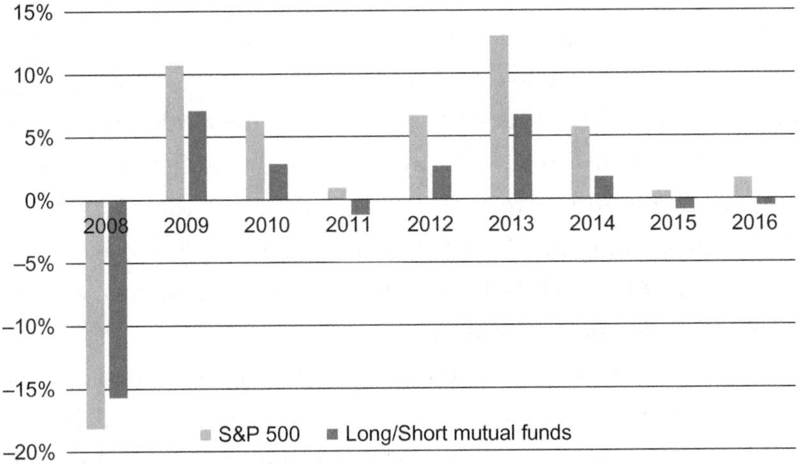

Source: CRSP data. Note: This figure shows the annual performance of the Lipper Long-Short Equity Funds Index relative to the S&P 500 index between 2008 and summer 2016.

(7%) by two percentage points. The relative outperformance of the S&P 500 continued between 2010 and 2016.

For the close to eight-year period examined, Lipper Long/Short Mutual Funds provide lower volatility compared to the S&P 500 Index: 7.2% vs. 9.6 %, respectively, but fail to deliver the return. The average annual return for long/short funds was 0.4%, while S&P 500 generated an annual 3.2% return. As a result, Lipper Long-Short Mutual Funds have a lower Sharpe ratio compared with the S&P 500 (0.04 vs. 0.32), implying that investors were actually punished for taking on more risk relative to a risk-free asset. The Sharpe ratio is calculated by dividing the excess return (0.4% − 0.1%) by the volatility (7.2%). A long-only equity strategy (S&P 500) provided a positive excess return or Sharpe ratio of 0.32.

Research on the long-short equity strategy focuses on hedge funds, not mutual funds. The research findings provide some support for the claims of "superiority" of this strategy.[10,11] However, generalizing the results for hedge funds to mutual funds is questionable because mutual funds differ from hedge funds on several dimensions, such as short-selling restrictions and using derivatives and leverage.

Figure 11.2 highlights the differences in the performance of long-short hedge funds and long-short mutual funds. Hedge funds provided investors with a much smoother ride through the financial crisis in 2008. The average annual hedge fund return between 2008 and 2016 was 1.6% and the volatility was 3.8%. The Sharpe ratio the Long/Short Hedge Fund index was 0.39 which implied a slightly better risk-adjusted return than was the S&P 500 index provided (0.32).

Aberdeen suggests that today's investment environment has been marked by several years of rising equity and fixed income market prices, low volatility, excessive liquidity, and slow economic growth. Aberdeen believes the next several years could bring different results with a pick-up in volatility and dispersion among financial assets, increasing opportunities for both long and short positions. The period 2011–2016 has not been too

Figure 11.2: Comparison of the Barclay Equity Long-Short Index (Hedge Funds) and the Lipper Long-Short Funds Index (Mutual Funds)

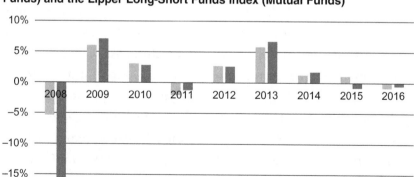

Source: CRSP data. *Note*: This figure shows the annual performance of the Barclay Equity Long-Short Index (hedge funds) relative to Lipper Long-Short Mutual Funds Index between 2008 and summer 2016.

successful for the Aberdeen Equity Long-Short Fund investor: As of June 30, 2016, the fund's cumulative return was 2.3% compared to 12.1% for the S&P 500 Index.[12]

Long-short equity mutual funds follow a seemingly straightforward strategy, which in reality entails relatively complicated transactions and active management. Thus, these funds represent a complex product for untrained investors. By promising equity-like returns with reduced volatility, these funds claim that they can provide a "free-lunch." As discussed previously, you don't get something for nothing in the investment world. Thus, you should be cautious and remember that although long-short mutual funds may deliver lower volatility, you should not expect excessive risk-adjusted returns.

Trap Judgment

Long-Short Equity Funds

Becoming a victim of investment fraud

Misrepresenting risky products as safe

Making unrealistic return expectations

Falling for mutual fund traps

Overpaying for products and services

Investing in complex products

Engaging in gambling disguised as investing

Relying on unsupported promises

STRUCTURED PRODUCTS

The Financial Industry Regulatory Authority, Inc. (FINRA) suggests that structured products can be attractive to investors because they can offer higher returns and may even feature a level of principal protection. However, these products can have major drawbacks such as credit and market risk, lack of liquidity, high hidden costs, inflexibility, and limited upside.[13]

No single, uniform definition of a structured product exists. Typically, structured investment products have the characteristic of combining a base instrument, such as a certificate of deposit (CD), note, or bond, with an embedded derivative that provides economic exposure to reference assets, indices or portfolios. They provide investors, at predetermined times, with payoffs that are linked to the performance of reference assets, indices, or other economic values. Examples of structured investment products targeted to retail investors are market-linked CDs, equity-linked notes (ELNs), and index-linked bonds. Structured investment products are advertised as tools that combine the upside potential of stock markets with guaranteed principal. For example, the Swedish bank SEB promotes index-linked notes on its website as follows:

> An Equity-Linked Note (ELN) is an instrument with its yield linked to share price performance, thereby combining the possibility of healthy returns of equities with the security of bonds. Regardless of any falling rates in the stock market, the ELN returns at least the nominal amount on the repayment date.

A structured financial product is a package consisting of two parts: a CD/note/bond and a call option. The call option typically has a market index such as the S&P 500 as the underlying asset and a strike price equal to the issue date value of the index or some predetermined modification of this value. A *strike price* is the *price* at which a specific derivative contract can be exercised. As an example, Morgan Stanley issued an equity-linked note in November 2013 with the following terms:[14]

Issuer: Morgan Stanley

Issue price: $1000 per note

Pricing date: November 22, 2013

Maturity date: May 27, 2021

Interest: None

Underlying index: S&P 500® Index

Supplemental redemption amount: $1000 (the index percentage change) (the participation rate), provided that the supplemental redemption amount will not be less than $0 or greater than $750 per note.

Morgan Stanley suggests that the "market-linked notes" offer investors exposure to the performance of equities and provide for the repayment of principal at maturity.

Essentially all equity-linked notes have an additional feature: a specific, predetermined participation rate. The *participation* rate is the factor by which the holder of the ELN will benefit from the returns of the embedded call option at maturity. For example, if the participation factor is 85% and the embedded option expires in the money, say the stock index is 20% above the option's strike price, the equity option will return 17% = (85%)(20%). Thus, the returns of such a product seem to be defined by two return-drivers: (1) the option value at maturity times the participation rate and (2) the yield of the zero-coupon note. In Morgan Stanley's "Market-Linked Notes" example, the participation rate is 100% but a maximum payment occurs at maturity of $1750 per note (175% of the stated principal amount). As attractive as the possible 75% return may sound, an investor should acknowledge that in 7.5 years, it would correspond to an annual return of about 8%. The investor has no rights to receive dividends with respect to the stocks that underlie the index.

Structured products have been a success story in retail finance. Low interest rates drove investors in search of structured products apart from traditional asset classes such as equities, fixed income, and real estate. Since their introduction in 1980s, structured products have become permanent members of product repertoires of nearly all major retail financial services providers all around the world, targeted almost exclusively to retail investors. However, just because structured products have gained in popularity doesn't mean that you should join the herd.

Structured products tend to have complicated contract terms making the valuation of the product difficult for retail investors. Conditions can include different averaging methods for starting and ending values and caps limiting the maximum price increase of the underlying asset (e.g., stock index) in which the investor will participate. The proper valuation of these products requires complicated financial modeling, which results in the product-issuing financial institution having a clear information edge over its clients. When these complicated contract terms are combined with an endless repertoire of different indices, the market of structured products becomes one in which each offered product is essentially unique. Calculating the true value of these products is extremely difficult because investors must know multiple valuation techniques.

Another potential problem related to index-linked bonds is that while these products are often marketed as alternatives for investing purely in bonds and notes, they have substantially worse liquidity. The payoff profile of a structured product is only offered at maturity, which might be several years away, and until then investors are stuck with poor secondary market prices tying up their investments. The issuers provide almost all of the liquidity and have incentives to offer poor bid/ask prices. This results in a situation where invested capital is essentially tied into the products from purchase to maturity.

Many naïve investors might also be missing a key aspect from the main selling argument of structured products: The capital security is subject to the issuer-institution's default risk because the issuer, not the government, secures the capital. Thus, even products with capital protection are exposed to issuer risk. Furthermore, the payoff profile of structured products may be highly complex. Here is an example of a product *Jayenne 4* distributed by Credit Agricole:

> *This is a growth product linked to a basket composed of the FTSE Euro First 80, the FTSE 100, the SMI and the NIKKEI 225. The Annual Performance is set at 5% for*

*the first three years. In the following years, if the perfor-
mance since the start date of the worst-performing index is
positive or null, then the Annual Performance for that
year is registered at 5%, otherwise 0%. The Basket
Performance since the start date is registered every six
months. The Final Basket Performance is calculated as the
average of all these six monthly readings, capped at a
maximum basket performance of 100%. After 8 years, the
product offers a guaranteed capital return of 100%, plus
the greater of either the sum of the Annual Performances,
or 100% of the Final Basket performance.[15]*

This example illustrates the complexity of a popular structured product, which contrasts with the likely level of financial sophistication of the average client of Credit Agricole. How can an investor without a PhD degree in finance estimate a portfolio's expected return from which three best-performing shares are removed every year? This task would be challenging even for a finance professor. Evidence shows that financial complexity in European markets has been steadily increasing. The more complex a retail structured product is, the more profitable it is for the bank.[15]

A Case Study: Equity Index-Linked Bonds in Norway

Here is a case study involving equity index-linked bonds. In 2000, Ivar Røeggen bought equity index-linked bonds at a price of NOK 500,000 (≈ €64,000) from DnB NOR, Norway's largest financial group. He financed this investment and related front-end fees by taking out a loan of more than NOK 520,000 (≈ €66,500) with a nominal interest rate of 7.95% also from DnB NOR. The deal was a textbook example of a loan-financed structured product. When the maturity date of the bonds approached in 2006, the options expired worthless. Although the bond had a guaranteed repayment of the nominal amount, Røeggen lost NOK 249,000 (≈ €31,850) in interest payments and other costs related to both the index-linked bond and his loan. The financial press later suggested that DnB NOR had sold at least NOK 60 million ($\approx$ €7.4 million) worth of similar package deals.

As a result of such a disappointing investment outcome, Røeggen filed a law suit against the bank. He claimed that considering the high interest rate on the loan (7.95% a year), the investment package as a whole had a negative or insufficiently positive expected return. That is, he challenged the suitability of selling such "loan-financed structured products" to retail investors.

DnB NOR's main defense against Røeggen's claims was that the bank saw the sale of structured products and the financing of these products as two separate transactions, suggesting that it didn't sell Røeggen the package as a whole, but as two separate parts. The bank defended its view that according to its valuation models, the expected return on the structured product was sufficiently positive given the loan financing of its purchase. However, an expert witness on the case questioned the legitimacy of the bank's models and eventually both parties agreed that Johnsen's far less optimistic models were more suitable for evaluating the product's expected return.

Based on expert testimony, the bank was irresponsible for pushing debt-financing of the index-linked bond. The high level of profitability created a strong incentive for the bank to endorse such a product for its clients. This product, which was targeted at retail investors, was highly complex. Furthermore, the product's structure made evaluating all its costs difficult, which in turn complicated the task of objectively evaluating the product's expected return. Given the product's target audience, the bank could easily include costs without the customers noticing.[16]

Yet, the bank's clients were not blameless. They had a responsibility to familiarize themselves with the product and exhibit more self-driven skepticism. The lessons to be learned from this case are two-fold. First, if you are naive, you are more likely to accept a product. Second, if you don't understand a bank product, you should stay away from it. The Supreme Court ruled that the Norwegian bank DnB NOR provided Mr. Røeggen with incorrect and overly optimistic information about the investment, the investment was loan financed, and he wasn't a professional investor. The bank had to compensate Røeggen for his losses and also needed to compensate other customers who had invested in misleadingly marketed savings products. The cost for DnB NOR was 450 million NOK.[17] Five years before this the rules for marketing and selling structured products had already been tightened. In 2008 the Finance Minister Kristin Halvonsen announced that the new regulations would effectively make it illegal to sell structured bonds and other complex instruments to retail investors.[18]

According to Frank Armstrong III, the founder of Principal Solutions, Inc. and the author of *Informed Investor*:

> *If you know where to look, Wall Street can crank out some amazingly good products. But they would much rather sell you garbage. Armstrong's Second Law states that the awfulness of the product is directly related to the profits to the firm and commissions to the broker. Just as sex sells, toxic pays. And no amoral, profit maximizing, commission driven broker or institution can afford to ignore a good toxic product.*[19]

Market participants often view financial innovation as something worthwhile. Some innovations allow investors to achieve desired payoffs unavailable in other financial instruments, enable risk management, provide tax benefits, circumvent regulations, and lower transaction costs. Despite the potential benefits of financial innovations, another side exists to the story. Some new products are predisposed to lead to a conflict of interests between issuers and their clients.

Structured products are complex and can be more risky than they seem. They typically have complicated contract terms with many restrictions and conditions making the valuation of the product extremely difficult for retail investors. Evidence shows a lack of support for the claim that they deliver highly customized risk-return profiles unattainable by traditional financial instruments. Proper valuation of these products requires complex financial modeling, which gives the issuer an edge over its clients. This leaves room for overpaying for such products.

A Case Study: Reverse Convertibles

A *reverse convertible*, also known as a reverse *exchangeable security* or *revertible note*, is a structured product that generally consists of a high-yield, short-term note of the issuer that is linked to the performance of an unrelated reference asset, which is often a single stock but in some cases a basket of stocks, an index or some other asset. Usually, the initial investment is $1000 per security, and maturity dates range from three months to one year. It is an unsecured debt obligation of the issuer, not the reference company, and thus carries the rating of the issuer. Reverse convertibles are popular in part because of the high yields they offer.

Reverse convertibles offer a steady stream of high-yield payments through the payment of a coupon rate often higher than that of a high-yield bond. If the stock's price stays above the "knock-in" level, which is typically 80% of the stock's price at the time of purchase, the whole time before the maturity, the investor will receive 100% of the initial investment at maturity of the convertible. However, if the stock's price at some point falls below the knock-in level and does not exceed the initial purchase price at the time of maturity, the investor will receive an investment in the form of equity ownership in the reference company. This means that the investor ends up with shares that are worth less than the original investment.[20]

In practice, when you buy a reverse convertible, you receive a yield-enhanced bond. Because you don't own the underlying asset such as the stock, you don't get to participate in any upside appreciation. However, you do participate in the downside price risk. The upside potential is limited to the stated coupon because the investor receives coupon payments regardless of the performance of the underlying reference shares. The risk potential is nearly the same as for the underlying security, less the coupon payment. Granted, the reverse convertible provides some conditional downside protection unavailable through owning the stock, because if the stock price declines but doesn't reach the knock-in level, you will receive 100% of your initial investment.

Despite the appeal of high-yield of reverse convertibles, investors should be very cautious before investing in them. In most cases, the investor is unlikely to fully comprehend the complexity of this structured product. A good example that illustrates the riskiness of these products is the investor alert issued by FINRA in 2011 concerning reverse convertibles. According to FINRA, "They are complex investments that often involve terms, features and risks that can be difficult for individual investors and investment professionals alike to evaluate."[20]

Some investors get confused and believe that reverse convertibles are safe. This belief enables brokers to misrepresent or omit important information about the investment's real risks and take advantage of unwary investors. Another factor that worsens the situation is that reverse convertibles pay high commissions to the brokers who sell them. The nickname of reverse convertibles used on Wall Street, "Nest Egg Slashers," also gives a hint of the true characteristics of the products.[21]

Reverse convertibles originated in Europe in the 1990s and first arrived to the U.S. markets in 2005. They are aimed at retail investors. Issuance of the notes in 2008 alone amounted to $7 billion. During the first five years in the U.S. markets, stock prices kept rising, so the downsides didn't emerge. In 2008 many perplexed investors received large equity positions and faced substantial losses on their initial investment.[21]

Reverse convertibles are at best similar to high-yield bonds and at worst like owning a stock. In a flat or rising markets, reverse convertibles do well, but in a falling market the opposite is true. Reverse convertibles might be a suitable investment for an investor who wants a higher stream of current income than is presently available from other bonds or bank products and who is prepared to give up any appreciation in the value of the underlying asset. Given that no "free lunches" are available for investors in the financial markets, the higher yield simply compensates investors for assuming greater risks on reverse convertibles. However, these risks include not only the risks that fixed income products normally carry such as inflation and default risk, but also any additional risks associated with the underlying asset. Given the secondary trading for most structured products is limited, the investment might turn out be highly illiquid. Furthermore, the issuers of reverse convertibles charge large up-front fees from investors, typically ranging from 1% to 8%, for packaging the reverse convertible from its individual components. In the prospectus, these fees are often called the "costs of hedging" or "built-in costs" and the specific amount is often undisclosed.

Considering the various features of reverse convertibles, FINRA's assessment of these financial instruments is appropriate. Reverse convertibles are complex investments that often involve terms and risks that can be difficult for both individual investors and investment professionals to evaluate.

A Case Study: SPARQS

Stock participation accreting redemption quarterly-pay securities (SPARQS) are a publicly issued structured equity product issued by Morgan Stanley in the United States. Introduced in 2001, the issuer targeted SPARQS specifically at retail investors. During their short lifetime, SPARQS evolved quickly into a billion dollar industry, as Morgan Stanley alone issued 69 different SPARQS between 2001 and 2005 with proceeds of about $2.2 billion. Other major financial institutions also issued large volumes of essentially identical products during the same period, including yield-enhanced equity-linked debt securities (YEELDS) offered by Lehman Brothers and stock return income debt securities (STRIDES) offered by Merrill Lynch.

SPARQS are a quarterly interest paying, callable note that is exchanged for shares of the underlying company at maturity. If called, holders receive all the future interest payments of the note, but waive their rights on the underlying equity at maturity. Just as with index-linked notes, SPARQS are obligations of the issuer, which in this case is Morgan Stanley, and not of the company whose shares act as the underlying equity of a specific SPARQS contract.

One study examines the offering prices of SPARQS, the most popular of the publicly offered U.S. retail structured equity products.[22] The offering prices of SPARQS were, on average, almost 8% higher than estimates of the products' fair market values obtained using objective option pricing methods. Under reasonable assumptions about the underlying stocks' expected returns, the mean expected return estimate on the structured products is slightly below zero. Because the products don't provide tax, liquidity, or other benefits, rationalizing their purchase is questionable for informed rational investors.

Wrap-Up of Structured Products

Issuers of structured products promote them as a way for investors to achieve desired payoff patterns unavailable with other financial instruments. Some products can be attractive to investors because they can offer positive returns and may even feature a level of principal protection. Yet, structured products often have major drawbacks such as credit risk, lack of liquidity, and high hidden costs. Proper valuation of these products requires complex financial modeling, which enables issuers to overcharge for these products. The inability of most retail investors to properly evaluate these products results when they tend to overestimate the expected returns. Do you clearly understand the structured product and its true value? If you don't, stay away.

Trap Judgment

Structured Products

Becoming a victim of investment fraud

Misrepresenting risky products as safe

Making excessive return expectations

Falling for mutual fund traps

Overpaying for products and services

Investing in complex products

Engaging in gambling disguised as investing

Relying on unsupported promises

LEVERAGED AND INVERSE EXCHANGE-TRADED FUNDS

An *exchange-traded fund* (ETF) is typically a marketable security that tracks an index, a commodity, bonds, or a basket of assets. ETFs are similar to index mutual funds but are listed and traded on exchanges at varying prices throughout the day just like stocks. In 1993 State Street Global Advisors launched the first ETF in the United States called the SPDR, which tracks the S&P 500 index. The name is an acronym for the Standard & Poor's Depositary Receipts. The ETF industry has grown rapidly and it is now even bigger than the more established business of hedge funds. Assets in the global ETF industry were $2.9 trillion at the end of 2015 but in 1999 the ETF industry was less than a tenth the size of its ritzier rival.[23]

ETFs share some basic characteristics with mutual funds but several operational and structural differences exist between these investment products. An ETF is a pooled investment vehicle with shares that can be traded throughout the day on a stock exchange at a market-determined price — just as the shares of any publicly traded company. In contrast, mutual fund shares are not listed on stock exchanges. Instead, investors buy and sell shares from the fund company. Pricing also differs between mutual funds and ETFs. Although mutual fund investors can place orders to buy or sell shares throughout the day, all orders placed during the day receive the same price, called the *net asset value* (NAV), which is calculated the next time it is computed. Most U.S. mutual funds calculate their NAV as of 4:00 p.m. eastern standard time because that is the time U.S. stock exchanges typically close. In contrast, the price of an ETF share is continuously determined on a stock exchange.[24]

An ETF originates with a sponsor — a company or financial institution — that chooses the ETF's investment objective. In the case of an index-based ETF, the sponsor chooses both an index and a method of tracking its target index. Although the majority of the ETFs are passive in that they track an index such as the S&P 500. ETF sponsors continue building on recent innovations by launching additional actively managed ETFs. The sponsor of an actively managed ETF determines the fund's investment objective and may trade securities at its discretion, much like an actively managed mutual fund. Until now active ETF markets have remained relatively small. In 2015, only 1% of the assets were tied to actively managed funds out of the $2.1 trillion U.S. listed ETF market.[25] Active ETFs are generally much more expensive than passive ETFs. You can buy a U.S. stock ETF such as the Schwab U.S. Board Equity ETF for as little as three basis points (bps), or $3 per $10,000 invested and get a portfolio of the largest 2500 stocks in the United States. By contrast, most active ETFs cost from 50 to 125 bps in the expense ratio.

The introduction of several subcategories of ETFs, namely leveraged and inverse ETFs, has expanded their popularity among individual investors. Leveraged ETFs provide daily returns that are a multiple or a negative multiple of the daily returns on a market index or benchmark. Inverse ETFs try to go up when the market drops and vice versa. Many investors fail to understand the risks associated with leveraged and inverse ETFs and believe they are similar to a normal ETF. In reality, these instruments are more suitable for professional traders than for long-term retail investors or anyone who cannot tolerate a high-risk portfolio. Thus, if you trade these financial instruments, you should fully understand what you're trading.[26]

Leveraged and inverse ETFs are complex products that use both leverage and different financial derivatives to achieve desired payoff. For example, a leveraged ETF portfolio manager might borrow 200% of the equity in the portfolio and invest 300% of the equity value in securities. A typical leveraged ETF has a 2:1 or 3:1 leverage ratio, which it tries to keep constant throughout the period of its activity. The portfolio manager of an inverse ETF effectively replicates short sales. Leveraged and inverse ETFs track most of the major international equity indices tracked also by ordinary ETFs such as the S&P 500, FTSE 100, and Dow Jones Industrial Average (DJIA).

Figure 11.3 shows the percentage of the $50.3 billion in total net assets held by leveraged and inverse ETFs as of August 25, 2015, held by different classes. The most popular among investors are Bear 1x and Bull 2x.

After being introduced in 2006, these products grew quickly to encompass a notable volume of the ETF market. As of June, 2015, leveraged and inverse ETFs had $63 billion of AUM. This rapid growth isn't surprising because the global investment community saw the products as a convenient alternative to the traditional approach for levering a portfolio. A total of 44% of the leveraged and inverse ETF assets were in bearish short and leveraged products and 56% were allocated to bullish double- or triple-leveraged funds.[27]

Unsophisticated investors who fail to understand that leveraged ETFs are a poor way of leveraging or selling short an index for a longer than a day or two may experience substantial investment shortfalls. The extent of the shortfall depends on the holding

Figure 11.3: Division of Total Net Assets of Leveraged and Inverse U.S. ETFs to Different Classes

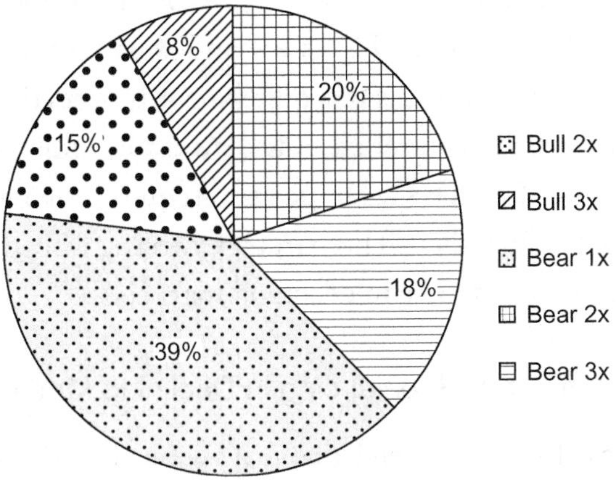

Source: ETF database, etfdb.com. *Notes*: This figure shows the percentage of the $50.3 billion in total net assets held by leveraged and inverse ETFs as of August 25, 2015 in different classes. The most popular among investors are Bear 1x and Bull 2x.

period of the investment and the returns and volatility of the underlying ETF.[28]

A main concern is that contrary to what the typical names of the products such as "ABC's 3x S&P 500" might suggest, leveraged ETFs only aim to, and are capable of, accurately replicating, amplifying, or inversing daily returns of the index they are tracking and not the long-term returns. For example, a leveraged ETF promising to provide three times the returns of the S&P 500, index (Bull 3x), actually aims and is designed to deliver three times the daily return of the S&P 500. In the long-run, this successful daily mimicking doesn't add up to an exact amplification of the index's long-term returns. As a result of daily rebalancing of the leveraged and inverse ETF portfolios to re-establish the same leverage or short ratio at the end of each day, both 200% and 300% leveraged ETFs and inverse ETFs are quite likely to have negative returns across long holding periods whether the underlying market returns are positive or negative.

Continuous fluctuations in the price of the underlying index change the value of the ETF's assets and thus require the ETF to adjust its index exposure. As this adjustment is needed continuously to maintain a constant leverage ratio, adjusting index exposure in accordance with the ETF's leverage ratio requires rebalancing at the end of each trading day. This strategy works well during rising markets but problems arise in declining markets.

Example of Rebalancing in Declining Markets

This example illustrates the problem of rebalancing in declining markets. Consider an initial $100 investment in a double-levered fund (Bull 2x). At the start, the levered investment has two parts: $200 in equity and $100 in borrowing. Next, assume that equity increases by 10% to $220 during the first trading day. At this point, the security is no longer a double-levered fund; it is a 2.2 times levered fund while the investor's initial stake has grown to $120. Typically, to maintain the two times leverage ratio, the portfolio manager rebalances the fund before the start of the next trading day. Borrowing an additional $20 further enhances the fund's equity position, which currently is $220. The $20 can be employed to buy an incremental $20 stake in the underlying security, so that the mix is now $240 equity and $120 borrowing — again double levered.

Assume that the equity decreases by 9.09% over the next trading day so that the underlying asset returns to its initial price. Now the fund's $240 in equity declines to $218.18 while the amount borrowed remains at $120. At this point the fund is a 1.82 times levered fund. To restore the fund to 2.0 times leverage, $21.82 in equity must be sold and the proceeds returned to the lender. Once this happens, the fund has $196.36 in equity with $98.18 in borrowing to yield a leverage ratio of 2.0. In this case, although the underlying equity's value has remained the same over the two-day period (+10%, −9.09%), the investor's initial stake of $100 has now shrunk to $98.18 for a two-day loss of 1.82%. Had the fund not rebalanced at the end of the first trading day, the investor's stake would have returned to $100 at the end of the second trading day leaving the investor flat for the two days. This example shows how the performance of a levered product depends upon the return patterns of the underlying security and the rebalancing decisions.

Figure 11.4 illustrates a real-life example. During the volatile period between December 1, 2008, and April 30, 2009, the Russell 1000 Financial Services Index gained 6.7%. The index fell by 35% by March 2009 but recovered well by the end of April. Correspondingly, an ETF seeking to deliver 3x the index's return (Bull 3x) fell by 53.5% over the five-month period. The return was much worse than 3x +6.7%. The 3x inverse ETF (Bear 3x) of

---

Figure 11.4: Performance of Russell 1000 Financial Services Index and Related Bull (3x) and Bear (−3x) ETFs

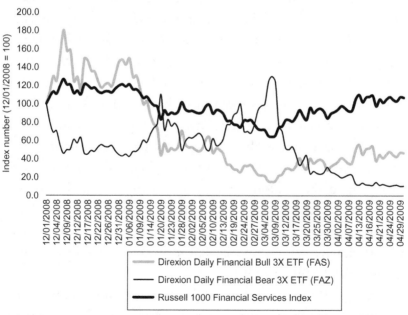

Direxion Daily Financial Bull 3X ETF (FAS)
Direxion Daily Financial Bear 3X ETF (FAZ)
Russell 1000 Financial Services Index

Sources: FAS and FAZ return data from the Center for Research in Financial Prices (CRSP), Russell 1000 Financial Services Index return data from http://uk.advfn.com/p.php?pid=charts&mode=java& symbol=A^RIFIN.X. *Notes*: The figure shows that between December 1, 2008 and April 30, 2009 the Russell 1000 Financial Services Index gained 6.7%, while an ETF seeking to deliver 3x the index's return fell by 53.5%. The 3x inverse ETF of the same underlying index declined by 89.6% during the same period.

the same underlying index declined by 89.6% during the same period. The return was much worse than 3x −6.7%.

Others report similar evidence for the Canadian ETF markets.[29] As the volatility of the return path of the underlying benchmark index increases, tracking error also increases. In this situation, *tracking error* is the difference between the ETF's realized returns and the returns anticipated by the promised leverage ratio. Tracking errors tend to be small for holding periods of up to a week, but become increasingly larger for longer horizons.

In 2009, FINRA stated its concern about the possibility of investors expecting long-term returns from these products that are consistent with the leverage ratios. The SEC also issued an alert about leveraged ETFs to clarify the concern about a potential mismatch between investor expectations and realities of the product.[30]

Both the SEC and FINRA asked the ETF issuer companies to communicate more explicitly their products' aim of mimicking daily rather than long-term returns of the index it is tracking. Despite increasing compliance, a question still remains about whether issuers have exerted sufficient effort to inform clients and unsophisticated investors about the risks related to their product.

Unlike mutual fund shares, investors buy ETF shares on an exchange through a broker, not directly from the company issuing the funds. Since ETFs are popular financial products, investors can gather information from many available sources. However, the issuing company is the only party that regulators require to disclose the potential risks related to an ETF product. Unfortunately, many investors fail to review this information or understand the investment.

Although issuing companies and others attempt to inform investors of the true nature of the leveraged and inverse ETFs, many investors still buy these complex financial products without fully understanding the risks. For example, untrained investors may expect the long-term returns to correspond with the returns of the index multiplied by the leverage ratio of the product. However, the performance of these ETFs can yield unexpected results, which may be far worse than anticipated. Consequently, a potential mismatch is likely to occur between investor expectations and real outcomes. Leveraged and inverse ETFs are unsuitable as long-term investments. As always, you should fully understand an investment's potential risks and rewards before committing your hard-earned capital.

Trap Judgment

Leveraged and Inverse ETFs

Becoming a victim of investment fraud

Misrepresenting risky products as safe

Making unrealistic return expectations

Falling for mutual fund traps

Overpaying for products and services

Investing in complex products

Engaging in gambling disguised as investing

Relying on unsupported promises

LESSONS LEARNED

Although complexity is a relative term, some financial products are much more complex than others. In many cases, the associated risks and costs are not immediately apparent or easily understood, even for experienced investors. To protect yourself and to avoid investing in too complex products, you should keep in mind the following lessons:

1. Don't invest in a financial product that you don't understand.

2. Make sure that you have the requisite knowledge and time to monitor an investment's risks over time.

3. Be aware that the name of a product may not reflect its true features.

4. Think twice about investing in a product based on a mixture of derivatives.

5. Reconsider an investment that relies heavily on assumptions of abundant market liquidity, low interest rates or low inflation.

6. Be aware that the credit rating of an issuing institution may change during the product's lifetime.

7. Understand an investment's total costs before investing because similar, less complex and less costly products may be available.

8. Seek further information from an unbiased, independent source if you don't fully understand an investment.

QUESTIONS

1. Explain a long-only strategy.

2. Differentiate between a long-short equity fund and a hedge fund.

3. Structured investment products are advertised as tools that combine the upside potential of stock markets with guaranteed principal. Explain whether a structured investment product is a "free-lunch."

4. Explain the meaning of an index-linked note.

5. Explain the participation rate of an index-linked note.

6. Discuss why reverse convertibles are called "nest egg slashers."

7. Compare and contrast actively managed and passively managed ETFs.

8. Differentiate between a traditional ETF and a leveraged and inverse ETF.

9. Explain the risks associated with investing in leveraged and inverse ETFs.

NOTES

1. Célérier, C., & Vallée, B. (2014). *What drives financial complexity? A look into the retail market for structured products.* Working Paper. University of Zurich and HEC Paris. Retrieved from http://www.hbs. edu/faculty/conferences/2013-household-behavior-risky-asset-mkts/ Documents/What-Drives-Financial-Complexity_Celerier-Vallee.pdf

2. BlackRock. Global long/short equity fund. *BlackRock.com.* Retrieved from https://www.blackrock.com/investing/literature/investor-guide/oef-global-long-short-equity-fund-investor-guide.pdf

3. Carlin, B. I., & Manson, G. (2011). Obfuscation, learning, and the evolution of investor sophistication. *Review of Financial Studies, 24*(3), 754 – 785.

4. International Organization of Securities Commissions (IOSCO). (2013). *Suitability requirements with respect to the distribution of complex financial products.* Retrieved from https://www.iosco.org/library/ pubdocs/pdf/IOSCOPD400.pdf

5. Alloway, T. (2015). Products tell us a lot about the global search for yield. *Bloomberg,* November 30. Retrieved from http://www.bloomberg. com/news/articles/2015-11-30/sales-of-structured-products-tell-us-a-lot-about-the-global-search-for-yield

6. Lumpkin, S. (2010). Consumer protection and financial innovation: a few basic propositions. *OECD Journal: Financial Market Trends, (1),* 1 – 23. Retrieved from http://www.oecd.org/finance/financial-markets/ 46010844.pdf

7. Morningstar. (2016). Long-short equity: total returns. *Morningstar.com,* September 23. Retrieved from http://news.morning-star.com/fund-category-returns/long-short-equity/$FOCA$LO.aspx

8. Aberdeen equity long-short fund. Retrieved from http://www.aberd-een-asset.com/aam.nsf/usretail/mutualequitiesLongShort

9. Michaud, R. O. (1993). Are long-short equity strategies superior?" *Financial Analysts Journal, 49*(6), 44 – 49.

10. Blackstone Group. (2013). *Taking stock: Long/short hedge funds and equity replacement.* Retrieved from https://www.cfainstitute.org/ learning/products/publications/contributed/altinvestment/Documents/bx_ takingstock_blackstone.pdf

11. Fung, W., & Hsieh, D. A. (2011). The risk in hedge fund strategies: Theory and evidence from long/short equity hedge funds. *Journal of Empirical Finance*, 18(4), 547 – 569.

12. Aberdeen Asset Management. *The quarterly factsheet of Aberdeen equity long-short fund*. Retrieved from http://www.aberdeen-asset.com/ aam.nsf/usretail/mutualequitiesLongShort

13. Financial Industry Regulatory Authority (FINRA). Grass isn't always greener – Chasing return in a challenging investment environment. Retrieved from http://www.finra.org/investors/alerts/grass-isnt-always-greener. Connon, H. (2013). Quick guide to structured products. *Interactive Investor*, June 19. Retrieved from http://www.iii.co.uk/tools-research/knowledge-centre/quick-guide-structured-products

14. Morgan Stanley. Retrieved from http://www.morganstanley.com/ structuredinvestments/docs/prospectus/prelim/ProspectusRed6 1761JMN6.pdf

15. Célérier, C., & Vallée, B. (2015). *Catering to investors through product complexity*. Working Paper. University of Zurich and Harvard Business School. Retrieved from http://papers.ssrn.com/sol3/papers.cfm? abstract_id=2289890

16. Folkestad, S. (2012). Historisk om bankprodukter i Hoyesterett. *NHH Bulletin*, No3-2012, pp. 16–21. Retrieved from https://issuu.com/ nhhalumni/docs/nhh_bulletin_nr_03_-_2012

17. Sundberg, J. D. (2013). *DnB tar 450 miljoner i tapp etter Roeggen-saken*. E24, April 19. Retrieved from http://e24.no/boers-og-finans/dnb/ dnb-tar-450-millioner-i-tap-etter-roeeggen-saken/20359958

18. Moskwa, W. (2008). Norway to tighten rules on structured products. *Reuters*, February 11. Retrieved from http://uk.reuters.com/article/norway-financial-idUKL1170675820080211

19. Armstrong, F. (2013). Equity linked CDs: More garbage wall street wants to feed you. *Forbes*, February 12, 2013. Retrieved from http:// www.forbes.com/sites/greatspeculations/2013/02/12/equity-linked-cds-more-garbage-wall-street-wants-to-feed-you/#2eae07441b7d

20. Financial Industry Regulatory Authority (FINARA). (2011). Investor alerts: Reverse convertibles — Complex investment vehicles. Retrieved from http://www.finra.org/investors/alerts/reverse-convertibles-complex-investment-vehicles

21. Light, L. (2009). Reverse converts: A nest-egg slasher? *The Wall Street Journal*, June 16. Retrieved from http://www.wsj.com/articles/ SB124511060085417057

22. Henderson, B. J., & Pearson, N. D. (2011). The dark side of financial innovation: A case study of the pricing of a retail financial product. *Journal of Financial Economics*, 100(2), 227–247.

23. Economist. (2015). Roaring ahead. Exchange-traded funds have overtaken hedge funds as an investment vehicle. *The Economist*, August 1. Retrieved from http://www.economist.com/news/finance-and-economics/21660169-exchange-traded-funds-have-overtaken-hedge-funds-investment-vehicle-roaring

24. Investment Company Institute. (2016). *2016 Investment Company Factbook*. Retrieved from https://www.ici.org/pdf/2016_factbook.pdf

25. Murphy, C. (2015). When, if ever, will active ETFs take off? *ETF.com.*, July 7. Retrieved from http://www.etf.com/sections/features-and-news/when-if-ever-will-active-etfs-take?nopaging=1

26. TradeKing. *Leveraged and inverse ETFs: A word of caution.* Retrieved from https://www.tradeking.com/education/etfs/leveraged-and-inverse-etfs

27. Shriber, T. (2015). Inverse, leveraged ETF assets reach a record $63 billion. *ETF Trends*, July 8. Retrieved from http://www.etftrends.com/2015/07/inverse-leveraged-etf-assets-reach-a-record-63-billion//

28. Guedj, I., Li, G., & McCann, C. (2010). Leveraged and inverse ETFs, holding periods, and investment shortfalls. *Journal of Index Investing*, 1(3), 45–57.

29. Charupat, N., & Miu, P. (2011). The pricing and performance of leveraged exchange-traded funds. *Journal of Banking & Finance*, 35(4), 966–977.

30. Avellaneda, M., & Zhang, S. (2010). Path-dependence of leveraged ETF returns. *SIAM Journal of Financial Mathematics*, 1(1), 586–603.

12

TRAPS 8 AND 9: ENGAGING IN GAMBLING DISGUISED AS INVESTING AND RELYING ON UNSUPPORTED PROMISES

Gambling: The sure way of getting nothing from something.
Wilson Mizner, American playwright,
raconteur, and entrepreneur

Promises are only as strong as the person who gives them.
Stephen Richards, Author,
film director, and producer

Successful investors must dodge costly investing mistakes, overcome behavioral biases, and avoid investment traps that could cripple their chances of reaching their financial goals. Two additional traps that lie in their path are engaging in gambling disguised as investing and relying on unsupported promises. This final chapter discusses these two investment traps and provides concluding remarks about becoming a successful investor.

GAMBLING DISGUISED AS INVESTING

According to some Wall Street skeptics, the stock market is the capitalist casino, a place where gambling wears a thin mask called investing. However, this cliché doesn't adequately differentiate between gambling and investing and represents a misinformed view. Investing isn't simply gambling by another name because gambling is a no-win venture whereas investing isn't.[1]

Not surprisingly, different views exist about gambling and investing and sometimes this distinction is difficult to see. One view is that the key difference involves "thrill." When thrill becomes the sole purpose of buying and selling securities, then investors have crossed the line into becoming gamblers.[2] If you want to play the game for thrill, then put some "play money" in a small account for entertainment purposes but don't confuse investing with gambling. As Terrence Murphy, an American free-lance writer, once wrote "A gambler never makes the same mistake twice. It's usually three or more times." Successful investors learn from their mistakes.

Another view is that both gambling and investing involve any activity in which money is put at risk for the purpose of making a profit but differ based on various characteristics. For example, gambling is characterized by at least some of the following: (1) conducts little or no research; (2) has unfavorable odds; (3) reflects risk-seeking behavior; (4) takes an unsystematic approach; (5) reflects emotions such as greed and fear; (6) concerns a discrete event or series of discrete events that are not part of a long-term plan; (7) is motivated solely by entertainment or compulsion; (8) involves no tangible ownership of something; and (9) results in no net economic effect. By contrast, the characteristics of investing are complete opposites of gambling. Consequently, investing involves at least some of the following: (1) conducts sufficient research; (2) has favorable odds; (3) reflects risk-averse behavior; (4) takes a systematic approach; (5) avoids emotions such as greed and fear; (6) concerns an ongoing activity as part of a long-term plan; (7) isn't motivated solely by entertainment or compulsion; (8) involves ownership of something tangible; and (9) results in a net positive economic effect.[3]

Despite some superficial similarities between the two concepts, major differences exist between gambling and investing. The main difference is that an investor's expected return is positive, whereas a gambler's expected return is negative. Two areas where gambling is disguised as investing, at least for individual investors, involve foreign exchange and excessive online trading.

Foreign Exchange

The foreign exchange market (FX, forex, or currency market) is perhaps the largest, most globally integrated, and most active financial market in the world.[4] The roles of FX are to (1) provide the institutional structure to exchange money between countries, (2) determine the rate of exchange between currencies, and (3) physically complete foreign exchange transactions. A *foreign exchange transaction* is an agreement between a buyer and a seller that a given amount of one currency is to be delivered at a specified rate for some other currency. The main economic task of foreign exchange transactions is to assist international trade and investment by enabling currency conversion.

Key participants in FX include foreign exchange dealers, participants in commercial and investment transactions, central banks and treasuries, foreign exchange brokers, and arbitrageurs and speculators. *Arbitrage* involves the simultaneous buying and selling of an asset to profit from small differences in price. *Currency speculation* involves buying, selling, and holding currencies in order to make a profit from favorable fluctuations in exchange rates. Some estimate that 95% of FX participants are currency speculators.[5]

Features of Currency Markets

Online traders desiring high-risk speculation have embraced the FX market. Currency trading by individual investors is not new. In 1972, the Chicago Mercantile Exchange introduced currency futures contracts, though spot trading by individual investors was not common until the late 1990s. Several developments spurred the market's growth. The end of the dot-com boom and the collapse of the NASDAQ index in 2000 sent day traders looking for new opportunities. *Day trading* is basically speculation in securities, specifically buying and selling the same security within the same trading day in a margin account. In the FX market, no such thing as a bear market exists because people can make money trading currencies by buying contracts or selling them short; up and down moves are equally playable.

Several features of the currency market attract certain types of retail investors. For example, FX is accessible to investors and does not require much money to get started. Investors can open an account over the Internet. Depending on the type of account (standard, mini, and managed), opening one requires between a few hundred and several thousand dollars.[6] Downloading a trading platform takes minutes. Trading takes place 24 hours a day and many firms have minimal or no commissions.

Another feature of FX is that investors can use financial leverage to magnify potential gains and losses. *Financial leverage* refers to using debt to acquire additional assets. The leverage on a standard trade is a breathtaking 100 to 1, meaning that someone who puts up $1000 controls 100 times that, or $100,000. Using borrowed money to trade magnifies small moves of one currency against another into big gains or huge losses. Thus, only a few minutes are necessary to realize a 100% gain on a position, or a total wipeout.

Finally, traders can focus on a few currencies rather than dealing with thousands of stock. The most frequently traded currencies in the world normally include the Euro (EUR), U.S. Dollar

(USD), Japanese Yen (JPY), Great British Pound (GBP), Australian Dollar (AUD), Swiss Franc (CHF), and Canadian Dollar (CAN). Foreign exchange rates are quoted in pairs with the six major currency pairs being the following: EUR/USD, USD/JPY, GPB/USD, USD/CHF, AUD/USD, and USD/CAD.[7]

Currency trading is not for everyone. Nonprofessional investors can be overwhelmed by the amount of information and the complexity of variables at play in FX. Changes in such economic factors as inflation and industrial production as well as geopolitical events, such as changes in a country's leadership, can lead to fluctuations in exchange rates. As one observer notes, "To follow the fundamentals of the FX market, it helps to be a maven of global macroeconomics and a fiend for geopolitics."[8] These and other factors can influence the decision of whether to buy or sell a currency pair. Before engaging in FX trading, you should carefully consider your investment objectives, level of experience, and risk appetite. FX trading should typically be left to the professionals.[5]

A Zero-Sum Game

Currency trading is a zero-sum game. This means that in FX trading, one's win is always another's loss. In fact when accounting for commissions and other expenses, FX trading becomes a negative-sum game. Given such a setting, profitable trading would require an ability to continuously predict currency movements correctly. A 50% correct prediction is the theoretical minimum for break-even, even though it would also depend on expenses and other factors.

For naïve investors, especially overconfident ones, who believe strongly in their capability of predicting currency movements better than chance alone, the odds might seem fine, but various studies show that even the world's top economic experts and academics aren't capable of predicting/modeling currency rates better than chance alone.[9] In fact, one study concludes that the experts actually perform worse than a random walk model, implying that their estimates would be more successful if done by a pure coin toss.[10]

As FX trading is a zero-sum game, retail traders compete with institutional investors and other professional investors for their profits. Unfortunately, for the retail investors, they would seem disadvantaged against such investors for two main reasons. First, professional traders who devote their full time and attention to currency trading are backed by powerful analytical resources. Therefore, they have an *information advantage* over retail traders, especially inexperienced ones. Second, and more importantly, assuming that currency movements are unpredictable in their nature, meaning that currency prices follow a random walk, professional traders nearly always have a *capital advantage* over retail traders, which subjects retail traders to the *gambler's ruin problem*. The laws of probability are in the casino's favor. A gambler with finite wealth will eventually go broke against an opponent with infinite wealth, even in a fair game where each side has zero value such as two players tossing a coin. In the gambling world, the casino is the opponent with infinite wealth. A player with a negative expected value game will go bankrupt even earlier. A retail speculator is almost certain to go bankrupt at some stage especially as commissions and other expenses make FX speculation a negative expected value "game." The speculator is "playing" against the entire market, which basically has endless capital.

Considering the two main disadvantages that retail traders have in FX trading, one could expect that rational retail traders would be unwilling to take part in currency speculation. However, the seemingly high popularity of online FX trading platforms would seem to suggest quite the opposite as hundreds of FX brokers target their services mainly to retail traders worldwide. These trading platforms such as FXCM and Saxo Bank seem to be targeted at retail investors given that institutional traders presumably have in-house brokers or other more sophisticated trading platforms.

Caveats

FX brokers have a clear incentive to promote FX trading to their clients, who are retail traders. An incentive for such promotion is created because the profits of an FX broker depend entirely on the trading volumes of their customers, not on whether the customers trade profitably or not. Therefore, the broker is the only party involved in FX trading that makes money from every trade, regardless of the trade's outcome. This attempt to promote FX trading to retail traders is present on various websites that are clearly targeted to inexperienced retail traders.

Not only does the offering of a high leverage ratio make FX speculation a risky endeavor for retail traders, it also provides additional evidence that online FX trading platforms are targeted primarily to retail traders because better capitalized professional investors do not require such high leverage ratios. Although professional currency dealers such as banks and hedge funds generally use leverage ratios of no more than 10:1, some FX brokers offer their clients leverage as high as 400:1. Advertising includes content especially relevant to retail traders found on different retail investor education websites such as Investopedia, FX discussion forums, and social media.

In some countries, FX brokers are essentially unregulated and don't fall under regulatory oversight. This means that no licenses are required to start a FX brokerage and no professional supervision exists; company actions are regulated only by general company and accounting laws, which often fail to account for specifics related to financial sector companies. As a result, basically anyone, regardless of their background or knowledge in the FX market, can start a FX brokerage.

Trading with a regulated broker is important to insure that the broker is regulated by an official body. The presence of regulatory authorities helps to assure a broker's economic strength and the integrity toward the traders. Examples of leading regulatory bodies are the National Futures Association and Commodity

Futures Trading Commission (CFTC), in the United States, and the Financial Services Authority (FSA UK) in Europe.

FX trading platforms targeted to unprofessional investors are gambling or at least speculation dressed up as investing. As previously noted, professional traders have two main advantages over retail investors: information and capital. As previously noted, even the world's top economic experts and academics aren't capable of predicting/modeling currency rates better than a naïve random walk model. As FX trading is a zero-sum game, any positive expected return is excessive.

Trap Judgment

FX Trading

Becoming a victim of investment fraud

Misrepresenting risky products as safe

Making unrealistic return expectations

Falling for mutual fund traps

Overpaying for products and services

Investing in complex products

Engaging in gambling disguised as investing

Relying on unsupported promises

Excessive Online Trading

In 2016, slightly more than half of Americans (52%) reported investing money in the stock market, matching the lowest ownership rate in Gallup's 19-year trend. Despite generally rising markets since the Great Recession, nearly half of U.S. adults are on the sidelines. This percentage differs markedly from prerecession levels that spanned 58–65%. The biggest drops in in stock ownership are among middle-aged and middle-income groups. In recent years, both confidence in the stock market and levels of financial literacy have suffered.[11]

How do individual investors often behave? Although such investors should attempt to maximize wealth while minimizing risk, empirical research reveals that they behave quite differently. Many hold poorly diversified portfolios, trade actively and speculatively often due to overconfidence, and underperform standard benchmarks such as a low-cost index fund due to incurring unnecessary investment costs, return losses, and tax liabilities.[12] Let's examine how overconfidence can lead to excessive online trading and harm investors.

Overconfidence

If overconfidence is a main driver behind frequent trading, what factors facilitate, if not drive, more active trading? Before the era of the Internet and computers, investors traded securities using the tedious, timely, and costly process of calling a stockbroker to make an order. This process changed in the 1990s with a huge increase in the speed and availability of Internet connections, which led to brokers creating online platforms allowing retail investors to carry out their own trades. *Online trading* involves placing buy/sell orders for financial securities and/or currencies using a brokerage's Internet-based proprietary trading platforms. Online trading also decreased transaction costs and commissions, making trading cheaper, quicker, and easier. Combined with overconfidence bias, trading volumes skyrocketed, for both institutional and retail investors. Online trading creates other problems such as allowing inexperienced and uninformed investors to trade and enabling platforms to exploit the investors' overconfidence and facilitate active trading for their own gain.

The platform providers should not be blamed for simply facilitating a bias that has always existed, but can be questioned for encouraging and feeding this bias even when it does not benefit investors. For example, E*TRADE's premier trading platform claims to "give investors the cutting-edge tools and technology to make faster, smarter market decisions,"[13] which is not something that should really be advertised given the previously discussed findings. Another questionable means of encouraging investors to trade more can be seen in fee structures. A common fee structure, found in E*TRADE, charges lower commissions and fees the more an investor trades.[14] The advantage for the platform is clear — more trades equals more total fees, but as already noted, no advantage exists to investors from more frequent trading.

An alternative pricing structure can be found when searching for "Online Trading" — Plus500. This platform claims to charge "no commissions" but a closer look reveals a "finance fee," a fee charged for holding a position open overnight, encouraging investors to open and close (i.e., buy and sell) on the same day. As discussed with FX trading, predicting price movements in such a short time period is difficult, and is closer to gambling than investing for a retail investor. Plus500 also charges an "inactivity fee," if the platform is unused or dormant for a period of three months.[15]

Lower Costs of Online Trading

Given that the cost of trading drives down the returns of active traders, surely lower costs associated with online trading should help bring these returns in line with the market. Evidence shows, however, this result is not the case.[16] In fact, those trading online do even worse than before the advent of online trading for several reasons. First, turnover is higher. Active investors who started to trade online, traded more actively and speculatively resulting in lower returns. This increased trading is not explained by lower costs and ease of access, but by overconfidence. Online trading augments both the illusion of knowledge and the illusion of control. The *illusion of knowledge* is the tendency for people to think they have a better understanding than they actually do about any topic, issue, concept, or problem. More inexperienced traders, who are the main targets of online platforms, tend to be more overconfident because they are likely to have success records that are unrepresentative of their abilities. The *illusion of control* is the tendency for people to overestimate their ability to control or at least influence outcomes or events over which they have no influence. For example, when investors who do considerable research before buying stocks believe that their analysis and knowledge gives them control over the future of stocks they own.[17]

Second, even if the direct costs and commissions are lower, a problem remains with the *bid-ask spread*, which is the difference between the highest price that a buyer is willing to pay for an asset (bid price) and the lowest price that a seller is willing to accept to sell it (ask price). Market makers inevitably push a bid-ask spread to allow them to buy low and sell high. A *market maker* is a dealer in securities or other assets who undertakes to buy or sell at specified prices at all times. Examples of a market maker are a standard online brokerage firm such as Charles Schwab or Merrill Lynch. Often e-brokerages get a cut from the market makers with whom they have existing contracts. The investor has limited knowledge of what such a spread may be, and so the market maker can increase the spread and thus pass the cost on to the investor.

As previously mentioned, Plus500 advertises it does not charge any commissions, which should be viewed skeptically. In fact, Plus500 is compensated for its services through the market spread. Plus500 passes the indirect cost to investors through the market spread, and the prices given to investors are not necessarily the best obtainable in the market.

High Frequency Trading

High frequency trading (HFT) is an automated trading platform used by large investment banks, hedge funds, and institutional investors using powerful computers to transact a large number of orders at extremely high speeds. Using computer algorithms, also known as *algobots*, HFT platforms enable traders to rapidly execute millions of orders and scan multiple markets and exchanges in a few milliseconds. Those using the platforms have an enormous advantage in the open market because they have the ability to front-run or execute orders before others due to getting information more quickly. They can arbitrage away extremely small price discrepancies that only exist over very short time horizons. By anticipating and beating the trends to the market place, high frequency traders can gain favorable returns on trades due to their prior knowledge and low bid-ask spreads.[18]

Should individual investors, especially those actively trading online, be concerned about HFT? The answer is typically no. Although front-running every order may be possible, it wouldn't be profitable so high frequency traders only front-run big orders by institutions and other large investors. These traders would gain no advantage by front-running trades unless they are frequent and unusually large orders. As a result, trades by retail investors are likely to be unaffected.[19]

Online trading platforms targeted to unprofessional investors are gambling disguised as investing. After going online, investors tend to trade more actively, more speculatively, and less profitably than previously. Evidence shows that individual investors destroy value through active trading. Service providers promoting superior trading technology also lead to excessive return expectations. In short, the typical online trader is no match for highly sophisticated institutional investors.

Trap Judgment

Online Trading

Becoming a victim of investment fraud

Misrepresenting risky products as safe

Making unrealistic return expectations

Falling for mutual fund traps

Overpaying for products and services

Investing in complex products

Engaging in gambling disguised as investing

Relying on unsupported promises

UNSUPPORTED PROMISES

Some financial products are sold using marketing claims unsupported by evidence. For example, long/short equity funds claim that they can provide a "free-lunch." The phrase "there's no such thing as a free-lunch" is often used to describe situations in which investors are unable to consistently make large profits without bearing the risk of a potential loss. Let's examine three examples of the investment trap of relying on unsupported promises involving socially responsible investing (SRI), investment clubs, and investment newsletters.

SOCIALLY RESPONSIBLE INVESTING

Socially responsible investing, also called ethical investing and green investing, is an investment approach that integrates environmental, social, and governance (ESG) considerations as a part of the investment process. Investors limit their investment alternatives to securities of firms whose products or actions they consider socially acceptable. Retail investors can make socially responsible investments in individual companies, follow SRI indexes, or use socially conscious mutual funds or ETFs.[20]

Screening Processes

SRI strategies apply a set of investment restrictions or screens to the general investment pool to identify companies from which investors can choose their investments. Restrictions are usually based on ESG or other ethical criteria. The screening process consists of two different methods: negative and positive screening. *Negative* or *avoidance screening* excludes companies that manufacturer or provide certain objectionable products or services. For instance, SRI investors using negative criteria have typically shunned investments related to companies in alcohol, gambling, tobacco, military weapons, nuclear power, civilian firearms, adult entertainment, and genetically modified organisms. *Positive* or *affirmative screening* involves selecting companies based on positive characteristics that show leadership in such areas as product design, employee policies, environmental protection, diversity, labor relations, human rights, or other practices.[21]

The SRI approach has become an increasingly popular investment philosophy for asset management funds over the past decade. SRI funds have experienced phenomenal growth. These funds have been offered widely to both retail investors and institutional investors in the form of mutual funds and other funds. From 2012 to 2014, SRI assets in the United States grew 76% from $3.74 trillion to $6.57 trillion. The number of stock and bond mutual funds that apply socially responsible mandates has also risen. Currently, the United States has more than 100 sustainable mutual funds. Globally, interest in SRI is even more impressive. Between 2012 and 2014, global SRI assets rose from $13.3 trillion to $21.4 trillion.[22]

SRI and Conventional Mutual Funds

SRI funds try to actively differentiate themselves from ordinary mutual funds. The criteria they use to do so are often ambiguous and fail to provide much insight into how SRI funds differ from ordinary mutual funds on a more practical level. SRI funds often provide bold claims or promises on the effect of these differences. For example, Trillium Asset Management claims that "companies that adhere to strong positive ESG policies have the potential to increase profitability and develop a competitive edge. We seek to lower portfolio risk and help identify the best managed companies by integrating ESG factors into the investment process."[23] Nordea suggests that "we are convinced that taking ESG issues into account in all our investments can lead to better performance."[24]

SRI funds tend to emphasize two key selling points. First, they claim that by affecting corporations' access to capital funding, SRI funds can change prevailing corporate practices. This means that investing in socially responsible companies will encourage other companies to adopt higher ESG standards for fear of becoming less competitive in the capital markets. They call this category of promises the "corporate change" category. Second, SRI funds claim they can outperform conventional actively managed funds as stable long-term returns come from sustainable businesses that foresee the problems of the future. They classify such promises as the "outperformance" category.[25] **Table 12.1** summarizes various claims made by SRI funds and their managers.

Performance of SRI Mutual Funds

A key issue for investors is whether securities selected by an SRI screening process exhibit different performance from conventional investments. Academic research on the performance of socially responsible mutual funds produces mixed results. Several studies report little evidence of a difference in risk-adjusted returns between these two types of funds. Yet, others report statistically significant costs associated with socially responsible mutual fund investing. These differences largely result from varying methodology and time period.[26] Evidence also shows that investors shunning "sin stocks" lost out on high returns.[27] A *sin stock* is an investment in a company or industry that some consider illegal, immoral, or unethical, such as tobacco companies or liquor distributors. Despite some exceptions, research typically shows no statistically significant performance difference between the socially responsible and conventional mutual funds.[28] Ultimately, SRI investors face a choice between expected payoffs and investing based on their values.

Table 12.1: Examples of Claims Made by SRI Funds and Their Managers

Fund	"Outperformance" claims	"Corporate Change" claims
AMP Henderson Global Investors	"Social or environmental issues can affect long-term profitability and share price performance."	"[Investing in specific companies acts to] encourage companies to adopt higher social and environmental standards."
Calvert (U.S.)	"[L]ong term rewards will come from those organizations whose products, services and methods enhance the human condition and the traditional American values of individual initiative, equality of opportunity, and cooperative effort.""[R]esponding to social concerns should not only avoid the liability that may be incurred when a product or service is determined to have a negative social impact … but … better position [a firm] to develop opportunities …"	
Challenger International	"Relative outperformance comes from investing in quality companies [who] will be re-rated to their true valuation at a later date."	"[I]dentifying the most socially responsive companies in each industry [may] encourage their competitors to improve on their own standards."
Continental Venture Capital	"Reducing negative externalities seen as consistent with long term profit maximization." "Environmental efficiency [attracts a] return premium."	–
Hesta	–	"[SRI will] encourage Australian companies to achieve better environmental practice." "Our 'best of sector' model encourages companies to compete for investment by improving their environmental performance."
Hunter Hall Investment Management	"The objective … is to increase the wealth of … investors by substantially outperforming the MCSI World Accumulation Net Return Index."	–

Table 12.1: *(Continued)*

Fund	"Outperformance" claims	"Corporate Change" claims
Vanguard Investments Australia	"Companies taking a lead in [sustainability-driven operations] will gain a competitive edge and outperform their industry peers."	–
Westpac	–	"Our unique best of sector approach to investing rewards companies with leading sustainability performance, while encouraging others to improve their practices."

Case: UBS International Sustainable Equity

Headquartered in Zurich, Switzerland, UBS is present in all major financial centers worldwide. It has offices in more than 50 countries. UBS Group AG employs more than 60,000 people around the world. UBS's strategy builds on the strengths of all of its businesses and focuses its efforts on areas in which it excels, while seeking to capitalize on the compelling growth prospects in the businesses and regions in which it operates. UBS claims that all of its businesses are capital-efficient and benefit from a strong competitive position in their targeted markets. As of June 30, 2016, UBS Asset Management, a business group of UBS, had $647 billion in assets under management (AUM) worldwide.[29]

Having managed institutional sustainable equity strategies for almost two decades, UBS claims that is has emerged as a leader in sustainable and responsible investing. The sustainable equity team of UBS leverages the firm's global equity research platform and its proprietary portfolio construction and risk management system. UBS suggests that using sustainability factors in addition to traditional investment factors can lead to better investment decisions.

UBS International Sustainable Equity Fund follows an international equity strategy seeking to maximize total return with a sustainable investment approach. The fund focuses on the alignment of a traditional investment discipline with the concept of sustainability — the potential for long-term maintenance of environmental, economic, and social well-being. At the end of June 2016, the past 10 years of the fund's historical returns do not provide evidence of outperformance, but the opposite. As Table 12.2 shows, the fund has clearly lost against the MSCI World Free Index over 1-, 5-, and 10-year periods.

The fund classes differ in fees. The Equity Class P contains a maximum front-end sales charge (load) of 5.5% while the Equity Class A has no load. Total annual fund operating expenses (net expense ratio) also differ. For Equity Class A, the annual net expense ratio is 1.25% while for Equity Class P it is 1.00% annually. In a 10-year period ending in June 2016, both fund classes outperformed the MSCI World ex-USA Index but clearly lost against MSCI World Free Index.

Which benchmark index is more relevant? The MSCI World Free Index (net) appears to be a strong contender for the proper benchmark index to evaluate the historical performance of the UBS International Sustainability Fund. In October, 2015, UBS Global Sustainable Equity Fund was renamed UBS International Sustainable Equity Fund. At the same time, the MSCI World

Table 12.2: Historical Performance of UBS International Sustainable Equity Fund Relative to Two Benchmark MSCI Indices as of June 30, 2016

	1 Year	5 Years	10 Years
UBS International Sustainable Equity Class P	−13.83	1.87	1.96
UBS International Sustainable Equity Class A	−14.07	1.62	1.73
MSCI World ex-USA Index (net)	−9.79	1.24	1.66
MSCI World Free Index (net)	−2.78	6.63	4.43

Source: The monthly report of UBS.[30]

ex-USA Index (net) replaced the MSCI World Free Index (net) as the fund's primary benchmark index. UBS suggests that it more closely aligns with the fund's investment strategy. As of June, 2016, this may be true because the fund had only 2.3% of its assets in U.S. equities. At the end of June 2015, as much as 33.8% of the fund's holdings had U.S. exposure.[31] As of June 30, 2016, the UBS International Sustainable Equity Fund has clearly lost against the MSCI World Free Index over 1-, 5-, and 10-year periods.

Although academic studies produce mixed results on the performance of SRI mutual funds, such funds generally perform similarly to investment styles that do not take SRI issues into consideration in investment decisions. Thus, the practice of touting SRI funds as outperforming their traditional peers is questionable.

SRI funds may derive their shareholder following for other reasons such emotional utility. For example, "By investing with Rathbone Greenbank, you can be confident that your money is supporting the issues you care about or corporate change. Rathbone Greenbank is a prominent activist on ethical and sustainability issues, engaging directly with companies and government to improve business practices." These alleged benefits delivered by SRI strategy also seem questionable for several reasons. For example, the market share of SRI may be insufficient to impact the market. Even if the amount of funds was sufficient "to matter," no guarantee exists that financial markets would see investment decisions of SRI funds as signals of undisclosed future revenue growth or costs.

Trap Judgment

Socially Responsible Investing

Becoming a victim of investment fraud

Misrepresenting risky products as safe

Making unrealistic return expectations

Falling for mutual fund trapsOverpaying for products and services

Investing in complex products

Engaging in gambling disguised as investing

Relying on unsupported promises

INVESTMENT CLUBS

An *investment club* is a group of individuals meeting on a regular basis for the purpose of pooling money and retail investing. These clubs have historically been formed mostly on a geographical basis such as local collectives of neighbors, colleagues, and church members. Some investment clubs focus on investing solely in stocks, mutual funds, bonds, or real estate, while others choose to invest in multiple asset classes. Investment clubs are usually formed as general partnerships, but may also be formed as limited liability companies, limited liability partnerships, corporations, or sole proprietorships. Typically, investment club members come together regularly to make decisions about the allocation of the money amassed from each member's regular contributions.

Investment clubs may either be beneficial or detrimental to the retail investor seeking to join one, possibly depending on the basis on which the club is formed. For example, investment clubs that are formed on a geographical basis may bring together people with complementary views and provide a "diversity premium" resulting in lower risks and higher returns. Investment clubs are also formed by colleagues in a certain industry, who share a similar background, and lead to less informed investment decisions through "herd mentality" and the lack of multiple perspectives. Despite being called clubs, most are similar to small companies than typical clubs such as a book or automobile club because the main purpose of these associations is to make money. Even if some members join the club mostly for the sake of social interaction, each member has his own money at stake, might incur substantial losses or profits, and might even be held personally responsible for the club's collective liabilities. An increasing number of clubs hold meetings and conduct other operations fully online.[32,33]

The first known U.S. investment club started in Texas in 1898 based on a European model dating back several generations.[34] Although investment clubs have existed in the United States for more than a century, they first started to receive country-wide notoriety in the 1980s and 1990s when the stock market began its unprecedented surge toward record-breaking levels. In 1998, investment clubs reached their peak — a record of 37,219 National Association of Investors Corporation (NAIC) enrolled investment clubs were registered and the number of individual club members exceeded 600,000. Together, investment clubs registered to NAIC hold about $125 billion in U.S. stock holdings, which is comparable to the assets of some of the world's biggest pension funds. Overall, the rise of investment clubs was a part of a bigger movement toward widening the demographic composition of the investor population, more specifically women. Another important contributor was the tripling of the number of participants in defined contribution plans who had to decide how to invest their pension funds.[32]

The media attention given to a few well-performing investment clubs created a public consensus that investment clubs tended to outperform the markets. The NAIC, also known as BetterInvesting, is a nonprofit, umbrella organization consisting of about 13,000 investment clubs. The organization actively endorses investment clubs to retail investors and aims to educate individuals in becoming successful long-term investors. According to BetterInvesting.org, "Investment club members enjoy extra dividends beyond watching their portfolio grow or taking a drawdown to pay for college or that dream vacation: long-term friendships and the self-confidence that comes from understanding stocks." Although investment clubs are forbidden from directly promoting their services, NAIC seems to actively endorse investment clubs an as "market-beating" investment alternative creating a positive public perception of investment clubs that may not be justified. In its marketing brochure and other content, NAIC emphasizes the strong performance of its BIXX 100 index. BetterInvestment 100 index (BIXX), tracks the 100 most bought stocks by individual investment clubs as indicated by member clubs in NAIC's annual survey. NASDAQ maintains the index. However, good performance of the index does not in itself provide any robust proof of good individual performance of any specific investment club. NAIC also conducts and publishes surveys of investment club performance that are potentially skewed but often show market-beating returns.[35] Yet, investors have reason to be skeptical about high expected returns.

In her book *POP Finance: Investment Clubs and the New Investor Populism*, Brooke Harrington studies the performance of investment clubs over a period of 12 years. Based on data collected by NAIC, 96% of a sample of 1,245 investment clubs underperformed the S&P 500 Index, and the average club underperformed by a large difference of 20.8%.[32]

One academic study denounces the widely suggested claims of general outperformance of the clubs.[35] Of a sample of 166 investment clubs, 60% underperformed the market. The study finds three major differences in the ways investment clubs invest when compared to individual investors and suggests that these are the key drivers of investment club underperformance:

1. The average investment club tilts its investments toward growth stocks more than an average individual investor.

2. On average clubs execute smaller trades than individual investors.

3. Clubs and individual investors have similar annual turnover, which eats up their returns due to too frequent trading.

According to Zack Miller, the number of Americans participating in local investment clubs had shrunken by 80% from 1998 to 2013. After five years of mediocre stock market performance, investment clubs have lost much of their cachet. Even the National Association of Investment Clubs changed its name to BetterInvesting to reflect the new reality — Americans just aren't that into investment clubs anymore. Old-school investment clubs have also given way to a new form of social investing that's happening online. Investors are increasingly turning to financial sites such as Morningstar.com and The Motley Fool to research investments and get advice.[36]

Advocates of investment clubs say that club members consider educational and social aspects at least as important as seeking good returns on their investments. In this sense, BetterInvesting can benefit investors because it provides its members with an ample amount of educational content, including both educational webinars and investment club seminars, conventions, and several other educational and social events for beginner investors around the United States.

According to Tess Vigeland, a veteran journalist and American radio host, the most interesting and useful portion of the club meetings is the time members spend researching and explaining aspects of the stock market and the economy. In an investment club, you can pose questions that can help you and others become smarter about money. This, in turn, can help empower you to have a fuller conversation with your own financial advisor. Sharing knowledge not only makes managing your money more fun, but also makes you more confident in your financial decision-making.[37] Larry Swedroe, a frequent writer on investments, shares a somewhat more skeptical view. The problem with most clubs is that they focus on stock selection. The academic evidence is overwhelming that trying to beat the market by identifying mispriced securities is a loser's game. He concludes that investment clubs can serve social functions such as fostering friendships, but individuals would be far better off joining a book club.[38]

Classic Case: Beardstown Ladies

Beardstown Ladies was an investment club formed by a group of elderly women who gained fame for their strong investment performance between 1984 and 1993. The group claimed to have exhibited an average annual return of 23.4% over this period, clearly beating the S&P 500's 14.9%. Such a strong performance combined with a sympathetic image of the group's members quickly made the grandmas from Beardstown Illinois celebrities and loved by the U.S. investing public. They started appearing in several different TV and radio shows both domestically and internationally. CBS featured them on the "This Morning" show in 1991 and again the next year. In 1993, they were commissioned to make a video, "The Beardstown Ladies: Cooking Up Profits on Wall Street."

Their Cinderella story hit the investing public's soft spot. The Ladies ended up authoring five investment books, one of which was the best-seller *The Beardstown Ladies' Common-Sense Investment Guide*, an investment book including stock-picking tips and recipes that sold more than 800,000 copies and was translated into seven languages.

Unfortunately, as often is the case with Cinderella stories, the reality wasn't all that beautiful. After several public suspicions about the returns claimed by the club, PWC performed an outside audit and found that the group's stated returns had included new invested capital from its members, which they were putting up on a monthly basis. PWC recalculated and confirmed an average annual return of 9.1% rather than 23.4%. This revelation led to harsh public criticism of the investment club and a class action lawsuit against Hyperion, the publisher of their books.

The publisher took the Ladies' books out of print. Later, it settled the case by offering to swap any Beardstown book for other Hyperion titles. Today, only used copies of the Ladies' books are available on Amazon.com and eBay.[39]

Beardstown Ladies exemplifies the problems surrounding invest-ment clubs in general: they are mostly amateur-run organizations with no compulsory regulatory authorities or any collectively defined "industry practices" that still aim to compete as serious alternatives for professional investment mediums such as mutual funds. Even though the Beardstown Ladies was only a single specific case, evidence challenges the view of investment clubs being serious investment alternatives on a more general level.

Given the lack of objective and easily accessible information centers or databases on investment clubs, the overly optimistic image of investment clubs seems unfounded. Limited evidence on the returns of investment clubs fails to support this image.

Trap Judgment

Investment Clubs

Becoming a victim of investment fraud

Misrepresenting risky products as safe

Making unrealistic return expectations

Falling for mutual fund traps

Overpaying for products and services

Investing in complex products

Engaging in gambling disguised as investing

Relying on unsupported promises

INVESTMENT NEWSLETTERS

Investment newsletters are typically subscription-based, weekly issues/publications offering investment advice targeted primarily at retail investors. Their aim is to transform retail investors from uninformed to informed investors. The focus of the investment newsletters across different categories varies dramatically. Some have a narrow and specific scope such as a newsletter that gives stock/derivative purchase recommendations by concentrating only on the analysis of different insider trading statistics. Other newsletters have a far more general scope such as focusing on evaluating the upcoming macroeconomic climate and its effects on some sectors of equity markets.

This diverse market of newsletters consists of around 1,300 different newsletters in the United States and Canada with an annual industry revenue of more than $3.4 billion.[40] These numbers indicate a clear demand for investment newsletters. Subscribing to a newsletter is a considerable investment for an average retail investor, as the average annual subscription fees paid by newsletter subscribers is $317. Some high-end newsletters charge as much as several thousand dollars annually. Given the costs incurred by newsletters' clients, they should expect to receive some benefits. Not surprisingly, various studies examine the investment performance of investment newsletters.

The Motley Fool is one of the world's market leaders in investment advice services and its flagship newsletter "Motley Fool Stock Advisor" is one of the world's most subscribed investment newsletters. An advertisement of the Motley Fool Stock Advisor, as shown on The Motley Fool website's newsletter section on August 8, 2016, shows Stock Advisor "outperforming the S&P by +122.38% since 2002!" The return percentage indicated on the advertisement may change daily. The cost of Stock Advisor is $199 a year.

Some general aspects related to this specific advertisement raise the following concerns:

- Stock Advisor boasts substantial outperformance relative to the S&P index. However, these are raw returns, not risk-adjusted returns. Thus, Stock Advisor is essentially dressing-up their returns when comparing their returns as "equals" to the S&P 500 index.

- Stock Advisor puts a strong emphasis on its high historical returns.

- The statement "The investment service that helps any level of investor beat the market, no matter how much time or money they have" is a promise that is too good to be true.

Several studies on investment newsletter performance find that securities recommended by investment newsletters don't outperform appropriate benchmarks and thus don't generate positive abnormal returns.[41] One study analyzes the equity-portfolio recommendations made by 153 investment newsletters and finds no evidence of superior stock-picking ability and abnormal short-run performance persistence or hot hands. After accounting for appropriate risk-factors, newsletters, on average, don't seem to exhibit any positive abnormal performance. Additionally, well-performing newsletters don't tend to continue to have positive risk-adjusted returns in the future. Instead, newsletters tend to recommend securities that have performed well in the recent past. Newsletters with poor past performance are more likely to go out of business.

The majority of newsletters can't outperform the broader market over the long term. Investors who subscribe to stock selection or market timing services and then attempt to specifically replicate the newsletter's suggested portfolio are unlikely to be successful. You should never use a newsletter as your only input into the investment process. Instead, you should attempt to collect as much information as possible before forming your own independent judgment, which you can then incorporate into your overall investment strategy. You can then research available newsletters with good long-term reputations, and incorporate them into your investment program.[42]

Case: Investment Newsletters by Doug Fabian

The following example involving Doug Fabian shows how investment newsletters tend to endorse themselves to potential clients. According to his website:

*Doug Fabian is the editor of three publications: Successful
ETF Investing, ETF Trader's Edge, and Fabian's Weekly
ETF Report. Doug was previously known as one of
America's top mutual fund advisors, but in recent years he
has made a revolutionary 100% shift to exchange traded
funds (ETFs).*[43]

Based on the data gathered by the *Hulbert Financial* Digest, the
past leading source of investment letter performance data,
Fabian's results aren't that impressive. Mark Hulbert closed his
Hulbert Financial Digest in March, 2016. When Hulbert began
publishing the digest in 1980, the market had 28 investment newsletters, which were printed on paper and came in the mail.
Hulbert subscribed to each of those 28 newsletters, and over the
years added more than 100 others. These data gave him a unique
view of the value of various newsletters and their many differing
approaches to making money. Hulbert also highlighted the performance of investment newsletters against the risk needed to get
superior investment results.[44]

The most important lesson his 36-year run revealed was the sheer
difficulty of trying to beat the market. Hulbert suggests that over 30
years, most investors would be better off in a S&P 500 index fund
or an ETF. In a 2013 column at Barron's, Hulbert indicates that
stock newsletters often claim excellent performance, but their actual
numbers don't stand up to scrutiny.[45] One of the examples Hulbert
mentions is Fabian's "Successful Investing" newsletter. In 1992,
Fabian became editor after taking over from his father, Richard
Fabian, who began the newsletter in the 1970s, when it was called
"Telephone Switch Newsletter." The elder Fabian claimed that his
trend-following system would produce 20% annualized returns
over any five-year period. Since 1980, however, which is when the
Hulbert Financial Digest began monitoring the newsletter, it never
produced a 20% annualized return over any five-calendar-year
period. The *Hulbert Financial Digest* calculates that its model portfolios over the last 33 years have produced an average annualized

return of 7.0%, markedly less than the 11.2% annualized return of the Wilshire 5000's total return index.

Hulbert cites the newsletter's website, where you can read that "For more than 30 years, Successful Investing (formerly the Telephone Switch Newsletter) has produced double-digit annual gains." and "Taking over the reins from his dad, Dick Fabian, back in 1992, Doug has continued to uphold the reputation of the newsletter as the #1 risk-adjusted market timer as ranked by Hulbert's Investment Digest." According to the *Hulbert Financial Digest*, Fabian's market timing advice since 1992 ranks in 21st place out of the 32 newsletters monitored over this period on a risk-adjusted basis.[45]

Unsurprisingly, the website of Doug Fabian does not provide any newsletter performance data or testable public market commentary. Disclaimers in his newsletters, such as the ETF Trader newsletter, offer the following level of accountability:

- *"Neither the Editor, the publisher, nor any of their respective affiliates make any guarantee or other promise as to any results that may be obtained from using the Newsletter."*

- *"To the maximum extent permitted by law, the Editor, the publisher and their respective affiliates disclaim any and all liability in the event any information, commentary, analysis, opinions, advice and/or recommendations in the Newsletter prove to be inaccurate, incomplete or unreliable, or result in any investment or other losses."*

- *"The Newsletter's commentary, analysis, opinions, advice and recommendations represent the personal and subjective views of the Editor, and are subject to change at any time without notice."*

- *"Neither the Editor, the publisher, nor any of their respective affiliates guarantees the accuracy or completeness of any such information."*

- *"Neither the Editor, the publisher, nor any of their respective affiliates is responsible for any errors or omissions in any Newsletter."*[46]

Hulbert offers several general rules to follow when confronted with investment performance claims:[45]

1. Be skeptical of all claims.
2. Look for objective confirmation from an independent source.
3. Apply a simple reality check to all performance claims. Assume that, because Warren Buffett's long-term return is 19.7% annualized, any claimed return above that is either (a) lying or (b) covers too short of a time period to be sustainable. Regardless, your proper response is to ignore it.

Endorsing investment newsletters as market-beating is a questionable practice because newsletters, on average, don't exhibit positive abnormal performance. Given that no proper regulation defines "industry practices," providers of investment newsletters can exaggerate historical returns in order to generate excessive return expectations.

Trap Judgment

Investment Newsletters

Becoming a victim of investment fraud

Misrepresenting risky product as safe

Having unrealistic return expectations

Falling for mutual fund traps

Overpaying for products and services

Investing in complex products

Engaging in gambling disguised as investing

Relying on unsupported promises

LESSONS LEARNED

Individual investors often confuse gambling with investing. Although gambling can be both exciting and entertaining, these characteristics aren't those of investing. You need to curb your enthusiasm. As George Soros notes, "If investing is entertaining, if you're having fun, you're probably not making any money. Good investing is boring." The most effective long-term investments are often the most boring such as low-volatility stocks, passively managed index funds, and low-cost ETFs. If investing is boring, you're probably doing something right. Being boring can make you rich. FX trading and excessive online trading can be thrilling but also involves elements of gambling.

"There's no such thing as a free-lunch" is a popular adage in the investment world. Yet, many investors find themselves drawn into all manner of get-rich-quick schemes such as investment clubs and investment newsletters. Or they buy the selling argument that SRI outperforms because better long-term returns come from sustainable businesses. Empirical evidence of the real performance of SRI funds, investment clubs, and investment newsletters reveals that they, on average, don't lead to over performance. You should keep in mind the following advice:

- Don't confuse investing with gambling.

- Use a small "play money" account for entertainment purposes.

- Don't get lured into the siren song of the trading world.

- Be skeptical of all claims of better than average returns.

- Look carefully into details when excellent historical performance of an investment strategy is promoted. Is the benchmark index appropriate? Are dividends included in the benchmark index? What about the riskiness of the strategy relative to the passive index?

- Always keep in mind that historical performance isn't necessarily indicative of future returns.

- Remember that the odds are against you in stock picking and market timing.

- Don't believe that you have an information advantage over others when buying or selling.

BECOMING A SUCCESSFUL INVESTOR

Financial markets can be a daunting place that can beat up not only beginners but also experienced and savvy investors so badly that that they limp out of the ring for good. But it doesn't have to be if you are wary of and avoid the investing mistakes and traps as well as behavioral biases that can be crippling. Doing diligent research and keeping your head on straight can improve your chances of long-term success. The guidance provided in Investment Traps Exposed can help you to be successful in staying in the investment ring and meeting your financial goals.

To help make better financial decisions, you need to be aware of two enemies: one is internal and the other is external. All investors suffer, often unknowingly, from behavioral biases that affect their sound judgment. Moreover, many investors get caught up in the latest investment fad instead of developing a sound long-term investment plan and sticking with that plan. They let emotions rule their decision-making instead of having the discipline to follow a well-designed plan. The results can be devastating. Acting impulsively is the last refuge of unskilled investors. As Benjamin Graham once noted, "The individual investor should act consistently as an investor and not as a speculator."

External forces can also affect your behavior. Financial products are sometimes sold aggressively and persuasively. Unfortunately, the goal of many seemingly legitimate people is to separate you from your hard earned money, not to help you achieve your financial goals. Investment frauds are ubiquitous and lurk just around the corner. Although some of these investment products may appear too enticing to pass up, you need to be constantly vigilant. Your task is to find out which products fit your investments plan and which don't. Keeping a watchful eye on your investment at all times is always good advice.

Making sound investment decisions is part of being financially literate. Along this journey you have taken the first step by reading this book. Chapters 2 and 3 highlighted 15 common investing mistakes that many investors, including financial professionals, make and provided advice on how to avoid them. Making mistakes is part of the learning process, but repeating them disregards what you've learned. Chapter 4 featured behavioral biases that can rob you of achieving your full potential as an investor.

The remaining chapters identified and explained nine major investment traps, illustrated them with real-life examples from around the globe, and provided insights and guidance on how to mitigate them. Successful investors recognize and avoid these costly traps. The investment world doesn't have to be a scary place if you are well-prepared to face it. Although you can't control the market, you can control yourself when dealing with it and successfully navigate the investment minefield.

QUESTIONS

1. Discuss two disadvantages that unprofessional investors face in FX trading.

2. Explain why individuals who engage in excessive online trading typically underperform their benchmarks.

3. Identify two selling points that SRI funds tend to emphasize.

4. Discuss the differences between negative and positive screening in SRI.

5. UBS suggests that using sustainability factors in addition to traditional investment factors can lead to better investment decisions. Discuss whether this approach has been realized with the UBS International Sustainable Equity Fund.

6. Explain three major differences in how investment clubs invest compared to individual investors.

7. Discuss why the popularity of investment clubs decreased in the United States.

8. Discuss whether investment newsletters are "market-beating."

9. Explain why you should be skeptical of claims made by investment newsletters.

NOTES

1. David, M. Investing vs. gambling: Where is your money safer?" *Investopedia*. Retrieved from http://www.investopedia.com/financial-edge/0512/investing-vs.-gambling-where-is-your-money-safer.aspx

2. Weidner, D. (2011, June 16). Gambler or investor? the truth about why we trade. *The Wall Street Journal*. Retrieved from http://www.wsj.com/articles/SB10001424052702303499204576388151661037330

3. Murcko, T. (2016). What is the difference between gambling and investing? *InvestorGuide.com*. Retrieved from http://www.investorguide.com/article/12525/what-is-the-difference-between-gambling-and-investing/

4. Potter, S. (2015, , July 14). *Trends in foreign exchange markets and the challenges ahead*. Federal Reserve Bank of New York. Retrieved from https://www.newyorkfed.org/newsevents/speeches/2015/pot150714

5. InvestorGuide Staff Writers and Editors. (2016). *Understanding the risks of currency speculation*. *InvestorGuide.com*. Retrieved from http://www.investorguide.com/article/11846/understanding-the-risks-of-currency-speculation-igu/

6. Hunt, D. Forex basics: Setting up an account. *Investopedia*. Retrieved from http://www.investopedia.com/articles/forex/08/forex-account-type. asp

7. England, W. (2014). Understanding the forex majors. *Daily FX*, January 3. Retrieved from https://www.dailyfx.com/forex/education/ trading_tips/daily_trading_lesson/2014/01/03/Understanding_The_ Forex_Majors.html

8. Egan, J. (2005). Check the currency risk. then multiply by 100. *The New York Times*, Money: Investing, June 19. Retrieved from http:// www.nytimes.com/2005/06/19/business/yourmoney/check-the-currency- risk-then-multiply-by-100.html?_r=0

9. Meese, R., & Rogoff, K. (1983). Empirical exchange rate models of the seventies: Do they fit out of sample? *Journal of International Economics*, 14(1−2), 3−24. Retrieved from http://scholar.harvard.edu/ files/rogoff/files/51_jie1983.pdf

10. Mitchell, K., & Pearce, D. (2007). Professional forecasts of interest rates and exchange rates: Evidence from the wall street journal's panel of economists. *Journal of Macroeconomics*, 29(4), 840−854.

11. McCarthy, J. (2016). Just over half of Americans own stocks, matching record low. *Gallup*, April 20. Retrieved from http://www. gallup.com/poll/190883/half-americans-own-stocks-matching-record- low.aspx

12. Barber, B. M., & Odean, T. (2000). Trading is hazardous to your wealth: The common stock investment performance of individual inves- tors. *Journal of Finance*, 55(2), 773−805. Barber, B. M., & Odean, T. (2011, September 7). *The behavior of individual investors*. Working Paper. University of California. Retrieved from http://www.umass.edu/ preferen/You%20Must%20Read%20This/Barber-Odean%202011.pdf

13. E*TRADE. (2016). *Active trading*. Retrieved from https://us.etrade. com/active-trading?ploc=p-TopNav

14. E*TRADE. (2016). *Active trading, pricing & rates*. Retrieved from https://us.etrade.com/active-trading/pricing#stocks

15. Plus500. (2016). *Instrument types & pricing*. Retrieved from http:// www.plus500.com/Help/HelpFees.aspx

16. Barber, B. M., & Odean, T. (2002). Online investors: Do the slow die first? *Review of Financial Studies*, 15(2), 455−488. Retrieved from

https://faculty.haas.berkeley.edu/odean/Papers%20current%20versions/
Online%20RFS.pdf

17. Khandelwal, V. (2013). Stock analysis and the illusion of control.
Safal Niveshak, October 8. Retrieved from http://www.safalniveshak.
com/stock-analysis-and-illusion-of-control/

18. Investopedia Staff. What is high-frequency trading? *Investopedia*.
Retrieved from http://www.investopedia.com/ask/answers/09/high-fre-
quency-trading.asp

19. Hoium, T. (2014). There's only 1 way to beat high-frequency trading in a rigged market. *The Motley Fool*, April 5. Retrieved from http://
www.fool.com/investing/general/2014/04/05/theres-only-1-way-to-beat-
high-frequency-trading-i.aspx

20. Baker, H. K., & Nofsinger, J. R. (2012). Socially responsible finance
and investing: An overview. In H. K. Baker & J. R. Nofsinger (Eds.),
*Socially responsible finance and investing: Financial institutions, cor-
porations, investors, and activists* (pp. 1–14). Hoboken, NJ: Wiley.

21. Social Funds. Screening your portfolio. *SocialFunds.com*. Retrieved
from http://www.socialfunds.com/page.cgi/article2.html

22. Global Sustainable Investment Alliance (GSIA). (2014). *Global
Sustainable Investment Review*. Retrieved from http://www.gsi-alliance.
org/wp-content/uploads/2015/02/GSIA_Review_download.pdf

23. Trillium Asset Management. *Trillium mutual funds*. Retrieved from
http://trilliummutualfunds.com/

24. Nordea. *Responsibility, responsible investments, 'how we work.'*
Retrieved from http://www.nordea.com/en/responsibility/responsible-
investments/how_we_work/

25. Haigh, M., & Hazelton, J. (2004). Financial markets: A tool for
social responsibility? *Journal of Business Ethics*, 52(1), 59–71.

26. Kiymaz, H. (2012). SRI mutual fund and index performance. In
H. K. Baker & J. R. Nofsinger (Eds.), *Socially responsible finance and
investing: Financial institutions, corporations, investors, and activists*
(pp. 425–442). Hoboken, NJ: Wiley.

27. Guenster, N. (2012). Performance implications of SR Investing: Past
versus future. In H. K. Baker & J. R. Nofsinger (Eds.),*Socially
Responsible finance and investing: Financial institutions, corporations,
investors, and activists* (pp. 443–454. Hoboken, NJ: Wiley.

28. Junarsin, E., Enrico, Libert, & Fendy. (2016). socially responsible mutual funds. In H. K. Baker, G. Filbeck, & H. Kiymaz (Eds.), *Mutual funds and exchange-traded funds: Building blocks to wealth* (pp. 248–267). New York, NY: Oxford University Press.

29. USB. (2016). *Key facts*. Retrieved from https://www.ubs.com/us/en/asset_management/financial_advisors.html

30. USB. *UBS monthly fund report*. Retrieved from https://www.ubs.com/us/en/asset_management/financial_advisors/mutual_funds/international_sustainable_equity.html

31. USB. (2015, June 30). The UBS funds — Equities, annual report.

32. Harrington, B. (2010). *Pop finance: Investment clubs and the new investor populism*. Princeton, NJ: Princeton University Press.

33. Investment Club. *Wikipedia*. Retrieved from https://en.wikipedia.org/wiki/Investment_club.

34. Thaler, R. (1992). Savings, fungibility, and mental accounts. In R. Thaler (Ed.), *The winner's curse: Paradoxes and anomalies of economic life* (pp. 107–121). Princeton, NJ: Princeton University Press.

35. Barber, B., & Odean, T. (2000). Too many cooks spoil the profits: Investment club performance. *Financial Analysts Journal, 56*(1), 17–25.

36. Miller, Z. (2013). The death of investment clubs: Why it could be a good thing. *LearnVest*, February 28, 2013. Retrieved from https://www.learnvest.com/2013/02/the-death-of-investment-clubs-why-it-could-be-a-good-thing/

37. Vigeland, T. (2013). Shedding a tear over vanishing investment clubs. *Forbes*, February 15. Retrieved from http://www.forbes.com/sites/nextavenue/2013/02/15/shedding-a-tear-over-vanishing-investment-clubs/#161b50872d6b

38. Swedroe, L. (2013). Don't get beaten with an investment club. *CBS Money Watch*, August 15. Retrieved from http://www.cbsnews.com/news/dont-get-beaten-with-an-investment-club/

39. Gongloff, M. (2006, May 1). Where are they now: The beardstown ladies once icons of an emerging investor class, they're still together — Buying and holding. *The Wall Street Journal*. Retrieved from http://www.wsj.com/articles/SB114596682916135186

40. Brown, S., Cao-Alvira, J. J., & Powers, E. (2013). Do investment newsletters move markets. *Financial Management, 42*(2), 315–338.

41. Metrick, A. (1999). Performance evaluation with transactions data: The stock selection of investment newsletters. *Journal of Finance, 54*(5), 1743–1775. Jaffe, J. F., & Mahoney, J. M. (1999). The performance of investment newsletters. *Journal of Financial Economics, 53*(2), 289–307. Kumar, A., & Ponsl, V. (2002). *Behavior and performance of investment newsletter analysts*. Working Paper. Cornell University and Yale School of Management. Sewell, M. V. (2012). The efficient market hypothesis: Empirical evidence. *International Journal of Statistics and Probability, 1*(2), 164–178.

42. Perry, B. (2014). Evaluating paid investing newsletters. *Investopedia*, February 8. Retrieved from http://www.investopedia.com/articles/trading/evaluating-paid-investing-newsletters.asp

43. Fabian, D. Home page. Retrieved from https://www.fabian.com/about-doug/

44. Merriman, P. A. (2016). What the Hulbert financial digest really taught us. *MarketWatch*, June 8. Retrieved from http://www.marketwatch.com/story/what-the-hulbert-financial-digest-really-taught-us-2016-06-08

45. Hulbert, M. (2013). Newsletter returns: Be skeptical stock newsletters often claim blow-out-the-lights performance, but their actual numbers don't stand up to scrutiny. Here's why that's a bad sign for the market. *Barron's*, October 3. Retrieved from http://www.barrons.com/articles/SB50001424053111903320604579109521642860630

46. Fabian, D. *Disclaimer*. Retrieved from https://www.fabian.com/disclaimer/

INDEX